The Chinese Dream and Law

The Chinese Dream and Law
The Third Surge of Utopianism, 2012–2024

SHIPING HUA

Published by State University of New York Press, Albany

© 2025 State University of New York

All rights reserved

Printed in the United States of America

No part of this book may be used or reproduced in any manner whatsoever without written permission. No part of this book may be stored in a retrieval system or transmitted in any form or by any means including electronic, electrostatic, magnetic tape, mechanical, photocopying, recording, or otherwise without the prior permission in writing of the publisher.

Links to third-party websites are provided as a convenience and for informational purposes only. They do not constitute an endorsement or an approval of any of the products, services, or opinions of the organization, companies, or individuals. SUNY Press bears no responsibility for the accuracy, legality, or content of a URL, the external website, or for that of subsequent websites.

EU GPSR Authorised Representative:
Logos Europe, 9 rue Nicolas Poussin, 17000, La Rochelle, France
contact@logoseurope.eu

For information, contact State University of New York Press, Albany, NY
www.sunypress.edu

Library of Congress Cataloging-in-Publication Data

Name: Hua, Shiping, 1956– author.
Title: The Chinese dream and law : the third surge of utopianism, 2012–2024 / Shiping Hua.
Description: Albany : State University of New York Press, [2025]. | Includes bibliographical references and index.
Identifiers: LCCN 2025000867 | ISBN 9798855803525 (hardcover : alk. paper) | ISBN 9798855803532 (ebook) | ISBN 9798855803518 (pbk. : alk. paper)
Subjects: LCSH: Legislation—China—History. | China—Politics and government—2002– | Xi, Jinping. | Utopias. | China—Foreign relations—21st century.
Classification: LCC KNQ2516 .H83 2025 | DDC 349.51—dc23/eng/20250114
LC record available at https://lccn.loc.gov/2025000867

For J. Blaine Hudson and Helen Lew Lang

Contents

Acknowledgments ix

Abbreviations xi

Chapter 1 The Question and the Argument 1

Chapter 2 The Chinese Dream, Utopianism, and Law 11

Chapter 3 A Reversal of the Dengist Reform? 27

Chapter 4 The Creation of the Security State 43

Chapter 5 The Politics of Anticorruption 59

Chapter 6 Civil Rights Chinese Style 77

Chapter 7 China's Vision for a New Global Order 95

Chapter 8 The Chinese Dream: A Story of Culture 115

Appendices 127

Glossary 209

Notes 211

Bibliography 251

Index 279

Acknowledgments

This book is dedicated to J. Blaine Hudson (1949–2013), former Dean of the College of Arts and Sciences at the University of Louisville, and Helen Lew Lang, from Louisville, Kentucky. Dean Hudson's leadership and the Lang family's generous donation made the creation of the Asian Studies Program at the University of Louisville possible. I am also grateful to Mary P. Sheridan, Director of Commonwealth Center for Humanities and Society at UofL, for the indexing costs that she covered.

The bulk of this book was completed during my sabbatical in the fall of 2023. I am grateful to Tricia J. Gray, chair of the Department of Political Science, and Dayna Touron, dean of the College of Arts and Sciences at the University of Louisville, for this generous support.

With the permission from University of California Press and Taylor & Francis, we are republishing parts of two articles: Chapter 3 "The PRC Fifth Constitutional Amendment: A Reversal of the Reform" was published in *Asian Survey* 60, no. 6 (November/December 2020): 1172–93. "Chapter 6: Civil Rights Chinese Style" was published in *Chinese Legality: Ideology, Law and Institutions* (London: Routledge 2023).

Chapters 3, 4, 6, 7 were presented at various conferences, including the American Political Science Association annual meeting in Philadelphia, September 5–8, 2024; the Mid-West Political Science Association annual meeting in Chicago April 4–7, 2024; the Association of Chinese Professors in Social Sciences (ACPSS) annual meeting at High Point University, North Carolina, October 11–13, 2024; ACPSS annual meeting at Pacific Lutheran University, Washington, October 20–23, 2023. The comments from the audience were very useful for the revision of this book.

Abbreviations

CASS	Chinese Academy of Social Sciences
CCDI	Central Commission of Discipline Inspection
CCP	Chinese Communist Party
EU	European Union
KMT	Kuomintang
NPC	National People's Congress
PRC	The People's Republic of China
UK	United Kingdom
UN	The United Nations
UNESCO	United Nations Educational, Scientific and Cultural Organization.
USSR	The Union of the Soviet Socialist Republics
WTO	World Trade Organization

Chapter 1

The Question and the Argument

> The Chinese Dream is the world's dream.
>
> —Ma Zhengang, Beijing's former ambassador to the United Kingdom (UK)

This book is the first comprehensive study of the Chinese Dream[1] undertaken by analyzing the major laws promulgated during the Xi Jinping era, including the Fifth Constitutional Amendment, the National Security Law, the National Supervision Law, the Civil Code, and the Law on Foreign Relations. This is done against the background of the politics and ideology of the Xi regime in general. The central question this study addresses is: Why and how does the Chinese Dream have to be realized through law?

The Xi regime claims that the current leadership's mission statement rests on the Chinese Dream[2] and that the dream is also embedded in the Chinese Communist Party (CCP)'s political manifesto and vision for the country.[3] In pursuit of this dream, the Xi regime refers to the law more often than any of the previous administrations in the People's Republic of China (PRC). In October 2014 "Ruling according to the law" was made the main theme of the fourth session of the Eighteenth National Party Congress. This was the first time in the history of the CCP that this theme has been addressed this way.[4]

In 2016 Xi stated that in order "to realize the Chinese Dream, we have to deepen the reform and continue to open up to the outside world, continue to rule comprehensively according to law, promote modernization, and raise the standard of living of the people."[5] For him, the realization of the Chinese Dream depends on holding fast to the leadership of the CCP, the notion that the people are the masters of the country, and rule according to law.[6]

What is the Chinese Dream? In 2016, Xinhua, the official news agency of the PRC, summarized Xi's Chinese Dream in the following way. For Xi, the Chinese Dream encapsulates the hopes of the nation. The long-term hope lies in the continuation of the Confucian *datong*, that is, the Great Harmony[7]; their modern hope is for "the rejuvenation of the Chinese nation," alluding to the belief that China suffered grievously from foreign invasions and humiliations since the Opium War in 1839; their short-term hope (he uses the term *xiaokang*, or lesser prosperity)[8], is to double the country's GDP from 2010 through 2020; and the instrument for achieving the Chinese Dream is the state.[9] Modern ideologies such as "socialism," "democracy," and "freedom" are notably missing from this list.

For some in the Xi regime, the "rejuvenation of the Chinese nation" marks the beginning of the third epoch of world civilization, following the first epoch of the axial age of Plato, Aristotle, and Confucius and the second epoch of the Industrial Revolution.[10] Ma Zhengang, Beijing's former ambassador to the United Kingdom (UK), declared that "the Chinese Dream is the world's dream."[11] The Chinese are not the only Asians to claim that their values are universal in application. Former Malaysian Prime Minister Mahathir Mohamad has stated: "Asian values are universal values. European values are European values."[12]

In contrast to China's low-key engagement in foreign affairs under Deng, China under Xi has recently started to prescribe solutions to world problems. On September 21, 2021, at the Seventy-Sixth UN General Assembly, Xi offered "An Initiative for Global Development"; on April 21, 2022, at the opening ceremony of the Boao Asian Forum, he made a keynote speech announcing "An Initiative for Global Security"; on March 15, 2023, at the Dialogue between the Chinese Communist Party and Parties of the Other Countries, he announced "An Initiative for Global Civilizations."[13] These three proposals, which were later codified in the PRC Law on Foreign Relations that came into effect on July 1, 2023, describe a world order that is different from the current one.

Xi's confidence in his solutions has some basis in fact. For instance, after four decades of rapid economic development, the Chinese rightly believe that China has not yet reached its zenith and therefore has much room for further growth. In 2021, China's share of the global economy in terms of GDP was 18.4 percent, compared with 23.3 percent in 1700.[14] The Chinese Dream is indeed no daydream.

But China's confidence cannot be taken too far. Some scholars believe that the political concept of the Chinese Dream is utopian and nostalgic.[15] The concept of datong, literally meaning "great harmony," promoted by Xi, was developed in central China twenty-five hundred years ago. It may not be applicable to the areas beyond central China that were considered "barbarian" at the time, and it may not be applicable in today's diverse world. In ancient China, areas that were not governed by the government officials who had passed the civil service examinations were considered barbarian. In addition, datong was meant to apply to ethnic Chinese, although in Confucius's discourse China equals the world.[16] The dramatic difference between domestic politics and world affairs is that while the former might aim for compassion and rule according to law, the latter aims at opportunism, as was noted by the ancient Chinese strategist Sun Tzu (544–496 BCE).[17] The Chinese Dream does not equal the world's dream.

In modern times, China experienced its first surge of utopianism in the late Qing and the early Republic era, when the Chinese intellectuals such as Kang Youwei (1858–1927 CE) promoted the idea of datong as part of their attempt to modernize Chinese society.[18] China experienced its second surge of utopianism during the Maoist era in gigantic efforts of social engineering such as the Great Leap Forward and the Cultural Revolution. Again, the idea of datong was one of the intellectual inspirations for these efforts.[19] If it is an exaggeration for Sun Yat-sen to say that "China has a population of 400 million and every one of them wants to be the emperor,"[20] it is probably true that many of its modern leaders, such as Kang, Mao, and now Xi, want not only to save China but also the world.

Because of the setbacks suffered in China during those utopian attempts at social engineering, this style of utopianism was dropped by the regime over the first three decades of the post-Mao reform period. Over the first two decades of the reform, Chinese consciousness turned to the worship of science. The utopian enthusiasm of Kang and Mao gave way to a low-key attitude of observing objective rules.[21] However, the current manifestation of the Chinese Dream can be characterized as China's third surge of utopianism in modern history.[22] Indeed, the model of the Chinese Dream has been normalized and reincorporated into the pathways of the country's quotidian political rhetoric since the late Qing, exemplified by Kang and Mao, in that it hopes to bring about datong in the long term, and xiaokang, a moderately prosperous society, in the short term; and it resorts to China's cultural tradition to justify contemporary politics. In this light, the three decades of reform before Xi look like an aberration, a deviation from the normal trajectory of the country's political development in the last century.

A Road Map of Legal Development

This study also aims to categorize the variety of scholarly opinions about China's legal reform during the Xi era. Studies in the West with a positive evaluation of China's legal system were largely published before Xi's second term and need to be updated. For instance, referring mainly to the period before Xi took office in 2013, Guanghua Yu analyzes China's constitutional law reform and finds that it is not only conducive to China's economic development but also enhances citizens' freedom.[23] Albert Chen reviews the trajectory of Chinese legal reform in the first fifteen years of the twenty-first century and argues that there was no "turn against law."[24] Similarly, Larry Catá Backer, writing in 2006, believes the Chinese legal system during the post-Mao era has legitimate elements.[25] Studies in the West published after this period tend to offer different conclusions.

The relationship between the timing on studies of China's legal system and the conclusions drawn has already been noted elsewhere. For Jacques deLisle, for instance, writing five years after Xi took office, "There are limits to what can be inferred from a relatively short period, especially following a leadership transition."[26] Elizabeth Economy notes that even after five years into Xi's regime, many China watchers in the West still did not know what Xi's intentions were.[27] For Robert Sutter, the United States' engagement policies toward China continued well into the last days of the Obama administration.[28]

To show the changes during the Xi regime from his two predecessors, Jiang Zemin and Hu Jintao, I use a comparative method in texts clearly indicating how Xi reversed his predecessors' legal reforms, for example, in the Fifth Amendment to the Constitution in 2018, as compared with the first four amendments of his predecessors, and the 2015 National Supervision Law, as compared with the previous supervision laws. Accordingly, here I compare the National Security Law of 2015 with its earlier version, the 1993 National Security Law.

In this way I address deLisle's remark about the uncertainty regarding China's legal development due to the short time Xi had been in office.

Elizabeth Economy remarks that "while his initiatives echo the ideas of past leaders, Xi has transformed them into policies. His willingness to embrace risk has largely allowed him to achieve his objectives."[29] This viewpoint is addressed by showing that Xi's thinking about legal reform, not only his ability to execute changes, differs from that of his predecessors.

Mary E. Gallagher believes that China's half-hearted attempt to institute the rule of law undermines the possibility of authoritarian rule, as it emboldens the working class to defend their interest through the legal system; however, she notes that those who do not have the skills to use the law to defend themselves sometimes resort to protests.[30] This situation, although it could very well be the case, may need to be viewed from a new perspective; however, the passing of the recent National Security Law has tightened the Chinese government's authoritarian control over the nation as a whole.

More recent studies from the West on the Chinese legal system tend to be critical of it. In 2020 Carl Minzner suggests that there was a "turn against law" in the first decade of this century.[31] For Jacques deLisle, the Xi version of the law appears to be more "Legalist," "Leninist," and "instrumentalist" than that of its predecessors.[32] Jeffrey E. Thomas believes that the CCP's domination of the state, together with the Chinese cultural tradition of tolerating centralized power, make it unlikely that China will attain Western ideals of the rule of law.[33] Rogier J. E. H. Creemers and Susan Trevaskes believe that it has become clear that the rule of law, as understood in the West, will not emerge in China during the Xi era anytime soon.[34]

In addition to the problem of timing, another source of confusion and diversity is the linguistic and cultural setting. China is a unique country and civilization with a unique legal development: thus, it is hard to describe the Chinese experience using another language. For example, such key concepts in this study as "utopianism" and "rule by law" have culturally based meanings. Because of this, some of the findings of the World Bank about China's legal development seem logically inconsistent with each other. For instance, the World Bank found that under the Xi regime, the index of the rule of law in China did not drop. That does not seem consistent with another finding by the World Bank; namely, that the index of voice and accountability as well as political stability, used as indicators of the increasing concentration of power in the CCP and Xi, had gotten worse during the Xi administration and are much lower than what is considered the norm in upper-middle income countries.

The current study finds the World Bank's first finding cited above puzzling but the second one convincing. According to this study, the newly instituted practice of *liuzhi* (the enforced detention by authorities of those suspected of crimes or flouting party discipline) in the 2018 Supervision Law is a retreat from the rule of law because it restrains defendants without giving them proper legal protection. It is possible that the World Bank did not distinguish "the rule of law" from the Chinese "rule by law." To clarify these seemingly inconsistent findings, chapter 2 offers a more detailed theoretical discussion.

Why Is Law a Good Reflection of the Chinese Dream?

Scholars have different views on how seriously we should treat the Chinese Dream. Roderick MacFarquar notes that Xi has mounted a crusade for moral purity within the party; yet, he argues, neither the "Chinese Dream" nor "socialism with Chinese characteristics" has the intellectual plausibility of Marxism-Leninism, and certainly neither arouses the mass fervor that Mao Zedong thought generated at its height.[35] Michael Peters, however, takes a positive position on the Chinese Dream. He believes it can draw upon huge narrative and cultural resources, including the discourse of Chinese cosmopolitanism that has been examined recently in a spate of publications. The efficacy of the Chinese Dream lies in its emphasis on past empires as well as China's contemporary relations with the United States and its future orientations.[36]

On this matter I take a nuanced position, arguing that the Chinese Dream is neither entirely negative nor entirely positive. Any evaluation of the Chinese Dream has to be based on solid ground, such as the legal documents in which it is addressed. Up to now, scholars who study the Chinese Dream have not related it to the law, and those who study the law have not related it to the Chinese Dream, although the intimate connection between the two are obvious.[37] This study aims to fill this gap.

As with the case of legal development, perspectives on the Chinese Dream also vary in the definitions used and the evaluations it attracts. The vagueness of the notion of the Chinese Dream is also widely acknowledged. "The China Dream is so broad that there's room [in it] for sweet dreams or nightmares."[38] Therefore, scholars often take very different positions on the Chinese Dream based on their impressions. For Michael Feng, for instance, it includes everything positive, such as "prosperity, democracy, civility, harmony, freedom, equality, justice, [the] rule of law, patriotism, dedication, integrity and friendship."[39] This study has found, however, the Chinese Dream is not about "freedom," as is clearly shown in the Civil

Code, which ensures people do not have the political right to challenge the state. Neither is it about "democracy," in the sense that practically all the major laws under study ensure the dominance of the leadership and the CCP, not the people, in decision-making.

Chris Ford believes that the current bloom of quasi-Confucian political thinking is deployed both to discredit Western ideals of democratic pluralism and to rationalize continued one-party rule in China.[40] For William A. Callahan, the Chinese Dream is inspired by state socialism and the Chinese civilization dynamic, which engages in the global competition of social models. The Chinese Dream is not necessarily a positive ideal, but centers on the notion that China faces a common enemy: liberalism, the West, and the United States.[41]

This study, however, takes seriously Xi's notion of "deepening the reform and opening up to the outside world" as relevant to the Chinese Dream. The state capitalism that is reflected in the reform and opening up to the outside world is the means through which to realize the Chinese Dream. As will be shown in the following chapters, many laws promulgated during the Xi period have their origins in the West. Laws that are conducive to China's economy are promoted, for example, the "liberalization of foreign investment law may advance under Xi."[42]

This shows that, generally speaking, the regime takes a pragmatic position on many issues. For instance, it does not care whether a policy promotes socialism or not: thus, the existence of a stock market that is by definition opposed to socialism is protected by the law. But should the legal system as perceived to have failed to guarantee social stability, and instead encourage workers to seek more personal freedom, then the Xi regime may switch to a more illiberal Legalist approach. If they have to abandon term limits to public office, as Xi did, they would do it without heeding what Westerners might say. The National Supervision Law does look like Legalism, and the Xi regime does not hesitate to use it.

The Chinese do not see the seeming contradiction between their utopian Chinese Dream and their pragmatic attitudes toward handling concrete socioeconomic and political issues. This spirit is embedded in the Taoist teaching of "adopting the unworldly [often high morality] attitudes to handle worldly matters" (yi chushi zhixin zuo rushi zhishi).[43] Some Western scholars tend to view the high morality expressed in this context as a scam to deceive the public. Kerry Brown for instance has made the admirable attempt to find the underlying meaning of the Chinese narratives and arts with regard to the Chinese Dream.[44]

8 | The Chinese Dream and Law

Because this is a study about the politics and ideology of the Xi regime I do not deal with the technical aspects of certain laws. For instance, here the massive Civil Code is studied only for its political and ideological implications, not its technical details.

About the Book

The structure of the book is as follows: Following the introduction, chapter 2 is the theoretical and historical reference that relates to all the core chapters of the book. Chapter 3 is the general ideological assessment of Xi's policies, as reflected in the Fifth Constitutional Amendment. Chapters, 4, 5, 6, and 7 deal with four core aspects of the Chinese society related to the Chinese Dream: the authoritarian social control through law, how to control the bureaucrats through law, how to control the citizens through law, and how Xi's foreign policy is reflected in law.

Chapter 1: The Question and the Argument.

Chapter 2 sets out the analytical framework for understanding the following five chapters that deal with concrete laws, to show the meanings of these laws in the broader project of the Chinese Dream. It discusses the continuing appeal of the Confucian datong in modern times. It examines the current legal system in China through the lens of Marxist, Soviet, and Maoist legal thought and practice; the logical relationship between the law and the current state capitalist system; and the way that the current legal system is moving toward Legalism.

Chapter 3 provides a comparative study of the Fifth Constitutional Amendment and the four earlier amendments. The amendment is largely a reversal of the reform of the law in China because it emphasizes the role of ideology, the CCP, and personality in decision making. The extension of the term in office of the PRC presidency is the most controversial. After the Cultural Revolution, there was almost a consensus within the CCP that the concentration of power in the hands of one person should be avoided. This law has undermined this consensus, reversed this trend, and made the Chinese political process more centralized.

Chapter 4 focuses on the 2015 National Security Law, whose background is the national rejuvenation of the Chinese Dream. This law is the blueprint for the creation of a security state. Compared with the 1993 version of this law, the 2015 one designates more areas as essential to national security, shows less commitment to the protection of individuals by the law, and enhances the power of the state apparatus.

Chapter 5 looks at the politics of anticorruption. Compared with previous versions, the 2018 National Supervision Law removes some of the independence of the judiciary and offers less protection of human rights during legal processes. By the same token, the 2018 law is consistent with Chinese legal culture, in which the law's primary purpose is to serve the pragmatic purpose of institution maintenance. It is also a tool for the leader to fight corruption and increase the power of the state. In spite of the achievements of the anticorruption campaign, this chapter casts doubt on the claim that freedom is part of the Chinese Dream.

Chapter 6 is a study of China's newly promulgated Civil Code, which is meant to give the people some leeway in the context of China's slower economic growth and a more confrontational international environment. This law has made progress in protecting people's socioeconomic rights but not necessarily political rights. The Chinese Dream promises to deepen the current reform, so this will allow the continuation of the state capitalist system.

Chapter 7 studies the Law on Foreign Relations, which marks the first time that China's foreign policy guidelines had been codified in law. This law emphasizes the role of Xi Jinping in foreign affairs by including his three initiatives for the future international order, that is, on development, security, and civilization. The law has led to ambiguity in China's approach to the current international order, which it claims it does not intend to challenge, for example, the civilization initiative points to a very different international order from the existing one. The law treats international norms and institutions creatively to suit China's national interests (e.g., the interpretation of human rights). This law also makes the Chinese Constitution supreme over international law and reconfirms its "one China" policy in foreign relations.

Chapter 8 concludes the book by offering some prospects of the Chinese Dream that include the cultural resilience of datong as a core human hope for the Chinese people, the long-held statism as against individuality-based human freedom, as well as the pragmatic nature of the CCP.

Chapter 2

The Chinese Dream, Utopianism, and Law

Datong is communism.

—Guo Moruo, *Karl Marx Enters the Confucian Temple*

This chapter provides an analytical framework to contextualize the following key chapters about concrete laws (chapters 3 through 7) in the broader Chinese political and legal culture and aims to answer the question why the Chinese Dream has to be realized through law. Chapters 3 to 7 answer the second part of the question addressed in this book: how the Chinese Dream is reflected in China's laws. The first section of this chapter discusses the origin of datong, the process leading to datong, xiaokang, and why the process leading to datong could be utopian while the origin of datong is not. The second section discusses the legal thought and experience in Marxist-Soviet-Maoist theory, the theoretical connection between state capitalism and the law, and how Legalism impacts on the current legal system.

The Chinese Dream and Utopianism

THE LONG-TERM HOPE: DATONG

Like the American Dream, the Chinese Dream is meant to inspire hope.[1] Xi's promotion of datong aims partly to reinvigorate classical Chinese culture.[2] This is part of the Chinese government's attempt to use the tradition to justify the present politics. Ye Zicheng said in 2017 that Confucianism, Legalism, and Taoism have implications for the modern era, not just for China, but also for the world.³ This attempt to reinterpret Chinese cultural traditions is also reflected by the fact that Lu Xun's (1881–1936) works condemning the Chinese tradition have been removed from middle-school textbooks in China.⁴ Similarly, some elements of ancient Chinese military thought, such as the works of Sun Tzu, are readily apparent in China's military doctrine and operations today.⁵ Xi Jinping tends to cite Confucian classics more than his predecessors, Jiang Zemin and Hu Jintao, to justify his views, and he uses Chinese history more often than they did to present China's domestic and foreign policies.⁶ This is reflected in some of the laws examined in this book, such as the National Supervision Law and the Foreign Relations Law.

What are the qualities of datong that make Xi and many other important modern Chinese political leaders believe that it can be used to mobilize the Chinese people? As a general inspiration for the Chinese, the concept of datong depicts a human paradise characterized by love and equality that can be achieved through human exertion. Political leaders also subsume all kinds of political agendas under the rubric of datong, in the name of pursuing this human hope. The concept of datong comes from the Confucian classic, *The Analects*. It is supposed to be based on a real human community that existed long before Confucius was born, during the Yao (around 2357–2256 BCE) and Shun (around 2255–2205 BCE) periods.⁷ This Confucian concept is not, therefore, a religious belief. According to this concept, a human community that exhibits datong can be described thus:

> When the Great Way was in practice, then the Empire was held in common. They chose people of talent and ability whose words were sincere, and they cultivated harmony. Thus people did not only love their own parents, not only nurture their own children. The elderly were cared for till the end of their life, the able-bodied pursued their careers, while the young were nurtured in growing up. Provisions were made to care for widows, orphans, childless men, and the disabled. Men had their part to play (work), while women had their home (marriage). Possessions were used, but not hoarded for selfish reasons. Work was encouraged, but not for selfish advantage. In this way selfish schemes did not arise. Robbers, thieves, rebels, and traitors had no place, and thus outer doors were not closed. This is called the Great Unity of Harmony (datong).⁸

Psychologically, datong, as a model of an ideal community, satisfies the Chinese human need for hope: a function that is fulfilled by religion in many other civilizations.[9] By contrast, Christians' hope for an afterlife is heaven, and they often view the present world as a sinful place. Hindus also place their human hope in the afterworld and say that people must live ethically so they can be reincarnated in a higher form. Russian Orthodox followers find this world awful by its very nature, and people are taught to wait for the savior. Believers in Japanese Shintoism worship nature: to them people and things are naturally beautiful as they are and therefore human achievements are not emphasized.[10]

Modern psychology shows that determination, motivation and perseverance, which are qualities required and encouraged by this special Chinese kind of hope, is a better predictor than talent for achieving goals.[11] Passion and commitment can be very powerful.[12]

Confucianism, especially the datong concept, was able to unite the Chinese in terms of political consciousness in ancient times, largely because of China's geographical isolation and because most Chinese belonged to the Han ethnic group. The achievement-oriented datong concept can sometimes be extremely constructive. It helped to produce ancient miracles like the Great Wall, which was designed for national defense, and the Grand Canal, which was largely intended as a means of transportation. China's ancient irrigation system is also among the most remarkable achievements in human history.[13] No other country has been able to feed so many people with so few resources for so many years. The arable land in China is about 6–7 percent of the world's total arable land, yet the Chinese population constitutes around 20–25 percent of the world's total, and China's freshwater resources comprise about 25 percent of the world average.[14]

Short-Term Hope: Xiakang (Lesser Prosperity)

The concept of xiaokang that appears in Xi's Chinese Dream mainly refers to the hope of improving living standards and other readily achievable socioeconomic goals in China in the short term. This improvement can take place along the way to achieving the perfect embodiment of datong. In the *Shi Jing*, or the *Book of Odes*, xiaokang applies to the administration of Yu (2205–2198 BCE), King Tang (?) in the Shang dynasty (1700–1027 BCE), and the reigns of Wen (1152–1056 BCE) and Wu (?–1043 BCE) in the Zhou Dynasty (1027–221 BCE).[15] Evil rulers such as King Jie (1706–1664

BCE) of the Xia dynasty (2070–1600 BCE), and King Zou (?–1046 BCE) of the Shang dynasty (1600–1046 BCE) are not included.[16]

The duality of the Chinese hope is that although the eventual goal is datong, the immediate goal is xiaokang. Although xiaokang is not as good as datong, it is an improvement on normal times. Moreover, modern political thinkers often consider not only that xiaokang is the first step toward achieving datong but that it also mirrors the concept of datong. Often the proposals advanced by modern political leaders mirror datong: indicating, therefore, that they often want to transform not only China but the whole world. They tend to draw inspiration from and romanticize China's ancient past to justify their current policies, and they favor putting in place a kind of egalitarianism achieved through authoritarian measures, which is a typical feature of modern utopianism.

As a result, the most prominent leaders of the modern period use the idea of datong as a clarion call for political mobilization.[17] The lower and more achievable practical goals embedded in the concept of xiaokang make it more realizable and, as it mirrors datong, serve as a useful strategy for achieving social transformation. Because it has little specific content it fits into different political orientations. Thus, while the goal of datong is always the same, xiaokang is always different.

This situation can be seen in the different strategies adopted by Chinese politicians in their modern attempts to transform Chinese society. In geopolitical terms, to modernize, China adopted a different strategy from that of its neighbor, Japan; in political terms, China adopted a different strategy from that of other republics such as the United States; and as a communist country, its strategy differed from that of the former Soviet Union.

In the late nineteenth century, Japanese politicians adopted a pragmatic, piecemeal approach to modernize Japan, while the efforts of Chinese politicians were marked by impatience and utopianism. The Japanese reform's strategy was to start gradually by changing people's consciousness first, then to engage in political reform, and finally to modernize its industries and technologies. Kang Youwei's (1858–1927) strategy reversed this approach. The late Qing reform failed partly because of their unrealistic hope, as demonstrated in Kang Youwei's *Da Tong Shu*, or *The Book of Datong*. Kang was keenly aware that his political agenda was the first stage toward datong. That is why he withheld the publication of his masterpiece when he was alive. It was not published until eight years after he died.

Kang reinterpreted the Confucian classics to justify his political platform of reform (tuo gu gai zhi). Like Confucius, Kang imagined that life in ancient China was better than in modern times, and his goal was to restore the glories of the past. This is similar to the Meiji Restoration, which imagined the past was better and the current elites just needed to restore the glorious past.[18]

As with the case of Kang Youwei, the strategies of Sun Yat-sen (1866–1925), the founder of modern China, also follow the three features of the Chinese hope: for an eventual human paradise on earth of datong, preceded by the first step of building a xiaokang republic, and using an imagined glorious past to justify this agenda.

Sun Yat-sen advocated datong. In fact, datong is mentioned in the national anthem of the Republic of China that was founded by Sun and the Kuomintang (KMT). Aiming at datong, Sun proposed a political platform that was summarized in the Three Principles of the People: nationalism, democracy, and the people's livelihood. Sun was aware that his political platform constituted the first step to datong. For instance, the principle of nationalism explicitly demands expelling the Manchus. This is certainly not in the all-loving spirit of datong. Sun's understanding of democracy incorporates the standard Western principles of elections, human rights, and press freedom.

What distinguishes Sun's political thought from that of other democracies such as the United States is his third principle, "the people's livelihood." For Sun, the people's livelihood can only be improved under state socialism.[19] His tendency toward some kind of socialism is also demonstrated by the fact that in 1925 and 1926 the KMT applied for membership to the Communist International, which was controlled by the former Union of Soviet Socialist Republics (USSR). Both attempts failed. In the early days, the CCP and the KMT had dual membership, which implies the two parties' ideologies were similar. China has never had a sizable libertarian right-wing party. In contemporary Taiwan, the income gap between the rich and poor is not that great.

But the concept of the people's livelihood is not like the Maoist concept of communism. Sun opposes capitalists, not capital per se because capitalists are exploiters and thus should be opposed. Although capital itself generates inequality, the state can effectively control it using state socialism. Sun's platform is not a form of extreme egalitarianism.[20] He believed that everybody should be equal in social status, although the division of labor exists. "When the peasants, workers, businessmen, and government officials fulfil their responsibilities according to the division of labor, datong could be realized."[21]

Like Kang, Sun drew inspiration from China's past to justify his policies. Sun believed that the Three Principles of the People, especially the people's livelihood, originated from the thought of Mencius. Improving people's livelihood comes about through socialism and communism.[22] Like that of Kang, Sun's revolution was unsuccessful. Although the Republic was established mainly through Sun's efforts, he was unable to maintain it. Yuan Shikai (1859–1916) was able to seize power from Sun and eventually restore the dynastical rule for a short period of time.

Similarly, Mao Zedong (1893–1976) also believes that the future of the world lies in bringing about datong.[23] In 1924, Guo Moruo (1892–1978) wrote a short story entitled *Makesi jin Wenmiao* (Karl Marx Enters the Temple of Confucius). In a fictional conversation, Confucius and Marx agree that Confucian datong and communism are the same concept.[24] After the decades of wars and chaos following the failed attempt by Kang Youwei to transform the Qing, China underwent another wave of utopianism during the Maoist era. In making adjustments to the communist system, the USSR took a temporary retreat from communism, for example, during the enactment of its New Economic Policy in 1924, while Maoist China tended to become even more radical, such as when it embarked on the Great Leap Forward and the Cultural Revolution.[25]

In the 1950s, Mao divided Chinese political development into two stages; a period under the so-called New Democracy or "the people's democratic dictatorship," and one under socialism, that is, the dictatorship of the proletariat. In the New Democracy period before 1957, there was political pluralism in China in the sense that besides the CCP, other political entities, including the smaller parties that were aligned to the CCP before the communist take-over in 1949, were still able to function in an independent manner. China's economy then was also a mixture of public and private ownership.

The New Democracy was supposed to evolve into socialism over a long period. But only a few years after it was initiated, following the Korean War (1950–1953), Mao was ready to initiate socialism, which he saw as the primary stage of communism. Thus, in 1958, Zhang Guozhong, the party secretary of Xushui County, Shandong Province, announced: "We should run headfirst into communism, instead of gradually evolving into it." He was awarded a Model Labor title in 1966, which was a major honor. The establishment of the People's Commune in 1958 marked the beginning of socialism and even the public dining halls in the countryside at the time seemed to embody communism.[26]

Mao drew inspiration for his People's Commune from Zhang Lu's (?–216 CE) utopianism of earlier times. For instance, Mao found similarities between the People's Commune he initiated in 1958 and Zhang Lu's egalitarian peasant rebellion. In 191, Zhang Lu led a faction of the Yellow Turban Rebellion, which was part of the general wave of peasant rebellions at that time. For the next three decades, Zhang Lu experimented with egalitarianism in central China. His government promoted the following principles: the public ownership of property; the use of manual labor as the only source of income; a social welfare system; and a redemptive instead of punitive approach to crime.[27]

The post-Mao reform reversed the political development model in use in China since the late Qing. Although the theory of "the primary stage of socialism"[28] insists that this is only the first stage for the eventual realization of full-blown socialism, datong and communism is either indefinitely postponed into the remote future or rarely mentioned in China's political agenda in the first three decades of the reform. As will be discussed later, the mentioning of the primary stage of socialism was deleted from some of those laws examined in this book. The three decades before Xi were also noted for their antitradition trend, exemplified by the late 1980s TV series *He Shang* (River Elegy).[29] In addition, over these three decades, China's income gap had increased from a minimal level immediately after the Mao era to one that was larger than that of the United States around 2011, before the Xi regime. This tendency runs counter to the vision of those major political leaders such as Kang, Sun, and Mao.

DATONG AND UTOPIANISM

Although the Chinese hope for worldly achievements sometimes produced miracles in ancient times, it often produced negative results in modern times, such as the failed reform led by Kang Youwei, and the disastrous Great Leap Forward and the Cultural Revolution by Mao. The negative impact of this concept on modern China has been noted by Li Zehou (1930–2021) and Liu Zaifu (1941–) in their influential book, *Gaobie geming* (Farewell to Revolution).[30] Western China watchers have used the term "utopianism" to describe these gigantic Chinese experiments in social reconstruction in modern times.[31]

How can we explain and describe the situation by which the idea of datong looks like utopianism in modern times? Its origin is not utopian, since it is supposed to have been a real human community in ancient times, not heaven as in the religious sense, or a Western utopia that is supposed to be a "no place"?[32]

As the only major civilization on earth to have existed uninterrupted for millennia,[33] the Chinese conception of hope is unique. In fact, the Chinese language does not contain the word "utopia." The Chinese created the equivalent of the concept of utopia by the sound, "wu-tuo-bang." Western scholars also use the terms "utopianism" and "optimism" interchangeably to describe the Chinese experience.[34] They refer to the same phenomenon as people's pursuit of happiness.[35]

Because datong is a "better place" for the Chinese that is realizable, all important Chinese political leaders have the tendency to do that. In the West, however, few nationwide efforts are made to do the seemingly impossible, except in sporadic small-scale social experiments or extremely unusual situations such as Winston Churchill during World War II. In many people's eyes, Churchill was doing the impossible. But he was eventually successful in working with the Allies to defeat the Nazis.[36]

The Chinese eagerness to succeed has been widely noted: "Never before has a nation so industrially backward and with so large and poor a population attempted so strenuously to acquire the military strength and stature of a major world power," the United States Central Intelligence Agency observed during the Cultural Revolution period.[37]

An obvious reason for the twentieth-century surges of utopianism is anachronism, that is, the time and the place are misplaced. Although the origin of datong is not utopian, but worldly and realizable, the processes and actions in the twentieth century and current are utopian because Chinese leaders tend to apply an ancient concept to today's world, which consists of diverse cultures, among which several not only believe in their own superiority but also have the capacity to defend their ways of living, especially the West.

Twentieth-century revolutionary enthusiasm associated with utopianism in China is also connected with the traditional Chinese way of thinking that is not rational,[38] in contrast to the teaching of Plato.[39] For Confucius, the essence of humanity is ethics; for Plato it is reason.[40] Thus this nonrational way of thinking, which can easily become irrational, as it was developed by neo-Confucians Zhu Xi (1126–1271 CE) and Wang Yangming (1472–1529 CE), has had an enormous impact on the social transformation of China in modern times.[41] It encourages the belief that radical social transformation is possible.[42]

Western scholars' tendency to use the word "utopianism" to describe the Chinese experience is also because the Chinese utopianism, such as that by Kang, Sun, Mao, is similar to that of the Western utopias in political platform: an equalitarian society ensured by some kind of authoritarian control. Utopian policies tend to dismantle the current order totally or in part.[43]

Why Must the Chinese Dream Be Realized through Law?

To explain why the Chinese Dream must be realized through the law, I will look at legal developments under Xi through the lens of the mainstream political thought and systems that China has experienced: the Marxist-Maoist system, state capitalism, and Legalism. The intimate relationship between the Chinese Dream and the law is also demonstrated by the fact that the various laws promulgated during the Xi period, such as the Fifth Constitutional Amendment (Art. 32), the National Security Law (Art. 1), and the Law on Foreign Relations (Art 1) explicitly state that these laws are designed for "the rejuvenation of the Chinese nation," which is the main feature of the Chinese Dream. I will show that "rule according to the law" has had different meanings in China over different periods.

China and Marxist-Soviet Legal Theory

According to Marxist theory, a country's legal system is an element of its superstructure and, like other such elements, is determined by its economic base. For Marx and Engels, social organization evolves directly out of the mode of production and commerce and forms the basis of the state and the rest of the ideological superstructure.[44] The legal and political superstructure arises from the relations of production that constitute the economic structure of the society.[45] A capitalist state is a committee to manage the common affairs of the bourgeoisie.[46]

But the Marxist theory of law was not well developed because it belongs to the realm of superstructure, and Marx devoted most of his attention to the nature of the economic base. Marxist theory is richest in the area of political economy. As a result, legal development in communist countries is not built on solid Marxist theory. This is especially the case in the PRC.

After founding the PRC, Mao was reluctant to design a constitution. It was only after pressure from Joseph Stalin (1878–1953) that it instituted its first constitution in 1954, which lasted, however, for only three years. The 1954 PRC Constitution was modeled on the 1937 Soviet one and, like the latter, it was underpinned by the Marxist theory of historical materialism. The main difference is that China located itself at a lower stage of development from the one that could be observed in the USSR at the time; calling it the New Democracy, similar to the situation of the USSR before 1937.[47] The main consequence of this was that the Soviet Constitution provided less space for private enterprise than the Chinese one because the USSR was already a socialist country but China was purportedly at a lower stage of development at the time.

Chinese communists do not seem to have a problem with law from a philosophical perspective but view law from a pragmatic angle to see whether it is useful for the purpose of governance. During the Cultural Revolution, there was the *ru fa zhi zheng* (debate between Confucianism and Legalism),[48] when Mao and his regime endorsed Legalism[49] against Confucianism although China had virtually no laws at the time.[50]

During the reform era, from 1978, law has been viewed as particularly useful for the regime. The endorsement of the law at the beginning of the reform was a rational response to the lawless Cultural Revolution when many government officials, including former PRC president Liu Shaoqi (1898–1969), were persecuted without the protection of the law. It is also essential for society to be regulated by the law if it is to attract foreign investment, when up to 64 percent of the country's GDP was earned through foreign trade in 2006.[51]

In Chinese political circles, law is thought to be less subversive to the regime than democracy. For instance, contract law, which is derived largely from the West, has been embraced in China because it does not challenge the dominance of the party. Loudly promoting the law also served to enhance China's image abroad during the reform era, when many Western observers complained about China's lack of progress in political reform. For a long time during the reform era, the law was endorsed by people both inside and outside China because it is hard to distinguish the Western notion of the rule of law and the various versions of the "rule by law"[52] that exist in China. Thus, in general, for the first two or three decades after the reform, Chinese legal reforms moved closer to the Western notion of the rule of law, although they fell far short of it.

Post-Mao reform is justified by the theory of "the primary stage of socialism" that was developed by the regime. Marxist historical materialism states that societies must undergo developmental stages; from primitive society (hunting/gathering) and slavery, to feudal, capitalist, socialist, and finally communist society.[53] According to this theory, Maoist China made the error of skipping the stage of capitalist development, and the post-Mao regime therefore had to make up the lesson of capitalism.

During the three decades of reform and opening up to the outside world before Xi, China was moving in a similar direction as the West in terms of its economic development model. The Chinese legal system was largely reliant on incorporating Western laws into its system, especially those borrowed from Anglo-American legal model.[54] The Chinese legal system at that time was a type of "thin constitutionalism," that is, quasi-constitutionalism.[55] Among the five amendments to the Constitution during the post-Mao era, the first four made before Xi moved in the direction of the West and the most recent one made by Xi reversed this trend.

The various laws since the post-Mao reform, especially before Xi, ensure that China has a predominantly capitalist economy. Chinese law is designed to accommodate the relations of production in China, where about 60 percent of the country's GDP is generated by the private sector. In addition, the laws have a class character, that is, they are ideological. As a result, the Civil Code, which protects private property and legitimizes the stock market, is more bourgeoise than proletarian in class character. This has been true even though the law was rapidly developed after the reform in order to meet historical contingencies, such as in response to the Cultural Revolution and foreign trade, rather than out of the ideological convictions of the leadership. The relationship between Marxism and today's political system is also ambiguous. Marx's communism was based on the Paris Commune, which practiced direct democracy and direct elections, neither of which we can expect to witness in China's foreseeable future.

State Capitalism and Rule by Law

In describing the Chinese Dream, Xi remarks that "we will comprehensively deepen the reform and opening up to the outside world. We will comprehensively promote rule according to the law."[56] Xi inherited from his predecessors a system that shares many similarities with the Western development model. In 2010 Scott Kennedy noted that, despite suggestions that China had developed a mode of economic development that was an alternative to the Washington Consensus, Beijing had in fact embraced eight of the ten policy instruments recommended in John Williamson's 1990 formulation.[57]

Capitalist market economy[58] needs laws in order to function.[59] Private property, the commodity market, and the stock market are protected by bodies of law, such as the Civil Code and Foreign Investment Law.

Over the last decade, China has undergone a process called *guojin mintui* (the advance of the state and the retreat of the people). This is in accordance with the Chinese Dream that prioritizes the state, which is public, over the family, which is private: "Without the state, how can family survive?" (*mei you guo, na you jia*). Xi stresses that the Chinese people's dream is built upon the dream of the nation and the dream of the state.[60]

Therefore, China's economy has been described as state capitalism. "Since the mid-2000s, China's political economy has stabilized around a model where most sectors are marketized and increasingly integrated with the global economy; yet strategic industries remain firmly in the grasp of an elite empire of state-owned enterprises."[61] State capitalism needs a legal system that the state can manipulate, that is, a type of "rule by law" unlike the Western rule of law, which is designed to meet the needs of rational capitalism.

Comparatively speaking, the economy of contemporary China is more capitalistic than the vision of Sun Yat-sen, who opposed capitalists, not capital. Xi wants to "let the market to play a decisive role in the allocation of resources." Xi also likes to call entrepreneurs, that is, capitalists, "zi ji ren" (our own).[62] As we see, in the Civil Code the term "exploitation" was removed from earlier civil laws, indicating that such things like stocks are protected by law. In the Marxist analysis, stocks that are used for investments are by definition exploitative. Private property, another feature of capitalist society, is also protected by the law. But under Xi, capitalism is manipulated by the state.[63]

Currently, the private sector regulated by the market plays an important role in the Chinese economy. According to the All-China Federation of Industry and Commerce, an official business group: "The combination of numbers 60/70/80/90 are frequently used to describe the private sector's contribution to the Chinese economy: they contribute 60 percent of China's GDP, and are responsible for 70 percent of innovation, 80 percent of urban employment and provide 90 percent of new jobs. Private wealth is also responsible for 70 percent of investment and 90 percent of exports."[64] On the relationship between law and the capitalist market, Weber argues: "On the one hand, capitalism was interested in strictly formal law and legal procedure. It was interested in having law function in a predictable way, possibly like a piece of machinery. On the other hand, the rationalism of officialdom in absolutist states led to the interest in codified systems and in homogeneous law to be handled by a rationally trained bureaucracy striving for equal, inter-local opportunities of promotion."[65] But the current Chinese system is not the kind of capitalism that the Western countries have, that is, rational capitalism, as Max Weber calls it. It is a kind of capitalism where the state is heavily involved. According to Wen Tiejun, about 70 percent of financial assets are controlled by state-owned banks. Land is state owned. About 70 percent of industrial assets are controlled by the state.[66] Under Xi, the state has made some advances against the private sector: "The private sector's share of China's largest listed companies continued to decline to 43 percent in the second half of 2022."[67]

Chinese state capitalism as it exists now was to some extent predicted by Max Weber more than a century ago. Max Weber remarks that although capitalism did not originate in China, China was able to adjust to a capitalist world. Chinese capitalism is "political capitalism," or state capitalism, as it is more commonly called today. It is difficult for China to have the kind of capitalism that the West has. For Weber, in the cultural context of China, human relations are unlimited, which is against the logic of business.[68] In other words, rational capitalism that calls for rule of law with minimum state involvement cannot function in the Chinese context because of unlimited human relations. China needs some kind of state capitalism in which the state is involved heavily not only in economic activities but also in the judicial process.

The core elements of the rule of law in liberal democracies include the separation of powers, the supremacy of the law, the protection of fundamental rights, and the independence of the justice system.[69] We see that the Chinese legal system does not protect citizens' political rights from the state, although their socioeconomic rights are mostly protected. However, Xi has retained some laws that are mostly Western in character, such as contract laws. In addition, there may be some commonality between traditional Chinese law and contemporary Western law, as Karen Turner has found.[70] For instance, Emperor Zhu Yuanzhang of Ming dynasty (1368–1644) believes that law is applicable to everybody, including the Emperor himself.

Commenting on the relations between market and law under Xi, Jacques deLisle remarks that the "market relies on legal frameworks to facilitate and diffuse voluntary transactions among diverse actors, and displace less law-centric modes for arranging economic relationships, such as state planning, status or informal connections. According to the Fourth Plenum's policy document, the socialist market economy 'is essentially a rule of law economy.'"[71]

Moving toward Legalism

Why has Xi's legal system become increasingly Legalist and less liberal than that it was during the first three decades of the post-Mao reform? One reason is that the liberal form of legal development during this period is no longer able to meet the needs of the regime in terms of governance and stability.[72] There was so much tension in society that China's spending on securing domestic stability started to overtake military expenditure under Hu Jintao.[73]

While the legal system was politicized to various degrees in the three decades before Xi, the current regime still finds it too liberal. The Xi regime started to find excuses to deflect the legal system he inherited even more from the rule of law in the Western sense. In defending the deflection from rule of law, a Chinese legal scholar argues that the national security law belongs to the area of "high politics" where other states also find it difficult to adhere strictly to the principle of rule of law.[74]

Historically, the Chinese legal system evolved independently from other legal systems and all Chinese institutions and ideologies that exist were invented and developed endogenously. China developed an agriculture-oriented legal system in which the protection and development of agriculture was its absolute and primary task and the closed, cyclical nature of agricultural production, in contrast to the open system of trading around the Mediterranean, also resulted in the closedness and conservatism of the legal system.

From the perspective of some Chinese legal scholars, "As an integral part of traditional Chinese culture, the Chinese (traditional) legal system is a precious fortune (windfall) for the construction of the socialist rule-of-law system with Chinese characteristics and [a] socialist country under rule of law."[75] Other Chinese legal scholars claim that the Chinese legal cultural tradition is useful not only for contemporary China but also for the world. Their argument is that the Chinese legal system was sufficiently diverse to incorporate the laws of other ethnic groups. The international legal system is diverse and uses not only the common law of the UK but also the continental law of France. It is possible or even constructive to add the Chinese legal system to world systems that are already diverse.[76]

In this context, Legalism, which was developed during the Warring States period (475–221 BCE) primarily in Qin (221–206 BCE), has inspired current scholars and government officials. Indeed, the current Chinese legal system resembles Legalism.[77] Showing his appreciation of the Qin system, Chen Zhiwu even argues that everything Qin did was correct: it failed only because they did it too fast.[78] Qin collapsed shortly after Emperor Shihuang of Qin (259–210 BCE) died, largely because the empire expanded too much and in too short a period.

Some Chinese scholars believe that the retreat from the law under Xi, for example, the National Security Law, is not only justified[79] but also admirable. Ye Zicheng and Long Quanlin claim that the country's highest level of legal development over the last 2,300 years was attained during the Qin Empire, when Shang Yang (390–338 BCE) and others developed Legalism. This is Legalism version 1.0. The legal system developed after Shang Yang was not as good a form of Legalism. The current legal system under Xi, according to them, is Legalism version 2.0.[80]

The main tool Qin used to make itself the most powerful among these kingdoms was the law. Generally speaking, however, the role of law in Chinese history has fluctuated over time, and it does not have the moral quality that Western law has. When law is necessary, it usually serves the pragmatic goal of being an instrument to implement policies. Historically, when there were periods of peace and unity Confucian order was executed while law was often placed in a subordinate position.

The Warring States period provides inspiration for the current regime. Qin's dream was to unify China during a very challenging time. The current international arena is similar to the Warring States period in the sense there is less consensus among the world's major countries than there was two decades ago. Furthermore, the United States, hitherto the strongest economy in the world, has been considerably weakened by the September 11 terrorist attack, the 2009 economic recession, and the more recent Covid-19 pandemic. In terms of freedom, Freedom House has estimated that democracy worldwide has been in decline for seventeen years. Countries are more likely to believe that in today's world, it is the law of the jungle that dominates more than the existence of a civil, rule-based international community.

The following principles of Legalism are relevant to the current legal system: (1) a political agenda to strengthen the country's power; (2) by strengthening the state and the top leader; (3) and by weakening the people politically while protecting their socioeconomic rights through law. Shang Yang (390–338 BCE), the architect of Legalism, believed that the government should concern itself with two things: economic activities, i.e., farming, and preparation for war, and these two goals can be realized only through the application of the law. For instance, the allocation of land was not based on nepotism as was the case with the aristocratic society before Qin, but based on how much contribution one made to the country, that is, how many enemies one kills on the battleground. Qin's strategy was to "enrich the state and empower the army" (fu guo qiang bing). For Han Fei (280–233 BCE), another key figure in promoting Legalism, "The ruler who respects the law and punishes the guilty will gain the trust and support of his subjects."[81] This is similar to Xi's agenda, advancing the economy and unifying with Taiwan through force, if necessary.

Xi's rule by law and Legalism promoted by Shang Yang and Han Fei are also similar in that both aim to use the law to enhance the power of the state and the leader. The Legalist Qin has been described as the first totalitarian state.[82] "The school perfected the science of government and art of statecraft to a level that would have greatly impressed Machiavelli."[83] Legalism is viewed as the policy of an absolute ruler who wants to control and dominate the state to achieve power and wealth. Legalists accept dictatorship and state-dominated polities.[84]

In addition, neither the regime's rule by law nor the Legalism attempts to empower the people politically. Shang Yang encourages the people to inform on each other to the government. One of the controversial dictums in the *Book of Lord Shang* states: "When the people are weak, the state is strong; hence the state that possesses the Way strives to weaken the people."[85] Moreover, "to prevent wrongdoing and stop transgressions, nothing is better than making punishments heavy. When punishments are heavy and [criminals] are inevitably captured, then the people dare not try [to break the law]."[86] For Han Fei, "A ruler should cultivate a sense of uncertainty and unpredictability to keep his subjects on their toes."[87] On the other hand, Han Fei continues, Legalism guarantees people's welfare, provided they contributed to the welfare of the state, largely by serving in the military. By doing so they will be rewarded materially, typically by being given land in accordance with their achievement, namely how many enemies they kill.[88]

We can see the similarities between this approach and the current Anti-Corruption campaign in China. Offenders are handed out heavy penalties: and even those who had retired many years ago have been taken out of the retirement and thrown into jail, such as Zhou Yongkang, a former Politburo Standing Committee member.

A combination of Legalism, or rule by law, not rule of law, and Chinese utopianism in the name of the Chinese Dream can be extremely powerful. In the following chapters, one will see in a specific way how the Chinese Dream is reflected in those major laws promulgated during the Xi era.

Chapter 3

A Reversal of the Dengist Reform?

> Correct ideas don't fall from heaven. They come from social reality.
>
> —Mao Zedong, *Where Do Correct Ideas Come From?*

China's 1982 Constitution was noted for its stronger emphasis on the protection of citizens' rights and the retreat of the Chinese Communist Party (CCP) from the daily work of government. The Four Constitutional Amendments promulgated from 1988 through 2004 continued this liberal trend, writing into the Constitution such important items as "human rights," "the protection of private properties," and "the rule of law." With thirty-one items in these four amendments, about two-thirds promoted economic reforms, and about a third dealt with political or technical reforms.[1] As a result of these developments, the United States viewed its bilateral relations with China in a positive light during the decades ending on the last day of the Obama administration.[2]

However, China's Fifth Constitutional Amendment, which was promulgated after Xi Jinping's first term as president of the People's Republic of China (PRC) in 2018 moved in a different direction. If, during the first few years of his term, observers in the West still believed that the post-Mao reform would continue along the old track set by Deng Xiaoping in 1978 and reinforced in 1992 in Deng's Southern Tour, this time it was clear that the old game was over. A new era had come.

This chapter is an examination of constitutional reform under Xi Jinping by analyzing the Fifth PRC Constitutional Amendment promulgated at the Thirteenth National People's Congress (NPC) in early 2018 that was preceded by the party constitutional amendment that had been adopted at the Nineteenth National Party Congress in late 2017.

This chapter tries to answer the following questions: To what extent was the Fifth PRC Constitutional Amendment under Xi a departure from the 1982 Constitution drafted under Deng Xiaoping and the four constitutional amendments that were mostly drafted under Jiang Zemin? How was this constitutional amendment related to China's prereform era and to the country's legal tradition? And how did officials present this transformation of the political direction under Xi as "the truth" at the philosophical level?

My study of the Fifth Amendment is a natural outgrowth of cumulative research on China's legal system and developments before the Xi era.[3] One such example is Jianfu Chen's study that examined the Fourth Constitutional Amendment adopted on March 14, 2004, by the National People's Congress (NPC), and compared it with the previous three amendments and the 1982 Constitution.[4]

In this chapter I try to determine which specific parts of Xi's ideological orientation are a continuation of the previous regimes and which are departures from them. The lack of transparency in Chinese politics will probably prevent us from ever knowing the real story, but it is hoped that this study on the Fifth Amendment, which may be viewed as a more accurate reflection of Xi's thought than the party's earlier policy announcements, will bring us one step closer to the truth. This chapter also attempts to complement the policy-level focus of most of current studies on the Xi regime that pay less attention to the philosophical underpinnings of the issues involved.[5]

In this study, I argue that the policy orientations reflected in the Fifth Amendment and the party constitutional amendment are a combination of a return to some elements of Maoism, with the emphasis on ideology, the party, and the cult of personality; a return to some constitutional formality during the Republic era, such as Sun Yat-sen's Five Powers Constitution (*Wu Quan Xian Fa*); and a return to some elements of the legal tradition of China's imperial past.

These policy orientations were justified by Maoist philosophical voluntarism. In this theory, the relative detachment of the "superstructure" and the "economic base" justified the current tolerance of Chinese cultural tradition and the view that the policy orientation of economic reform did not necessarily have to go hand in hand with political reform. When it mentions those areas that posed no imminent threat to the regime, such as the economic sphere and law in general, the Fifth Amendment is purposefully vague to give the regime flexibility in policymaking.

In general, the Fifth Amendment is a departure from the liberal policies that are reflected in the previous four constitutional amendments promulgated from 1988 through 2004. The regime felt comfortable making the transition under the philosophical assumption that correct ideas, as they are formulated in documents such as constitutional amendments, do not emerge from abstract principles, such as human rights or freedom. They come only from social practice. When social circumstances change, the state documents need to reflect these changes.

The Return to Maoist Politics: Ideology, the CCP, and the Cult of Personality

Stressing the Role of Ideology

The 1982 Constitution played down the concept of "class" by characterizing the nature of the Chinese society as the "people's democratic dictatorship" rather than "the dictatorship of the proletariat." Implying that the CCP does not have to consist only of the working class, Jiang Zemin stated that before the founding of the PRC, party membership largely consisted of peasants and intellectuals, and not the working class.[6]

However, ideology is now at the core of China's political system.[7] This was reflected in the constitutional amendments of both the party and the state. In the General Outline of the new party constitution, the following aims were added, to "raise the soft power of the state, [s]tick to the leadership role of ideological work, increasingly consolidate the leadership role of Marxism, [and] consolidate the common ideological base of the party and the people in their common struggle.[8] (CCP Art. 5)

For the new PRC constitution, the clause, "socialist core values," was added, after "The state advocates. . . ." Now, it reads, "The state advocates 'socialist core values,' the love of the country, the love of the people, labor, [and] science and socialist public virtues." (PRC Art. 39).

In recent years, terms such as "universal values" and "constitutionalism" have been viewed with increasing negativity by the Chinese media.[9] This contrasts with the fact that the previously four state constitutional amendments added the following goals to the document: the "protection of private properties"

(2004 Amendment, Art. 22, 13), the "rule of law" (1999 Amendment, Art. 13), and respect for "human rights (2004 Amendment, Art. 24).

Some Western observers have seen this as a return to Maoism. This view is reinforced by Xi's remark: "One cannot use the past three decades to renounce the experience of the three decades before that since the founding of the PRC,"[10] implying that events such as the Cultural Revolution were no longer considered to be a disaster. On September 10, 2018, it was reported that the textbooks for the Chinese school system had reevaluated the Cultural Revolution and changed its description from that of a "disaster" to the more neutral, even positive, terminology of "a hard struggle and exploration."[11] Wang Weiguang, the former president of the Chinese Academy of Social Sciences (CASS), also threatened to use "the proletarian dictatorship to carry out class struggle."[12] This expression was widely used during the Cultural Revolution.

Stressing the Role of the CCP

The 1982 Constitution signaled the retreat of the CCP from the daily work of government. For instance, it deleted the phrase in the 1978 Constitution: "The CCP is the core leader of the Chinese people" (1978, Art. 2). Although the 1978 Constitution was promulgated shortly after Mao's death, it retained many of the ideological elements of the Cultural Revolution. And it was identical in many ways to the 1975 Constitution made during the Cultural Revolution.

The 1982 Constitution also deleted the item in the 1978 Constitution that "citizens must obey the leadership of the CCP" (1978 Art. 56). In the words of Deng Xiaoping: "While we are correcting unhealthy tendencies and cracking down on crime, we must leave the matters that fall within the scope of the law to judicial institutions; it is not appropriate for the party to concern itself with such matters. The party should concern itself with inner-Party discipline, leaving legal problems to the government."[13] In the early part of the reform era, the party's role was de-emphasized to such an extent that it was limited to the roles of leadership in the areas of politics, ideology, and organization. In the new party constitution adopted in 2017, the tone was changed, signifying the return of ideology.[14]

The new party constitution also says that "the party takes overall leadership of the country."[15] Similarly, in the new PRC constitutional amendment, the following was added: "The most basic characteristic of socialism with Chinese characteristics is the leadership role played by the CCP" (PRC

Art 36). Moreover, the Xi regime is determined to strengthen the CCP. On August 26, 2018, "The Regulation on Punishment of the CCP," was announced. Its most severe punishment is reserved for CCP members who do not adhere to party discipline.[16] Referring to Mikhail Gorbachev's failure to defend the party, Xi charged that "proportional to the population, the Soviet Communist Party had more members than we do, but nobody was manly enough to stand up and resist [Gorbachev]."[17]

The National News and Publication Bureau that controlled China's TV, broadcasting, and print media used to be under the jurisdiction of the State Council. It is now under the CCP Central Committee's Propaganda Department. As chapter 5 on the supervision law explains, the anticorruption campaign under Xi relied largely on the Party's Disciplinary Inspection Commission, not the judiciary.

Stressing the Role of Xi

The 1982 Constitution deleted the 1978 Constitution item reading, "The commander in chief of the armed forces is the chairman of the CCP" (1978 Art. 19). This is a departure from the Maoist era cult of personality. It also ended the life tenure of leaders. In this constitution, everybody has a maximum of two terms in office, including the PRC president.[18]

In a reversal, the nineteenth party constitution (Art. 23) adopted in 2017 added a clause that "the Central Military Commission reports to its Chairperson."[19] Similarly, the PRC constitutional amendment in 2018 also ended the term limit of the PRC president (PRC: Item 45). The *New York Times* reported that the way that the amendment was made did not follow the usual procedures.[20] This persistence of authoritarian politics in China has greatly disappointed Western observers.[21]

The cult of personality coincides with the issue of the income gap between rich and poor that then threatened the regime. To address the problem, the new party constitution changed the policy of "allowing a few to become rich" in the 1980s to "more equality" (CCP General Outline).[22]

Compared with the experience of Scandinavian countries, where equality is ensured by democracy, the Chinese are more familiar with its own history, when dictators such as Emperor Zhu Yuanzhang (1328–1398 AD) in Ming (1368–1644 AD)[23] and the peasant rebellion leader Hong Xiuquan (1814–1864 AD) of the Taiping Rebellion (1850–1864 AD) sometimes addressed the issue of equality.[24] The Mao era was certainly noted for his emphasis on the equality in outcome.

Defending the new constitutional amendment that eliminated term limits for the PRC president, the official English-language newspaper *China Daily* argued that "these naysayers against the elimination of the term limit casually disregard the fact that China's political system has developed and is evolving in accordance with the country's unique national conditions."25

The Return to Maoist Philosophical Voluntarism

Official ideology is extremely important in communist countries, because in a sense, it is the "soul" of the communist movement. For instance, Mikhail Suslov (1902–1982) in the former Soviet Union, Chen Boda (1904–1989), and Zhang Zhunqiao (1917–2005) during the Maoist era occupied very prominent positions in the party because they were the ideology tsars during these periods. An analysis of a policy's philosophical underpinnings is necessary because these underpinnings are seen as bestowing a moral truth on policy changes, so they appear to be more than merely temporary adjustments in the face of empirical contingencies.26

Theory: A Return to Maoist "Voluntarism"

As with the case of policy orientations where the elites can see no options beyond a combination of Western liberal, Maoist, and Chinese cultural traditions, the philosophical underpinnings of the new policy are also unsophisticated. For China, this is an era characterized by a paucity of theories. An understanding of the relative importance of Marxist philosophical notions of "the economic base" and "the superstructure" is often key to understanding the philosophical underpinnings of the CCP policy orientations.

According to this theory, known as "historical materialism," the "economic base," which largely refers to "productive forces," plays a more decisive role in social change than the "superstructure," which includes the political system and values and which plays a secondary role, although occasionally the superstructure can be more decisive. This rhetoric enables the regime to switch back and forth along the spectrum of the relative importance of the "superstructure" and the "base" as needed.27

During the Maoist era, a stronger emphasis was placed on the superstructure to emphasize human initiative, that is, voluntarism, instead of the economic base that provides a justification for observing "objective rules," that is, economic determinism. Maurice Meissner and Frederic Wakeman analyzed Mao's voluntarism, which inverts economic determinism in historical materialism. The drastic social changes of the collectivization in 1957 and the Cultural Revolution[28] were based on the notion that people's consciousness (which is part of the superstructure), is more decisive than objective rules in terms of historical changes. Mao did not have the patience to wait until China's productive forces were developed to the stage that would automatically change the relations of production (which is part of the superstructure).[29]

The theory of the primary stage of socialism, the main theory Deng used to justify capitalism-oriented reform, was based on a form of historical materialism that once again reversed Maoist voluntarism. In defending this theory, which was developed in the late 1970s and early 1980s and placed more emphasis on the role of the productive forces as an agent of change, that is, the base, Jiang Zemin cited Karl Marx's *The Critique of Political Economy* to argue that productive forces have a determining force over relations of production. He therefore seemed to suggest that the Russian October Revolution in 1917 was premature in that the country's productive forces had not developed to such a level as to warrant the establishment of a state socialist system. But Jiang praised Lenin's capitalism-oriented New Economic Policy in the 1920s, which, in the words of Lenin, is a "retreat" from communist ideals.[30]

With the political connotations, the base/superstructure paradigm is an old discussion in world Marxist theoretical debates. On the eve of the October Revolution in 1917, Georgi Plekhanov (1856–1918) wanted the moderate Mensheviks to lead the revolution because the needs of the bourgeoisie revolution come before the dictatorship of the proletariat according to the theory of historical materialism, while Vladimir Lenin (1870–1924) did not have the patience to wait for this to be brought about. In the 1950s, the CCP, again based on the stage theory in historical materialism, originally wanted to allow the New Democracy (xin minzhu zhuyi geming) to last at least fifteen years before the Socialist Revolution was to start. In fact, it lasted only three years, after which Mao decided it was time to launch the Socialist Revolution.

The primary stage of socialism was developed in the 1980s by liberal academics such as Su Shaozhi, who argued that Maoist policies had committed the error of skipping the stage of capitalism before jumping into the socialism stage. What China had to do, then, was to make up the lesson of the capitalist stage of social development.[31] Based on this theory, Jiang Zemin wanted to allow the primary stage of socialism to last for "several dozens of generations," again emphasizing the generative power of the economic base.

Accordingly, at the CCP Fourteenth National Conference in 1992 under Jiang, the party claimed that China was at the primary stage of socialism, which could last for over a hundred years. Criticizing the Maoist voluntarism that existed between 1956–1976, the party made it clear that "we cannot jump over this stage."[32]

Following the 1992 Southern Tour by Deng Xiaoping, who pushed for more reform, the 1993 constitutional amendment proclaimed again that "China is at the primary stage of socialism" (PRC Art. 3). The 1999 constitutional amendment restated that "China will be in the primary stage of socialism for a long time to come" (PRC Art. 12).

Even non-Marxist scholars note the close relationship between economics and politics. David Shambaugh argues that there was a positive relation between economic growth and political democracy. China's authoritarianism had been successful in promoting the country's economy over the previous four decades. In the future, Shambaugh insists, this would not do. China has to liberalize its political system in order to succeed.[33] This is the theoretical base, that is, the modernization theory, on which the West had expected inevitable political change, given that China's economic structure had changed profoundly over the previous four decades.

However, according to the theoreticians in the Xi regime, the transition does not have to be as long as Jiang believed. Since the superstructure is independent of the base, according to voluntarism, society can both move forward, as Lenin and Mao believed, and it can also move backward toward China's past, as some of Xi's policies indicate.

Yang Guangbin claims theories that existed over the last six decades were not enough. "We must have new theories," he states.[34] This is partly to question the major theoretical framework in place since the start of the Dengist reform four decades ago, that is, the primary stage of socialism derived from historical materialism. The theories in the Xi era do not represent paradigmatic shifts but rather a difference in the emphasis on different notions of the old Marxist historical materialism, such as the base and the superstructure.

Turning the primary stage of socialism upside down and restoring the Maoist emphasis on human initiative, the new party constitution deleted the phrase "[comprehensively execute the party's basic line during the primary stage of socialism" (General Outline). The theories under the Xi administration resemble those that were promoted during the Maoist era in emphasizing the role of the superstructure, including political systems, values, and culture—instead of productive forces—in bringing about change. This is symbolized by the Central Party School's removal in 2015 of the epigraph at the gate by Jiang Zemin, who had worked with Deng to lay down the theoretical foundation of the reform, which is the idea of the primary stage of socialism.³⁵

Although this term is deemphasized in the amendment, the phrase was not eliminated from it. After all, constitutions by definition are products of political compromise, and they do not have to be theoretically rigorous. The term "the primary stage of socialism" is broad and is easy to qualify. Essentially, it means that China should adopt some elements of capitalism at this stage. This compromise in the constitutional amendment is intended to secure the continuity of China's political development.

Economic Reform Does Not Have to Go with Political Reform

In contrast to the view expressed in the 1982 Constitution that the primary stage of socialism would continue for a long time, some leading scholars under Xi have announced that by 2022, the end of Xi's second term in office, China's political system would have become well established, implying reform is no longer necessary.³⁶ This was against the background that although economically China looks more capitalistic than ostensibly capitalist societies such as the United States, the United Kingdom or Australia; politically, it is an authoritarian regime.³⁷ Some scholars in the Xi administration call the historical materialism on which the primary stage of socialism theory was based "vulgar historical materialism." What matters is not whether it is a democracy or an authoritarian system. The importance of judging whether a system is good or not is whether it leads to effective governance.³⁸

Reforming China's political system is not a goal of the Xi regime. For Xi, the idea of deepening reform refers to economic reforms, and rule by law, not political reform. Xi's reforms apply to areas such as unbalanced, uncoordinated, and unsustainable development, promoting scientific and technological innovation, the distortion of the industrial structure, the income gap between urban and rural areas, income disparities among population, reforms to education, social security, medical services, housing, the environment, food, drug safety, workplace safety, law enforcement and the administration of justice, sensual and materialistic self-indulgence, and bureaucratism.³⁹

Cultural Traditions Do Not Have to Disappear with a New Economic Structure

Another political implication of the stronger emphasis on the superstructure is that although the Chinese economy has changed profoundly, China's cultural tradition is seen as an integral part of the superstructure and thus will continue to influence politics and society. Yang Guangbin remarks that "culture" belongs to the category of "social existence" (shehui cunzai), which is located in the economic "base," not "social consciousness" (shehui yishi) which is located in the superstructure.[40] This unusual classification is intended to justify the continued existence of the Chinese cultural tradition.

Xi has also remarked that cultural pluralism will lead to political pluralism, indicating that China will develop in a unique way.[41] Some leading scholars under Xi complain that in the last thirty years, Chinese leaders have been ambiguous about the legitimacy of Chinese cultural tradition. Xi used Chinese culture as a tool not only in justifying domestic policies but also in foreign policy. The new constitutional amendment added the clause "ren lei mingyun gongtongti," meaning "a community of shared future for mankind" (PRC Art. 35). This is an attempt to move away from the Western notion of "nation-state."

Against this background, the Xi regime brought in the datong concept. Indeed, Xi's agenda displays the three characteristics of the Chinese hope: an eventual human paradise on earth (datong), taking concrete steps towards datong (xiaokang), and a strategic glorification of the past. The Xi regime is not committed to modern ideologies, such as democracy, freedom, and socialism, as the laws examined in this study demonstrate. For Xi, datong is the dream of the nation and the dream of every Chinese person.[42] As he said in 2014, "The Chinese dream is about contributing to the welfare of the world. Mencius said, 'When people are successful, they improve the world. When people are poor, they make themselves alone good.' With this cherished attitude of morality and aspiration, China will govern itself well."[43] Later, in 2015, Xi also remarked that "the lesser prosperity is the prosperity of the Chinese people as a whole; [the aim that] nobody should be left out. In the next five years we will have to lift 30 million of those living under the poverty line out of poverty."[44]

Under Xi, modernization discourse changed in a fundamental way. Li Zehou's comment on the modernization of China during the three decades before Xi assumed power is salient. He says that the tragedy of Chinese modernization lies in the fact that jiu wang yadao qimeng (the salvation of the Chinese nation precludes enlightenment). This means that Western values such as socialism, democracy, and freedom are desirable, but cannot be put into practice because China is too busy protecting itself from a series of disasters, especially foreign incursions, to do so.

Over most of the twentieth century the Chinese cultural tradition was cited as the main reason why the country lagged behind other industrialized countries. Lu Xun used his comic fictional character Ah Q to ridicule China's experience in the early part of the twentieth century, saying: "We used to be wealthier."[45] Jiang Zemin embraced Western culture, and was critical of the Chinese cultural tradition. He believed that "advanced culture" can be found in other countries as well.[46] Jiang uses the negative example of the Qing dynasty (1644–1911 CE) to demonstrate that it is necessary to learn Western ideas, noting that under Emperor Qian Long (1736–1795 CE), China's economy was the largest in the world. But because of its arrogance and refusal to open up to the outside world, Qing was defeated by Western powers and the dynasty fell.[47]

Nowadays, these criticisms of the Chinese cultural tradition are no longer included in the Chinese Dream. China does not have to embrace Western concepts of modernization. For example, junior middle schools and all classes below grade nine are no longer allowed to study foreign texts.[48] In recent years, schools of Chinese studies or (guo xue yuan) have been established in many major universities. Even the college entrance examination in China resembles the traditional civil service examination in the sense that it is designed to facilitate social mobility, that is, to provide an avenue for children in poor families to move up the social ladder.

In recent decades some Chinese scholars cite the contribution of China's glorious past to the country's rise. Urbanization is an example. It has been noted, for instance, that in Song dynasty (960–1279 CE) 22 percent of the population was urban, just as in 1980. In 1949, when the PRC was founded, it was around 10 percent. Xi has stressed the positive aspects of China's cultural tradition more often than Mao Zedong, Deng Xiaoping, Jiang Zemin, and Hu Jintao ever did during their time at the helm.[49] This positive evaluation of the Chinse cultural tradition is also reflected in the new party constitution, which was adopted in 2018 (Art. 3).[50]

As a result of all these changes, Tang Wenming has proposed that Kang Youwei, not Sun Yat-sen, or Mao Zedong, should be considered the law maker of modern China, because he valued the Chinese cultural tradition more by updating Confucianism to serve as the dominant ideology.[51] Many scholars believe that if the late Qing reform under Kang had been successful, China might have become a constitutional monarchy, like modern Japan.

Under Xi, China has been moving in the direction of equality, or gong tong fu yu (collectively shared wealth), in a way that reflects the eventual ambition to achieve datong. Evidence for this comes from World Bank data showing that China has lifted millions out of poverty in the last decade.[52] As a result, the income gap between the rich and the poor has narrowed under Xi. China's Gini was 43.7 in 2010 but dropped to 38.2 in 2019. China Gini is now slightly lower than the United States, indicating that it is more equal than the latter.[53] One report notes that "the satisfaction gap between privileged and more marginalized populations in China is beginning to close, in large part owing to efforts by the Hu Jintao and Xi Jinping administrations to rebalance the gains of economic growth and shift resources towards the populations most overlooked during China's first few decades of reform."[54]

Mao: "Correct Ideas Come from Social Practice"

In constitutional making, Chinese communists never believed in abstract concepts based on some kind of general principle, such as "freedom," or "human rights," as was the case in the U.S. Constitution. For them, ideas are derived from social reality and after these ideas have been summarized and systemized in the form of documents, they can be used to guide social practice in social movements and campaigns. As Mao asks, "Where do correct ideas come from? From Heaven? No. Correct ideas can only come from social practice."[55]

According to this logic, the CCP did not see anything wrong when the party promoted the adoption of the U.S. constitutional model instead of the Soviet one in its 1946 constitutional reform. That was because not only the United States was the supreme power at the end of the Second World War, but also because the U.S. constitutional model would allow the CCP to survive better within the alliance dominated by Kuomintang (KMT). If they had adopted a Soviet constitutional model at that time, this would have given the dominant KMT more power and would have decreased the space for the survival of the smaller CCP.

Similarly, the CCP was prepared to use the Four Constitutional Amendments to move in the direction of liberalism during the period from 1988 through 2004 when the United States dominated the world in most areas and the main item on China's agenda was to develop its productive forces. In both these two periods, when the CCP was seriously leaning towards a U.S. constitutional model, the Chinese communists were not led by an embrace of U.S. ideals, but by their pragmatic need for the survival of the CCP and for making China into a strong nation.

The Fifth Amendment is no exception to this pragmatic approach. It was a response to the international scene as well as the domestic situation that China faced at that time. Xi Jinping came to power under very different international and domestic environment compared with his two predecessors. The Fifth Amendment was promulgated against the background of the rapid growth of the Chinese economy. The International Monetary Fund (IMF) estimated that China's economy was larger than that of the United States in terms of its purchasing power parity (PPP) as early as 2014.[56] According to official Chinese data, during Xi's first term from 2012 to 2017 the country's GDP increased from 54 trillion RMB (7.9 trillion USD) to 80 trillion RMB (11.6 trillion USD), second largest economy in the world.[57] According to the World Bank, China has since 1990 lifted 800 million people out of poverty.[58]

The economic depression of 2008 was also a factor for China's switch in policy orientation. In terms of its overall impact, the IMF concluded that it was the worst global recession since the Great Depression in the 1930s.[59] Although China's exports suffered as a result of the recession, on the whole, the country did not experience a recession because the Chinese government controlled the country's banking system more strictly than Western countries did. The economic slowdown in the West encouraged some Chinese establishment intellectuals to brag about China's power, e.g., the claim by Hu Angang in 2015 that China had surpassed the United States in all major areas.[60]

Going hand in hand with the West's economic slowdown was the decline in confidence in the Western economic and political model.[61] The effectiveness of the American democracy was called into question.[62] A World Bank President remarked: "With the 19th Party Congress of October 2017, China has positioned itself as an example to emulate. President Xi Jinping's speech signified a departure from China's past aspirations. The Chinese model offers a new option for other countries and nations who want to speed up their development while preserving their independence; and it offers Chinese wisdom and a Chinese approach to solving the problems facing mankind."[63] This contrasted to the "Third Wave of Democratization" of the 1980s and 1990s.⁶⁴ Actually, the global situation after the 2008 depression resembled that in the 1930s following the 1929 Great Depression in that some countries such as Germany, Italy, and Japan lost confidence in the Western model of development and turned to Nazism, Fascism, and militarism. In recent years, growing number of strongmen has emerged in many countries in the world, such as China, Russia, Turkey, and India, in defiance of Western liberalism.⁶⁵

The diversity and confusion of Western theories has reinforced people's doubt about democracy. The American scholar Francis Fukuyama, who had claimed in the 1990s that democracy had won throughout the world⁶⁶ now called the U.S. democracy inefficient and dysfunctional.⁶⁷ Earlier, Eric Hobsbawm described the failure of all systems, state socialism, capitalism, and nationalism.⁶⁸ Some Chinese intellectuals also took notice of the earlier work by Joseph Schumpeter who remarked that all politics were within the elites, not about the masses, thus casting doubt about modern liberal democracy.⁶⁹

The CCP was also faced with a serious domestic challenge at the time. The first was that the income gap between the rich and poor had grown dramatically during the reform era. This was ironic for a country that claims to follow the model set by Karl Marx who preached equality. Some among the Chinese elites believed that the old way of governance over the past four decades was unable to resolve this problem and a return to some Maoist practices, such as egalitarianism guaranteed by an emphasis on ideology, the party, and a strong ruler seem to be the answer.

Furthermore, official corruption has reached unprecedented levels that called for a greater role of the law in curbing this phenomenon. A Western report estimated that about 170 ministerial-level officials had been purged, and around 1.34 million officials had been dismissed or punished between 2012 and 2017.⁷⁰ The explosive nature of Chinese society is illustrated by the fact that in 2018 China spent more money on *weiwen*, that is, stamping out social unrest, than on military spending.⁷¹ A drastic change of leadership style is required to avoid ungovernable social unrest.

To deal with this situation, the CCP changed its policy orientations. In a major article collectively written by a study group within the Central Party School (a think tank under the CCP Central Committee), the new era was launched, announcing a transition from "focusing on incentives so that a few can get rich first to a focus on growing the common wealth of all the Chinese people," reflecting the regime's concern about the growing income gap; from "liberating people's thought from leftism (immediately after the Cultural Revolution) to "centralizing political ideas along the line of the party," implying a tightening of control of people's thought; and from Deng Xiaoping's "hiding one's capabilities to bide one's time" (tao guang yang hui) to launching an assertive foreign policy in world affairs.[72]

In a sense, the historical circumstances in the first decade of the twenty-first century called for a new kind of leader who was different from Jiang Zemin, an engineer from Shanghai, China's most modern city. In other words, the switch in politics was probably more structural than personal. Xi Jinping (1953–) was the first major leader born after the 1949 communist take-over. When the Cultural Revolution (1966–1976) broke out, he was thirteen. He witnessed the harsh nature of politics during the chaos, especially given the fact that his father, former Vice Premier Xi Zhongxun (1913–2002) was jailed for political reasons. Xi Jinping then was sent to the northwestern part of China to live in a cave with poor peasants.

As a princeling,[73] he is more likely to view himself as inheriting the communist tradition represented by his father, unlike Hu Jintao (1942–) and Wen Jiabao (1942–) who are viewed by some as "temporary managers" of the government because they had roots among the common folk. Many among Xi's generation of leaders were also active participants in the Cultural Revolution and their activities turned them into seasoned politicians. They were different from Hu and Wen, a generation whose world outlook was shaped in the 1950s and was noted for producing politicians who were obedient to their supervisors. The 1950s was a time when the CCP enjoyed prestige and most young people had little difficulty in being the "obedient tools of the party."

Xi also differed from the previous two generations of Chinese leaders in terms of his academic background. While the generation of Jiang Zemin and Hu Jintao was noted for being technocrats who were typically not interested in philosophical issues such as socialism, capitalism, and democracy—both Jiang Zemin and Hu Jintao were engineers—Xi studied Marxism at Tsinghua University.

Conclusion

In modern history, China has experienced three traditions: communist, traditional, and Western liberalism. These three traditions are like building blocks that the Chinese leaders during different periods place in a different order. During the period of the four constitutional amendments from 1988 through to 2004, the liberal block was at the top, while the communist and the traditional blocks were at the bottom, in a triangle. During the time of the Fifth Constitutional Amendment, the two blocks of communism and Chinese tradition were at the top while the liberalism block was at the bottom, in an inverted triangle upside down. In both these circumstances, none of the three pieces was abandoned. It was just a matter of emphasis.

The flexible nature of the post-Mao reform can also be seen from the fact that Wang Huning served as the ideology tsar for the three regimes of Jiang Zemin, Hu Jintao, and Xi Jinping.[74] The thread that runs through all the three regimes is the idea of sticking to the CCP leadership, that is supposed to be the most important in Deng Xiaoping's Four Cardinal Principles, that is, sticking to socialist path, people's democratic dictatorship, the CCP leadership, and Marxism-Leninism Mao Zedong Thought.

The Fifth PRC Amendment in 2018, as well as the new party constitutional amendment adopted in 2017, symbolized the reversal of China's constitutional reform in its emphasis on ideology, the CCP, the personal role of the top leader, and some aspects of China's legal tradition.

This is a departure from the previous four constitutional amendments. The first three amendments were promulgated, for the most part, during Jiang's regime. Although the fourth amendment was promulgated in 2004, when Hu was the party secretary, Jiang's influence was obvious. Jiang's theory of "Three Represents," was added to the fourth amendment, not Hu's trademark notion of a harmonious society. Therefore, we can say that the four amendments were largely the theories of Jiang.

In general, the new constitutional amendments were a response to the international and domestic challenges that China faced towards the end of the first decade of the twenty-first century. These challenges include an international environment in which freedom had been in decline for more than a decade; and the domestic situation in which official corruption and the income gap between the rich and poor reduced the trust of the Chinese people in the government to a record low. Many felt that the country was on the verge of a revolution.

Having examined the general ideological orientation of the Xi regime through analyzing the five constitutional amendments, focusing on the Fifth one, in the following four chapters we will turn to the study of the four concrete issues that the Xi regime has dealt: how to control the Chinese society through law; how to control the bureaucrats through law; how to control the people through law and how Xi's foreign policy is reflected in law.

Chapter 4

The Creation of the Security State

This chapter compares the National Security Law of 2015 (SL15) with the National Security Law of 1993 (SL93). Western scholars have not made a comprehensive study of the SL15. This is odd because there is a considerable body of literature on the Central National Security Commission (CNSC) which was established in 2013, the institution that carries out the policies and laws embodied in the SL15. For instance, Ji You and Richard Hu have made detailed studies of the organization and functions of the CNSC, in which You emphasizes the domestic function of the institution, while Hu claims that it is both domestic and international.[1] Joel Wuthnow complains that CNSC is not transparent because the Chinese Communist Party (CCP) is secretive about its activities.[2] Similarly, David Lampton raises more questions about the CNSC than he answers, saying that the maturation of the institution may take years.[3] But the general view of scholars is that the aim of Commission is to centralize power in matters of national security. The opaque operations of CNSC make it necessary to study SL15 that is supposed to guide the operations of the institution.

The concept of national security has not been clearly defined in the literature. It is generally taken to have a self-evident meaning, or as an ambiguous symbol.[4] The evolving conception of this term poses a challenge to the interpretation and application of international law.[5] Nevertheless, in general the concept of national security since the end of the Second World War has been based on the notions of nation-state and sovereignty and generally refers to the case when a country faces no danger to its territories, citizens, economy, and other institutions, especially the state.

Considering that enormous global changes have affected the meaning of traditional national security concepts in recent years, Anton Grizold argues that a new "cooperative model of international security may represent the starting point for the forming of a new and more efficiently adjusted national and global security structure."[6] This model includes the nontraditional aspects of national security, such as its economy, technology, and natural resources. In 2017 Congyan Cai wrote an article promoting the concept of new national security, which she sees as representing a twenty-first-century paradigm characterized by "multiple actors, wide covering, low predictability, subjective perception, dual nature, and rampant diffusion." She claims that Chinese conception of national security has its own Chinese characteristics.[7] In a related way, SL15 defines national security as: "The state in which China's political power, sovereignty, unity, and territorial integrity, the wellbeing of the nation, the sustainable development of the economy and society and other important national interests are relatively free of any danger or domestic or foreign threat, and the ability to maintain a continuously secure state."

The Western media consequently interprets Chinese national security as what "Chinese leaders see as three sacrosanct rights of the nation: maintaining the political system, with unquestioned rule by the CCP; defending sovereignty claims and territorial integrity; and economic development."[8] This is a departure from the SL93 that defines national security in Article 3 as mostly related to domestic security and to citizens who collaborate with outside forces to harm China's national security. While SL15 has eighty-four articles covering a much wider area of national security—including sovereignty and territorial integrity, politics, economics, finance, energy, food, science and technology, culture, religion, information, terrorism, outer space, deep sea, and polar regions—the 1993 law has thirty-four articles that are largely designed to combat espionage.

The SL15 aims at the national rejuvenation of the Chinese people (Art 1), which is a key component of the Chinese Dream. This is also the mission of the CNSC, which is intended to meet the needs of China's growing power and Xi's aspiration to play big power diplomacy in world affairs as well as his ambition to make overall reforms of foreign and national security policymaking institutions in China.[9] The SL15 was promulgated in response to the fact that the world had become more globalized since 1993, and China had developed more contacts with the outside world. In contrast to the early 1990s, when China was in a period of isolation—partly because of the government's crackdown on Tiananmen demonstrators in 1989,[10] by 2014 China had established 72 partnerships with 67 countries.[11] China is now the largest trading partner with eighty countries in the world, while the United States is the largest trading partner with fifty countries.[12]

Institutional deficiency is another reason why China found it necessary to promulgate SL15. Many of the top leaders believe that the power structure, which was decentralized during the Hu Jintao and Wen Jiabao era, needs to be recentralized.[13] Examining Chinese institutional structures and the structural distribution of resources and authority during the post-Mao era, Kenneth Lieberthal uses the term a "fragmented authoritarianism model" to describe its internal dynamics and the source of its institutional deficiencies.[14] For instance, the Chinese government's handling of the US bombing of China's Belgrade Embassy in 1999 was widely believed to be inept.[15]

1. Political Security

The Security of the CPP and Ideological Threats

Political security is the most important of the many areas of national security defined by the SL15, because it addresses the security of the regime and the CCP.[16] The ruling elites have realized that the security situation for China has become more challenging than before. Zheng Shuna, deputy director of the National People's Congress (NPC)'s Legislative Affairs Commission, remarked that the law was in part necessitated by China's "increasingly grim" security situation, which was now "more complicated than at any other time in history."[17] In Xi's report at the Twentieth CCP National Conference, he mentions the term "struggle" seventeen times and "security" fifty times.[18]

The key to political security is ideological security. Barry Buzan argues that the referent object of political security is ideology.[19] As a constituent part of the system of national security, "ideological security" refers to the situation where the state's dominant ideology is relatively secure and free from internal and external threats, as well as to its ability to ensure it can continue unchecked.[20] This connection is especially marked in the case of the CCP because it obtains legitimacy not via democratic elections but via a theory, that is, Leninist-Maoist thought. This theory and thought state that the Communist Party is the vanguard of the proletariat and therefore entitled to lead because the party has no self-interest.[21]

For SL15, "the state adheres to the orientation of the advanced socialist culture, carrying forward the excellent traditional culture of the Chinese people, cultivating and practicing the Core Socialist Values,[22] guarding against and resisting negative cultural influences, taking hold of dominance in the ideology and culture." (Art 23). SL93 does not mention ideology.

Ideology and culture were included in China's national security against the background that throughout the world culture has come to be regarded as an integral part of national security. For instance, "Culture has become fashionable in mainstream international relations scholarship in the post-Cold War era. One of the most surprising aspects of the renaissance of scholarly interest in culture has been the emerging consensus in national security policy studies that culture can affect significantly grand strategy and state behavior."[23] Similarly, Tang Aijun claims that "the core of national political security is the security of the regime and the political system. Maintaining regime security and political system security requires demonstrating and publicizing the rationality and legitimacy (of the regime) . . . to elevate ideological construction to a strategic position in national security and formulate and implement a national ideological security strategy."[24] For the Chinese, culture and ideological security also refers to the concern that the Chinese cultural tradition that should not be replaced by Western culture.[25]

The ruling elites may also have been concerned that if the liberal trends that had been developing before Xi were not stopped, China may have become another Taiwan or South Korea, where multiparty politics would emerge and threaten the CCP monopoly of power.

Evidence of Threats: Foreign, Religion, and Rights Awareness

In the SL15, a top national security concern is the spread of foreign influence in China (Art 27). This is exemplified by the comment by Xi Jinping: "Hostile Western forces have always regarded China's development and growth as a threat to Western values and institutional models. They have not for a moment ceased their ideological infiltration of China."[26] Before Xi came to power, some foreign donors and international nongovernmental organizations (NGOs) funded, initiated, and designed training programs that introduced their Chinese recipients to what they call "best practices" in "NGO management." These efforts were regarded as successful from the perspective of the West. Despite recurring Chinese suspicions that the concept of civil society and NGOs were a new weapon of foreign imperialism, the structures and practices promoted by foreign donors mesh well with state's efforts to channel new social energies into governable organizational forms.[27]

I directed a research project funded by the US State Department in collaboration with China's Central Party School to promote legislative reforms in China from 2006 through 2011 when it was successfully completed.[28] We held workshops in Sichuan, Anhui, Beijing, and Shanxi, and hosted delegations from provincial party schools for visits in the United

States. In the first three decades after the reform, these activities were viewed by the Chinese authorities as more constructive than subversive. However, these projects that attempted introducing Western ideas to China were not always successful, especially with the recent policy switch. As the chief editor, I edited a book series that translated Western political science books into Chinese published by Renmin University Press. The series had published twenty-three titles before it was discontinued in 2020. Another example was the Carter Center's efforts to promote grassroots elections in China. The center used the platform of the internet and held workshops to demonstrate to the Chinese how elections work in the West. This project was eventually stopped by the regime, who believed it was subverting the stability of China.[29]

Another area of national security concern is that of religious activities, especially religions that originate in foreign countries. Before Xi came to power, there were estimated to be as many as 130 million protestants in China, who held many of their religious activities in secret.[30] This reminded us of the Falun Gong cult movement in the 1990s, which also had more than a hundred million followers.[31] Falun Gong has now either gone underground or exists in exile in foreign countries. Both have a larger membership than the CCP, which has about ninety-eight million members. China's capitalism-oriented reform with the "emerging market is exciting and perilous, accompanied by widespread moral corruption, which prompts many individuals to seek a theodicy, or a religious worldview, to put the seemingly chaotic universe into order."[32] To minimize these dangers, the SL15 decreeds that the state will prevent, stop, and lawfully punish the exploitation of religion as a way of conducting illegal and criminal activities that endanger national security and oppose foreign influence and interference into domestic religious affairs. Thus, the state will shut down cult organizations in accordance with the law (Art 27).

Against this background churchgoers attempted to meet these new rules. For instance, church leaders are quick to reinforce the idea that their organizations are purely religious in character and harbor no political ambitions. As one preacher explained, most church services begin with prayers for China and CCP leaders (even though party members are required to uphold atheism), signaling their open commitment to patriotism.[33]

A third source of national security concern is China's rising consciousness of human rights. Modernization theory predicts that the rise in China's economic prosperity and trade will lead to the endorsement of democracy and human rights by the Chinese people,[34] although China's political elite may hope for the demise of the political domination of the West.[35] According to a study by Peter Lorentzen and Suzanne Scoggins conducted before Xi came to power, the Chinese were exhibiting a rising "rights consciousness," and some observers suggested that this phenomenon was driving political change. Thus, it is thought that the rights consciousness resulting from this change in values was a threat to the continued rule of the CCP.[36]

It is not just Western observers who hold this view. The regime under Xi believes that such values as democracy, freedom, and human rights are threats to China's ideological security. For the regime, "the main method of Western ideological penetration has been to promote 'universal values' and to dissolve China's dominant ideology."[37] This approach has changed radically from that of Jiang Zemin, who was able to recite the Gettysburg Address to *60 Minutes CBS News*.[38]

The CCP now feels that the party, rather than the government, has to be in charge of national security. While the State Council oversaw national security in the SL93 (Art 2), SL15 now stipulates that the CCP is in charge of national security (Art 4, 15). The CNSC is under the jurisdiction of the Central Committee of the CCP and Xi Jinping, the general secretary of the Central Committee.

Territorial Security

DOMESTIC: ETHNIC MINORITIES

There are fifty-six ethnic groups in China, the largest of which is the Han. About 114 million people in China are officially recognized as belonging to one or another ethnic minority.[39] Among these ethnic minorities, the deepest separatist tendencies can be observed in Tibet and Xinjiang. One factor contributing to this is that these two autonomous regions are geographically the most distant from the center of Chinese civilization, that is, central China.[40] As historically nomadic tribes, their way of living is also much different from that of central China: farming. It is also because the religions they practice are largely very distinct from Confucianism. Many Tibetans believe in Lamaism, a religion close to Buddhism.[41] Most Uyghurs identify themselves as Muslims and practice Sunni Islam. This also conflicts with Confucianism. Once in a while riots and protests against the government emerge from these two areas.

The three decades before Xi saw a change in government policies toward ethnic minorities, starting with a policy of assimilation during the Maoist era to one of pluralism in 1982. "The 1982 Constitution and the Law on National Regional Autonomy of 1984 have granted national minorities the most pluralistic rights in comparison with any of the previous legislation. The loosening of political and economic restrictions and the return to pluralistic policies led to a revival of nationalist consciousness in many parts of the minority areas."[42] Due to the fact that these minorities have disproportionately suffered adverse effects from China's rapid socioeconomic transition, together with the growing inequality between the rich and the poor—not to mention the failure of the local authorities to properly implement government policies—ethnic issues had become an increasing source of dissatisfaction, conflict, and even violence before Xi came to power.

The government policies under Xi have reversed this trend and are moving back from pluralism to assimilation. The issue of ethnic minorities is raised in the SL15 to the level of national security, while it is not mentioned in the SL93. The new law calls for ethnic separatism to be stopped and punished and for the nation to defend national integrity, the unity of all ethnic nationalities, and social harmony (Art 26).

But this recent policy change under Xi does not seem have improved matters in the sense that the conflicts between ethnic minorities and the regime seem to have become worse. For instance, in 2023 the United Nations noted that around a million Tibetan children were adversely affected by Chinese government policies aimed at assimilating the Tibetan culturally, religiously, and linguistically by instituting a residential school system.[43] The situation in Xinjiang is also troubling. According to a report by the Council on Foreign Relations, the Chinese government has since 2017 subjected many Uyghurs to intense surveillance, religious restrictions, forced labor, and forced sterilization.[44]

GREATER CHINA: HONG KONG, TAIWAN, AND THE SOUTH CHINA SEA

Xi's political gestures toward greater China, that is, Hong Kong, Macau, Taiwan, and disputed territories, have also become more assertive. The Xi regime insists, with respect to Hong Kong, that "the Hong Kong Special Administrative Region, and Macao Special Administrative Region shall fulfill responsibilities for the preservation of national security." (Art 40) By contrast, Hong Kong and Macau are not mentioned in the SL93. A more detailed document, the National Security Law for Hong Kong (NSLHK) makes activities that are viewed by the regime as secession and subversion punishable with a maximum life sentence. Under the NSLHK Beijing's national security staff are not subject to the jurisdiction of local government, although they have jurisdiction for serious security offenses in Hong Kong.[45]

This is a drastic departure from the 1984 Sino-British Joint Declaration that stipulates that the "One Country, Two Systems" arrangement would remain unchanged for fifty years starting from 1997. The new law has serious consequence for Hong Kong in terms of human rights, and it led to massive protests in 2019 and 2020 in opposition to the erosion of the rule of law, the decline of liberal society, and the downgrading of the electoral system in Hong Kong.[46]

Another hot-button issue for China's national security is Taiwan. Beijing's policy toward Taiwan has undergone three stages in the last four decades. In the 1980s, Beijing was actively engaged in seeking political reunification with Taiwan. With the election of Lee Tenghui (1923–2020) as the president of the Republic of Taiwan (ROC) and his subsequent visit to the United States as an alumnus of Cornell University, Beijing's strategy became more passive: as long as Taiwan did not declare its independence, things were considered to be acceptable.[47] Lee is a Taiwan native and in the eyes of Beijing has the tendency for Taiwan's independence from the mainland. Since the voices advocating the liberation of Taiwan by force have become louder, and since Xi came to power, Beijing's attitude toward Taiwan has entered a third stage. The Xi regime has stated that "the sovereignty and territorial integrity of China cannot be encroached upon or divided. Preservation of national sovereignty and territorial integrity is a shared obligation of all the Chinese people, including compatriots from Hong Kong, Macao, and Taiwan" (Art 11, 21). This means Taiwanese who want the island to remain independent of China are acting illegally and are therefore punishable accordingly. In protest, the Taiwanese government insists that ROC is a country of sovereignty. "Our policy is to stick to the ROC constitution, keep the status quo of 'no reunification, no independence and no armed conflicts.'" Both the ruling Kuomintang (KMT) and the opposition Democratic Progressive Party (DPP) oppose the SL15.[48]

In January 2024, Lai Ching-te, the candidate of the DPP was elected ROC president. Lai is known for his proindependence posture. This is the third time that the DPP has won the presidential elections in Taiwan. It is clear that Taiwan is drifting further away from the mainland, a situation that could cause serious conflicts across the Taiwan Strait.

China's policies toward disputed border areas and territorial waters have also become more aggressive. Among these are the Senkaku (Diaoyu) Islands of which China, Taiwan, and Japan all claim sovereignty, although it is under the control of Japan. Besides fishing resources, the area is also rich in crude oil. During the Deng administration, the Chinese government intended to shelve the issue and leave it for future generations to deal with.[49] But the regime under Xi has raised issues like this to the level of national security that need to be dealt with urgently. According to SL15, "The State increases the construction of border defense, coastal defense, and air defense, taking all necessary defense and control measures to defend the security of continental territory, internal water bodies, territorial waters and airspace, and to maintain national territorial sovereignty and maritime rights and interests (Art 17)."

China's assertion of its claim to the Senkaku Islands has led to its increased military and paramilitary forays around the island's waters and airspace and the risk of a Sino–Japanese crisis has reached unprecedented heights. The increased frequency and proximity at which vessels and aircraft encounter one another have led to an increased risk of conflict.[50] A recent national security controversy involves changes made to the standard map of China. Since 1949 China had always claimed that its territory is 9.60 million square kilometers. But in the 2023 standard map it increased China's territory to 10.45 million square kilometers, expanding it to include the disputed territories in the Philippines, Malaysia, Vietnam, Taiwan, and India.[51] This contrasts with its behavior during Jiang Zemin's administration, when China settled most of its territorial disputes with its neighbors with an accommodating attitude.[52]

Economic Security

The SL15 has raised issues related to economics to the level of national security, stating that China will defend the country's economic system (Art 19). Under this law, transnational corporations do not merely operate in China for economic gain; their presence is a matter of national security and therefore needs to be monitored. For instance, now China requires transnational corporations operating in the country to host groups that monitor their compliance with the CCP orthodoxy. In addition, the CCP has started to establish party cells within these corporations operating in China.[53]

China also wants to make sure that transnational corporations are unable to gather intelligence in the country. China's recent Anti-Espionage Law bans the transfer of information related to national security from China to other countries. This law is vague in content and leaves the boundary between legal and illegal activities unclear, a situation that alarms the United States because it believes that foreign companies in China could be punished for undertaking ordinary business activities.[54]

China is not the only country that has elevated economic activity and technology to an urgent matter of national security. The United States also wants to block China from developing chip technology. The *New York Times* reports that "the effects (of this ban) will go far beyond cutting into Chinese military advancements, threatening the country's economic growth and scientific leadership too."[55] Emily Kilcrease, a senior fellow at the Center for a New American Security and a former US trade official, believes that "there are key tech areas that China should not advance in. These happen to be the areas that will power future economic growth and development."[56] Xi Jinping has voiced his opposition to the use of economic measures and technology for strategic purposes.[57]

The US-China trade war that started in 2018 is yet another example of economic issues being elevated to a national security concern. Since joining the World Trade Organization in 2001, China's trade behavior had always been a concern of Western countries, including China's blockage of market access to foreign companies, the government's subsidies of export products, violation of the protection of intellectual property rights, and its forced technology transfer imposed upon foreign corporations.[58] But the conflicts at the time were generally manageable because the United States tolerated some of China's malpractices in international trade for the strategic reason of encouraging China to move in the direction that the West desired.[59]

This strategy was similar to the US approach to its trade relations with Japan following the end of the Second World War in the 1950s and 1960s. Despite the lack of reciprocal access to the Japanese market, the United States largely refrained from resorting to aggressive trade tactics against the Japanese in an effort to keep Japan on the side of the Western bloc during the Cold War. However, it changed course in the 1970s and 1980s when the Japanese economy became large enough to threaten US economic interests.

The trade conflicts between the United States and China became a war in 2018 partly because of Xi's change of course from Deng Xiaoping's reforms in the late 1970s, a shift that is dampening the hopes in the West that China would pursue a more liberal path. It also is a result of the changes in the balance of power. In addition to China's rapid economic growth (from 10 percent of the US economy in 2010 to about 70 percent around 2021), the United States believes that China now has increased its military power considerably. Some experts in the United States believe that China has a larger number of land-based (stationary and mobile) intercontinental ballistic missile launchers than the United States. The real Chinese military budget is probably far higher than its alleged budget of $224.79 billion.[60]

Human Rights and National Security

HUMAN RIGHTS AND NATIONAL SECURITY

In general, national security issues are different from other issues regarding the rule of law: while the rule of law is regarded as innately constructive in most respects, it is not as straightforward when it comes to national security. When national security conflicts with the right to privacy, some are inclined to protect the former at the expense of the latter, while others lean toward protecting human rights. In times of war, national security is often stressed, while in times of peace, a democratic country tends to pay more attention to civil rights.[61] People's expectations of the rule of law in national security are low because national security is supposed to be high-end politics. Even some democracies may sometimes surrender the protection of privacy over the question of national security.[62] A typical case is the US government's detention of about 120,000 Japanese Americans during the Second World War.[63]

To make things more complex, in China the understanding of human rights is different from that of many other countries. Societal and cultural differences acquired in the last few thousand years cannot be overcome within mere decades. The world has not become flat culturally. This surely has an impact on people's understanding of human rights and the rule of law.[64]

Historically, Chinese rulers permit citizens fewer rights and freedoms than many other countries, such as Japan and Russia.[65] For instance, the current Chinese regime is highly punitive when it comes to wrongdoing. Amnesty International reports that China executes more people than all other countries combined.[66] The retention of death penalty in China is grounded on its so-called national circumstances that require the death penalty to achieve crime control, incapacitate criminals, and appease public anger.[67]

Although the PRC is a signatory to a number of UN human rights conventions, the Chinese government has reservations about the implementation of some of the conventions that could influence its national approach to human rights issues. For instance, China does not recognize the International Court of Justice's mandate to settle disputes on human rights, nor does it allow the individual complaint procedure that is provided for in the International Convention on the Elimination of All Forms of Racial Discrimination to be followed in China.[68]

Implications of SL15

Of all the laws examined in this book, the SL15 is weak in protecting human rights, such as Civil Code and National Supervision Law. It is also weaker than the SL93. For instance, in the SL93, citizens' rights against "unlawful detention," "excessive or abuse of power," and "confession by torture" committed by the national security forces are missing from the SL15 (see Table 4.1). This is in spite of the fact that the SL93 is not up to the standards of the rule of law in the first place. It also allocates excessive power to the government. It entrusts broad powers, ranging from intelligence-gathering to law enforcement to the Ministry of State Security and does not give people the right to protest against unfair decisions. Judicial institutions such as the courts had no say in the enforcement of national security law.[69]

In protest against the SL15, the ambassadors of the United States, Canada, Germany, and Japan co-signed a letter in Beijing addressed to the government of China, expressing their disquiet with it, saying that "we believe the new legislative measures have the potential to impede commerce, stifle innovation, and infringe on China's obligation to protect human rights in accordance with international law."[70] Similarly, in response to the SL15, a UN official said, "I regret that more and more governments around the world are using national security measures to restrict the rights to freedom of expression, association and peaceful assembly, and also as a tool to target human rights defenders and silence critics."[71] Furthermore, legal scholar Jerome Cohen noted that this "reflects the party's determination to create a garrison state." William Nee, from Amnesty International criticized the law for its vague provisions, as well as the lack of detail on what Beijing deems offenses and what penalties would apply to them. Such ambiguities would "make it impossible for people to know what behavior is actually prohibited" and allow the authorities to prosecute anyone they deemed to be a threat.[72]

Going hand in hand with the decrease in human rights enjoyed by ordinary citizens in China is the increased power of the ruling elites on national security. For example, the SL15 gives President Xi a lot more power than presidents had in the past, including the power to declare a state of emergency. This item was not included in the SL93. Western observers believe that the Chinese government intends to strengthen national security through Xi's leadership,[73] and Xi will use the CNSC to gain personal power.[74] These scholars believe that expansion of the definition of security may allow the CNSC to wield unlimited power.[75]

Conclusion

The post-Mao reform has witnessed three approaches to development: the first was "economic development is the hard truth (fazhan shi yingdaoli)," that is, achieving economic development was the primary aim, mostly in the 1990s under Deng and Jiang; the second was the view that "considerations of stability override everything else (wending yadao yiqie)," which was prevalent mostly during the Hu-Wen era. The third attitude is that "security is the hard truth (an quan shi ying daoli)" and found mostly under Xi. In the last four decades, China has become increasingly insecure.

When Xi came to power, he encountered three daunting problems that threatened to tear society apart: the people hated the government (chou guan); the people hated the rich (chou fu); and the people had no spiritual faith. As one of the characters says in a TV series entitled *In the Name of the People (renmin de mingyi)* sponsored by the Supreme People's Procuratorate in 2017, "In the past, people did not believe that the government would do bad things; nowadays, people don't believe that the government will do good things." The introduction of the TV series in Baidu, the Chinese version of Google, received over sixty million hits, indicating that the fictional view struck a chord in the hearts of the people.[76]

To address these problems, Xi had two options: moving forward along the relatively liberal line unleashed by Deng's reform or moving backward to the Maoist line. He chose the second option because he is familiar with it and because the international conditions (a perceived weaker US) allow him to do so. More importantly, to move along the line of political reform will lead to problems that the CCP does not want to encounter. Political reform will force the CCP to share power with other sectors of society, such as entrepreneurs who have accumulated wealth. For instance, Jack Ma, who owns a giant online retail company, is starting to establish so-called universities that resemble the club of successful entrepreneurs because the prerequisite for enrollment is huge amounts of money.[77] The primary purpose of Ma's university is networking: more for political purposes than gaining scientific knowledge.

In adopting the Maoist method of relying on the CCP to clean up corruption, Xi seems to have made some headway in addressing two of the most important problems he encountered in 2012: the income gap between rich and poor has narrowed, and corruption has been efficiently addressed. But during the process, he has made other problems worse. For instance, China's economic growth, which was the basis of the CCP's legitimacy during the post-Mao era, was cut in half during the Xi regime. By moving against the democratization process, Xi also alienated major Western countries, especially the United States. China, and especially the CCP, has become less secure, and Xi therefore makes security the top priority in policy making as discussed in this chapter.

Table 4.1 Comparison of the National Security Laws of 1993 and 2015 on Human Rights

1993	2015
Article 22: Any citizen or organization has the right to address the state security organ at a high level or a relevant department to expose or complain about the excessive use or abuse of power or other unlawful acts committed by a state security organ or its functionaries. This high-level state security organ or department shall ascertain the facts without delay and be responsible for the handling thereof. No one may suppress or retaliate against any citizen or organization that has assisted a state security organ in its work or made reports or charges according to law.	Article 81: Where citizens and organizations suffer a loss of assets because they supported or assisted national security work may follow the relevant national provisions to obtain compensation; where physical injury or death is caused, they may follow relevant national provisions to obtain bereavement benefits.
Article 31: Any party concerned, if not satisfied with a detention decision, may apply for it to be reconsidered within 15 days after receipt of the decision to the organ at a higher level over the one that has made the decision; and if they are still not satisfied with the reconsideration decision, the party concerned may bring a suit in a people's court within 15 days after receipt of the reconsideration decision.	Article 82: Citizens and organizations have the right to raise criticisms and recommendations to state organs regarding national security, and they have the right to file complaint appeals, accusations or reports regarding the unlawful activity of state organs and their personnel.

The Creation of the Security State | 57

1993	2015
Article 32: Any state security official who neglects their duty or engages in malpractices for personal interests, if the offence constitutes a crime, shall be punished in accordance with the provisions of Article 187 or Article 188 of the Criminal Law. Any such person who practices unlawful detention or extorts a confession by torture, if the offence constitutes a crime, shall be punished respectively in accordance with the provisions of Article 143 or Article 136 of the Criminal Law.	Article 83: In national security work, when special measures are required that restrict the rights and freedoms of citizens, they shall be conducted in accordance with the law, and limited by the actual need to safeguard national security.
Article 9: As necessitated by the maintenance of state security, a state security organ may, when necessary and in accordance with the relevant provisions of the state, have priority in use of any means of transport or communication, site or building belonging to any organ, organization, enterprise, institution or individual, and shall make a timely return after its use and pay an appropriate fee, and, in case of any damage or loss, shall make compensation therefor.	Article 7: The safeguarding of national security shall abide by the Constitution and the law, persist in the principles of the socialist rule of law, respect and ensure human rights, and protect the rights and liberties of citizens according to the law.
Article 13: State security organs and their functionaries, in their work of state security, shall act strictly according to law, and refrain from overstepping or abusing their powers and infringing upon the lawful rights and interests of any organization or individual.	

Chapter 5

The Politics of Anticorruption

The Supervision Law of the People's Republic of China (NSL) was promulgated by the National People's Congress (NPC) in March 2018. This was the third supervision law to be created after the 2010 Administrative Supervision Law of the People's Republic of China[1] and the 1990 Administrative Supervision Statutes of the People's Republic of China.

All the three supervision laws target corruption, defined as ranging from traditional economic corruption such as bribery, embezzlement, and misappropriation to the neglect of duties and unethical behavior such as gambling and the sexual vices of state functionaries.[2] In this chapter we ask what is new about the third one, compared with the previous two laws; examine how it is situated in key theoretical and ideological issues of the post-Mao era, and inspect the changing role of the CCP in relation to the structuring of institutions to address corruption and judicial independence.

At 9,305 Chinese characters in length, China's 2018 NSL is roughly the same length as the first two supervision laws combined. Corruption is mentioned only in the 2018 NSL, not in the two previous ones. The 1990 Supervision Law is called a "*tiaoli*" (regulation), which has lower juridical force than "*fa lu*" (law), under which the 2010 and 2018 supervision laws were promulgated. In addition, the 1990 regulation was put into effect by the State Council, which ranks lower down the power structure than the NPC, which promulgated the 2010 and 2018 variants. This demonstrates the increasing urgency with which the Chinese government addresses official corruption and its growing interest in using the law to govern society.

The NSL mirrors the images of the Chinese legal tradition such as the Legalism of Qin (221–206 BCE) and the anticorruption endeavors of Emperor

Zhu Yuanzhang (1328–1398 CE) of the Ming Dynasty (1368–1644). As an integrated part of Xi's policy, this law stresses the role of Xi's personality, the party leadership, and the centralization of power. In a reversal of the post-Mao trend to separate the CCP from the government's daily operations (*dang zheng fen jia*), the newly created National Supervision Commission (NSC) combines the powers of the party's Central Commission of Disciplinary Inspection (CCDI), the NSC, and the Procuratorate. In a clarification of the post-Mao debate as to which was more powerful, the CCP or the law (*dang da hai shi fa da*), it was learned that the judiciary had been stripped of some of its independence, not only in practice, but also in principle. The NSC now handles criminal cases, such as the embezzlement of public funds, as well as the politically deviant behavior of government officials, whether they are party members or not. This signals the regime's retreat from its commitment to protect human rights during the judicial procedure.

The current research project builds upon some previous studies on the topic, albeit with a different focus. These previous studies include topics such as the NSC, not the NSL;[3] the procedures for interrogation in investigations;[4] the relationship between the NSC and the judiciary;[5] and the relationship between lower-level and top-level supervision institutions.[6]

This chapter is structured as follows. The first section explains the historical background to the various supervision laws. The next section analyzes Chinese legal culture and the NSL, starting with the premodern Chinese state's method of handling bureaucrats. The third section discusses the ideological orientation of the NSL and the structure of the NSC. The final section discusses domestic and overseas anticorruption operations. It deals with such issues as the connection between judicial independence and human rights, focusing on liuzhi (the enforced detention and involuntary disappearances by authorities of those suspected of crimes or flouting party discipline or possible crimes) and shuanggui (questioning a potential criminal at an appointed time and place.) as well as the difficulties in overseas anticorruption operations.

Why Was the NSL Considered Necessary?

The NSL was developed to prevent official corruption (2018 Art. 1). Historically, communist countries have addressed wrongdoing by government officials, which often consist of a mixture of criminal and political offenses, using a variety of methods. The former Soviet Union (USSR) relied largely on the secret police, Cheka, to address corruption[7] and under Mao China relied on a combination of the party's disciplinary inspection offices and political campaigns.

The PRC's first attempt to deal with official corruption was in 1952 using the San Fan Movement (the Three Antis Movement), which consisted of "Anti-Corruption, anti-waste, and anti-bureaucratism, i.e., the attitudes of being out of touch with the masses." The new regime's monopoly of power made it easy for government officials to embezzle public funds. According to official sources, as many as nine million people were investigated, and 4.5 percent of them were found guilty or problematic. Some received a reprimand from the party while 9,942 were found guilty and sentenced. Forty-two of the latter were executed.[8]

The Hundred Flowers Movement in 1956[9] and the Cultural Revolution[10] had many targets and one of them was corruption. But the corruption during these periods was small in scale because public resources had by now been tightly controlled after the San Fan period. Another difference was that while the San Fan Movement was led by the party, the Hundred Flowers Movement and the Cultural Revolution were mass mobilization campaigns that were manipulated by the top leadership, with the personal involvement of Mao himself. What these campaigns had in common is that they were not regulated by law.

During the post-Mao era, official corruption became considerably worse because central control had relaxed and fiscal policies had become more flexible, especially at the local level. Due to China's fiscal decentralization and lack of relevant supervision and management, government officials were easily able to abuse public resources.[11] To make the situation worse, although China's legal system has undergone tremendous changes in the last four decades, it still does not have well established laws and institutions to control corruption. China remains one of the few countries where public officials don't have to disclose their income publicly.

Another contributor to corruption is *guanxi,* the Chinese term for personal connections.[12] The Chinese are known for valuing personal relations very highly, often at the expense of the public good. Confucian love is graded in stages of familiarity; it is not an equal and universal love. Belonging to the same family, coming from the same hometown, having studied at the same school, means a lot to Chinese people. In addition, unlike some other civilizations, including the Christian belief that the rich find it harder to get to heaven than the poor, the Chinese tend to view wealth as having unlimited value.[13]

Corruption had dire consequences for the country and the regime. For instance, in the late 1990s, economic losses due to corruption were estimated to have amounted to around 13.2 to 16.8 percent of China's total GDP.[14] In addition, this corruption has triggered social unrest.[15] Despite Hu Jintao's emphasis on harmony, some estimate that "mass protests incidents" in China had grown to approximately 180,000 in 2010 from 90,000 in 2006.[16] "In March 2011, international news outlets reported that spending on internal security in China had, for the first time, surpassed its expenditure on external defense."[17] The NSL's purpose is to control the official corruption that has endangered the very survival of the regime.

Historically, China had had more peasant rebellions than many other civilizations.[18] A major source of this social unrest is official corruption. Unlike the tradition of other East Asian countries such as Japan, Confucianism permits and justifies the popular overthrowal of the government, if the latter does not govern properly in line with Confucianism. China's peasant rebellions have been among the largest in history.[19] For the Confucian sage Mencius, the people are like the water and the government is like the boat. The water can either carry the boat or overturn it.[20]

Learning from the Past in Dealing with Corruption

The 2018 NSL emphasizes the relevance of Chinese cultural tradition in dealing with corruption (2018 Art. 6). This was not included in the earlier supervision laws. The current leadership believes that they can learn from the country's past to deal with corruption by using the law. The current anticorruption campaign through the NSL mirrors Legalism, when reformers like Han Fei (280–233 BCE) and Shang Yang (390–338 BCE) advocated the idea of governance using the law instead of personal arbitrary dictatorships. For Han Fei, the state will guarantee the people's safety and material necessities on condition that they surrender their political rights, such as the right to participate in the country's decision making. This arrangement was ensured not by personal dictatorship, but through the use of the law.[21]

The premodern Chinese legal system was far from being independent from the monarch. The emperors often made arbitrary judgments. During the Wei and Jin period (220–420 CE), when it came to determining the death penalty, no punishment could ever be executed without submitting it to the emperor in advance for his approval. The emperor held both legislative and judicial powers.[22] What is more, he could at will punish anyone who fell under his rule, regardless of law or statute. Since Zhou (1046–256 BCE), the practice has dominated: "Ritual propriety (*li*), music (*yue*) and punitive campaigns are initiated by the emperor."[23]

Nevertheless, the role of the monarch in the legal process was not always clear. For instance, Zhu Yuanzhang believes that law should be applicable to the emperor as well.[24] Mao Zedong considers Zhu Yuanzhang one of the two most talented administrators among the Chinese emperors. The other is Emperor Li Shimin (598–649 CE) of the Tang dynasty (618–907 CE), who was known for not only the achievement of expanding the territories during his reign,[25] but also the cruelty of killing his father and two brothers in competition for power. Shang Yang designed a comprehensive legal system for the Qin era that was very strictly followed. Even the Crown Prince was subjected to punishment if he violated the law. Ironically, when Shang Yang fell from power and was trying to escape from Qin, a hotelier en route would not allow him to stay there because he did not have the proper paperwork, as the law designed by Shang Yang himself required. He was therefore caught and executed.[26]

In order to control the official corruption that is the major source of peasant rebellion, Chinese rulers have sometimes adopted very severe measures to punish offenders. Zhu Yuanzhang enhanced centralized power and combated corruption with very strict penalties, including lynching. Undesirable political activities, such as developing factions within the court, were also punishable by death. As Zhu remarked:

> Those of you in charge of money and grain have stolen them for yourselves; those of you in charge of criminal laws and punishments have neglected the regulations. In this way grievances are not redressed and false charges are ignored. . . . Occasionally these unjust matters come to my attention. After I discover the truth, I capture and imprison the corrupt, villainous, and oppressive officials involved. I punish them with the death penalty or forced labor or have them flogged with bamboo sticks in order to make manifest the consequences of good and evil actions.[27]

The emperor sometimes became personally involved in investigating and judging cases. Zhu used his bodyguards, the *jin yi wei*, who were under the control of the eunuchs, to investigate cases bypassing legal procedures. He also relied on secret agents operating outside the law to fight corruption, such as the *dongchang* (Eastern Yard) and *xichang* (Western Yard).[28]

The threat of heavy penalties was not the only means by which bureaucrats were controlled. Historically, Chinese rulers used both Confucian ethics and legal instruments to govern society, with a different focus during different periods. The relationship between Confucianism and Legalism is not agreed upon in the literature. Some scholars believe that there is no contradiction between Confucianism and Legalism. Roger Ames and Henry Rosemont note that "in *The Analects* of Confucius, there is a saying '[l]ead the people with administrative injunctions and keep them orderly with penal law, and they will avoid punishments but will be without a sense of shame. Lead them with excellence and keep them orderly through observing ritual propriety, and they will develop a sense of shame, and moreover, will order themselves,' which emphasizes the guiding function of propriety towards law."[29] Zhu Yuanzhang also believed that the two can coexist. But he believed that law should be subordinated to Confucian ethics.[30] Confucianism has had a variable impact on corruption. The family is not only the foundation of Confucian ethics but also one of the unique features of the Chinese legal system. In the Qing period the son was permitted to conceal a crime committed by his father without being subject to punishment by the legal system. When the Confucian scholars took the civil service examination, whose contents were mostly Confucian classics about high morality, candidates had to pledge that once they were selected to be government officials, they would serve the people—not their own interests.

Because of the high ethical content of Confucianism, government officials who passed the civil service examinations were not paid highly. Those who were true believers in Confucianism, such as Tian Wenjing (1662–1733 CE), a provincial governor during Emperor Yong Zheng's (1678–1735 CE) reign in the Qing era (1636–1644 CE), were unable to support their families properly if they relied only on their salary, without resorting to such practices as taking bribes. Government officials also engaged in corrupt practices for political reasons. In an environment where everybody was corrupt, officials like Tian Wenjing found themselves in a dangerous situation because of the jealousy of their colleagues who were worried that this incorruptible official might report their illegal activities to the anticorruption institutions. Tian survived largely due to Emperor Yong Zheng's personal protection.[31] Because of the low pay of the government officials and the prevalence of corruption, receiving extra income in the form of corruption in addition to a salary was considered normal.

This situation has led to what Westerners would call hypocrisy. In Chinese, there is no word for "hypocrite." Therefore, a new term "wei jun zi" or "fake gentleman" was created, implying that honesty is not as important as appropriateness in demeanor. For the Chinese, courtesy is more important than honesty.[32] The Chinese do not consider it necessarily hypocritical to project a self-image that is better than the reality. Rather, it is considered necessary to remold oneself to match the self-image and be a better person and, consequently, to make a better society for everybody.

The situation with the PRC is similar. Government officials are supposed to serve the people. In fact, at the entrance of the Zhong Nan Hai, the compound of the Chinese government, there is a motto by Mao Zedong, "To Serve the People." But living standards of government officials are much higher than the average people, not necessarily because their salaries are higher, but because they have access to income in gray areas or downright corruption. That is why the current civil service examination is extremely competitive, although the salary is not much higher than that of other professions.[33] The situation is similar in Japan.

The ambiguity of Chinese legal traditions—for example, the unclear relationship between Legalism and Confucianism and the possible discrepancy between what people say when they take the civil service examination and what people do after they are selected as government officials—makes it easier for the current regime to take a pragmatic attitude toward tradition in legal matters. For instance, in the Civil Code, parts of the Chinese tradition are endorsed, such as a stable family; others are forbidden, such as the marriage dowry. While still others are not mentioned, such as same-sex marriage. On the supervision of bureaucrats, the approach is similar. The incorporation of some elements of the Legalist thought and the practice of Zhu Yuanzhang does not necessarily contradict the official ideology that "governance with morality (*yi de zhi guo*) must be followed."

The NSL's Ideological Orientation and the NSC's Structure Issues

The emphasis of the leader's personality and the role of the party in the NSL is clear. Unlike in the first two laws, which were silent about Deng Xiaoping (the paramount leader), and Jiang Zemin (who was the PRC president when they were promulgated), in the third Supervision Law, Xi is mentioned by name along with Karl Marx, Vladimir Lenin, Mao, and Deng. However, the names of his predecessors, Jiang Zemin and Hu Jintao, are noticeably missing from the list.

During the post-Mao reform starting in 1978 Deng rowed back on the CCP's cult of personality. At the time of his death, Deng had never held a top party or government position: the only title he had held was that of Honorary President of China's Bridge Player's Association. The Cultural Revolution was reversed in other areas as well.

But when Xi Jinping came to power in 2012, there was a far greater personalization of power, and this disrupted the norms and balances that previous leaders had put in place. As a result, political institutions have become weaker,[34] and Xi's power has increased.[35] Another notable difference between the 2018 NSL and its predecessors is that it mentions the party leadership (2018 Art. 2). Part of Deng's reform was intended to separate the party from the government. The goal then was to allow the CCP to provide general oversight but to stay out of the daily operations of government. As Backer notes, "The problem of rule of law in China is indeed the problem of the Chinese Communist Party."[36]

The CCP's increasing role in government affairs became obvious before the NSL was enacted. For instance, in an article in 2013, Western scholars noted the party's advance on civil society in Shanghai, such as taking over urban grassroots society.[37] The NSL was drafted by the CCDI to meet political demands such as strengthening the state rather than in consultation with legal minds."[38]

The efforts to increase the CCP's power has intensified in recent years. For instance, until about half a dozen years ago, the party secretary's responsibility in colleges and universities lay largely in the areas of human resources, making sure personnel management meet the ideological and political standards required, and in student affairs in such areas as disciplinary management. But since Xi's second term in office, it has assumed a great deal more power to the extent that all important decisions have to be scrutinized by the party secretaries.

Similarly, the National School of Administration, which was created in 1994 under the State Council and was meant to make governance more administratively professional and less political, has been combined with the Central Party School. This has meant the virtual elimination of the National School of Administration. Similarly, the Office of Overseas Chinese under the State Council was recently transferred to the jurisdiction of the United Front Department of CCP Central Committee, so that matters related to overseas Chinese are under the direct leadership of the party.

The Chinese Communist regime has survived for over seventy years without the use of critically important ingredients to secure legitimacy, such as holding democratic elections. It is widely believed that the regime's resilience is due in part to its construction of effective institutions. Although this view has been challenged in recent years, the importance of maintaining strong institutions to the CCP is beyond doubt.[39]

The establishment of the NSC has drawn inspiration from China's past. For instance, the *jian cha*, meaning the system of supervision, was developed in the Qin dynasty and ran through all subsequent dynasties. In many of these dynasties, the head of the supervision system was called the *yushi daifu*, or royal censor. The system was hierarchical and largely isolated from the bureaucracy. The royal censor reported directly to the emperor. His primary function was to discipline government officials.

In formal terms, the NSC also shares some similarities with the Control Yuan in Sun Yat-sen's *Wu Quan Xian Fa*, or "Five Powers Constitution" which was promulgated in 1936. In addition to the division of power into the legislature, the executive, and the judiciary, as is commonly found in the West, the Five Powers Constitution includes two more powers: the Control Yuan that disciplines bureaucrats and the Examination Yuan that selects the bureaucrats. This model is distinctly Chinese. As China is a country with a tradition of strong government, the recruitment and supervision of government officials plays a more important role in governance in China than it does in the West. In the Five Powers Constitution, supervisory power includes the power to investigate, inspect, impeach, and supervise financial issues. Although in English the mainland supervisory commission reads differently from the Control Yuan, that is, the former uses the word "commission" but when Taiwan uses the sound of "yuan," in Chinese, it is the same: jian cha. The Control Yuan is parallel to the Legislative Yuan, but the NSC comes under the Standing Committee of the NPC.

Before the establishment of the NSC, supervisory power was divided among three agencies so that the CCDI regulated party members in accordance with party rules. Administrative supervisory institutions such as the Ministry of Supervision oversaw civil servants in accordance with the 2010 Administrative Supervision Law, and procuratorates had the power to prosecute state functionaries for corruption.

Also before this structural merge, China had undertaken the accelerated politicization of the Procuratorate, especially after 2014, when Xi announced his policy to consolidate the party in terms of decision making as well as to undertake the clean-up of the organization (*cong yan zhi dang*). The Procuratorate sometimes did not have to follow legal procedures, because the CCDI was also involved. For instance, it did not have to follow the

Criminal Procedure Law that stipulates that the duration of interrogation by summons or forced appearance may not exceed twelve hours. After the merger took place, the legal protection of those under investigation decreased.

The CCP has always been able to overrule decisions by government supervisory institutions, such as the Ministry of Supervision and the Procuratorate. The relationship between CCDI and the Procuratorate was hierarchical in both political and legal ways.[40] This is because the CCDI secretary has a higher political rank in the party than the chief procurator and also that he possesses the power of veto, which has a substantial impact on the career advancement of the chief procurator.

The CCDI played a leading role in drafting the NSL, working together with the NPC's Legislative Work Committee.[41] The 2018 NSL aims to legalize the unification of state supervision and party disciplinary inspection and allow them to share resources. The CCDI and the NSC staff work in the same physical office space and share resources. The NSC ranks higher than the Supreme People's Court and the Supreme Procuratorate. According to an official interpretation, "The reform would unify the Communist Party of China and state supervisory systems and is designed to serve as a guiding law against corruption and for state supervision."[42]

Those who advocated this structural change insist that while the Commission of Disciplinary Inspections (CDIs), which operates below the CCDI, had more power than the Procuratorate, only 20 to 30 percent of the cases to be investigated were initiated by the CDIs. Most of these cases were handled by the Procuratorate. In addition, because 80 percent of civil servants and 95 percent of senior officials are party members, the tasks of CDIs and state supervision overlap to a great extent. The merger is supposed to have not only strengthened the supervision role of the CCP, but also made the system more efficient.[43]

It seems that the NSC strives for efficiency, often at the expense of judicial independence. Legal scholars are concerned that although the integration of the CCP disciplinary institutions with Procuratorate's anticorruption powers will enhance the party's capacity to curb corruption, it may bring new uncertainties to China's political and legal system. As a CDI officer remarked, "In daily practice, we need to understand the National Supervision Law from a political angle, rather than from a legal perspective."[44]

Although the establishment of the NSC has significantly strengthened the party's control over corruption at all levels, it has weakened the power of the Procuratorate and the courts in processing corruption cases. It has also significantly weakened their independence and professionalism when handling corruption cases, leading to superficial and unjust prosecutions and trials. This is in spite of the fact that the CCDI has not been perceived to be effective in fighting corruption and the decentralized arrangements for fighting corruption were effective. Some have even suggested the anticorruption efforts are mainly for political purposes.[45] Xuezhi Guo hence criticized the CCP and Xi's reluctance to use the Western legal model to deal with corruption thusly: "The CCP continually rejects the methods ingrained in liberal democracy of separation of power and checks and balances, and the party's internal control structure has impeded the institutionalization of a depoliticized legal system. Instead, it strives to promote internal supervision and a mechanism of checks and balances within the system."[46]

The power to fight corruption was not only horizontally integrated, in the sense that the CCDI, the Ministry of Supervision, and the Supreme Procuratorate now worked together: it was also integrated vertically, through the bottom-up centralization of power. The reform started by Deng in 1978 was a gradual process of decentralization. This is reflected in the supervision system. Moreover, decentralized local initiatives in the past seem to have produced some good results, as Ting Gong remarks: "In contrast to the early campaign style Anti-Corruption strategy based on nationwide uniformity, disparate local integrity initiatives and programs have proliferated in China in recent years. Local innovation in managing government integrity has been encouraged by the Center."[47]

Although the decentralized system seems to have worked, the NSL has made the system more centralized vertically. This centralization is based on the belief that local supervisory institutions were not efficient, because local leaders can intervene by investigating and even judging cases.[48] The Procuratorate and CDIs were controlled by the local government in terms of finance support before the reform of the judicial system and therefore, a case could be manipulated by local government using finance as leverage to influence the judicial decision.[49] The Procuratorate and CDIs were connected closely to local government leaders. Since some procurators were under the mayors and party secretaries, it was hard for them to investigate leaders who were their superiors. The reformed system, now integrated and centralized, is supposed to be able to prevent local leaders from interfering in investigations.

These centralization efforts also include strengthening the party's vertical control over CDIs. The heads of the CDIs are appointed by CDIs on the next level, and the upper-level CDIs lead the anticorruption work of the lower ones in terms of personnel appointments and approval of the decisions made by the lower level CDIs. Structurally, the CDIs are the managers in the supervisory commission system. Consequently, horizontal control by local party leaders has been weakened. Unlike other authoritarian regimes that have political parties, the CCP is in a dominant position within the state. But this monopoly is through administrative arrangements, not constitutional safeguards.[50] In general, as an institution the NSC has centralized power at the same time that the power of the local authorities has decreased. The Procuratorate's power has also decreased[51] (Art. 46).

Li Jianguo, Vice Chairman of the Standing Committee of the Twelfth NPC, has remarked that the new system aims to integrate resources and forces combatting corruption, strengthen the CCP's centralized and unified leadership, build a centralized, unified, authoritative and efficient national supervision system, and supervise all public officials.[52]

The centralization of power in these Anti-Corruption efforts reflects the centralization of power of the state in general under Xi, as we found in our examination of the Fifth Constitutional Amendment. This process seems to have been accomplished without much resistance. One reason for this is that China is used to having a centralized state, unlike Japan or western Europe. China's premodern system is properly described as an all-encompassing system (*da yi tong*).[53]

The 2018 NSL also gives the NSC wider jurisdiction power than the previous supervision laws. Since it was enacted the jurisdiction of the NSC covers both party and non-party members. It covers state-owned enterprises (2018, Art. 12) and so-called democratic parties (2018 Art 15.1) which are the small political parties that pledge loyalty to the CCP. These small parties have their origins before the communist take-over in 1949, when they had collaborated with the CCP as against the Kuomintang. They are not mentioned in the 1990 and 1997 supervision laws.

According to Carl Minzner, "The top-down vision of legal reform developing under Xi Jinping's administration may have more in common with current trends in the party disciplinary apparatus or historical ones in the imperial Chinese censorate than it does with Western rule-of-law norms."[54] This is very different from laws promulgated in 1990s, when many Chinese legal scholars believed that China had borrowed massive number of foreign laws during the reform era from Anglo-American models.[55]

Anticorruption Operations Domestic and Overseas

The establishment of the NSC was a step toward wielding greater control of citizens' lives. Granting the NSL the power to place people in custody without going through legal procedures (Art. 22, 43), it is a step backward from the due process in China's Criminal Procedure Law, as amended in 2012. It is similar to the power granted to the CCDIs by the liuzhi, which bypasses legal procedures. Before the 2018 Supervision Law, shuanggui, which is legally based on the 1990 administrative supervision statutes by the State Council,[56] was the standard way of investigating official corruption.

Shuanggui and liuzhi are specially created terms that are used specifically for the supervision system. They are used only in the Chinese context and cannot be easily translated into English. In most studies written in English that deal with the Chinese supervision system, the word "detention" is not used, because liuzhi is extra-legal, while detention is more frequently used as a legal term. By comparing the two terms, shuanggui and liuzhi, we hope to show the ideological direction in which supervision in China has been moving in the last four decades.

The first way in which liuzhi differs from shuanggui is that it is a new system that was directly created by the CCP. Moreover, while shuanggui is used to discipline only party members, liuzhi also can be used to investigate nonparty members whose work is related to the government. Furthermore, the number of days one can spend under liuzhi has greatly increased. When liuzhi was first implemented under the 1995 People's Police Law, it could be used for only forty-eight hours. Under the 2018 Supervision Law, people can be detained for up to ninety days. Similarly, those giving bribes in the private sector could not be detained under shuanggui, whereas they can under liuzhi.

Another difference is that the new system appears less committed to protecting individuals' rights. The 2010 Administrative Supervision Law stipulates that no detention or quasi-detention is allowed without going through the correct legal procedure (Art. 20, 2010).[57] This phrase has disappeared in the 2018 NSL. The new law is also silent on whether a detained individual must have access to a lawyer. The general conclusions observers draw from this is that detainees may be denied access to a lawyer.

But the new NSL seems to have made some progress in the professionalization and institutionalization of the system. For instance, shuanggui did not make it clear about the means which investigations should employ. This gray area was clarified in the 2018 Supervision Law.

In spite of the differences between shuanggui and liuzhi, neither of them is completely clear on protecting individuals' rights, and there are contradictions in the different legal documents. The previous system under shuanggui contradicts the Administrative Supervision Law stipulating that detention or quasi-detention without going through the legal procedure is not allowed. The new supervision law with liuzhi does not include the phrase that people can sue for unlawful detentions.

The promulgation of the NSL has drawn criticism from both inside China and abroad. Chinese scholar Tong Zhiwei argues that "the draft law on national supervision marks a retreat from the protection of human rights, because the power of the supervisory commission is too broad and lacks external checks." The reason for using the NSL rather than the Criminal Procedural Law to regulate the investigations of duty-related offences by government officials is to increase the party's ability to control corruption by removing public officials' constitutional rights (for example, their access to lawyers).[58]

Amnesty International's East Asia Regional Director Nicholas Bequelin has said: "The Supervision Law is a systemic threat to human rights in China. It places tens of millions of people at the mercy of a secretive and virtually unaccountable system that is above the law. It by-passes judicial institutions by establishing a parallel system solely run by the Chinese Communist Party with no outside checks and balances."[59]

The 2018 NSL covers efforts to stamp out both domestic and international corruption whereas the first two supervision laws cover domestic operations only. This was a response to the increasing importance of foreign trade in the Chinese economy during the reform era, especially since 2001 when the country joined the World Trade Organization. Although the 2018 NSL is already more detailed than the first two supervision laws, the Chinese enacted even more detailed regulations in 2021 in the Implementation of the Supervision Law of the PRC (Regulation). This was an attempt to make its anticorruption efforts more professional. It also explicitly insists on China's uniqueness by including Xi's so-called Four Self-Confidences, that is, self-confidence in following the path of socialism with Chinese characteristics; in the theory of socialism with Chinese characteristics; in the system of socialism with Chinese characteristics; and in Chinese culture (Regulation Art. 2). This was announced by Xi Jinping at the celebration of the ninety-fifth anniversary of the CCP in 2016.[60]

The problem of corruption overseas is mostly in the form of persons escaping from China with funds and assets obtained through questionable means. Because of the transitional nature of the reform, the boundaries between legal and illegal activities are not always clear and the laws are not vigorously followed. Many people rely on their gray income for a comfortable life. This includes expensive gifts or contract kickbacks. China does not have very tough control over receiving expensive gifts such as luxurious watches or cars. What these sources of gray area income have in common is that they are not reported to the taxman; a practice that is considered illegal in the West.

China's tolerance of gray area income also comes from the fact that when Zhu Rongji was Premier (1998–2003) he allowed many money-losing state-owned enterprises to declare themselves bankrupt. This resulted in laying off approximately 35 percent of the workforce, or forty million workers, over five years.[61] Many of these unemployed workers became street vendors, and collecting taxes from them is not easy because of the scale of the businesses and people's sympathy for them for losing their jobs. But those corrupt officials took advantage of this people's tolerance of illegal activities.

In 2013, the National Economic Research Institute of China estimated that Chinese citizens had hidden as much as $2.34 trillion RMB ($369 billion) in gray income each year from the government, or roughly 20 percent of the country's GDP at the time. These sums are often earned from dubious and off-the-books income, such as kickbacks for contracts.[62]

Since it is hard to safeguard gray income through legal means, those who have access to such resources understandably worry about the safety of their money as well as of themselves. To exit the country altogether is often the preferred option. According to an official source, in 2011 alone, people with investable assets valued at $ 1 million or more transferred 2.8 trillion RMB ($458.3 billion) of their 33 trillion RMB ($5.45 trillion) in total assets out of the country; a sum that at the time constituted about three percent of the country's GDP.[63]

Because of the risk of being caught, some government officials choose to stay in China to continue making money while sending their family members abroad with their assets so that they can later emigrate from the country more easily. These are called "naked officials." In 2013, there were an estimated 1.2 million naked officials with financial assets and families outside China, according to official sources.[64] A 2014 survey found that 47 percent of the 2,000 wealthy Chinese polled, each worth over $1.5 million in assets, planned to emigrate within the next five years.[65] From the mid-1990s to 2011, as many as 18,000 corrupt government officials had fled abroad, taking $123 billion of their assets with them. The most attractive destinations for these people are the United States of America, Canada, Australia, and the Netherlands.[66] In response, the Chinese government has expanded their anticorruption operations overseas, as exemplified by their Operation Fox Hunt and Skynet and in 2015, it released a list of the one hundred most-wanted fugitives who had emigrated abroad. By 2017, forty people on the list had been forcibly repatriated back to China.[67]

According to another official source, in 2018, 1,335 emigrants were returned to China and fifty-six of the top one hundred who were under a "Red Notice" were arrested. A Red Notice is issued by Interpol, the International Criminal Police Organization that coordinates collaboration among over 190 countries to deal with cross-country criminal activities. It flags individuals for arrest and possible extradition to face the law. China also reclaimed 3.5 billion RMB ($500 million) in that year.[68] Between 2018 and 2020, the NSC claimed in its first work report that it had repatriated 3,848 fugitives from abroad and reclaimed about 10 billion RMB ($143 million) in illegal funds.[69]

These overseas anticorruption operations are officially led by the NSC's Bureau of International Cooperation (Regulation Art 240). The Regulation repeatedly pledges that the NSC's operations abroad will respect the law in those foreign countries and they will stick to UN principles and international laws (Regulation Arts 243, 246, 247). However, since its domestic anticorruption efforts combine judicial and political considerations, it is hard for the NSC to separate the two in its overseas operations.

As a result, China's anticorruption operations abroad have led to much controversy. Western observers focus on the legality of these operations, together with China's attempts to change international norms, and its use of international organizations like Interpol. Western governments, research institutions, and the media emphasize the political expediency of these operations. Former United States Assistant Attorney General John Demers said in 2021 that China sets a dangerous precedent when it pursues expatriates, because it violates United States laws and abuses human rights in both the United States and China, remarking that the Fox Hunt reflects "the authoritarian nature of the Chinese government and their use of government power to enforce conformity and repress dissent."[70]

China is also criticized for trying to change international norms. According to Freedom House, "The anticorruption campaign is also a vehicle for the CCP to seek to change international norms to better suit its objectives and interests. Chinese officials and media present the anticorruption campaign as part of a global effort to shape anticorruption norms. This includes endorsing the 2014 'Beijing Declaration' on fighting corruption, a product of that year's Asia-Pacific Economic Cooperation forum (APEC), and the G20 Anti-Corruption Action Plan of 2017–18."[71] For Bertram Lang, "China aims to transform itself from an 'international norm-taker' to an 'international norm initiator' and thus influence the international anticorruption order."[72]

China's role in Interpol is another source of controversy. While its constitution prohibits countries from using the organization for political purposes, Interpol has been criticized for assisting states seeking to silence dissent abroad. As Bradley Jardine and Natalie Hall state: "Chinese police have issued 200 or more red notices per year since 2014, and possibly as many as 612 in 2016 alone. Before, China issued around 30 red notices per year. This dramatic escalation aligns with China's increasing securitization and pursuit of dissidents and opposition figures abroad, including Uyghurs."[73] It is of interest that Meng Hongwei, China's former Deputy Minister of Public Security, served as Interpol president during the period 2016–2018 until he himself was arrested by the Chinese government for corruption. Another problem with the red notices is that few on the list are high-ranking government officials. This may reflect loopholes in the Chinese anticorruption system that is criticized for enabling officials with guanxi to evade investigation and legal prosecution.[74] It is called by critics "selective Anti-Corruption."

Conclusion

The 2018 Supervision Law is a dramatic deviation from the two previous supervision laws. It enables the party to play a greater role in anticorruption activities. The merger of the three institutions of the CCDI, the Ministry of Supervision, and the procuratorate into NSC may have deviated from the existing legal procedures. In a departure from most liberal democracies in requiring government officials to disclose income to the public, Xi's China requires cadres above the level of county magistrates and departments disclose their income to the CCP, not to the public.[75]

Yet the 2018 NSL is consistent with the Fifth Constitutional Amendment that was promulgated under Xi. In the same way that the NSL is very different from the first two supervision laws, the Fifth Amendment also deviates from the ideological orientations of the first four constitutional amendments before Xi's administration. This shows that Xi is making changes from the reforms instituted by Deng Xiaoping in the late 1970s.

But the 2018 Supervision Law does not deviate from Chinese legal culture per se, as it has been practiced over history. Instead, it displays all four characteristics of traditional Chinese legal culture: pragmatism, instrumentalism, statism, and the inequality of citizens before the law. The law serves the pragmatic purpose of maintaining institutions. It is a tool for the leadership to use to fight corruption. It increases the power of the state and it decreases the judicial independence in which everybody is supposed to be treated equally according to the law.

The anticorruption operations under Xi have produced positive results as well. As part of the initial result of structural change, the number of whistleblowers reporting corruption and other malpractices handled in three pilot locations (Beijing, Shanxi province, and Zhejiang province) increased in the first eight months of 2017, compared with the same period in the previous year, by 29.7 percent in Beijing, 40.4 per cent in Shanxi, and by 91.5 percent in Zhejiang.[76] According to official sources, the total number of officials under investigation in Beijing increased from 210,000 before the reform to 997,000 as of December 2017.[77] Within a year after the promulgation of the NSL, supervisory institutions nationwide investigated 1.7 million cases of corruption and cases of political disciplines violations.[78]

For Andrew Wademan, the regime has been willing and able to attack the nexus between the official, the police, and the criminal. He suggests that the regime is far from being crippled as a result, let alone heading toward a potentially serious crisis of governance. He believes that the regime's efforts are effective partly because the fight against organized crime is led not only by the police but also by the court and the party.[79] In 2014, two years after Xi came to power, Transparency International's Corruption Perception Index score (CPI) for China was thirty-six. In 2021, it gradually improved to forty-five.[80] According to official sources, from 2012 to 2022, supervisory institutions investigated 4.516 million cases; among which 4.439 million people were penalized.[81]

Chapter 6

Civil Rights Chinese Style

This chapter is a study of the Civil Code of the People's Republic of China (PRC) that went into effect on January 1, 2021. The Civil Code consists of seven parts: General Rules, Property Rights, Contracts, Personality Rights, Marriage and Family, Right of Inheritance, and Tort Liability with a total of 1,260 articles.

In the last decade, the West has become increasingly concerned about the the reversal of the post-Mao reform, at least in some key areas, such as personality cult, more emphasis on ideology, and more political control.[1] Yet, in communist countries, such as the former Soviet Union, the promulgation of civil laws usually indicates a relaxing of communist fanaticism. What kind of messages of policy orientation and ideological trends that the regime has sent through this Civil Code?

This is the fifth time that the PRC has tried to make the Civil Code: the four previous failed attempts were made in 1954, 1962, 1979, and 2001. Why was it successful this time? In comparison with the previous civil laws, what is new in this Civil Code that is supposed to protect civil rights? How serious is this Civil Code in restricting state rights? To what extent does the Civil Code reflect the Chinese tradition or the regime's attitudes toward foreign experiences? Western scholars have noted such terms as *civil rights, freedom, democracy, equality*, and *rule of law* have different meanings when used in the Chinese context.[2] How is this reflected in the Civil Code?

This study is not a systematic introduction to the Civil Code, which is a conglomeration of civil laws promulgated over the years. In addition, some fruitful studies have been done that tried to explain the various civil laws, such as general provisions,[3] contracts laws,[4] private property laws,[5] and the impact of civil laws on sustainable development.[6] This project focuses on the issue of human rights by highlighting those new provisions that have political and ideological connotations. My approach is similar to some of the most recent studies on the Civil Code that focus on one particular dimension of the large document.[7]

This study shows that the Civil Code has successfully been completed in the midst of a time when China's economy had experienced a decline of growth for a decade and an increasingly challenging international environment exemplified by the US-China trade war. The regime intends to give the public more breathing space in those areas that don't hurt the state monopoly of power, for example, protecting the civil rights among nonstate actors. This situation is similar to the post-1989 Tiananmen Incident period when political control was tightened, while other areas such as the control of the economy were loosened, symbolized by Deng Xiaoping's 1992 Southern Tour.[8] The promulgation of the Civil Code is also a reflection of a more modernized Chinese society.

At least in principle, the Civil Code is a step forward from the previous civil laws in protecting private properties, privacy, and contractual relations. It seems even more significant in hindsight: four decades ago, the idea of the public-private divide, property rights, and even individualism had no root in the Chinese legal academia. Nevertheless, the rights as stipulated in the Civil Code are by and large among individuals and other nonstate actors, not vis-à-vis the state. Restricting state rights is mostly done in an abstract sense. When it involves concrete issues, it mostly occurs in small areas, such as "Lost & Found." When the state is a party vis-à-vis the legal persons or natural persons, it is mostly in the areas of economics, not politics.

Some new contents in the Civil Code seem to indicate that the economic reform will continue. For instance, the so-called exploitation was cut from the previous civil laws, indicating that "exploitation" such as stocks is allowed in state socialism; "a variety of forms of ownership" was added, indicating private ownerships are considered to be part of state socialism; the party's dominant theory of "primary stage socialism[9] that was formulated at the beginning of the reform was cut in some places, indicating that the allowance of "exploitation" and "private ownership of the means of production" will be part of the Chinese system for a long time, not merely a part of the transition. This does not contradict the fact that under Xi Jinping, China's political control has tightened, not loosened, as shown in chapter 4 on national security.

The Civil Code is also there to decrease social tension: for example, to protect the middle class and the poor in terms of property. This was against the background of the new party constitution in 2017, which changed the policy of "letting a few become rich" in the 1980s to "more equality" (CCP General Outline).

The Civil Code also reflects the regime's pragmatic attitudes toward the Chinese tradition and the foreign experience. Some aspects of the Chinese tradition such as the strong emphasis on family were protected; others such as dowry were banned. While endorsing some foreign experiences, especially in contract laws, the Civil Code seems to have distanced itself from some of the other foreign experiences.

The chapter is divided into four sections. It first lays down the historical background against which the Civil Code was promulgated, such as that of communist countries' past experience including that of the USSR and China in drafting civil laws. Then it discusses civil rights as included in the Civil Code for a legal person and a natural person. The following section discusses the Civil Code's limitations in restricting the rights of the state. The next section discusses the regime's pragmatic attitudes toward the Chinese tradition and the foreign experience, as reflected in the Civil Code. The conclusion consists of reflections on some historical and theoretical issues related to the Civil Code.

China's Previous Attempts for the Civil Code

Modern law came from the West, and all laws in modern China are connected with foreign laws. China's first attempt to promulgate a civil code began as early as 1911, with the Draft Civil Code of the Great Qing Dynasty that was accomplished with the help of Japanese scholars Yoshimasa Matsuoka and Kotaro Shida.[10]

This situation is consistent with the fact that the Qing constitution, China's first, was also based on that of Japan, that is, the Meiji constitution. The Chinese elites in the early twentieth century believe that learning from Japan is a "short cut" for China's modernization because of Japan's success in learning from the West. Japan accomplished its modernization drive in three or four decades after the Meiji Restoration in 1868. The Qing court was also fond of the Japanese elites' attitudes of being in favor of modernization without eliminating the monarchy.

In communist countries, the promulgation of civil laws usually signals taking a break from communist fanaticism, that is, reform that promoted private initiative, personal stimuli of labor and energy, and free accumulation of private property. The promulgation of the Soviet Civil Code went hand in hand with the New Economic Policy in 1921–1924 that was a "retreat" from communist ideals, in the words of Vladimir Lenin. The Soviet Civil Code was passed in October 1922, taking effect in January 1923. The code intended to uphold and regulate private property relations, which was a departure from War Communism in the first few years after the October Revolution in 1917.[11]

Compared with its communist neighbor of Russia, China is rather late in adopting a civil code. In fact, China under Mao was reluctant to adopt even a constitution. It was under pressure from Joseph Stalin that China adopted its first constitution in 1954.[12] Although the Chinese 1954 constitution was largely modeled after the 1937 Soviet constitution, it gave people less rights than the Soviet one. This is consistent with the fact that the late Qing Constitution, although modeled after the Meiji constitution, also gave the people less rights than the Japanese one.[13]

China's first attempt in 1954 to make a civil law went hand in hand with the first PRC constitution that was promulgated in the same year. It was partly based on the 1922 Civil Code of the then Soviet Union. The attempt was aborted because the country went into turmoil two years later first with the Hundred Flowers movement and then the Anti-Rightist Campaign.[14] The 1954 constitution itself was cast aside a few years after its promulgation.

The second attempt for a civil code was in 1962. It went hand in hand with Liu Shaoqi/Deng Xiaoping's "responsibility system," which was supposed to give people a break from leftist fanaticism as demonstrated during the Great Leap Forward, which was responsible for the deaths of millions of Chinese. It was aborted because the country went into another round of leftist fanaticism with the first being the Four Cleanings in 1964 and then the Cultural Revolution in 1966.[15]

The third one started following the 1978 Third Plenum of the CCP Central Committee that started the post-Mao reform.[16] The NPC Standing Committee re-commenced the drafting of a civil code in an attempt to meet the needs of building a market-oriented economy in 1979. In 1982, they worked out a fourth draft of the civil code after drawing on the experience of civil codes in the Soviet Union and Hungary. The foreign connection is obvious in that the 1982 constitution was also based on the PRC constitution of 1954 that was in turn based on the Soviet one in 1937. Apparently, the complexity of the Chinese society unleashed by the reform made it harder for the civil law to go into completion.

Since the 1980s, a series of standalone civil laws was enacted with the expectation of codifying them in the future. Those separate statutes include the 1980 Marriage Law (amended in 2001); 1985 Inheritance Law; 1986 General Principles of Civil Law (amended in 2009); 1991 Adoption Law (amended in 1998); 1995 Security Law; and 1999 Contracts Law.

The fourth attempt for a civil code was made when China joined the World Trade Organization in 2001. China's legislature submitted it for review in late 2002. It was not approved. China was probably too preoccupied with raising the productivity and GDP to enact the large and complex civil code. Therefore, China continued with the piece-by-piece approach instead of the codification of the civil laws. The 2007 Rights in Rem Law and 2009 Tort Liability Law were introduced.

The fifth attempt to codify the civil law coincided with Xi's ascendance to power in 2012, when the Communist Party's eighteenth NPC called for progress in drafting the unified civil code. The NPC passed the General Provisions in 2017. The Civil Code in its finalized form was thus presented to and adopted by the NPC at its annual session on May 28, 2020, concluding the country's six-decade journey to enacting a comprehensive Civil Code.

The successful enabling of the Civil Code resembles the previous attempts that occurred in the correction of extreme politics. The Hu Jintao era witnessed a substantial increase in both registered and unregistered social organizations, with registered social organizations doubling in number, from 244,509 to over 499,268, between 2002 and 2012.[17] Despite Hu's emphasis on "harmony," some estimated that "mass incidents" in China had grown to approximately 180,000 in 2010 compared to 90,000 back in 2006.[18] The Hu regime reportedly spent more money on the maintenance of social order than its military expense.[19]

It also coincided with Xi regime's louder voice on the market and law, because the heightened political control made the private sector worried. In the new party constitution, the role of the market has been changed from "essential role" to "decisive role," implying a more important role by the market (CCP General Outline). The principle of "rule according to law" was emphasized. In the Civil Code, "rule according to law" was added at least three times (Articles 237, 238, and 262, compared with the 2007 law). In Xi's report to the 19th National Party Congress in 2017, he mentioned "rule according to law" fifty-five times.

Without legal protection, private businessmen don't feel safe. The survey showed that they think there is a 22.5 percent chance of danger to themselves and a 26.8 percent chance that their assets are at risk.[20] Private sector investment in China slowed sharply from more than 20 percent growth when Xi assumed power to single digits in recent years. It fell 13 percent during the coronavirus-battered first four months of 2020, compared with a 7 percent decline for state-owned companies.[21] China under Xi had experienced a decade of decline in economic growth. To make the matters worse, the US started a trade war against China in 2017 soon after President Donald Trump came to power. China needs the private sector to boost up the country's economy, and it needs foreign investment as well.

The fifth attempt to codify the civil code also coincided with Xi's more assertive stands in foreign policy, for example, in 2014, China started to build artificial islands that could be used for military airports in the South China Sea.[22] It also went hand in hand with Xi's slogans of the Chinese Dream and Bainian weiyou zhi dabianju (a great change that has not happened in a hundred years). In a departure from the Hu regime that was noted for its emphasis on "harmony" and "stability," Xi wants to do something great.

The codification of the Chinese civil laws was viewed by Chinese scholars as significant as the French Civil Code of 1804 that embodied a legacy of the Napoleonic era. It was also regarded as significant as the German Civil Code of 1896 that grew out of a desire for a national law that would override the various customs and codes of the German territories. The Chinese Civil Code was also viewed as important as the Japanese Civil Code of 1898 that was the result of the modernization drive following the Meiji Restoration.[23]

The inspirational vision of the codification of the Chinese civil laws did not finish here. Ten years after the codification of the Napoleonic law, the dictator was defeated in 1814. Two decades after the promulgation of the German Civil Code, Germany was defeated in World War I. The Japanese Civil Code surely ushered Japan into the modern era with remarkable success including its defeat of Russia six years later. Nevertheless, Japan was defeated during World War II. It is not settled if the analogy of the Chinese civil code and that of these powers bears good or bad omens for China.

Civil laws and other lesser laws such as criminal laws and election laws complement the constitution, including the five constitutional amendments. Generally speaking, the Four Amendments in 1988, 1993, 1999, and 2004 were largely for the reform. The Civil Code is not a good reconfirmation of such principles as rule of law, human rights, and private property, as embodied in the first four constitutional amendments. The Fifth Amendment serves as a correction of the previous four amendments in the sense that it restored some of the prereform policies such as a stronger emphasis on personality leadership, the emphasis on ideology, and centralization of power. It deviated from the quasi-capitalism of the "primary stage capitalism," which was more prominent in the first Four Constitutional Amendments, but less so from the Fifth Constitutional Amendment.[24] The Civil Code could be viewed as a correction or complement of the Fifth Constitutional Amendment in that the tightening of political control is complemented with the protection of certain individual rights, especially economic rights, on the condition that it did not threaten the political monopoly of power of the CCP.

Civil Rights

Rights of a Legal Person

Regarding the rights of a legal person, the Civil Code is highly pragmatic in the sense that it strives to deal with the most urgent problems of Chinese society today, that is, housing: "Implementation of the code, which incorporates existing laws including those covering property, contracts and torts, reflects concerns among business owners over protection of personal and property rights."[25]

From 2007 to 2017, city dwellers grew from around 42 to 57 percent of the population. China's urban population now accounts for around 820 million people, and by 2030, the number will be over one billion, meaning almost another 200 million people will be living in cities.[26] In China, more than 90 percent of households own houses, with 87 percent in urban and 96 percent in rural areas.[27]

Among those housing issues are what the house owners should do after the seventy-year land-use right expires for their houses. In China, the state owns all land, and residents have a seventy-year land-usage right. As expirations approach, people are worried about what they should do with their homes. Homeowners need legal protection for their properties. Although the previously promulgated PRC Property Law allows the automatic renewal of construction land use for residential property upon the expiry of the contractual term, it does not have the stipulations on the requirements for such renewal. The Civil Code (Article 359) makes it clear that when construction land use rights for residential property are automatically renewed, the payment and the reduction or exemption of relevant renewal fees shall be made.

Another example of the Civil Code to protect the rights of the property owners is that in terms of the repair fees of buildings, the new Civil Code raised from two-thirds to three-quarters of property owners' agreement (Article 278 of the Civil Code as compared with Article 76 of 2007 law). The codification of "change of circumstances" (most comparable to a disruption to the business foundation) is another issue in protecting the interest of property owners. In particular, during the COVID-19 crisis and the legal problems caused by disruptions in supply chains, and the invocation of force majeure and change of circumstances in particular, numerous legal disputes arose. In this respect, the corresponding legal regulation on the change of circumstances, which was previously only addressed in a corresponding interpretation of the Supreme People's Court on the contract law, can now provide more legal certainty.[28]

In addition, the provisions related to contracts and property could impact foreign companies operating in China. For example, in the areas of factoring, guarantee contracts, property management contracts, partnerships, mortgages, pledges, and provisions were introduced.[29] Enacting the Civil Code that was labeled as "the basic law of a market economy" shows that the Chinese leadership wants to continue to open to the outside world.[30]

Rights of a Natural Person

On the rights of a natural person, the provisions with regard to the right to reside were added compared with the 2007 law. This is in response to the fact that more people are renting now. It is to protect the poor who can't buy houses against the property owners. Property owners can't cut water, electricity, and so on to pressure the tenants into paying rent (Articles 366–371). Legal experts called to separate the rights of property occupation and ownership to protect the rights of renters for a long time.

The Civil Code also made the attempt to protect the interest of villagers regarding collective property. The provision was added that members have the right to check and copy the financial record (Article 264, compared with the 2007 version).

Consumers domestic and international have long complained about the quality of Chinese products.[31] In response to this situation, the provision was added to the effect that those who sell commodities that have defects are legally liable (Article 1206). Intellectual property rights violation in China is another area that irritates lots of people, both domestic and international. For instance, in 2015, China and Hong Kong reportedly represented 86 percent of the global counterfeit industry, which is around 400 billion USD each year. About 80 percent of the world's counterfeit goods reportedly come from China, and many of the market's consumers are in China as well.[32] The Civil Code added a provision to ban intellectual property rights violations (Article 1185).

The Civil Code not only codifies the rights of a natural person on business and commercial matters but also strengthens the protection of the rights of privacy and personal information.[33] These things were unimportant when China was poor. Now a large middle class has emerged in China and people have started to care not only about their material life but also increasingly about a decent spiritual life. China's middle class has been among the fastest growing in the world, swelling from 39.1 million people (3.1 percent of the population) in 2000 to roughly 707 million (50.8 percent of the population) in 2018.[34] The Civil Code added the provision that those who suffer spiritual damage can sue for compensation (Articles 996 and 1183).

It also added the provision that allows people to choose to die with dignity (Article 1002). This is in response to the situation where some long-suffering patients cannot die with dignity because the medical workers don't want to take the responsibility of letting those patients who have no hope of survival die and the children of the patients don't want to be blamed for not having the proper behavior of piety that is supposed to be the top moral requirement for children in the Confucian tradition.

The Civil Code has more detailed regulations on sexual harassment, not restricted to the workplace (Article 1010). The concept of "sexual harassment" is defined for the first time. Employers are now required to be proactive in preventing sexual harassment and to implement concrete procedures to handle complaints and take disciplinary action accordingly. According to the new code, a person may be held liable "for speech, words, images or bodily actions that have been used to carry out sexual harassment against a person's wishes" (Article 1010). As a social phenomenon, sexual harassment is a relatively new thing in the last three decades. Before the reform, with the Maoist sexual asceticism, it rarely happened in China.[35]

It also has more detailed protection of privacy (Article 1032). Provisions were added that if the media don't use personal information properly, such as name, portrait, and other personal information, the person involved can sue the media (Article 999). Therefore, the new Civil Code may have a positive impact on famous foreigners looking to protect their rights in China. For example, Bruce Lee's heir sued a fast food chain for portrait right infringement, and Michael Jordan has several disputes with Qiaodan Sports Co., Ltd. ("Qiaodan" is the Chinese translation of "Jordan") over use of his name and likeness and recently won a victory on the trademark side.

But there are also compromises in the code's efforts to protect privacy. Compared with the EU General Data Protection Regulation (GDPR), which is considered the toughest privacy and security law in the world, China's new Civil Code falls short in regulating how long data collectors can keep people's information and under what circumstances they must delete data.[36]

Civil Rights and the State

Key Concepts

The Civil Code indicates the regime's new definition of socialism. It defines socialism as the following: the country sticks to the principle that the public ownership of the means of production is the base, while a variety of ownerships coexist; to each according to his/her contribution is the base, while a variety of the form of distributions co-exist; socialist market economy, etc. These are characteristics of a socialist system (Article 206).

Some key differences in this definition are noted in comparison with the 2004 Constitution's description of China's "socialist system." First, the term "exploitation" was cut, indicating an endorsement of such economic mechanism as stocks that by nature are supposed to be exploitative.[37] Stocks were not allowed under the Maoist regime or the Soviet regime before Mikhail Gorbachev.

Another item to be noted is that "a variety of ownerships co-exist" was added, because the Chinese economy has become more diverse. According to the official *China Daily*, the number of private companies accounted for 84.1 percent of all enterprises in 2018 in China.[38] In addition, the phrase "primary stage socialism" was cut, indicating the current regime's judgment that regards the current Chinese society as more established, not in transition from one mode of production (i.e., pre-socialist) to the next (i.e., socialist), compared with the 2004 Constitution, Article 6).

Another key conceptual issue is how to define "civil rights." "Civil law modulates the personal and property relationships between natural persons, legal persons, and non-legal-person organizations that are equal entities" (Article 2). Civil rights are defined as "natural persons enjoy the right to life, body rights, the right to health, name rights, image rights, reputation rights, honor rights, privacy rights, the right to marital autonomy and other such rights." For legal persons and unincorporated organizations, they "enjoy name rights, reputation rights, honor rights and other such rights" (Article 110).

But the bottom line is this does not involve the state rights. It does not include political rights, whereas civil rights in the Western setting do include political rights such as voting rights or the rights for a fair trial.[39] In the West, the concept of civil rights is defined as "the rights that constitute free and equal citizenship and include personal, political, and economic rights."[40] In China, the official explanation of the term of "civil rights" is separated from "political rights." Therefore, it does not contradict the Fifth Constitutional Amendment that strengthens the state power, state ideology, and personality cult. Nor does it contradict the 2015 National Security Law that tightens the country's political control. The Civil Code is largely to clarify the rights and interests, mostly in economic setting, among nonstate entities.

Relations with the State

In the West, the protection of civil rights inevitably involves restricting the state's rights. In the Civil Code, however, restricting the state's rights is either in an abstract sense (slogans) or on some economic rights, or on some trivial matters, such as Lost & Found, not in restricting the state's rights in politics. Equal protection of state and private properties was included in the civil code. Noticeably, the word "equally" was added to the code (Article 207 as compared with the 2007 Property Law Article 4).

This is significant that in the eyes of some Chinese legal scholars, the implementation of the principle of equal protection of public property and private property as was stipulated in the earlier Property Law (Draft) was unconstitutional.[41] But this is largely in the area of economics. "Usufruct," that is, one person's right to "possess, use, or benefit from" another's property (Article 323), is one example. After setting forth some general provisions, the subpart prescribes more detailed rules on various types of usufructs: right to land contractual management; right to the use of land for construction (e.g., businesses' right to use state-owned land for real estate development); and right to the use of house sites (e.g., rural residents' right to use land to build homes). This is important in the Chinese context because of the state and collective ownership of all lands.

It also includes some small things that the individual's rights are protected vis-à-vis the state. For instance, with Lost/Found, if nobody claims it for a period of time, then it belongs to the state. The time period was changed from six months to one year (Article 318, compared with Article 113 in the 2007 law).

Examples of limitations in restricting the state's rights include that those who infringe upon the name, likeness, reputation, or honor of a hero, martyr, harming the societal public interest, shall bear civil liability (Article 185). The Civil Code also added that for the property owners' meeting and the election of the owners' committee, both the local government and the residents' committee shall provide guidance and assistance (Article 277).

This situation made legal experts worry that the new civil code will apply only to disputes between private parties. It does not grant businesses any added privacy rights or legal protections in cases of criminal charges.[42] Legal experts added that "since the Civil Code only covers civil disputes, it does not help protect property rights against seizure of assets by the state, a most important concern among entrepreneurs."[43]

For individuals, the Civil Code carves out the country's first definitions of private spaces and private information. However, this applies only to private individuals and organizations. It does not enumerate any new privacy rights that apply to state snooping.[44] This is one reason that some say the code can be more of a symbol than substance, although there is also hope that it will reduce bureaucratic meddling and abuse.[45]

Another difficulty is the implementation of those provisions that are supposed to protect civil rights. For instance, the Civil Code imposes civil liability on illegally confining people and illegally searching people's bodies (Article 1011). But legal experts noted that although China has a comprehensive system of laws, people are concerned about their enforcement rather than the laws themselves.[46]

"Though the Civil Code is a step in the right direction for privacy rights, the fact that it does not establish independent courts means that it will be enforced at the pleasure of the government."[47] As courts are not independent and ultimately answer to the party, legal reforms in recent years have aimed to give judges more independence and rein in local officials' influence over courts.[48] Experts noted that although there are fairly strong privacy laws on the books, it is entirely at the discretion of the government as to whether they will be respected and enforced; it is unclear to what extent the new Civil Code will change that state of affairs.[49]

Another area of ambiguity is that with China's use of artificial intelligence and the thousands and thousands of surveillance video cameras installed in large cities, protection of personal information, including somebody's whereabouts, becomes questionable (Article 1034). Contradictions in the different legal documents have also been noted. The Civil Code added the new provision that people can sue for illegal detention (Article 1011).

However, this contradicts the National Security Law about Liu Zhi, which allows the government to detain people without going through proper legal procedures.

Modernization: Chinese Cultural Tradition and Foreign Experience

The regime has taken a pragmatic attitude in the Civil Code toward Chinese cultural tradition in the sense that some aspects of the Chinese tradition were endorsed, such as stable marriages, and others were discouraged, such as dowry. Stable families are important for the stability of the Chinese society.[50] However, Chinese families have become less and less stable in recent decades. In 2019, some 4.15 million Chinese couples divorced—up from 1.3 million in 2003, when couples were first allowed to divorce by mutual consent without going to court. Before then, divorce had to be obtained by one spouse suing another in court.[51]

In response to the rise of divorce in China in recent decades, the Civil Code added a cooling-off period of thirty days. Within that time, either party can withdraw the divorce application (Article 1077). In addition, one year after a child was born, the husband can't divorce the wife. Within half a year after abortion, the husband can't divorce the wife. The provision of promoting morality within the family was also added (Article 1043).

On the other hand, the provision of forbidding dowry was added to the Civil Code (Article 1042). Dowry is part of the Chinese tradition when girls were more or less treated by the parents as properties for sale. In recent decades, dowry in different forms existed for different reasons, one being China's one-child policy adopted in 1979 that resulted in the unbalanced ratio of gender. There are reportedly 118 men for every 100 women in China, with an "extra" 40 million males in the country. Consequently, in some areas, the price for brides has skyrocketed, especially in the countryside.[52]

The Civil Code is pragmatic in the sense that it did not try to deal with all the problems in Chinese society. For instance, the legalization of same-sex marriage was not included. Relatedly, there is no provision for nonmarital cohabitation. These issues are controversial, and lawmakers have never been sure of how to deal with them. On foreign experiences, the Civil Code also takes a pragmatic attitude in emphasizing some foreign experiences such as the contract laws and rejecting others. Contract laws are a large part of the Civil Code. Lots of the provisions in the contract laws are borrowed from foreign countries. The structure of the Civil Code is believed to be an adoption of the German Pandekten system, which contains an introductory section about general principles, followed by several specific sections.[53] To ensure that the new code contributes to a better business environment, lawmakers used the criteria in the World Bank's "Doing Business" report as reference for drafting articles related to business guarantees.[54]

However, regarding foreign companies operating in China, the following is cut: for those cases involving foreign parties, if domestic laws are not available, the law that another country used in the most similar circumstances can be used (Article 467). This is part of the regime's efforts to show its wenhua zixin (confidence in the Chinese culture). The Civil Code also de-emphasizes "primary stage socialism," as was the case with Fifth Amendment. "Primary stage socialism" was based on the Soviet version of Marxism. This is part of the efforts by the regime to reflect the official characterization of the so-called Xi Jinping New Era Socialism with Chinese Characteristics,[55] lilun zixin (confidence in theories).

Conclusion: Some Historical and Theoretical Considerations

In communist countries, the promulgation of civil codes usually occurrs when the leaders want to take a break from revolutionary fanaticism. The recent promulgation of China's Civil Code came out in the midst of the country's economic slowdown, the US–China trade war, and other social tensions. Compared with the previously promulgated civil laws, the Civil Code has made it clearer about the protection of non-state actors' rights, such as property rights and citizens' privacy. It has taken a pragmatic attitude toward Chinese tradition and foreign experiences.

However, the "civil rights" in the Civil Code do not include political rights. Other difficulties include the poor implementation of these laws with the Chinese Communist Party's dominance and its inconsistency with some provisions in other legal documents. The regime is willing to yield some rights to its citizens, mainly in the areas of economics, among the nonstate actors such as natural persons, legal persons, and unincorporated organizations, as long it does not threaten the dominance of the party.

The promulgation of the Civil Code needs to be comprehended in comparison with other important legal documents such as the recently promulgated Fifth Constitutional Amendment which include some policies similar to those prior to the reform. These documents complement each other: the regime intends to give the republic some breathing space in those less political, nonstate areas, as is the case with the Civil Code, while tightening the state's political control of society, as is the case with the National Security Law.

The emphasis on the state did not start with Xi or the CCP in general. For instance, Sun Yat-sen in the early twentieth century provided China with a recipe for a mobilizational guardianship rather than democracy. Sun was adamant in holding that the state will significantly regulate the market. He also portrayed ordinary citizens as impetuous, unjustifiably confident in their claims to understand political matters based on their experiences, and unable to grasp fully the knowledge necessary to make policy on a routine basis.[56]

The promulgation of Civil Code is also a result of the Xi administration's strong emphasis on law. In Xi's report to the 19th National Party Congress in 2017, he mentioned "rule according to law" fifty-five times. But Xi's "rule according to law" is certainly not rule of law in the Western sense. The emphasis of law can go hand in hand with centralization of power.[57] It is rule by law, not rule of law.[58]

China's legal reform also needs to be viewed in comparison with the former Soviet Union's experiences. In the eyes of the Chinese leaders, the collapse of the USSR was because of Mikhail Gorbachev's simultaneous push for not only economic reform but also political reform. Following the transitional period of Boris Yeltsin who was more liberal minded, Vladimir Putin seems to turn back to Russian tradition, that is, the Orthodox Church, to remold the political consciousness of the Russians. Now, again, the two countries seem to follow similar paths: authoritarianism rooted in indigenous cultural tradition.

To what extent are Xi's policies an ideological departure from his predecessors? It is hard to cut an ideological line among Jiang Zemin, Hu Jintao, and Xi Jinping, although some differences in their political and ideological attitudes can be detected. Jiang Zemin said to Mike Wallace on TV that the uneducated peasants are the reason China does not have democracy.[59] Wen Jiabao said the same thing in 2004. Both seemed to suggest China's condition for democracy was not ripe, although value-wise, democracy is good. But on other occasions, the ideological line is not clear. For instance, Jiang Zemin asserted that the CCP would make entrepreneurs bankrupt.[60]

Xi glorified the communist revolution by ordering the cadres to go back to such earlier communist bases of the earlier times as Jing Gangshan and Yan'an for revolutionary education, bu wang chu xin (never forget about the original goals of the CCP). As the domestic and international situation of China became more challenging, the way the Xi regime handles law became more political. Legal experts noted that if the law did not stipulate clearly, then the court can rule based on ideological considerations.[61] Previously, the Chinese law ruled that in those cases involving foreign parties, if domestic laws are not available, the law of another country in similar circumstances can be used.

However, even for the Xi regime, the ideological line is not always clear. This is reflected in the regime's inconsistency in treating the Cultural Revolution. Sometimes, the Cultural Revolution was regarded not as a total disaster but as a hard exploration by the CCP to look for the path of socialist development.[62] Sometimes, the interpretation is similar to that of the 1978 Third Plenum in which the Cultural Revolution was totally renounced.[63] Xi himself condemned the Cultural Revolution at the celebration of the fortieth anniversary of the post-Mao reform in December 2018.[64]

Theoretically speaking, the separation between economic rights and political rights as demonstrated in the Civil Code is not properly explained by Marxist theories. Marxism is known for its strong emphasis on the close relations between the economic base and superstructure to such an extent that before Deng's reform in 1978, economics was not a social science discipline. There was "political economy" though.

The Civil Code's emphasis on economics to the neglect of political rights is also inconsistent with the modernization theory where a large middle class will demand to defend not only their economic rights but also political rights.[65] For modernization theory, economic prosperity will bring about a large middle class that is well educated and who naturally would want to have a voice in the governance of the country. Democracy will by necessity follow substantial economic development. The theory was influential also because it demonstrated validity in the developments of some other countries, such as South Korea, Taiwan, and Singapore.[66]

Accidentally, the present promulgation of Civil Code at the theoretical level provides intellectual support to those who disfavor the American legal model advocating the idea that law should be understood from the perspectives of social sciences such as history, sociology, and economics, and to endorse the European continental model, because they are specific and concrete laws, and legal theoreticians don't have to debate about the fundamental nature of the Chinese legal system. During much of the reform era, Chinese law transplantation was predominantly Anglo-American.[67]

Scholars have viewed the Chinese experience from different perspectives. Some argue that human rights, including political rights, are interrelated, that is, private property law will promote human rights, including political rights, in general.⁶⁸ These scholars have taken an apologist position toward the Chinese way (Gottfried Wilhelm Leibniz admired the rational social order of premodern China, the respect for law, the social stability, and the moral system) are not alone.⁶⁹ Others disagree by saying that China's legal development has to follow the path of major industrialized societies, therefore implying that the Chinese legal system needs much improvement.⁷⁰

Chapter 7

China's Vision for a New Global Order

> Domestic politics is for law and compassion, but international relations is for opportunism.
>
> —Sun Tzu, *The Art of War*

Responses from scholars and the media in the West to the Foreign Relations Law (FRL) promulgated in July 2023 vary. Some believe the law contains nothing new, because most of the contents had been published previously in other forms and venues. They believe that the purpose of this law is to put Xi's personal stamp on it because it includes his own initiatives on civilization, security, and development. Others view it primarily as a tool for retaliating against sanctions from other countries, especially from the United States. Still others view it as constituting a serious challenge to the West.[1]

This chapter clarifies some of the issues related to the FRL, focusing on the three global initiatives by Xi Jinping that are codified in the law. As for the other laws I examine in this book, the FRL is intended as an instrument to bring about the great rejuvenation of the Chinese nation, which is an important part of the Chinese Dream (Art 1). As Xi remarks, "Now, we turn to discussing the Chinese Dream. I think that the dream to rejuvenate the Chinese nation is the greatest dream we have had since the beginning of modern times."[2]

One of the most important impetuses for the proposed initiatives embodied in the FRL is that the United States is currently hesitant about its leadership role in the world. Donald Trump, who has the support of about half of the American voters, has made it clear that the United States does not want to be the world leader. When he was in office, Trump's engagement with China was primarily in economic terms. For instance, he is the only US president not to raise the issue of human rights when he visited China, and he alienated the United States from its NATO allies and Japan by insisting that the allies must hitherto contribute more to defense, instead of relying on the United States to foot the NATO security bill.

Trump's attitude is partly a response to the decline of people's confidence in democracy globally since the twenty-first century, especially the belief that economic liberalization will lead to political democratization. While "for decades, political scientists have suggested that, in order for a country to become a highly developed, complex economy, its political system must be based on the principles of liberal democracy, the rule of law, and the protection of civil liberties."[3] This did not happen in many developing countries, and especially not in China. In addition, Americans' trust in the government has been in decline over the last few decades, casting doubt on the idea that democracy is a universal value.[4] This has encouraged some Chinese ruling elites, especially some of the establishment intellectuals,[5] to seize the opportunity and help China play a key role in global governance.

Unlike the Trump regime, the Biden administration's relations with China encompass not only the economic perspective but also the ideological and political realms. Under Biden, the US government wanted to restrain China in a comprehensive way, and the West was more united against authoritarian regimes, especially China. This concerted attempt is driven less by the belief in the eventual triumph of democracy than the protection of the relative superior, although declining, role held by the United States as global leader.[6] In the eyes of some Western scholars, Xi not only has the vision but also a strategy to restore the dominant regional role that China had enjoyed for centuries before the nineteenth century. If Xi succeeds, China will offer the rest of the world unprecedented political, economic, and military challenges.[7]

We can thus see that it is China's interest to push the world in the direction of pluralism and diversity and oppose the "unilateralism" and "hegemony" of the United States. In addition, over 70 percent of the Chinese polled in 2023 believe that China should be more actively involved in international affairs, according to a survey by Tsinghua University.[8] Beijing's foreign relations approach under Xi Jinping has shifted steadily away from that of the Jiang Zemin era of "keeping a low profile (tao guang yang hui)," when the then Foreign Minister Qian Qichen and leading theoretician Zheng Bijian advocated China's peaceful rise onto the world stage.[9] Xi's policy switch goes hand in hand with the increased confidence of the Chinese in world affairs. According to a poll recently undertaken by Tsinghua University, more than half the Chinese interviewed believe that China plays a more important role in the world than the United States.[10]

When Deng Xiaoping was alive, China played a passive role in foreign policy. For instance, it almost never used its power of veto in the UN Security Council from 1978 when the reform started to 1997, when Deng died. By contrast, the Xi regime wants to develop international cooperation in terms of military security and carry out "military actions in U.N. peacekeeping, international rescue, maritime escort, and protection of the State's overseas interests, and [preserve] State sovereignty, security, territorial integrity, [and] development interests" (Art 18). China also wants to "actively collaborate with foreign governments and international organization for exchange in international security, [and] fulfill China's obligations in maintaining international security" (Art 10).

A main driving force behind this change of policy is Xi himself. Since 2012, Xi's personal leadership has played a key role in transforming Chinese foreign policy, under the slogan of "major country diplomacy with Chinese characteristics."[11] Xi takes "noticeably greater interest in harnessing the Chinese Communist Party's coercive forces as his personal domestic power base and foreign policy instrument complementing China's hard economic power."[12]

The CCP under Xi is thus reverting to a form of personalized authoritarianism by eliminating the key political norms that previously distinguished China's collective leadership during the Hu-Wen era.[13] This "party-state realism," as Steve Tsang calls it, "puts the interests of the Communist Party at the core of China's national interest calculation; and on this basis adopting an instrumentalist approach; adopting a party-centric nationalism; and adhering to a neoclassical realist assessment of the country's place in the international system and its relative material power in advancing national interest."[14]

A major tool used by China to achieve this change of policy is the law. The fact that the CCP, not the government, runs China's foreign relations (Art 5) was implied previously. It is now codified into law.[15] The country has witnessed a proliferation of laws on foreign policy in recent decades.[16] By June 2023, there are about 150 laws that deal specifically with foreign relations.[17] Among the latter, China has implemented a host of statutes that target export control and sanctions against Chinese companies.[18] According to Wang Yi, Minister of Foreign Affairs, the role of the FRL is to emphasize rule according to the law. It is a toolkit for achieving this goal.[19]

The Civilization Initiative

The Goal: Diversity in Global Politics

According to Xi, "All civilizations created by human society are splendid. They are where each country's modernization drive draws its strength and where its unique feature comes from." He argues that nations need to keep an open mind in appreciating the perceptions of values by diverse civilizations, and refrain from imposing their own values or models on others and from stoking ideological confrontation about these values.[20] Similarly, the FRL claims to endorse the idea that we must respect the rich diversity of civilizations, against the dominance of the Western civilization, and the ideological dichotomy of democracy versus authoritarianism. It also claims to advocate the idea that all countries should rise above their national, ethnic, and cultural differences and uphold the values of peace, development, equity, justice, democracy, and freedom, which are common values of humanity (Art 23).

To interpret the official position, Zhao Tingyang says that "to be a true world power the PRC needs to excel not just in economic production but also in 'knowledge production.' It needs to stop borrowing ideas from the West, and exploit China's own indigenous 'resources of traditional thought' to 'create new world concepts and new world structures.'"[21] *Qiu Shi*, the official CCP journal, claims that "Going hand in hand with China's economic success, the Chinese development model has become more and more influential in the world."[22] In addition, the Xi regime has in recent years discouraged the teaching of Western ideas to Chinese students. Chinese civil society groups and NGOs are also discouraged from working with foreign NGOs.[23]

The emphasis on civilization, a broad and more general concept instead of ideology that is more directly related to politics by Xi and some Western scholars, arises from various considerations. Samuel Huntington's use of the term *civilization* instead of *ideology* to describe the twenty-first century world order is intended to refute Francis Fukuyama's influential argument in the 1990s that world history had come to an end with triumph of democracy as the ultimate human value.[24] However, the Chinese government wants to blur the boundaries between ideology and civilization, in an attempt to defuse the US division of the world into the two camps of democracy and authoritarianism. Joe Biden emphasizes ideology by calling the war between Russia and Ukraine one between authoritarianism and democracy, and this has negative connotations for China's international relations. China does not want to be identified as belonging to the authoritarian camp.

THE CHARACTERISTICS OF THE CHINESE CIVILIZATION

Although Xi and the FRL do not specify what the future will look like in terms of civilization, some Chinese scholars have already made attempts to do so by using the concept of tianxia, which literally means "everything under heaven, or the universe." In ancient times, tianxia sometimes refers to China[25] and at other times it refers to the world.[26] In current usage, it describes a future state where everything under heaven is under one political sovereign. This, according to Sheng Hong, is a better arrangement than the current global order characterized by the existence of separate nation-states.[27] Within tianxia, some countries are supposed to be superior to others that are inferior.[28] Endorsing the idea of using tianxia to conceive of a new global order, Lin Gang states that Chinese expansion is benevolent because it is based on the idea of tianxia, while Western expansion is not because it takes place by conquest.[29] Borrowing from Lucian Pye's observation that China is a civilization that pretends to be a nation-state while Western nation-states pretend to be a civilization, Xu Jilin believes that the Confucian order is better than the current world order.[30] Ye Zicheng believes that it is possible to realize a state of tianxia in which a benevolent China is the center of the world.[31]

To discredit the mainstream realist Western international relations theory from a methodological perspective, Zhao Tingyang questions the concept of "rationality," a key notion of realism in Western international relations theory. He argues that it is too rigid to divide international relations theory into schools of thought of "realism" and "idealism," saying that "political realism does not work well unless it is idealistic, which is the same thing as saying that political idealism cannot work unless it is realistic."[32]

Shuchen Xiang justifies the idea of tianxia by saying that there are important similarities between this concept and the decolonized, postracial world envisioned by decolonial thinkers of the Global South, whose concepts of "internalization," "relationality," and "amelioration," and a world order of mutual and cultural synthesis that decolonial thinkers refer to.[33] Xiang's "decolonial thinkers of the global south" refer to those theoreticians in developing countries that are critical of the current Western realist international relations theories that are based on such concepts as "sovereignty" and "nation-states."

June Dreyer, however, criticizes the tianxia concept as a trope for a hierarchical Sinocentric relationship among countries governed according to Confucian principles of benevolence. This Chinese explanation of tianxia is not consistent with China's current public commitment to the principles of the United Nations and the Five Principles of Peaceful Coexistence.[34] Dreyer argues that tianxia might have worked in premodern times but it will not work in the current diverse world in which several other civilizations claim they are superior.[35]

Barry Buzan also warns about the danger of being Sinocentric. He believes that the civilization initiative should address the concept of "civilization" in plural form, as a single form might indicate a Sinocentric global order. Recalling that China talked about its "peaceful rise" during the Hu-Wen years, Bazan criticizes China's recent more assertive foreign policy by noting that the Chinese government rarely talks about it nowadays.[36] However, Buzan gives some credit to Xi by noting that Xi's denial that Western civilization is superior is shared by some prominent Western scholars.[37]

There is a certain amount of cosmopolitanism in the Chinese cultural tradition that may serve, consciously or unconsciously, as one of the driving forces of the Chinese vision of a global order. In the words of John King Fairbank, Chinese nationalism is cultural nationalism, that is, a way of life, less of a political nationalism that is based largely on territories and ethnicities.[38] Both the Beijing government and Taipei government gave up war reparations against Japan after World War II. Even on military strategy, some Western strategists like Little Hart and political leaders such as the US Congressman Ike Skelton believe that some elements of the Chinese tradition are applicable to the world. Little Hart believes that for modern warfare, Sun Tzu's *Art of War* is more efficient than the military thought of Carl von Clausewitz, which serves as mainstream Western military thinking. Sun Tzu promotes an indirect strategy in wars, believing that the best strategy is to win over the enemy instead of killing him. Deception is a supreme strategy (bing zhe, gui tao ye).[39] Ike Skelton sent a list of "must read" to the U.S. National Defense University and Sun Tzu's *Art of War* is the second on the list, next only to the US Constitution.[40] Therefore, Xi's "civilization initiative" has some cultural basis.

The moderate temperament of the Chinese is possibly connected to the fact that historically the Chinese economy is based on farming, a way of life that encourages conservative behavior, unlike the nomadic tribes in the north such as the Mongols and Manchus and Mediterranean societies that rely on trade. For about four hundred years during the last millennium, the Han Chinese were ruled and oppressed by ethnic minorities, that is, the Mongols (Yuan 1279–1368 CE) and the Manchus (Qing 1644–1911 CE), whose productivity level was much lower than the Chinese and whose population was below 10 percent of Han (the main ethnic group among the Chinese). The focus of the Han Chinese is the family. As long as they can lead a Confucian way of life, they do not care who is in power. This is reinforced by their belief in the Confucian Mandate of Heaven, which states that the ruler does not have to ask the ruled for their consent.[41]

Wang Dongyue, however, offers a different understanding of the Chinese temperament from that argued by Weber and Fairbank. Wang claims that the Chinese look benevolent toward outsiders because historically and geographically, central China (zhongyuan) (i.e., roughly the current five provinces of Hebei, Shandong, Henan, Shanxi, and Shaanxi) was surrounded by high mountains or areas where nomadic tribes lived, and the land was not useful for farming. So the Chinese did not wish to seize territories outside central China because they found nothing desirable in them. For instance, the Chinese preferred to fend off the Xiongnu, a nomadic tribe to the north that existed from the third century BCE, by offering them women and gifts, or driving them away to faraway places instead of killing them because the Chinese had no desire to conquer areas inhabited by the Xiongnu.[42] That is also why they built the Great Wall instead of investing in building a powerful army to conquer other places. But among themselves, the Chinese are very cruel: the only way to expand land ownership is to seize it from each other, as we can see from the Warring States periods (475–221 BCE).[43]

The universal claim embodied in the tianxia conception has significant global connotations. In the 1980s, when the Japanese economy was strong and Japan appeared to emerge as a dominant power in Asia, some Western political leaders were alarmed. But scholars noted that Japanese culture did not make universal claims to preeminence and therefore Japan did not have the soft power to be the leader of Asia (although it might have the hard power of wealth and technology).[44] The Japanese tend to believe that Japanese culture is superior and unique and not applicable to all humankind.[45] In this sense, Japanese culture is similar to Judaism, in that it is largely practiced within a particular ethnic group. China differs from Japan in the sense that it not only has economic might and military strength, but also has the soft power[46] of datong that not only claims universal applicability but is also pragmatic and achievement oriented.

Western scholars are not certain about whether China's rise will be peaceful. Mainstream international relations theory posits that democracies are inherently peaceful and that authoritarian regimes are more prone to wars. They point to the empirical fact that no wars were fought between two democracies in the twentieth century and that wars occur when at least one party is an authoritarian state.[47] That is why many Western scholars are skeptical that China's rise will be peaceful, since the country has such a long authoritarian tradition and, as the various laws promulgated during Xi's regime show, it continues to become more authoritarian still.

Other Western scholars view the situation differently. Comparing the Confucian view of the world and that of Puritans, Max Weber notes that the Puritans believe that human relations with the universe are in tension, while Confucians believe they are in harmony with nature. Puritans want to dominate nature, while the Confucians want to adjust to it.[48] John King Fairbank made similar observations. Likewise, Arnold Toynbee claims that the Chinese way of life is better than that of the West.[49]

Samuel Huntington notes that the West won its world dominance not by the superiority of its ideas, values, or religion but rather by its superiority in applying organized violence. Although Westerners often forget this fact, non-Westerners never do. Huntington believes that at the root, the clash between the United States and China is a clash of civilizations. With increased economic power, China will seek hegemonic power in East Asia. This is only natural because that is exactly what Western countries like Great Britain and the United States did before.[50]

The Security Initiative

THE UN AND UNIVERSAL VALUES

The FRL promises to respect the current world order. The FRL states that China will pursue its independent foreign policy of peace and observe the Five Principles of Peaceful Coexistence (Art 4).[51] Although he has remarked that China is committed to respecting the sovereignty and territorial integrity of all countries and to upholding non-interference in other countries' internal affairs, Xi also notes that countries must "respect the independent choices of development paths and social systems made by people in different countries."[52] This means that China reserves the right to pursue its own "development path"; namely, state capitalism, and its own "social system," which is authoritarian in character. After all, the term *sovereignty* means that a country can do whatever it wants within its own territory.

Critics say although China has appeared to follow traditional Westphalian principles, at heart its compliance with international law is instrumentalist and to be used when it suits China's interests.[53] In addition, the FRL makes very clear that the Chinese Constitution takes precedence over international law. This instrumentalist attitude was adopted against the background of China's changing relations with the UN and the US. China fought against the UN forces during the Korean War (1950–1953) and was barred from being a member of the UN until 1971. Mao described the UN as a tool used by the United States during this period: the US picked up the UN when it was useful and dropped it when it was no longer of use.[54] When Deng was the supreme leader of the country (1978–1997), China kept a low profile at the UN, trying not to confront the Unites States. During the Xi era, however, China increasingly uses the UN to confront what China calls the "American unilateralism."

The Chinese also adopted a pragmatic attitude over the changing relations between the United States and the UN. During the Korean War, the United States was able to fight under the banner of the UN against North Korean communist expansion and the Chinese military that helped North Korean forces.[55] But in recent decades, the US no longer has the same degree of influence over the UN as it did immediately after the Second World War, as exemplified by the expulsion of Taiwan from the UN against the will of the United States in 1971. Currently the United States wants to increase the membership of the UN Security Council, in what has been an unsuccessful attempt to prevent China and Russia from using their veto power against the wishes of the United States. Similarly, China is reluctant to support the United States at the UN Security Council in condemning the recent Russian invasion of Ukraine. In the UN General Assembly, most of the countries are part of the Global South, and it is not easy for the United States to use the UN for its own purpose. In recent years the United States has demonstrated its increasing unhappiness with the UN by failing to pay its membership dues, and President Donald Trump pulled out of the United Nations Educational, Scientific and Cultural Organization (UNESCO), although Joe Biden rejoined it. The decline of US influence in the UN makes China eager to use that organization for its own purposes.

On the issue of universal values, the FRL promises to abide by the principles of the UN Charter and to reject the Cold War mentality, oppose unilateralism and group politics, bloc confrontation, such as that between the NATO the other countries, and "long-arm jurisdiction," as when the

US intervenes in the domestic affairs of other countries.[56] Similarly, the FRL commits China to respecting the international system with the UN at its core, the international order underpinned by international law, and the norms governing international relations based on the principles of the UN Charter (Art 19).

This diplomatic posture does not seem to be consistent with the fact that the concept of "universal values" in a domestic sense was treated by the Chinese media increasingly negatively in recent years.[57] China interprets such universal values as "human rights," "freedom," and "democracy" differently from the generally accepted meanings. Although China claims to observe and protect human rights, it states that its observance is conditional, that is, "in light of the realities." That is to say, China reserves the right to define human rights as it sees fit (Art 22). Similarly, the FRL commits China to "respect and protect human rights and to the principle of the universality of human rights and its observance in light of the realities of countries." (Art 22).[58] For the current regime, however, the term human rights generally refers to socioeconomic rights, not political rights, as was discussed in the chapter on the Civil Code. This has led the UN to criticize China's treatment of the Tibetans and Uighurs for its violations of their political human rights.[59]

Other examples of China's creative interpretation of international laws to suit the country's national interest include its different treatment of the Sino-British Joint Declaration on Hong Kong. Faced with the charges by the British and US governments that Beijing's violation of human rights in Hong Kong deviated from the joint declaration, the Chinese Ministry of Foreign Affairs claimed that the joint declaration was out of date.[60] On the issue that the British government allowed some Hong Kong citizens who have British National Overseas passport (BNO) to migrate to the UK, the State Council's Office of Hong Kong and Macau Affairs accused the British government of violating the joint declaration.[61]

On the question of freedom, although the UN definition of human rights includes freedom of opinion and expression, this is not included in China's definition of freedom. Xi promised to guarantee people a degree of socioeconomic freedom, e.g., he promised to "remove institutional barriers that block the social mobility of labor and talent, and ensure that all of our people have the chance to pursue a career through hard work."[62] But the list of Xi's statements about freedom compiled by the official Xinhua News Agency, makes no mention of the freedom of speech.[63]

China's democracy is what it calls "whole-process people's democracy," which does not include popular elections. It is a model of political decision-making with a focus on consequences, that is, how well the government can improve the socioeconomic lives of citizens, rather than being based on democratic processes with the key component of direct elections.[64] An example of this whole process people's democracy is that during the Xi regime, while the World Bank index of China's tolerance of dissent and voice considerably worsened, the income gap between the rich and poor had narrowed. In addition, official corruption had been reduced, according to Transparency International. This was done not according to the rule of law, as we understand it in the West, but largely through administrative measures that are controlled by the CCP.

How can we explain the situation that while the regime clearly regards universal values that include democracy, human rights, and freedom as subversive,[65] it nevertheless endorses them on paper in foreign policy statements? Sun Tzu's wisdom may provide an insight into this. He says that domestic politics is where compassion and law are needed, while international relations are where opportunism is required.[66] China is not alone in this approach to international relations. The statements contained in the FRL are, after all, designed to be diplomatic remarks and cannot be evaluated according to their face value.

East Asian International Relations

An important part of Xi's security initiative is China's relations with its neighboring countries. He remarks that "we should resolutely safeguard peace in Asia. The Five Principles of Peaceful Coexistence and the Bandung Spirit (was) first advocated by Asia." He also says that Asian countries should vigorously advance Asian cooperation and promote Asian unity.[67] Accordingly, the FRL promises that China will promote coordination and interaction with its neighboring countries in accordance with the principles of friendship, sincerity, mutual benefit, and inclusiveness, and adopt the policy to enhance friendship and partnership with its neighbors (Art 17).

In a tone that is unusual in diplomatic discourse, Chinese Foreign Minister Wang Yi said in July 2023, "Europeans and Americans can't distinguish between Chinese, Japanese, and South Korean individuals. No matter how much we dye our hair yellow or how sharp we make our noses, we can't become Westerners. We should always remember our roots."[68] Wang's breach of professional decorum is part of a change in China's diplomatic attitudes and is called "wolf warrior diplomacy" (zhan lang wai jiao), which is typified by the utterances of Zhao Lijian, former deputy head of the Information Bureau of the Ministry of Foreign Affairs.

To what extent are China's relations with other East Asian countries different from its relationships with non-East Asian countries? Historically, China's foreign policy has often been based on a tributary relationship in the sense that neighboring countries acknowledged the superiority of the Central Kingdom while China offered them in return some kind of protection.[69] However, the tributary relationship was not stable throughout history. When the Chinese dynasty was strong, such as during the Ming era (1368–1644 CE), the tributary relationship existed; when the Chinese empire was weak, such as during the late Qing period (1644–1912 CE), it vanished.[70] But even when tributary relationships were strong, things were not always smooth. For instance, during the Ming Dynasty, a Japanese prince wrote to Emperor Zhu Yuanzhang (Ming Taizu) (1328–1398) to express his defiance of Ming. He accused China of intending to wage war with Japan, but warned that Japan had ways of defending itself.[71] Similarly, during the reign of Zhu Yuanzhang, the ruler from Korea chastised the Ming emperor for attempting to scare Korea, like an adult threatening children, instead of relying on moral standards to exert its authority.[72] On another occasion, Zhu Yuanzhang threatened to send troops to Vietnam if the latter did not submit itself to Ming rule. But Vietnam insisted on maintaining its independence.[73]

When Japan invaded China during the Second World War, it was with the intention of emulating the precedents of the Mongols and Manchus. Thus, an ethnic group with a lower level of productivity and a smaller population than the Chinese was able to conquer and also rule the Chinese who are supposed to have a mild temperament. In the Qing era the Manchus did not have to work, because they could live on the annual stipend provided by the government.

This unique East Asian tradition has had an ambiguous impact on contemporary international relations and therefore scholars naturally interpret it in different ways, each of which is valid to various extents. Chin-Hao Huang, basing his argument against the realist school of thought in international relations,[74] notes that as a result, East Asian international relations resemble that of neighbors, not a jungle.[75] David Kang says that sometimes East Asian states believe that a strong China functions to stabilize the region, while a weak China tempts other states to try for regional domination. However, Kang is careful to point out that this tells us nothing about what their future attitudes may be.[76] Alastair Iain Johnston remarks that Confucian-Mencian discourse is sometimes "divorced from the strategic preferences that emanated from the classics on strategy." In other words, the Chinese may not be as benevolent as some people believed in international relations.[77]

Empirically, the international relations among East Asian nations in modern times do not present a rosy picture and Japan's role is particularly noteworthy. The governments of Beijing and Taipei both gave up claiming war reparations against Japan after the Second World War, although the International War Tribunal had ordered Japan to do so. However, the other Asian countries that had been occupied by Japan at the same time received war reparations in one way or the other.[78] At the entrance of the Memorial of the Second World War in Taipei, a banner reads: "We return vice with virtue (yi de bao yuan)," suggesting that the Chinese did not intend to revenge Japan for their crimes during the war. In return, Japan gave millions of dollars worth of low interest government loans to China in the early part of the post-Mao reform that don't make any sense financially, although nobody claims that these are war reparations in disguise.

However, in 1900 when eight foreign powers evaded China, Japan's actions against China were the most aggressive among the invading countries, and it contributed more troops than the other seven powers (Russia, Germany, France, the United States, Italy, the United Kingdom, and Austro-Hungary).[79] Korean nationals living in Japan after the Second World War were discriminated against to such an extent that they were not even allowed to become school teachers.[80] According to Louis Hayes, Japanese racism is directed toward other Asians, not toward Caucasians.[81] The current Japanese opinion of the Chinese is very low and vice versa. South Korea and Japan are close to the United States and distant from China, because of the perceived Chinese threat.

THE ORIGINS OF THE SECURITY INITIATIVE

China's realist version in foreign affairs is partly inspired by the country's traditional security culture, exemplified by Sun Tzu's *Art of War* that is essentially a realist approach through indirect means. It is not idealist, because it aims at increasing the country's power and meeting its interests, not at an ideal. Sun Tzu states that it is always better to win the enemy over than to kill them. *The Art of War* is so remote from the Confucian belief in benevolence as a foundation for human action that it was kept secret from the public for a long time.[82] Because he recommends this indirect approach to warfare, people often believe it is different from the mainstream realist approach of the West, arguing that the Chinese way is a benevolent way, unlike that of the West.[83]

China's foreign policy is also inspired by the country's response to its hundred-year-long experience of national humiliation in modern times.[84] This was an eventful and painful history. After having been the world's largest economy from the tenth to the eighteenth century,[85] China was greatly weakened by a series of foreign incursions that went alongside domestic peasant rebellions. For instance, after its defeat by Japan in 1895, the Qing government signed the Maguan Treaty. "By the terms of the treaty, China was obliged to recognize the independence of Korea, over which it had traditionally held suzerainty; to cede Taiwan, the Pescadores Islands, and the Liaodong (south Manchurian) Peninsula to Japan; to pay an indemnity of 200,000,000 taels (of silver) to Japan; and to open the ports of Shashi, Chongqing, Suzhou, and Hangzhou to Japanese trade."[86] During the Japanese occupation in the Second World War 15 to 20 million Chinese died.[87] China's GDP per capita steadily declined from $600 in 1829, to $530 in 1870, $552 in 1913, and $439 in 1950.[88]

But over the last four decades, China's impressive growth has reversed this decline. In 1980, China's GDP was 10 percent of US GDP, as measured by purchasing power parity (PPP); 7 percent of its GDP at current US dollar exchange rates; and 6 percent of the US in exports. Its foreign currency reserves were only one-sixth the size of those of the US reserves. By 2014, those figures were 101 percent of the US GDP in terms of PPP; 60 percent at the US dollar exchange rates; and 106 percent of US exports. China's reserves in 2014 were twenty-eight times larger than that of the United States.[89] On the other hand, this picture may also be complicated by what many believe; namely, that the West has been in decline for some time, at least in some areas. Samuel Huntington claims the West took four hundred years to reach the peak of its power around 1900 and has since then started to decline.[90] This is certainly another a great impetus for China to restore its previously dominant position in Asia.

Driven by realist and practical considerations, Chinese foreign policy is opportunistic, as taught by Sun Tzu, and China is not alone on this. When it comes to the issue of Hong Kong and Taiwan, China uses current international standards, such as sovereignty and national integrity, insisting that a country can do whatever it wants within its territory based on its claim Hong Kong and Taiwan are parts of China. When talking about international relations in the future, they resort to the supposedly special East Asian international relations that have roots in the tributary system in ancient times, insisting that the peculiar nature of East Asian international relations may be a better way to conduct international affairs.

As a result of this complexity, trust is hard to find in China's international relations, especially with the United States. Wang Jisi notes that underneath the appearance of "mutual cooperation" that both countries project, the Chinese believe that they are likely to replace the United States as the world's leading power, while Washington is working to prevent such a rise. Similarly, Ken Lieberthal notes that many US officials believe their Chinese counterparts see the US-Chinese relationship in terms of a zero-sum game in the struggle for global hegemony.[91]

The Development Initiative

ECONOMIC STRUCTURAL CHANGE

The development initiative is mostly about concrete economic issues, especially those related to the sanctions by the United States and the West on issues such as microchips, rare metals, Huawei, and the Belt and Road Initiative (BRI). Among the three initiatives, this one attracts more attention from the Western media than the other two, because of its concrete relevance. Although the FRL does not explicitly outline the restrictive measures or penalties related to the sanctions from the West, it is still significant in addressing the current issues.[92]

Xi remarked, "Protectionist moves will boomerang; anyone attempting to form exclusive blocs will end up isolating himself; maximum sanctions serve nobody's interest, and practices of decoupling and supply disruption are neither feasible nor sustainable."[93] Chinese Foreign Minister Wang Yi added that China opposes all forms of hegemony and power politics, unilateralism, protectionism, and bullying.[94]

Similarly, the FRL defines China's commitment to advancing a thoroughgoing economic opening-up of the country, actively promotes and protects foreign investment in China, encourages external economic cooperation including outbound investment, and promotes the development of the BRI. It is committed to upholding the multilateral trading system, opposes unilateralism and protectionism, and works to build an open global economy (Art 26).

This development initiative was formulated against a history in which two or three decades ago, the two economies of the United States and China were largely complementary, with the latter producing lower-end products such as textiles and the former producing high-level ones such as electronics and other high-tech products.⁹⁵ In order to make sure that China benefits from foreign investments, the regulations ruled that Chinese personnel had to be involved in the technological sector of foreign companies. The foreign high-tech companies were then given priority. For instance, in the early stage of the reform, China did not give priority to American companies operating in the consumption sector, such as McDonald's or Starbucks, while it encouraged such high-tech companies as Pittsburgh Paint and Glass to invest in China. Foreign companies operating in the consumer industry came later.

Today, things are different. China now is not only able to produce and export high-end products such as automobiles and electronics, but also compete with the West in top high-tech areas. Some Chinese companies such as Huawei are rapidly catching up and the structure of collaboration between the two economies have changed. In addition to economic competition, the US also worries that China's advance in high technology can be used for military purposes.

To deal with this situation, the US pressured China to raise the value of the Chinese currency, Renminbi, since the low value of the Chinese currency gives China an advantage in exports as was the case with Japan in the 1980s. The US also feels that a more effective way to slow down the Chinese economy is to control China's access to advanced technology, especially microchips, the key component for technological advancement. After all, China is not only an Asian country like Japan, but also a communist country and its rise therefore poses more challenges to the West.

This is similar to Japan's economic development after the Second World War. In the 1950s, the Japanese and US economies were complementary in the sense that Japan produced low-end products while the United States produced high-end ones. However, this started to change in the 1970s and 1980s, when Japan was able to produce some high-end products such as automobiles and electronics. The United States then had to limit the Japanese exports of high-end products, because they hurt the American companies in these areas. The United States therefore pressured Japan to raise the value of its currency so that the Japanese exports became less competitive on the international market.⁹⁶

The development initiative was also formulated against the history of differences in the speed of development of the economies of the United States and China. These differences are astonishing. From 1980 through 2016, the Chinese income grew by 831 percent while the United States one grew by 63 percent.⁹⁷ China's high speed in economic growth is caused by multiple factors. China takes advantage of globalization to catch up, for example, China's rapid growth is directly related to its joining of the WTO. China can also use latecomer's advantage, that is, to use the most updated technology developed in the West to catch up, because as a late comer, China does not have to invest too much in basic research.

The United States sees the FRL as a step taken by China to strengthen the country's position against the extraterritorial application of foreign laws, such as foreign sanctions and export controls by the Western countries.[98] China has thus been subjected to many sanctions from the United States, over high-tech products such as microchips and as well as related to the Uyghurs, Tibetans, and Hong Kong.[99]

Specific Issues

Specifically, the development initiative is related to issues such as microchips, rare metals, Huawei, and the BRI. The US is the birthplace of the advanced silicon chip. In 1990, about 37 percent of the world's microchips were produced in the United States. But it has been losing its market share to Asia, where 79 percent of the world's microchips were produced in 2020. By 2020 the US was producing only 12 percent of all microchips worldwide.[100] However, "even as China seeks to achieve self-reliance and encourage indigenous innovation, it is still highly dependent on technology transfers from the US."[101] China imports about $200 billion worth of microchips a year.

The United States first imposed restrictions on the export of microchips to China in 2015. It continued to do so in 2021 and again twice in 2022. The Biden administration intends to choke off China's access to the purchase of high-end AI microchips, US-made microchip design software; US-built semiconductor manufacturing equipment; and US-built components. In addition, US law requires a license for any US citizen, permanent resident, anyone who lives in the US, and US companies that collaborate with Chinese companies producing semiconductors in China.[102]

The United States' efforts to slow down China's development of microchips is exemplified in the case of Meng Wanzhou, Huawei's chief finance officer and daughter of Ren Zhengfei, the company's founder. Meng was arrested at Vancouver International Airport by Canadian police upon a request from the US government on December 1, 2018. The US Department of Justice handed out an indictment on January 28, 2019, charging her for bank and wire fraud in relations to transactions conducted by Skycom, which had functioned as Huawei's Iran-based subsidiary, in violation of US sanctions.¹⁰³ Meng admitted that she had made untrue statements to HSBC Bank to enable transactions in the US that supported Huawei's work in Iran in violation of US sanctions. She was released on September 24, 2021, shortly after the Chinese government released two Canadian citizens who were charged for spying in China, a move that was in apparent retaliation for the arrest of Meng by Canada.

In retaliation for sanctions by the United States and EU aiming to restrict China's access to advanced microchips, China has in turn imposed restrictions on the export of gallium and germanium, which are key materials for the production of semiconductors. These metals are also used in military equipment and weapons. China requires exporters of the two metals to apply for licenses detailing the information about the buyer and the application or usage of the metals. China is the largest producer of gallium and germanium, producing about 94 percent and 83 percent of global production, respectively.¹⁰⁴

Taking a broader perspective, China has launched the BRI in an attempt to export its excess productive capabilities to other regions. By 2023 China has entered into agreements with over 150 countries and 30 international organizations in the BRI. Many developing countries have welcomed the BRI because it addresses their desperate need for the construction of infrastructure such as roads, sea ports, and railways, although the implementation of the BRI has problems.¹⁰⁵

This has made the West anxious about China's intentions and its ability to change the world economic order. For Eyck Freymann, the BRI "is primarily a campaign to restore an ancient model in which foreign emissaries paid tribute to the Chinese emperor, offering gifts in exchange for political patronage. Xi sees himself as a sort of modern-day emperor, determined to restore China's past greatness."¹⁰⁶

Conclusion

This chapter focuses on Xi Jinping's three initiatives on civilization, security, and development codified in the FRL. The civilization initiative calls for a pluralistic and diverse world order, claiming that every civilization is splendid. However, some Western scholars have warned this idea may increase global conflict and fuel the Chinese enthusiasm for a Sinocentric world order.

Xi's security initiative was inspired by Sun Tzu's *Art of War* that is realist in an indirect way and the Hundred-Years of Humiliation that drives

China's desire to be the premier country once again. Although the Chinese government pledges that China will conform to universal values and the UN Charter on an abstract level, it interprets these values in its own way. Thus, Xi's "freedom" does not include freedom of speech, his "democracy" does not include popular elections, and his "human rights" does not include people's political rights. This law also makes the Chinese Constitution supreme over international law.

The development initiative that promotes free trade against sanctions and "protectionism" by the West is a result of the changed economic structure between China and the West and the discrepancy in the speed of the two economies. Starting off in the 1980s as a producer of low-end products, China now can compete with the West on high-end products, taking advantage of its latecomer status to use the most advanced technology invented by the West without having to invest a great deal in basic research.

Chapter 8

The Chinese Dream

A Story of Culture

This study has observed that the Chinese Dream constitutes the third surge of utopianism in modern history, following that by Kang Youwei in the late Qing period and that by Mao. Like most modern utopias, it displays an egalitarian tendency backed by some form of authoritarian control. The three decades before Xi represent a deviation from the normal trajectory of modern Chinese development over the last century. The legal system under Xi is a combination of the Chinese Legalist tradition, prereform practice, and some Western legal elements, although it is increasingly moving more toward Legalism. It is statist, instrumentalist, and pragmatic, and it does not accommodate a belief in judicial independence. This exemplifies the resilience of culture and tradition and its impact on current politics, which has been greatly underestimated by Western scholars. The euphoria expressed by Francis Fukuyama three decades before Xi assumed the helm has given way to deep pessimism about the future of the country among Western China watchers today.

Specifically, this study deals with the substance of the Chinese Dream in five chapters. It has found that (1) the general ideological and political orientation in China under Xi is an emphasis on ideology as well as the preeminent role of the CCP and the supreme leader (the Fifth Constitutional Amendment); (2) matters of national security are under the strict control of the CCP and take precedence over civil liberties (the National Security Law); (3) The CCP is responsible for the supervision of government officials at the expense of judicial independence and the law (the National Supervision

Law); (4) civil rights are taken to mean people's socioeconomic rights, not their political rights (the Civil Code); and (5) on issues of foreign relations, the civilization initiative paints a different global order than the current one and the security initiative pledges to uphold the UN Charter and universal values, while insisting that China has the right to interpret universal values such as "democracy," "freedom," and "human rights" in its own way (the Foreign Relations Law).

In the first three decades after the reform China generally moved toward initiating economic reform and pluralistic politics, largely in light of the failure of the Cultural Revolution and in grasping the benefits that China would reap in terms of economic growth by joining the world community. Although the Hu Jintao-Wen Jiabao era is characterized as a lost decade for political reform, it can also be described as a golden era in terms of economic growth and political stability.[1] Xi's return to the Chinese cultural tradition in his strong endorsement of the Confucian concept of datong and his adoption of elements of Legalism is connected to contemporary international and domestic changes.

Internationally, the number of countries that endorse freedom has been in decline globally for more than a decade.[2] The trust of US citizens in their government has also been in decline, falling from a record 77 percent of the population in 1960 to the current 25 percent.[3] As an example of democracy, the US is no longer as appealing as before. Fewer countries are democratizing as they had been doing in the 1990s, and more are looking back to their own past for inspiration. Global conflicts are increasingly civilizational, such as the ongoing Russia-Ukraine War and the Israel-Palestine conflicts. Even in economic terms, China no longer depends on foreign trade as much as before. In 2005, the share of foreign trade in China's GDP was 64.5 percent at its peak. In 2020, it was around 34 percent.[4]

Theoretically speaking, political culture is a soft independent variable, not an accurate parameter of social change. Sometimes it is assertive, as is the case in China at present, sometimes it is oppressed, as was the case during the early part of the post-Mao reform. Culture matters, but its importance depends on circumstances and the use to which it can be put.[5]

The impact of outside forces on a country's political process has been widely observed. One example of this is Japan, with its cultural worship of the military spirit. Japanese militarism sometimes is assertive, sometimes oppressed. Before the Tokugawa period (1603–1867), Japan had undergone more than a century of civil war. The militaristic spirit was so strong at that time that Japan decided to try to conquer China via Korea, largely because the thousands of samurais left after Toyotomi Hideyoshi (1537–1598) unified Japan through war had no other skills except as warriors.[6] However, Western nations, horrified by the destruction wrecked by the First World War, decided to constrain militarism, including that of Japan. Japan accordingly was obliged to give up its ambitions of military expansion and entered the era of Taisho Democracy (1912–1926). After the 1929 Great Depression started, showing up the deficiencies of both capitalism and democracy, Japan took a different path and decided to start military expansion again.

The Resilience of Cultural Traditions

THE HUMAN HOPE OF DATONG

Datong is the spiritual and cultural origin of Chinese thought. Various versions of utopianism with datong at their core will continue to emerge with the unpredictable consequences, as happened in the twentieth century. In this sense, datong is similar to Christianity for Westerners—nation-states may come and go, but Christianity will stay intact. For Xi datong has connotations similar to those that the Orthodox Church has for Vladimir Putin. That is why, in spite of the repeated failures of those who tried to put it into practice over time, such as Kang Youwei, Mao Zedong, and Sun Yat-sen, Xi continues to find it appealing.

The concept of datong depicts an ideal but unreachable world, unlike the pragmatic concept of xiaokang, which paints a situation that is both attainable and believable. Both concepts have proved highly resilient in Chinese culture and history and, because of their vagueness and applicability in different contexts, can be used by leaders as a goal to encourage and motivate the general public in the preferred direction. In this way it is like Confucianism, which is a broad school of thought that can be interpreted in different ways.

Thus, while many modern thinkers, such as Lu Hsun (also spelt as Lu Xun, 1881–1936), believe that Confucianism is inhuman, or a form of "cannibalism" (chi ren),[7] others believe that Confucianism is compatible with democracy.[8] This is illustrated by the conflicting pronouncements attributed to Confucius. He is well known for saying, "small-minded men and women are hard to deal with," a statement implying sexism.[9] But the Confucian scholar is also known for believing that "husbands and wives are equals (qi zhe, qi ye)."[10] This ambiguity is not unique to the Confucian belief system: other religions that have endured over time, such as Christianity, have similar qualities.[11] Both Confucianism and Christianity have the quality of adaptability in different times and conditions, partly because of their ambiguity and flexibility.

This situation has implications for the Chinese identity: What does it mean to be Chinese? Two scholars put it in a very unusual way: for Tu Wei-ming from Harvard, a Chinese person is anybody who is interested in China. In other words, the Chinese identity is not based on ethnicity. For Ying-shih Yu from Princeton, China is wherever he goes. In other words, the Chinese identity is not based on territory.[12] Chih-yu Shih from Taiwan discusses the diversity and flexibility of the Chinese identity by saying that "Chineseness is constantly negotiated and reproduced."[13]

STATISM AND HUMAN FREEDOM

The Qin dynasty (221–206 BCE), which had conquered six other kingdoms to eventually unify China, is known for the idea that the state takes priority over the individual. Qin was successful largely because during this time every individual was dependent on the state for their survival. This strategy worked well in an environment where warfare was constant and occasionally once a city was conquered both the soldiers and civilians were slaughtered by the enemy forces indiscriminately (tu cheng). For instance, Fan Ju (?–255 BCE) a councilor of Qin, advised the king to kill not only enemy soldiers, but also civilians, because civilians will have children that will grow up to become soldiers in their turn.[14] Under these circumstances, individuals had to depend on the state for survival and there was no room for individual freedom. This tradition continued up to modern times. The Nanjing Massacre (1937), when tens of thousands of civilians suffered casualties and abuses in the hands of the Japanese, reminds the Chinese that without the protection of the state individuals cannot survive.[15]

For many among the ruling elites, a strong state needs a unified ideology to control people's political beliefs. Freedom of thought by individuals was believed to be subversive to a centralized state. Emperor Shihuang of Qin (259–210 BCE) therefore burned all existing books, except for some technical ones such as those in medicine and farming, and he had many scholars killed (fen shu keng ru).[16] The people's beliefs were later unified and systemized in Han (202 BCE–220 CE) by Dong Zhongshu (179–104 BCE), a councilor and scholar. Han is an important dynasty in that the Chinese characterize themselves as belonging to the Han ethnic group.

The beginning of the Han dynasty was relatively peaceful because people needed respite from the many previous years of warfare. So Emperor Wen of Han (203–157 BCE) and Emperor Jing of Han (188–141 BCE) initially adopted the Taoist philosophy of letting things evolve by themselves and noninterference of people's lives (shang shan ruo shui).[17]

But in the long run, this form of governance was not effective from the perspective of the ruling elites who prefer an all-encompassing power structure to fend off outside invaders such as the nomadic tribes from the north. Therefore, during the reign of Emperor Wu of Han (156–87 BCE), Dong Zhongshu promoted Confucianism as the official ideology. This is largely because Confucianism supports the all-encompassing power structure of the state and the family, the basic unit of farming.[18] Dong Zhongshu's imposition of one ideology on bureaucrats led to the institutionalization of the civil service exam for all Chinese officials. The civil service examination was formally established in Sui (581–618 CE), modified in Tang (618–907 CE), and became well established in Song (960–1279 CE), later becoming widespread in Ming (1368–1644 CE), and Qing (1644–1911 CE). It was abolished in the late Qing in 1905.

Although the civil service examination discourages freedom of speech and thought, it was a vehicle that men could use to climb up the social ladder, at least in theory. The civil service examination largely replaced the aristocratic system of Zhou (1046–256 BCE), which persisted for much longer in Europe. Japan, and Korea, both of which borrowed much from China's methods, restricted the civil service examinations to aristocrats, and did not allow commoners to sit it. The stabilizing role of these civil service examinations can still be seen today.[19]

Because of the civil service examination system, China was traditionally ruled over by civilians, unlike in many other societies where military generals often rule. Even during times of war, the supreme commander was often a civilian, as in the case of Zeng Guofan (1811–1872 CE), who put down the Taiping Rebellion (1850–1864 CE).[20] Mao Zedong is another example of a civilian taking the role of supreme commander of communist military forces. Because of this, Westerners who first came to East Asia two centuries ago had the impression that Chinese society looks feminine, while Japanese society looks masculine.[21]

Premodern Chinese society based on Confucianism was so well developed that it has been called an ultra-stable system. Jin Guantao argues that over the last two millennia, dynasties periodically fail, but the system remains standing. In fact, the periodic collapses of dynasties allow the system to adjust, as, for example, providing a mechanism for eliminating the over-concentration of land in the hands of the few and reducing the population that the land cannot sustain.[22] The Confucian "Mandate of Heaven" justifies the people's periodic overthrow of the governments. For Mencius, "Water can carry the boat and it can also overturn the boat," meaning if the government does not rule benevolently, people have the right to overthrow the government.[23] This is a departure from the Japanese cultural tradition that discourages people's rebellion against the government. The Chinese ruling elites are always on the edge, fearful of people's possible uprisings.

In addition to policies that unified beliefs and culture, another contributor to China's authoritarian politics is its well-developed irrigation system, which requires maintenance by the state, given that the private sector does not have the resources to maintain it. This reinforces the role of the state.[24] The du jiang yan irrigation system in Sichuan was built around 256 BCE by Qin. It is still working today, benefiting millions of farmers living in the area. The Grand Canal running from Beijing to Hangzhou, which was built during the reign of Emperor Yang of the Sui in 609 CE also served the purpose of irrigation and transportation. China's irrigation system is believed to be the most developed in the world in premodern times.[25]

Efficient Governance Instead of Democracy

Just as the Chinese philosophical tradition exhibits similarities to European utopian conceptions and critical philosophy,[26] the Chinese political tradition also exhibits elements similar to modern conceptions, which makes it resilient and contributes to its longevity. The Chinese ideas and practices did not come out of the blue. In addition to the conception of equality that underlies the civil service examination, which has been compared favorably with the European tradition of rule by aristocrats whose noble birth does not necessarily qualify them to be good administrators, the Confucian "Mandate of Heaven" (tian ming) justifies situations when the people rise up to overthrow the government.[27] This approach has been compared favorably with the Japanese tradition that views the government as always correct. Even during the Meiji Restoration, the slogan is "the government is praised and the people are stupid."[28] Chinese emperors were sometimes obliged to engage in zui ji zhao, or public self-criticism. An example of this is Emperor Chongzhen of Ming (1628–1644 CE), who apologized to the people six times during his reign of seventeen years.[29]

Modern democracy is built on freedom of the individual. If there is no human freedom, there will be no democracy. This contradicts Confucius' doubt of the people's capacity for making sound judgments: "People should be allowed to know what things are; not why things are (min ke you zhi, bu ke zhi zhi)."[30] However, even without freedom people may still benefit from the efficient governance by an authoritarian regime, even a foreign one. Ezra Vogel found that in the first half of the twentieth century, when Taiwan and Manchuria were colonies or de facto colonies of Japan, their socioeconomic development was actually higher than that in the rest of China. Local resistance to the Japanese dominance was therefore not strong.[31]

This tradition seems to continue to the present. In most countries, when entrepreneurs become economically powerful, they seek political rights. However, the newly wealthy Chinese during the reform era chose either to collaborate with the regime or to exit the country and migrate, instead of seeking political representation. Wealthy people leave China, not because of their human rights concerns, but because they desire better educational opportunities (21 percent), persistent quality-of-life problems in China: environmental pollution (20 percent), food safety (19 percent), social welfare (15 percent) and poor health care (11 percent). These factors were trailed by economic issues such as assets security (8 percent) and tax concerns (1 percent).[32]

The Chinese tradition of efficient governance, instead of democracy, may therefore endure. In assuming office, Xi must deal with three most serious challenges to the regime: people's resentment of government officials, their resentment of the wealthy, and their loss of faith (chou guan, chou fu, xinyang que shi). Under Xi, the first two problems were effectively addressed in the first ten years through the anticorruption campaign and by lifting millions out of poverty, according to the data by World Bank and Transparency International. In addition, some of people's socioeconomic rights, not political rights, have been legalized.

However, Xi's anticorruption campaign was not conducted through an independent judicial system that ensures impartiality and justice but through the CCP. As a result, government officials with posts above the county and department level had to disclose their properties and earnings to the CCP, not to the public; a practice that strengthens not only the authoritarian rule of the party but that of Xi himself. Xi also relies on the CCP for lifting the poor out of poverty.[33] For the regime, the rule of law practiced in Western countries cannot even address their own income gap, so it would be absurd for China to try using it to fix its own problems. From the perspective of the regime, Xi has been pretty efficient in addressing these two most urgent problems while strengthening the party.

A third issue that needed to be tackled was that the Chinese are very materialistic and lack spiritual pursuits. Xi wants to give them a spiritual life. The American Dream is no longer as attractive as it used to be, given the decline in confidence in the U.S. government. Datong's Chinese Dream is a useful way of inspiring the Chinese population. Thus, the degree of power which Xi has amassed is partly because he largely fulfilled the mission commissioned to him by the party.

Compatibility between the Forces of Politics and Economics

Modernization theory holds that an essential component of a liberal democracy is freedom: the political democratic system ensures that individuals can freely select their leaders through the vote; the market economy ensures that individuals can freely participate in economic activities through employment or investment; social freedom ensures that the individuals can choose their lifestyles.[34] For Milton Friedman, a free market economy is the guarantor of human freedom in modern times.[35] It is obvious that the current Chinese political system does not follow the logic of modernization theory: people have considerable economic freedom in spite of certain amount of state intervention and they also have considerable freedom in their lifestyles, although there are limitations to this freedom as well. However, the strict political control of the CCP is not compatible with Chinese society's relatively free economic and social activities.

In certain areas, the Chinese nowadays have less political rights than their ancestors in the dynasties. For instance, in the premodern system government officials were recruited on merit through objectively based and transparent civil service examinations, while the recruitment of party members today is based on their subjectively measured loyalty to the CCP. The current civil service examination exists to recruit entry-level civil servants, but key leadership positions in the civil service are occupied by CCP members.

Will the discrepancies in Xi's strategy of limited economic reform without political reform cause a social explosion and lead to a revolution? Theoretically, it is not certain. Both Karl Marx's work and modernization theory recognize the important effects of the economic sphere on the political process. But both realize this effect is not invariable. Thus, Marx argues that although the economic base determines the superstructure, under certain circumstances, the situation is reversed.[36] Gabriel Almond suggests that theories in the social sciences such as the modernization theory are like clouds, unclear and constantly changing, not accurate and stable like clocks, in the case of the natural sciences.[37] Moreover, a pure free market economy as a guarantor of human freedom in modern times has never existed in the way Milton Friedman had hoped for. A certain amount of state intervention in the economies of liberal democracies has been quite common after the Second World War.[38] The Chinese tolerance of their lack of freedom as humans is consistent with their tolerance of an economy that is not totally free, such as state capitalism.

Empirically, a variety of social trends can be identified in China today. Some move in the direction of Maoism; others prefer the status quo; still others favor the continuation of the capitalism-oriented reform. A Phoenix TV network survey in Hong Kong in 2023 found that about 58 percent of the Chinese who were polled welcomed the recurrence of the Cultural Revolution, while 42 percent opposed the recurrence.[39] Albert Walter has identified a bottom-up revolt against Western ideas of modernity, including political pluralism, the rule of law, and the free market economy.[40] Jude Blanchette suggests that China is undergoing a revival in a contemporary, unapologetic embrace of extreme authoritarianism that draws direct inspiration from the Maoist era.[41]

Other studies show, however, that in spite of three-year lockdown for Covid 19 from 2019 to 2021, which led to a great deal of resentment by citizens, most Chinese are not opposed to the regime. For instance, a 2020 survey conducted by Harvard University finds that the Chinese citizen's satisfaction with the government had increased across the board since 2003 when the survey started.[42] Yasheng Huang attributes people's lack of enthusiasm for radical political change to the country's long tradition of statism, especially the role played by the civil service examination in discouraging diversity in opinions and actions.[43]

Others believe that some Chinese, especially those who live in the big cities and are well educated, tend to endorse Western values in general. China has the largest middle class in the world.[44] As a result of the setbacks China has suffered since 2018 during the US-China trade war, some of the elites, especially the intellectuals, have been loudly calling for another round of reform (dao bi gai ge), such as opening up China's market even more, decreasing subsidies to state-owned enterprises, and abiding by the rules of the World Trade Organizations (WTO). Long Yongtu, China's chief negotiator during talks to join the WTO, publicly criticized establishment intellectuals such as Hu Angang, whose exaggerations of China's power alarmed the United States.[45] Chinese economist Wu Jinglian expresses concern about the recent government attempts to promote state-owned enterprises at the expense of privately owned ones.[46]

Against this background, the current market economy is likely to continue. In the new party constitution, the role of the market has been changed from having "an essential role," to playing a "decisive role," implying a more important role has been envisaged for the market (CCP General Outline). Some marketization efforts have been identified. For instance, university professors since 2018 are no longer state employees enjoying life tenure, as they used to be. Instead, they are currently employed by the universities and their employment is subject to market forces.[47] The most important factor that makes Xi's regime think twice before giving up economic reform is that China's growth since he came to office had been cut in half, from more than 10 percent in the Jiang and Hu eras to the current 5 percent. Such low growth may cause not only economic problems but also social unrest.

The intervention of the state in the market is also likely to continue. The new party constitution changed from the 1980s policy of "letting a few to become rich" to one of promoting "more equality" (CCP General Outline).[48] In 2018 the BBC reported that the current regime has given up Jiang's "Three Represents" policy, which tried to recognize the role played by entrepreneurs. More and more privately owned companies have had to give up part of their independence to work with state-owned companies.[49] Theoretically, market forces by necessity will generate inequality in outcome if the government does not intervene.[50] To avoid this growth in inequality state intervention in the market is found in many contemporary liberal democracies as well, such as in France under Francois Mitterrand.[51]

In this uncertain environment, it is in the interest of the CCP not to continue the liberal trend of the first three decades of the reform. If the liberal tendency continues, the multi-party system will inevitably emerge. The experience of the Cultural Revolution, which gave people the right to participate in politics, that resulted in chaos and the post-Soviet experience in the former Union of Soviet Socialist Republics (USSR) also made the Xi regime reluctant to encourage the citizenry's active participation in politics. The collapse of the USSR did not produce a well-functioning democracy. Instead it led to an oligarchy rule and then to Putin's personal authoritarianism.[52]

Chinese leaders are deeply pragmatic and consider their political survival more important than the ideological convictions. After the failure of the Second Revolution in 1913, Sun Yat-sen wanted his followers to be loyal to himself rather than to the newly established party, a practice that contradicted his professed support of democracy. As a result, his closest ally, Huang Xing (1874–1916 CE), left him in protest.[53] Mao never wanted a constitution, so the 1954 one was valid for only three years. But when he was under pressure after the failure of the Great Leap Forward, after Liu Shaoqi discouraged him from attending the Seven Thousand Cadres Conference in January 1962 (and Deng Xiaoping advised him not to speak at it), he produced the PRC Constitution in protest.[54] Similar contradictions between ideology and pragmatic considerations are illustrated by the next example. Liu Shaoqi paid no heed to the law when he led the Four Cleanings Campaign (si qing) in 1964, during which many officials were purged with no legal procedure.[55] However, when he himself was purged during the Cultural Revolution, he used the Constitution to defend himself.[56] In the same way, immediately after Jiang Zemin came to power following the Tiananmen Massacre, his intention was to penalize the new entrepreneurs and push back on the reform. Yet Jiang swiftly backtracked after Deng threatened to fire anybody who opposed the reform.[57]

Conclusion

To conclude, in extraordinary situations, Chinese leaders may follow the path of modernity. It was thus possible for the Qing Dynasty to reform and modernize after being defeated by the Japanese in 1894, after the failed attempt to rely on economics and technology without political reform. It was possible for the Republic to try to reshape people's political awareness in 1920s during the New Culture Movement,[58] after the failure of the Late Qing Reform in 1898 proved that political reform cannot be accomplished without changing people's political awareness. It was possible for CCP to endorse US-style democracy against Soviet communism, as was the case during the constitution-making conference in 1946. And it was just as possible for China under the CCP to endorse quasi-liberalism and thin constitutionalism in the first three decades of the reform.

In similar situations, however, the Chinese culture of authoritarianism seems to have a more powerful impact on its modernization drive than its East Asian neighbor of Japan and its communist/postcommunist comrade, the former Soviet Union. Although Russia and Japan are not known to have a liberal tradition, for China this is even less so, in that it tends to permit less freedom in comparable situations. China's first modern Constitution in the late Qing was largely copied from the Japanese Meiji Constitution. Yet China allows people less freedom than Japan does. China's first communist constitution in 1954 was modeled after the 1937 Soviet constitution. Yet, again, China permits its people less freedom than the former Soviet Union did.[59]

In origin, the Soviet New Economic Policy (1924) and the Chinese Cultural Revolution are structurally similar in the sense that communism as a social system did not function effectively, and communist leaders had to make adjustments to carry the country through. But the leaders of the two countries used different strategies in these circumstances. While Vladimir Lenin (1898–1924 CE) moved in the rightist direction by taking a break from communist ideals, Mao moved in the leftist direction to radicalize the movement.[60]

China's opening up to the modern world has been painful. It started with the Opium War in 1839; the Chinese remember this bitterly as a critical point of the hundred-year-long humiliation they have endured at the hands of foreign powers. However, the Japanese treat their equally painful opening up to the West, that is, Matthew Perry's expedition to Japan in 1815, as beneficial to Japan because, however humiliating the experience was at the time, Japan might still be living in the dark ages had it not happened. Therefore, the Japanese nowadays celebrate Perry's coming to Japan in an annual Black Ships Festival.

How much appeal does the Chinese Dream have for people in the rest of the world? Given that the beautiful Chinese Dream has to be achieved through authoritarian means in this diverse world, at least for now and in the near future, the Chinese Dream is not the world's dream. The utopianism that could lead to a "better place" in the Chinese context, has increasingly become seen as a "no place" in the global context.[61]

Appendix A

The Fifth Constitutional Amendment of the
National People's Congress of the People's Republic of China

This English version is provided by the Communist Party of China Central Committee Institute of Party History and Literature. http://en.npc.gov.cn.cdurl.cn/laws.html

No. 1

The Amendment to the Constitution of the People's Republic of China has been adopted by the First Session of the Thirteenth National People's Congress of the People's Republic of China on March 11, 2018 and is hereby promulgated to take effect.

Presidium of the First Session of the Thirteenth National People's Congress of the People's Republic of China

March 11, 2018 in Beijing

Amendment to the Constitution of the
People's Republic of China

(Adopted by the First Session of the Thirteenth National People's Congress on March 11, 2018)

Article 32. In the seventh paragraph of the Preamble to the Constitution, "the guidance of Marxism-Leninism, Mao Zedong Thought, Deng Xiaoping

Theory and the Theory of Three Represents" is amended to read "the guidance of Marxism-Leninism, Mao Zedong Thought, Deng Xiaoping Theory, the Theory of Three Represents, the Scientific Outlook on Development and Xi Jinping Thought on Socialism with Chinese Characteristics for a New Era;" "improve the socialist legal system" is amended to read "improve socialist rule of law;" before "work hard in a spirit of self-reliance" the words "apply the new development philosophy" are inserted; and "promote coordinated material, political and cultural-ethical advancement, in order to build China into a socialist country that is prosperous, strong, democratic and culturally advanced" is amended to read "promote coordinated material, political, cultural-ethical, social and ecological advancement, in order to build China into a great modern socialist country that is prosperous, strong, democratic, culturally advanced, harmonious and beautiful, and realize the great rejuvenation of the Chinese nation." This paragraph is accordingly amended to read: "Both the victory in China's New Democratic Revolution and the successes in its socialist cause have been achieved by the Chinese people of all ethnic groups under the leadership of the Communist Party of China and the guidance of Marxism-Leninism and Mao Zedong Thought by upholding truth, correcting errors, and surmounting many difficulties and obstacles. Our country will long remain in the primary stage of socialism. The fundamental task for our country is to concentrate on achieving socialist modernization along the road of socialism with Chinese characteristics. We the Chinese people of all ethnic groups will continue, under the leadership of the Communist Party of China and the guidance of Marxism-Leninism, Mao Zedong Thought, Deng Xiaoping Theory, the Theory of Three Represents, the Scientific Outlook on Development and Xi Jinping Thought on Socialism with Chinese Characteristics for a New Era, to uphold the people's democratic dictatorship, stay on the socialist road, carry out reform and opening up, steadily improve the socialist institutions, develop the socialist market economy and socialist democracy, improve socialist rule of law, apply the new development philosophy, and work hard in a spirit of self-reliance to modernize step by step the country's industry, agriculture, national defense, and science and technology and promote coordinated material, political, cultural-ethical, social and ecological advancement, in order to build China into a great modern socialist country that is prosperous, strong, democratic, culturally advanced, harmonious and beautiful, and realize the great rejuvenation of the Chinese nation."

Article 33. In the tenth paragraph of the Preamble to the Constitution, "Through the long process of revolution and development" is amended to read "Through the long process of revolution, development and reform;" "a broad patriotic united front, including all socialist working people, people involved in building socialism, patriots who support socialism, and patriots who support China's reunification" is amended to read "a broad patriotic united front, including all socialist working people, people involved in building socialism, patriots who support socialism, and patriots who support China's reunification and are dedicated to the rejuvenation of the Chinese nation." This paragraph is accordingly amended to read: "The cause of building socialism must rely on workers, peasants and intellectuals and unite all forces that can be united. Through the long process of revolution, development and reform, a broad patriotic united front has formed under the leadership of the Communist Party of China, with the participation of other political parties and people's organizations and including all socialist working people, people involved in building socialism, patriots who support socialism, and patriots who support China's reunification and are dedicated to the rejuvenation of the Chinese nation. This united front will continue to be consolidated and developed. The Chinese People's Political Consultative Conference is a broadly representative organization of the united front, and has played a significant historical role. In the future, it will play an even more important role in the country's political and social life and its friendly foreign activities, in socialist modernization and in safeguarding the unity and solidarity of the country. The system of multiparty cooperation and political consultation under the leadership of the Communist Party of China will continue and develop long into the future."

Article 34. In the eleventh paragraph of the Preamble to the Constitution, "Socialist ethnic relations of equality, unity and mutual assistance are established and will continue to be strengthened" is amended to read "Socialist ethnic relations of equality, unity, mutual assistance and harmony are established and will continue to be strengthened."

Article 35. In the twelfth paragraph of the Preamble to the Constitution, "The achievements of China's revolution and development would have been impossible without the support of the world's people" is amended to read "The achievements of China's revolution, development and reform would have been impossible without the support of the world's people;" after "China pursues an independent foreign policy, and observes the five principles of mutual respect for sovereignty and territorial integrity, mutual nonaggression, mutual noninterference in internal affairs, equality and mutual benefit, and peaceful coexistence" the words "keeps to a path of peaceful development, follows a mutually beneficial strategy of opening up," are inserted; and "works to develop diplomatic relations and economic and cultural exchanges with other countries" is amended to read "works to develop diplomatic relations and economic and cultural exchanges with other countries, and promotes the building of a human community with a shared future." This paragraph is accordingly amended to read: "The achievements of China's revolution, development and reform would have been impossible without the support of the world's people. The future of China is closely bound up with the future of the world. China pursues an independent foreign policy, observes the five principles of mutual respect for sovereignty and territorial integrity, mutual nonaggression, mutual noninterference in internal affairs, equality and mutual benefit, and peaceful coexistence, keeps to a path of peaceful development, follows a mutually beneficial strategy of opening up, works to develop diplomatic relations and economic and cultural exchanges with other countries, and promotes the building of a human community with a shared future. China consistently opposes imperialism, hegemonism and colonialism, works to strengthen its solidarity with the people of all other countries, supports oppressed peoples and other developing countries in their just struggles to win and safeguard their independence and develop their economies, and strives to safeguard world peace and promote the cause of human progress."

Article 36. In paragraph 2 of article 1 of the Constitution, after "The socialist system is the fundamental system of the People's Republic of China." a new sentence is inserted to read: "Leadership by the Communist Party of China is the defining feature of socialism with Chinese characteristics."

Article 37. Paragraph 3 of article 3 of the Constitution, which reads "All administrative, adjudicatory and procuratorial organs of the state shall be created by the people's congresses and shall be responsible to them and subject to their oversight." is amended to read: "All administrative, supervisory, adjudicatory and procuratorial organs of the state shall be created by the people's congresses and shall be responsible to them and subject to their oversight."

Article 38. In paragraph 1 of article 4 of the Constitution, "The State shall protect the lawful rights and interests of all ethnic minorities and uphold and promote relations of equality, unity and mutual assistance among all ethnic groups." is amended to read: "The state shall protect the lawful rights and interests of all ethnic minorities and uphold and promote relations of equality, unity, mutual assistance and harmony among all ethnic groups."

Article 39. In paragraph 2 of article 24 of the Constitution, "The state shall advocate the civic virtues of love for the motherland, for the people, for work, for science and for socialism" is amended to read: "The state shall champion core socialist values; advocate the civic virtues of love for the motherland, for the people, for work, for science and for socialism." This paragraph is accordingly amended to read: "The state shall champion core socialist values; advocate the civic virtues of love for the motherland, for the people, for work, for science and for socialism; educate the people in patriotism and collectivism, in internationalism and communism, and in dialectical and historical materialism; and combat capitalist, feudal and other forms of decadent thought."

Article 40. In article 27 of the Constitution, a new paragraph is added as paragraph 3 to read: "State employees, when assuming office, should make a public pledge of allegiance to the Constitution in accordance with the provisions of law."

Article 41. In article 62 of the Constitution, a new item is added under "The National People's Congress shall exercise the following functions and powers" as item 7 to read "(7) electing the chairperson of the National Commission of Supervision," and items 7 through 15 are accordingly changed to items 8 through 16.

Article 42. In article 63 of the Constitution, a new item is added under "The National People's Congress shall have the power to remove from office the following personnel" as item 4 to read "(4) the chairperson of the National Commission of Supervision," and items 4 and 5 are accordingly changed to items 5 and 6.

Article 43. Paragraph 4 of article 65 of the Constitution, which reads "Members of the National People's Congress Standing Committee shall not hold office in an administrative, adjudicatory or procuratorial organ of the state." is amended to read: "Members of the National People's Congress Standing Committee shall not hold office in an administrative, supervisory, adjudicatory or procuratorial organ of the state."

Article 44. In article 67 of the Constitution under "The National People's Congress Standing Committee shall exercise the following functions and powers," item 6, which reads "(6) overseeing the work of the State Council, the Central Military Commission, the Supreme People's Court and the Supreme People's Procuratorate," is amended to read "(6) overseeing the work of the State Council, the Central Military Commission, the National Commission of Supervision, the Supreme People's Court and the Supreme People's Procuratorate;" and a new item is added as item 11 to read " (11) appointing or removing, based on recommendations by the chairperson of the National Commission of Supervision, vice chairpersons and members of the National Commission of Supervision," and items 11 through 21 are accordingly changed to items 12 through 22. In paragraph 1 of article 70 of the Constitution, "The National People's Congress shall establish an Ethnic Affairs Committee, a Law Committee, a Financial and Economic Committee, an Education, Science, Culture and Public Health Committee, a Foreign Affairs Committee, an Overseas Chinese Affairs Committee and such other special committees as are necessary." is amended to read "The National People's Congress shall establish an Ethnic Affairs Committee, a Constitution and Law Committee, a Financial and Economic Committee, an Education, Science, Culture and Public Health Committee, a Foreign Affairs Committee, an Overseas Chinese Affairs Committee and such other special committees as are necessary."

Article 45. Paragraph 3 of article 79 of the Constitution, which reads "The president and the vice president of the People's Republic of China shall have the same term of office as that of the National People's Congress and shall serve no more than two consecutive terms." is amended to read: "The president and the vice president of the People's Republic of China shall have the same term of office as that of the National People's Congress."

Article 46. In article 89 of the Constitution under "The State Council shall exercise the following functions and powers," item 6, which reads "(6) directing and managing economic work and urban and rural development," is amended to read "(6) directing and managing economic work, urban and rural development and ecological conservation;" and item 8, which reads "(8) directing and managing work such as civil affairs, public security, judicial administration and supervision," is amended to read "(8) directing and managing work such as civil affairs, public security and judicial administration."

Article 47. In article 100 of the Constitution, a new paragraph is added as paragraph 2 to read: "The people's congresses of cities divided into districts and their standing committees may, provided there is no conflict with the Constitution, laws or administrative regulations, or with the local regulations of their province or autonomous region, formulate local regulations in accordance with the provisions of law, which shall go into force after submission to the standing committee of the people's congress of their province or autonomous region and the receipt of approval."

Article 48. In paragraph 2 of article 101 of the Constitution, "Local people's congresses at or above the county level shall elect, and have the power to remove from office, presidents of people's courts and chief procurators of people's procuratorates at their respective levels." is amended to read: "Local people's congresses at and above the county level shall elect, and have the power to remove from office, chairpersons of the commissions of supervision, presidents of the people's courts and chief procurators of the people's procuratorates at their respective levels."

Article 49. Paragraph 3 of article 103 of the Constitution, which reads "Members of the standing committee of a local people's congress at or above the county level shall not hold office in an administrative, adjudicatory or procuratorial organ of the state," is amended to read: "Members of the standing committee of a local people's congress at or above the county level shall not hold office in an administrative, supervisory, adjudicatory or procuratorial organ of the state."

Article 50. In article 104 of the Constitution, "oversee the work of the people's government, the people's court and the people's procuratorate at their respective level" is amended to read "oversee the work of the people's government, the commission of supervision, the people's court and the people's procuratorate at their respective levels." This article is accordingly amended to read: "The standing committees of local people's congresses at and above the county level shall discuss and decide on major issues in all areas of work in their administrative areas; oversee the work of the people's government, the commission of supervision, the people's court and the people's procuratorate at their respective levels; revoke inappropriate decisions and orders made by the people's government at the same level; revoke inappropriate resolutions adopted by the people's congress at the next level down; decide on the appointment or removal of employees of state organs according to the authority invested in them as prescribed by law; and, when people's congresses at their level are out of session, remove from office and elect to fill vacancies individual deputies to the people's congress at the next level up."

Article 51. Paragraph 1 of article 107 of the Constitution, which reads "Local people's governments at and above the county level shall, according to the authority invested in them as prescribed by law, manage administrative work related to the economy, education, science, culture, public health, sports, urban and rural development, finance, civil affairs, public security, ethnic affairs, judicial administration, supervision, family planning, etc., within their administrative areas; and shall issue decisions and orders, appoint or remove, train, evaluate, and award or punish administrative employees," is amended to read: "Local people's governments at and above the county level shall, according to the authority invested in them as prescribed by law, manage administrative work related to the economy, education, science, culture, public health, sports, urban and rural development, finance, civil affairs, public security, ethnic affairs, judicial administration, family planning, etc., within their administrative areas; and shall issue decisions and orders, appoint or remove, train, evaluate, and award or punish administrative employees."

Article 52. In Chapter III of the Constitution titled "State Institutions," a new section is added as Section 7 titled "Commissions of Supervision;" and five new articles are added as articles 123 through 127. The content is as follows:

Section 7

COMMISSIONS OF SUPERVISION

Article 123. Commissions of supervision of the People's Republic of China at all levels are the supervisory organs of the state.

Article 124. The People's Republic of China shall establish a National Commission of Supervision and local commissions of supervision at all levels. A commission of supervision shall be composed of the following personnel: a chairperson, vice chairpersons, and members. The chairperson of a commission of supervision shall have the same term of office as that of the people's congress at the same level. The chairperson of the National Commission of Supervision shall serve no more than two consecutive terms. The organization, functions and powers of the commissions of supervision shall be prescribed by law.

Article 125. The National Commission of Supervision of the People's Republic of China is the highest supervisory organ. The National Commission of Supervision shall direct the work of local commissions of supervision at all levels; commissions of supervision at higher levels shall direct the work of those at lower levels.

Article 126. The National Commission of Supervision shall be responsible to the National People's Congress and the National People's Congress Standing Committee. Local commissions of supervision at all levels shall be responsible to the state organs of power that created them and to the commissions of supervision at the next level up.

Article 127. Commissions of supervision shall, in accordance with the provisions of law, independently exercise supervisory power, and shall not be subject to interference from any administrative organ, social organization or individual. The supervisory organs, in handling cases of duty-related malfeasance or crime, shall work together with adjudicatory organs, procuratorial organs and law enforcement authorities; they shall act as a mutual check on each other.

Section 7 is accordingly changed to Section 8, and articles 123 through 138 are accordingly changed to articles 128 through 143.

Appendix B

National Security Law of the People's Republic of China

Published July 1, 2015
By: Rogier Creemers
   https://digichina.stanford.edu/work/national-security-law-of-the-peoples-republic-of-china/
   NOTE: *This translation was originally published on the China Copyright and Media blog, a project of DigiChina's Prof. Rogier Creemers of the University of Leiden. It has not been edited, double-checked, or standardized with DigiChina's original content.*
   Passed at the 15th Meeting of the 12th National People's Congress Standing Committee on 1 July 2015)

Chapter I: General Principles

Article 1: In order to safeguard national security, defend the people's democratic dictatorship regime and the system of Socialism with Chinese characteristics, protect the fundamental interests of the people, ensure the smooth progress of reform, opening up and Socialist modernization construction, and realize the great rejuvenation of the Chinese nation, in accordance with the Constitution, this Law is formulated.

Article 2: National security refers to a situation in which the national regime, sovereignty, unity and territorial integrity, the welfare of the people, the sustained development of the economy and society and other major State interests are not in danger or under internal or external threat, as well as the capacity to ensure a sustained situation of security.

Article 3: National security work shall persist in a comprehensive national security view, take the security of the people as purpose, take political security as the foundation, take economic security as the basis, take military, cultural and social security as guarantee, take stimulating international security as a support, it shall safeguard national security in all areas, build a national security system, and march the path of national security with Chinese characteristics.

Article 4: [We must] persist in the leadership of the Chinese Communist Party over national security work, establish centralized, unified, effective and authoritative national security leadership structures.

Article 5: The Centre's national security leading body is responsible for policymaking, discussion and coordination of national security work, for researching the formulation and guiding the implementation of national security strategies and relevant major doctrines and policies, comprehensively planning and coordinating major affairs and major work concerning national security, and promoting the construction of national security rule of law.

Article 6: The State formulates and incessantly perfects national security strategies, comprehensively evaluates international and domestic security circumstances, and clarifies the guiding principles, middle and long-term objectives for national security strategy, as well as national security policies, work tasks and measures in focus areas.

Article 7: The safeguarding of national security shall abide by the Constitution and the law, persist in the principles of Socialist rule of law, respect and ensure human rights, and protect the rights and liberties of citizens according to the law.

Article 8: The safeguarding of national security shall be coordinated with economic and social development.

National security work shall comprehensively take account of internal security and external security, territorial security and citizens' security, traditional security and non-traditional security, our own security and common security.

Article 9: The safeguarding of national security shall persist in giving preference to prevention, treating both root causes and symptoms, integrating specialist work and the mass line, [it shall] fully give rein to the functions and roles of specialist bodies and other relevant bodies in safeguarding national security, and broadly mobilize citizens and organizations to prevent, curb and lawfully sanction acts harming national security.

Article 10: The safeguarding of national security shall persist in mutual trust, mutual benefit, equality and cooperation, in launching vigorous security exchange and cooperation with foreign governments and international organizations, the implementation of international security duties, the stimulation of common security, and the safeguarding of world peace.

Article 11: Citizens of the People's Republic of China, all State bodies and armed forces, all political parties and people's organizations, enterprises, undertakings, organizations and all other social organizations have the responsibility and duty to safeguard national security.

The sovereignty and territorial integrity of China brook no violation or separation. The safeguarding of national sovereignty, unity and territorial integrity is the common duty of all Chinese citizens, including Hong Kong and Macau compatriots, and Taiwan compatriots.

Article 12: The State issues awards and commendations to individuals and organizations making prominent contributions to safeguarding national security work.

Article 13: Where personnel of State bodies abuse their power, commit dereliction of duty, or engage in favouritism in the course of national security work or activities affecting national security, their legal liability will be punished according to the law.

Where any person or individual, in violation of this Law and relevant laws, des not uphold national security duties or engages in acts harming national security, their legal liability will be punished according to the law.

Article 14: 15 April of every year will be a national security education day for the entire population.

Chapter II: The Tasks of Safeguarding National Security

Article 15: The State persists in the leadership of the Chinese Communist Party, upholding the system of Socialism with Chinese characteristics, developing Socialist democratic politics, completing Socialist rule of law, strengthening constraints and supervisory mechanisms for the use of power, and guarantees all rights of the people, who are masters of their own affairs.

The State prevents, curbs and lawfully sanctions any act of treason, separatism, incitement of rebellion, subversion or incitement of subversion of the people's democratic dictatorship regime; it prevents, curbs and lawfully sanctions theft or divulgement of State secrets and other such acts harming national security; it prevents, curbs and lawfully punishes infiltration, destructive, subversive and separatist activities by foreign forces.

Article 16: The State upholds and develops the fundamental interests of the broadest people, it defends the people's security, creates good existence and development conditions and stable work and living environments, and guarantees citizens' lives, assets, security and other lawful rights and interests.

Article 17: The State strengthens the construction of border defence, maritime defence and air defence, it adopts all necessary defence and control measures, safeguards the security of the territory, internal waters, territorial waters and territorial airspace, and safeguards national territorial sovereignty and maritime rights and interests.

Article 18: The State strengthens the revolutionization, modernization and regularization of the armed forces, and constructs armed forces suited to the needs of ensuring national security and development interests; it implements vigorous doctrines for defensive military strategies, to guard against and curb aggression, and to curb armed subversion and separation; it launches international military security cooperation, it implements military operations for United Nations peacekeeping, international aid, maritime escorts and to safeguard overseas national interests, to safeguard national sovereignty, security, territorial integrity, development interests and world peace.

Article 19: The State safeguards the basic system of the national economy and the order of the Socialist market economy, it completes structures and mechanisms to prevent and dissolve economic security risks, to safeguard the security important sectors, crucial areas, focus industries, major infrastructure and major construction programmes as well as other economic interests that affect the lifelines of the national economy.

Article 20: The State completes mechanisms for cautious macro-level financial management and the prevention and management of financial risk, it strengthens the constructions of the financial infrastructure and basic capabilities, and it prevents and dissolves systemic and regional financial risk, and prevents and resists damage by external financial risks.

Article 21: The State reasonably uses and protects natural resources and energy, it effectively controls the development of strategic natural resources and energy, strengthens the storage of strategic natural resources and energy, it perfects the construction of strategic channels for the transportation of natural resources and energy, as well as measures for the protection of their security, it strengthens international natural resource and energy cooperation, comprehensively enhances emergency response capabilities, and ensures that the natural resources and energy required for economic and social developments can be provided in a sustained, reliable and efficient manner.

Article 22: The State completes food security protection system, it protects and raises comprehensive food production capacities, it perfects food storage structures, distribution systems and market regulation mechanisms, it completes food security early warning structures, and guarantees food supply, quality and security.

Article 23: the State persists in the progressive orientation of advanced Socialist culture, it inherits and carries forward the excellent traditional culture of the Chinese nation, it fosters and practices the Socialist core value view, it prevents and resists the influence of harmful culture, it grasps the initiative in the ideological area, and strengthens the overall power and influence of culture.

Article 24: The State strengthens the construction of indigenous innovation capabilities, it accelerates the development of indigenous, controllable and strategic high and new technologies and central or key technologies in important areas, and it strengthens the use and protection of intellectual property rights and the construction of science and technology secrecy protection, and guarantees the security of major technologies and projects.

Article 25: The State constructs a network and information security protection system, it upgrades network and information security protection capabilities, strengthens the innovation, research, development and application of network and information technologies, it realizes the security and controllability of core network and information technologies, crucial infrastructure and information systems and data in important areas; it strengthens network management, it prevents, curbs and lawfully sanctions online attacks, online hacking, online theft of secrets, the dissemination of unlawful or harmful information and other such online unlawful and criminal acts, it safeguards national sovereignty security and development interests in cyberspace.

Article 26: The State persists in and perfects the ethnic autonomous region system, it consolidates and develops Socialist ethnic relationships of equality, unity, mutual assistance and harmony. It persists in the equality of all ethnicities without exception, it strengthens ethic interaction, exchange and mingling, it prevents, curbs and lawfully sanctions acts of ethnic separatism, it upholds national unity, ethnic unity and social harmony, and realizes the common united struggle and common flourishing and development of all ethnicities.

Article 27: The State lawfully protects citizens' freedom of religious belief and regular religious practices, it persists in the principles of religious independence, autonomy and self-organization, it prevents, curbs and lawfully sanctions the use of the name of religion to conduct unlawful and criminal acts harming national security, it opposes interference by foreign forces in domestic religious affairs, and safeguards the order of regular religious activities.

The State lawfully bans heretical organizations, it prevents, curbs and lawfully sanctions heretical unlawful and criminal activities.

Article 28: The State opposes all forms of terrorism and extremism, it strengthens the construction of capabilities to prevent and manage terrorism, it lawfully engages in intelligence, investigation, protection, management as well as financial supervision work to lawfully ban terrorist activities and groups, and strictly punishes acts of violent terrorism.

Article 29: The State completes effective structures and mechanisms to effectively prevent and dissolve social contradictions, it completes public security systems, to vigorously prevent, reduce and dissolve social contradictions, it appropriately handles sudden events in public health, social security, and in other areas influencing national security and social stability, it stimulates social harmony, and safeguards public security and social security.

Article 30: The State perfects protection structures and systems to protect the ecological environment, it strengthens ecological construction and environmental protection, it delimits red lines for ecological protection, strengthens early warning and prevention of ecological risks, appropriately handles sudden environmental incidents, guarantees that the natural environment and conditions on which the people rely for their existence, including air, water, soil, etc., are not threatened or destroyed, and stimulates the harmonious development of humanity and nature.

Article 31: The State persists in the peaceful use of nuclear energy and nuclear technology, it strengthens international cooperation, prevents nuclear proliferation, perfects anti-proliferation mechanisms, strengthens security management, supervision and protection of nuclear facilities, nuclear materials, nuclear activities and nuclear waste processing, it strengthens emergency response systems and emergency response capacity building for nuclear accidents, it prevents, controls and eliminates ecological and environmental harms from nuclear accidents to citizens' lives and health, it incessantly strengthens capabilities to effective respond to and prevent nuclear threats and nuclear attacks.

Article 32: The State persists in the peaceful exploration and use of outer space, the international seabeds and the polar regions, it strengthens its capacity for secure comings and goings, scientific observation, exploitation and use, it strengthens international cooperation, and safeguards the security our country's activities, assets and other interests in outer space, the international seabeds and the polar regions.

Article 33: The State lawfully adopts necessary measures to protect the security and proper rights and interests of Chinese citizens, organizations and bodies abroad, and to protect national interests abroad from threat and harm.

Article 34: The State incessantly perfects the tasks of protecting national security on the basis of the needs of economic and social development, and national development interests.

CHAPTER III: THE DUTIES OF SAFEGUARDING NATIONAL SECURITY

Article 35: The National People's Congress decides on questions of war and peace and exercises other powers concerning national security provided in the Constitution, according to the provisions of the Constitution.

The National People's Congress Standing Committee decides on the declaration of the state of war, decides on general national mobilization or partial mobilization, decides on entering a state of emergency nationwide or in individual provinces, autonomous regions and municipalities, and exercises other powers concerning national security as provided in the Constitution and as empowered by the National People's Congress, according to the provisions of the Constitution.

Article 36: The Chairman People's Republic of China declares entry into a state of emergency, declares the state of war, issues the order for mobilization, and exercises other powers concerning national security as provided in the Constitution, according to the decisions of the National People's Congress and the decisions of the National People's Congress Standing Committee.

Article 37: According to the Constitution and the law, the State Council formulates administrative regulations concerning national security, stipulates relevant administrative measures, and disseminates relevant decisions and orders; it implements national security laws, regulations and policies; it decides on the entry into a state of emergencies of partial regions within provinces, autonomous regions and municipalities; and exercises other powers concerning national security as provided by the Constitution and the law, and as authorized by the National People's Congress and its Standing Committee.

Article 38: The Central Military Commission leads the armed forces nationwide, it decides on military strategy and the warfare doctrines of the armed forces, it has unified command of military operations to safeguard national security, formulates military regulations concerning national security, and issues relevant decisions and orders.

Article 39: All departments of Centre and State bodies, according to their powers and the division of labour, implement and exercise national security doctrines, policies, laws and regulations, manage and guide national security work in their systems and localities.

Article 40: All local levels' People's Congresses and local county-level or higher levels' People's Congress Standing Committees ensure the observance and implementation of national security laws and regulations within their administrative areas.

All local levels' People's Governments manage national security work within their administrative areas according to the provisions of laws and regulations.

The Hong Kong Special Administrative Region and Macau Special Administrative Region shall fulfil the responsibility of safeguarding national security.

Article 41: The People's Courts exercise judicial powers according to the provisions of the Constitution, the People's Procuratorates exercise prosecutorial powers according to the provisions of the Constitution, to punish crimes violating national security.

Article 42: National security bodies and public security bodies collect intelligence and information concerning national security according to the law, and exercise the powers of investigation, detention, inquiry and arrest, as well as other powers provided in the law in national security work according to the law.

Relevant military bodies exercise corresponding powers in national security work according to the law.

Article 43: State bodies and their work personnel shall, when exercising their responsibilities, implement the principle of safeguarding national security.

State bodies and their work personnel shall, when carrying out national security work or activities concerning national security, strictly exercise their duties according to the law, they may not exceed their powers or abuse their powers, and may not infringe the lawful rights and interests of individuals and organizations.

CHAPTER IV: THE NATIONAL SECURITY SYSTEM

Section 1: Ordinary Provisions

Article 44: The Centre's national security leading body implements a national security work structure and work mechanisms that combine centralization and decentralization, are coordinated and highly effective.

Article 45: The State establishes work coordination mechanisms for focus areas of national security, and comprehensively coordinates the work conducted by relevant functional Centre bodies.

Article 46: The State establishes national security work supervision, inspection and responsibility investigation mechanism, and guarantees that the national security strategy and major deployments are implemented.

Article 47: All Departments and all localities shall adopt effective measures to implement the national security strategy.

Article 48: On the basis of the needs of safeguarding national security work, the State establishes cross-departmental consultation work mechanisms, to engage in consultation and decision-making concerning major national security affairs, and put forward opinions and suggestions.

Article 49: The State establishes joint operational mechanisms concerning national security between the Centre and the localities, between departments, between military regions and between regions.

Article 50: The State establishes national security policymaking consultation mechanisms, organizes analysis and deliberation of the national security situation by experts and relevant parties, to move scientific policymaking in national security forward.

Section 2: Intelligence and Information

Article 51: The State completes intelligence and information collection, deliberation and use structures with uniform authority, flexible response, high accuracy and efficiency, and smooth operations, and it establishes intelligence and information work coordination mechanisms, to realize the timely collection, accurate deliberation and effective use and sharing of intelligence and information.

Article 52: National security bodies, public security bodies and relevant military bodies collect intelligence and information concerning national security according to the law, on the basis of their duties and the division of labour.

All State bodies' departments shall, in the process of carrying out their duties, timely report relevant information concerning national security they obtain.

Article 53: When engaging in intelligence and information work, modem scientific and technological methods shall be fully utilized, and the differentiation, screening, synthesis, deliberation and analysis of intelligence and information shall be strengthened.

Article 54: The submission of intelligence and information shall be timely, accurate and objective, it is not permitted to delay reports, fail to report, give false reports or lie about reports.

Section 3: Risk Prevention, Assessment and Early Warning

Article 55: The State formulates and perfects plans to respond to national security risks in all areas.

Article 56: The State establishes national security risk assessment mechanisms, to regularly launch investigation and evaluation of national security risks in all areas.

Relevant departments shall regularly submit national security risk evaluation reports to the Centre's national security leading body.

Article 57: The State completes national security risk monitoring and early warning structure, to timely issue corresponding early risk warnings on the basis of the extent of national security risks.

Article 58: County-level or higher local People's Governments and their relevant controlling departments shall, with regard to incidents harming national security that may soon occur or have already occurred, immediately report the matter to the People's Government and their relevant controlling departments of one level higher, and when necessary, may report the matter in a manner skipping levels.

Section 4: Examination and Supervision

Article 59: The State establishes national security examination and supervision structures and mechanisms, to conduct national security examination of foreign investments that influence or may influence national security, specific goods or core technologies, online information technology products and services, construction projects involving national security affairs, as well as other major affairs and activities, to effectively prevent and dissolve national security risks.

Article 60: All departments of Centre and State bodies exercise national security examination duties according to laws and administrative regulations, make national security examination decisions or put forward security examination opinions, and supervise their implementation according to the law.

Article 61: Provincial, autonomous regions and municipalities are responsible for national security examination and supervision work within their administrative regions.

Section 5: Crisis Control

Article 62: The State establishes national security crisis control structures with unified leadership, coordinated joint action, which are orderly and highly effective.

Article 63: When major events endangering national security occur, relevant Centre departments and relevant localities, on the basis of the uniform deployment of the Centre's national security leadership body, initiates emergency response plans, and adopts management, control and handling measures according to the law.

Article 64: When especially grave incidents endangering national security occur, and it is necessary to enter a state of emergency, a state of war or engage in general or partial mobilization, the National People's Congress and the National People's Congress Standing Committee or the State Council will decide on the matter according to the powers and procedures provided in the Constitution and relevant laws.

Article 65: After the country decides to enter a state of emergency, a state of war or to engage in national defence mobilization, relevant bodies exercising national security crisis management responsibilities, according to the provisions of laws or the National People's Congress Standing Committee, have the power to adopt special measures to limit the rights of citizens and organizations and increase the duties of citizens and organization.

Article 66: Relevant bodies exercising national security crisis management duties that adopt measures to deal with a national security crisis, shall adapt to the nature, extent and scope of the harm that the national security crisis may create; where there are many kinds of measures that may be chosen, the measure that benefits the protection of the rights and interests of citizens and organizations to the greatest extent shall be selected.

Article 67: The State completes national security crisis information reporting and dissemination mechanisms.

After the national security crisis incident occurs, relevant bodies exercising national security crisis management duties shall report the matter accurately and timely according to regulations, they shall also uniformly announce occurrence of the national security crisis incident, its development, management, handling and aftermath to society.

Article 68: After national security threats and dangers are controlled or eliminated, control and management measures shall be abolished timely, and the aftermath work shall be done.

Chapter V: National Security Guarantees

Article 69: The State completes national security protection systems, and strengthens capabilities to safeguard national security.

Article 70: The State completes national security law systems and structures, to promote the construction of national security rule of law.

Article 71: The State expands investment into all areas of construction concerning national security, and guarantees funding and equipment needed for national security work.

Article 72: Work units undertaking storage tasks of strategic assets for national security shall, according to relevant State regulations and standards, conduct the storage, preservation and safeguarding of national security assets, regularly adjust and update, and ensure the usability, efficacy and security of stored assets.

Article 73: Scientific and technological innovation in the area of national security is encouraged, to give rein to the role of science and technology in safeguarding national security.

Article 74: The State adopts the necessary measures to recruit, foster and manage specialist national security work talents and particular talents.

On the basis of the needs of safeguarding national security, the State protects the identity and lawful rights and interests of relevant bodies' personnel especially engaging in national security work, and expands their personal protection and security arrangements.

Article 75: National security bodies, public security bodies and relevant military bodies that engage in specialized national security work may adopt necessary ways and methods according to the law, relevant departments and localities shall provide support and coordination within the scope of their duties.

Article 76: The State strengthens news, propaganda and public opinion guidance concerning national security, it conducts national security propaganda and education activities in many forms, it will bring national security education into compulsory education systems and public servant education and training systems, and strengthens the national security consciousness of the entire population.

Chapter VI: The Duties and Rights of Citizens and Organizations

Article 77: Citizens and organizations shall have the duty to carry out the following matters to safeguard national security:

(1) abiding by the provisions in the Constitution, laws and regulations concerning national security

(2) timely reporting clues concerning acts harming national security;

(3) truthfully providing evidence involving acts harming national security of which they are aware;

(4) providing convenient conditions or other kinds of assistance to national security work;

(5) providing the necessary support and assistance to national security bodies, public security bodies and relevant military bodies;

(6) keeping State secrets of which they are aware;

(7) other duties as provided in laws and administrative regulations.

No person or organization may act in a manner harming national security, or may provide any kind of assistance or cooperation to individuals or organizations harming national security.

Article 78: Bodies, people's organizations, enterprises, undertakings and other social organizations shall educate these work units' personnel about safeguarding national security, mobilize and organize these work units' personnel to prevent and curb acts harming national security.

Article 79: Enterprises and undertakings shall, according to the demands of national security work, cooperate with relevant departments that adopt corresponding security measures.

Article 80: Citizens and organizations who act to support or assist national security works are protected by the law.

Where the personal security a person or their near relatives is endangered because of assistance in national security work, they may request protection with public security bodies or national security bodies. Public security bodies and national security bodies shall adopt protection measures jointly with relevant departments, according to the law.

Article 81: Where citizens or organizations support or assist national security work leading to damage to assets, compensation shall be granted according to relevant State regulations; where it results in personal harm or death, preferential treatment shall be extended to the bereaved according to relevant State regulations.

Article 82: Citizens and organizations have the right to put forward critical suggestions concerning national security work to State bodies, and have the right to put forward complaints, accusations and reports against unlawful acts or acts of neglect by State bodies and their work personnel in national security work.

Article 83: When it is necessary to adopt exceptional measures limiting citizens' rights and liberties in national security work, it will be handled according to the law, and be delimited by the real needs of safeguarding national security.

CHAPTER VII: SUPPLEMENTARY PRINCIPLES

Article 84: This Law takes effect on the date of promulgation.

Appendix C

Civil Code of the People's Republic of China

National People's Congress of the PR Website: http://en.npc.gov.cn.cdurl.cn/pdf/civilcodeofthepeoplesrepublicofchina.pdf

Adopted at the Third Session of the Thirteenth National People's Congress on May 28, 2020.

Notes: 1. This translation is for reference only. In case of discrepancy between the English translation and the original Chinese text, the Chinese text shall prevail. 2. In this translation, third-person singular male pronouns should be construed to include the corresponding female and neuter pronouns except where the context clearly requires otherwise.

Book One: General Part

Chapter I: General Provisions

Article 1: This Code is formulated in accordance with the Constitution of the People's Republic of China for the purposes of protecting the lawful rights and interests of the persons of the civil law, regulating civil-law relations, maintaining social and economic order, meeting the needs for developing socialism with Chinese characteristics, and carrying forward the core socialist values.

Article 2: The civil law regulates personal and proprietary relationships among the persons of the civil law, namely, natural persons, legal persons, and unincorporated organizations that are equal in status.

Article 3: The personal rights, proprietary rights, and other lawful rights and interests of the persons of the civil law are protected by law and free from infringement by any organization or individual.

Article 4: All persons of the civil law are equal in legal status when conducting civil activities.

Article 5: When conducting a civil activity, a person of the civil law shall, in compliance with the principle of voluntariness, create, alter, or terminate a civil juristic relationship according to his own will.

Article 6: When conducting a civil activity, a person of the civil law shall, in compliance with the principle of fairness, reasonably establish the rights and obligations of each party.

Article 7: When conducting a civil activity, a person of the civil law shall, in compliance with the principle of good faith, uphold honesty and honor commitments.

Article 8: When conducting a civil activity, no person of the civil law may violate the law, or offend public order or good morals.

Article 9: When conducting a civil activity, a person of the civil law shall act in a manner that facilitates conservation of resources and protection of the ecological environment.

Article 10: Civil disputes shall be resolved in accordance with law. Where the law does not specify, custom may be applied, provided that public order and good morals may not be offended.

Article 11: Where there are other laws providing special provisions regulating civil-law relations, such provisions shall be followed.

Article 12: The laws of the People's Republic of China shall apply to the civil activities taking place within the territory of the People's Republic of China, except as otherwise provided by law.

Chapter II: Natural Persons

Section 1: Capacity for Enjoying Civil-law Rights and Capacity for Performing Civil Juristic Acts

Article 13: A natural person shall, from the time of birth until the time of death, have the capacity for enjoying civil-law rights, and may enjoy civil-law rights and assume civil-law duties in accordance with law.

Article 14: All natural persons are equal in their capacity for enjoying civil-law rights.

Article 15: The time of birth and time of death of a natural person are determined by the time recorded on his birth or death certificate as applied, or, if there is no birth or death certificate, by the time recorded in the natural person's household registration or other valid identity certificate. If there is sufficient evidence overturning the time recorded in the aforementioned documents, the time that is established by such evidence shall prevail.

Article 16: A fetus is deemed as having the capacity for enjoying civil-law rights in estate succession, acceptance of gift, and other situations where protection of a fetus' interests is involved. Provided, however, that a stillborn fetus does not have such capacity ab initio.

Article 17: A natural person aged eighteen or above is an adult. A natural person under the age of eighteen is a minor.

Article 18: An adult has full capacity for performing civil juristic acts and may independently perform civil juristic acts. A minor aged sixteen or above whose main source of support is the income from his own labor is deemed as a person with full capacity for performing civil juristic acts.

Article 19: A minor aged eight or above has limited capacity for performing civil juristic acts and may perform a civil juristic act through or upon consent or ratification of his legal representative, except that such a minor may independently perform a civil juristic act that is purely beneficial to him or that is appropriate to his age and intelligence.

Article 20: A minor under the age of eight has no capacity for performing civil juristic acts, and may perform a civil juristic act only through his legal representative.

Article 21: An adult unable to comprehend his own conduct has no capacity for performing civil juristic acts, and may perform a civil juristic act only through his legal representative. The preceding paragraph is applicable to a minor aged eight or above who is unable to comprehend his own conduct.

Article 22: An adult unable to fully comprehend his own conduct has limited capacity for performing civil juristic acts and may perform a civil juristic act through or upon consent or ratification of his legal representative, except that such an adult may independently perform a civil juristic act that is purely beneficial to him or that is appropriate to his intelligence and mental status.

Article 23: The guardian of a person who has no or limited capacity for performing civil juristic acts is the legal representative of the person.

Article 24: Where an adult is unable to comprehend or fully comprehend his conduct, any interested person of such an adult or a relevant organization may request the people's court to declare that the said adult be identified as a person with no or limited capacity for performing civil juristic acts.

Where a person has been identified by the people's court as a person with no or limited capacity for performing civil juristic acts, the people's court may, upon request of the person, an interested person thereof, or a relevant organization, and based on the recovery of his intelligence and mental health, declare that the said person becomes a person with limited or full capacity for performing civil juristic acts.

A relevant organization referred to in this Article includes a residents' committee, a villagers' committee, a school, a medical institution, the women's federation, the disabled person's federation, a legally established organization for senior people, the civil affairs departments, and the like.

Article 25: The domicile of a natural person is the residence recorded in his household registration or other valid identification registration system; if a natural person's habitual residence is different from his domicile, the habitual residence is deemed as his domicile.

Section 2: Guardianship

Article 26: Parents have the duty to raise, educate, and protect their minor children. Adult children have the duty to support, assist, and protect their parents.

Article 27: The parents of a minor are his guardians. Where the parents of a minor are deceased or incompetent to be his guardians, the following persons, if competent, shall act as his guardians in the following order: (1) his paternal grandparents and maternal grandparents; (2) his elder brothers and elder sisters; or (3) any other individual or organization that is willing to act as his guardian, provided that consent must be obtained from the residents' committee, the villagers' committee, or the civil affairs department in the place where the minor's domicile is located.

Article 28: For an adult who has no or limited capacity for performing civil juristic acts, the following persons, if competent, shall act as his guardians in the following order: (1) his spouse; (2) his parents and his children; (3) any other close relatives of him; or (4) any other individual or organization that is willing to act as his guardian, provided that consent must be obtained from the residents' committee, the villagers' committee, or the civil affairs department in the place where the adult's domicile is located.

Article 29: A parent who is the guardian of his child may, in his will, designate a succeeding guardian for his child.

Article 30: A guardian may be determined through agreement among the persons who are legally qualified to be guardians. The true will of the ward shall be respected in determining the guardian through agreement.

Article 31: Where a dispute arises over the determination of a guardian, the guardian shall be appointed by the residents' committee, the villagers' committee, or the civil affairs department in the place where the ward's domicile is located, and a party not satisfied with such an appointment may request the people's court to appoint a guardian; the relevant parties may also directly request the people's court to make such an appointment.

When appointing a guardian, the residents' committee, the villagers' committee, the civil affairs department, or the people's court shall respect the true will of the ward and appoint a guardian in the best interest of the ward from among the legally qualified persons.

Where the personal, proprietary, and other lawful rights and interests of a ward are not under any protection before a guardian is appointed in accordance with the first paragraph of this Article, the residents' committee, the villagers' committee, a relevant organization designated by law, or the civil affairs department in the place where the ward's domicile is located shall act as a temporary guardian.

Once appointed, a guardian may not be replaced without authorization; where a guardian has been replaced without authorization, the responsibility of the originally appointed guardian is not discharged.

Article 32: Where there is no person legally qualified to be a guardian, the civil affairs department shall act as the guardian, and the residents' committee or villagers' committee in the place where the ward's domicile is located may also act as the guardian if they are competent in performing the duties of guardian.

Article 33: An adult with full capacity for performing civil juristic acts may, in anticipation of incapacity in the future, consult his close relatives, or other individuals or organizations willing to be his guardian, and appoint in writing a guardian for himself, who shall perform the duties of guardian when the adult loses all or part of his6capacity for performing civil juristic acts.

Article 34: The duties of a guardian are to represent the ward to perform civil juristic acts and to protect the personal, proprietary, and other lawful rights and interests of the ward.

A guardian's rights arising from performance of his duties as required by law are protected by law.

A guardian who fails to perform his duties or infringes upon the lawful rights or interests of the ward shall bear legal liability.

Where a guardian is temporarily unable to perform his duties owing to an emergency such as an unexpected incident, thus leaving the ward in an unattended situation, the residents' committee, the villagers' committee, or the civil affairs department in the place where the ward's domicile is located shall make arrangement as a temporary measure to provide necessary life care for the ward.

Article 35: A guardian shall perform his duties in the best interest of the ward. A guardian may not dispose of the ward's property unless it is for protecting the interests of the ward. When performing his duties and making decisions relating to a minor's interests, a guardian of a minor shall respect the true will of the minor based on the latter's age and intelligence.

When performing his duties, a guardian of an adult shall respect the true will of the adult to the greatest extent possible, and ensure and aid the ward in performing civil juristic acts appropriate to his intelligence and mental status. The guardian may not interfere with the matters that the ward is capable of independently managing.

Article 36: Where a guardian has performed any of the following acts, the people's court shall, upon request of a relevant individual or organization, disqualify the guardian, adopt necessary temporary measures, and appoint a new guardian in the best interest of the ward in accordance with law: (1) engaging in any act which severely harms the physical or mental health of the ward; (2) being indolent in performing the duties of guardian, or being unable to perform such duties but refusing to delegate all or part of the duties to others, thus placing the ward in a desperate situation; or (3) engaging in any other act which severely infringes upon the lawful rights and interests of the ward.

The relevant individual and organization referred to in this Article include any other person legally qualified to be a guardian, the residents' committee, the villagers' committee, a school, a medical institution, the women's federation, the disabled persons' federation, a child protection organization, a legally established organization for senior people, the civil affairs department, and the like.

Where the aforementioned individual and organization other than the civil affairs department, as stated in the preceding paragraph, fail to request the people's court to disqualify the guardian in a timely manner, the civil affairs department shall initiate such a request to the people's court.

Article 37: A parent, child, or spouse legally obligated to pay for his ward's support shall continue to perform such obligations after being disqualified as a guardian by the people's court.

Article 38: Where a ward's parent or child, who has been disqualified as a guardian by the people's court for reasons other than having committed an intentional crime against the ward, and who has truly repented and mended his ways, applies to the people's court for reinstatement, the people's court may, upon considering the actual situation and upon the satisfaction of the prerequisite that the true will of the ward is respected, reinstate the guardian, and the guardianship between the ward and the guardian appointed by the people's court after the disqualification of the original guardian shall thus be terminated simultaneously.

Article 39: A guardianship is terminated under any of the following circumstances: (1) the ward has obtained or regained full capacity for performing civil juristic acts; (2) the guardian has become incompetent to be a guardian; (3) the ward or the guardian deceases; or (4) any other circumstance in which the people's court determines to terminate the guardianship. Where a ward is still in need of a guardian after the termination of the guardianship, a new guardian shall be appointed in accordance with law.

Section 3: Declaration of a Missing Person and Declaration of Death

Article 40: If a natural person's whereabouts have been unknown for two years, an interested person may request the people's court to declare the natural person as a missing person.

Article 41: The period of time during which a natural person's whereabouts is unknown shall be counted from the date when the natural person has not been heard of ever since. If a person is missing during wartime, the time of his whereabouts becoming unknown shall be counted from the date the war ends or from the date as determined by the relevant authority.

Article 42: A missing person's property shall be placed in the custody of his spouse, adult children, parents, or any other person willing to take such custody. Where a dispute arises over the custody of a missing person's property, or the persons provided in the preceding paragraph are unavailable or incompetent for such a purpose, the property shall be placed in the custody of a person appointed by the people's court.

Article 43: A custodian shall properly manage the missing person's property and safeguard his proprietary interests. The taxes, debts, and other due payment obligations owed by a missing person, if any, shall be paid by the custodian out of the missing person's property. A custodian who, intentionally or due to gross negligence, causes damage to the property of the missing person shall be liable for compensation.

Article 44: Where a custodian fails to perform his duties of custodian, infringes upon the proprietary rights or interests of the missing person, or if the custodian becomes incompetent to be a custodian, an interested person of the missing person may request the people's court to replace the custodian. A custodian may, with just cause, request the people's court to appoint a new custodian to replace himself.

Where the people's court appoints a new custodian, the new custodian is entitled to request the former custodian to deliver the relevant property and a property management report in a timely manner.

Article 45: Where a missing person reappears, the people's court shall, upon request of the said person or an interested person thereof, revoke the declaration of his being missing. A missing person who reappears is entitled to request the custodian to deliver the relevant property and a property management report in a timely manner.

Article 46: An interested person may request the people's court to make a declaration of the death of a natural person under either of the following circumstances: (1) the natural person's whereabouts have been unknown for four years; or (2) the natural person's whereabouts have been unknown for two years as a result of an accident. The two-year requirement for a natural person to be declared dead does not apply where the person's whereabouts have been unknown as a result of an accident and if a relevant authority certifies that it is impossible for the said natural person to survive.

Article 47: Where an interested person requests the people's court to declare the death of a natural person, while another interested person requests to declare the person being missing, the people's court shall declare that the person is dead if the conditions for declaration of death as provided in this Code are satisfied.

Article 48: For a person declared dead, the date when the people's court makes a judgment declaring his death is deemed as the date of his death; for a person declared dead because his whereabouts is unknown as a result of an accident, the date of the occurrence of the accident is deemed as the date of his death.

Article 49: The declaration of the death of a natural person who is still alive does not affect the effects of the civil juristic acts performed by the person during the period the death declaration is effective.

Article 50: Where a person declared dead reappears, the people's court shall, upon request of the person or an interested person thereof, revoke the declaration of his death.

Article 51: The marital relationship with a person declared dead ceases to exist from the date the declaration of his death is made. Where the declaration of death is revoked, the aforementioned marital relationship shall be automatically resumed from the date the declaration of death is revoked, unless the spouse has married to someone else or states in writing to the marriage registration authority the unwillingness to resume the marriage.

Article 52: Where a child of a person declared dead has been legally adopted by others during the period when the declaration of death is effective, the person declared dead may not, after the declaration of his death is revoked, claim that the adoption is invalid on the ground that his child is adopted without his consent.

Article 53: Where a declaration of the death of a person is revoked, the person is entitled to request those who have obtained his property under Book Six of this Code to return the property, or make appropriate compensation if the property cannot be returned. Where an interested person conceals the true information and causes a natural person to be declared dead so as to obtain the latter's property, the interested person shall, in addition to returning the wrongfully obtained property, make compensation for any loss thus caused.

Section 4: Individual-run Industrial and Commercial Households and Rural-land Contractual Management Households

Article 54: A natural person who operates an industrial or commercial business may register it, in accordance with law, as an individual-run industrial and commercial household. An industrial and commercial household may have a trade name.

Article 55: Members of a rural economic collective who, in accordance with law, have been granted an original contract to operate a lot of rural land and engage in the operation of the land on a household basis form a rural-land contractual management household.

Article 56: The debts of an individual-run industrial and commercial household shall be paid from the assets of the individual who operates the business in his own name or from the individual's family assets if the business is operated in the name of the household, or, if it is impossible to determine whether the business is operated in the name of the individual or in the name of the individual's household, from the individual's family assets.

The debts of a rural-land contractual management household shall be paid from the assets of the household that is engaged in the operation on the contracted rural land, or from the portion of the assets of the family members who actually engage in such operation.

Chapter III: Legal Persons

Section 1: General Rules

Article 57: A legal person is an organization that has the capacity for enjoying civil-law rights and the capacity for performing civil juristic acts, and that independently enjoys civil-law rights and assumes civil-law obligations in accordance with law.

Article 58: A legal person shall be established in accordance with law. A legal person shall have its own name, governance structure, domicile, and assets or funds. The specific conditions and procedures for the establishment of a legal person shall be in accordance with laws and administrative regulations. Where there are laws or administrative regulations providing that the establishment of a legal person shall be subject to approval of a relevant authority, such provisions shall be followed.

Article 59: A legal person's capacity for enjoying civil-law rights and capacity for performing civil juristic acts are acquired when the legal person is established, and cease when the legal person is terminated.

Article 60: A legal person independently assumes civil liability to the extent of all of its assets.

Article 61: The person with the responsibility of representing a legal person in conducting civil activities in accordance with law or the legal person's articles of association is the legal representative of the legal person.

The legal consequences of the civil activities conducted by the legal representative in the legal person's name shall be assumed by the legal person. Any restrictions on the legal representative's power to represent the legal person which is stipulated in the articles of association or imposed by the governing body of the legal person may not be asserted against a bona fide counterparty.

Article 62: Where a legal representative of a legal person causes damage to others while performing his responsibilities, the civil liability thus incurred shall be assumed by the legal person.

After assuming the aforementioned civil liability, the legal person has the right to indemnification, in accordance with law or its articles of association, against its legal representative who is at fault.

Article 63: The domicile of a legal person is the place where its principal administrative office is located. Where a legal person is required by law to be registered, the place of its principal administrative office shall be registered as its domicile.

Article 64: Where, during the term of existence of a legal person, there is any change in a matter that has been recorded upon its registration, the legal person shall apply to the registration authority for modification of the registration in accordance with law.

Article 65: The actual situation of a legal person, which is inconsistent with what is recorded upon registration, may not be asserted against a bona fide counterparty.

Article 66: The registration authority shall, in accordance with law, post in a timely manner a public notice of the information recorded by a legal person upon registration.

Article 67: In case of a merger between or among legal persons, the rights and obligations of such legal persons shall be enjoyed and assumed by the surviving legal person. In case of a division of a legal person, the rights and obligations of the legal person shall be enjoyed and assumed jointly and severally by the legal persons established after division, unless otherwise agreed by its creditors and debtors.

Article 68: If any of the following causes exists, a legal person is terminated after it has completed liquidation and de-registration in accordance with law: (1) the legal person is dissolved; (2) the legal person is declared bankrupt; or (3) there exists any other cause as provided by law. Where there are laws or administrative regulations providing that the termination of a legal person shall be subject to approval of the relevant authority, such provisions shall be followed.

Article 69: A legal person is dissolved under any of the following circumstances: (1) the term stipulated in its articles of association expires, or there exists any other cause for dissolution as is stipulated in the articles of association; (2) the governing body of the legal person makes a resolution to dissolve the legal person; (3) the legal person has to be dissolved because of a merger or division; (4) the legal person's business license or registration certificate is legally revoked, or the legal person has received an order of closure or been dissolved; or (5) there exists any other circumstance as provided by law.

Article 70: Where a legal person is dissolved for reasons other than a merger or division, a liquidation committee shall be formed in a timely manner by the persons with the duty of liquidation to liquidate the legal person.

Unless otherwise provided by laws or administrative regulations, members of the legal person's executive or decision-making body, such as the directors or councilors, are the persons with the duty to liquidate the legal person.

The persons with the duty to liquidate the legal person who fail to perform their duties in time and thus cause damage to others shall bear civil liability; the competent authority or an interested person may request the people's court to appoint the relevant persons to form a liquidation committee to liquidate the legal person.

Article 71: The procedure for liquidating a legal person and the authorities of a liquidation committee shall be in compliance with the provisions of relevant laws; in the absence of such a provision, the relevant rules provided in corporate laws shall be applied mutatis mutandis.

Article 72: During the period of liquidation, a legal person continues to exist but may not engage in any activity unrelated to the liquidation.

Unless otherwise provided by law, upon completion of the liquidation, any residual assets of a liquidated legal person shall be distributed in accordance with its articles of association or the resolution made by its governing body. A legal person is terminated after liquidation and de-registration is completed; a legal person that is not required by law to be registered is terminated upon completion of the liquidation.

Article 73: A legal person declared bankrupt is terminated upon completion of the bankruptcy liquidation and de-registration in accordance with law.

Article 74: A legal person may establish branches in accordance with law. Where there are laws or administrative regulations providing that such a branch shall be registered, such provisions shall be followed. A branch of a legal person engages in civil activities in its own name and the civil liability thus incurred shall be assumed by the legal person; alternatively, the civil liability may also be paid first from the assets managed by the branch, and any deficiency shall be paid by the legal person.

Article 75: The legal consequences of the civil activities conducted by an incorporator for the purpose of establishing a legal person shall be assumed by the legal person; or, in the event that no legal person is successfully established, by the incorporator, or the incorporators jointly and severally if there are two or more of them.

Where an incorporator engages in civil activities in his own name for the purpose of establishing a legal person and thus incurs civil liability, a third person creditor may elect to request either the legal person or the incorporator to bear the liability.

Section 2: For-profit Legal Persons

Article 76: A for-profit legal person is a legal person established for the purpose of making profits and distributing the profits among its shareholders and other capital contributors.

For-profit legal persons include limited liability companies, joint stock companies limited by shares, and other enterprises that have the legal person status.

Article 77: A for-profit legal person is established upon registration in accordance with law.

Article 78: The registration authority shall issue a business license to a legally established for-profit legal person. The date of issuance of the business license is the date of establishment of the for-profit legal person.

Article 79: To establish a for-profit legal person, there shall be articles of association formulated in accordance with law.

Article 80: A for-profit legal person shall establish a governing body. The governing body has the authority to revise the articles of association of the legal person, elect or replace members of the executive or supervisory body, and perform other responsibilities stipulated in the articles of association.

Article 81: A for-profit legal person shall establish an executive body. The executive body has the authority to convene meetings of the governing body, decide on business and investment plans, establish internal management structure, and perform other responsibilities stipulated in the articles of association of the legal person.

Where the executive body of a legal person is the board of directors or the executive director, the legal representative shall be the chairman of the board of directors, the executive director, or the manager, as is stipulated in the articles of association. Where there is no board of directors or executive director established, the person with the principal responsibilities as stipulated in the articles of association shall be the executive body and the legal representative of the legal person.

Article 82: Where a for-profit legal person establishes a supervisory body such as a board of supervisors or a supervisor, the supervisory body has, in accordance with law, the authority to inspect the financial matters of the legal person, supervise the performance of duty by the members of the executive body and the senior management officers of the legal person, and perform other responsibilities stipulated in the articles of association.

Article 83: A capital contributor of a for-profit legal person may not abuse his rights as such to harm the interests of the legal person or any other capital contributor. A capital contributor abusing such rights and causing harm to the legal person or any other capital contributor shall bear civil liability in accordance with law.

A capital contributor of a for-profit legal person may not abuse the legal person's independent status and his own limited liability status to harm the interests of the legal person's creditors. A capital contributor abusing the legal person's independent status or its own limited liability status to evade repayment of debts and thus severely harming the interests of the legal person's creditors shall be jointly and severally liable for the legal person's obligations.

Article 84: The controlling capital contributors, actual controllers, directors, supervisors, and senior management officers of a for-profit legal person may not harm the legal person's interests by taking advantage of any affiliated relations, and shall compensate for any loss thus caused to the legal person.

Article 85: A capital contributor of a for-profit legal person may request the people's court to revoke a resolution which is made at a meeting of the governing body or executive body of the legal person if the procedure for convening the meeting or the voting method thereof is in violation of the laws, administrative regulations, or the legal person's articles of association, or, if the content of the resolution violates the articles of association. Provided, however, that any civil juristic relationship already formed between the legal person and a bona fide counterparty based on such a resolution may not be affected.

Article 86: A for-profit legal person shall, when engaging in operational activities, observe commercial ethics, maintain the security of transactions, subject itself to the supervision of the government and the public, and assume social responsibilities.

Section 3: Non-profit Legal Persons

Article 87: A non-profit legal person is a legal person established for public welfare or other non-profit purposes which may not distribute any profit to its capital contributors, incorporators, or members. Non-profit legal persons include public institutions, social organizations, foundations, social service institutions, and the like.

Article 88: A public institution established for the purpose of providing public services to meet the needs for economic and social development attains the status of a public-institution legal person if it satisfies the requirements for being a legal person and is legally registered as such; where the law does not require such a public institution to be registered, it attains the status of a public-institution legal person from the date of its establishment.

Article 89: Where a public-institution legal person establishes a council, the council is its decision-making body unless otherwise provided by law.

The legal representative of a public-institution legal person is elected in accordance with the provisions of laws, administrative regulations, or the legal person's articles of association.

Article 90: A social organization established upon the common will of its members for a non-profit purpose, such as public welfare or the common interest of all members, attains the status of a social-organization legal person if it satisfies the requirements for being a legal person and is legally registered as such. Where the law does not require such a social organization to be registered, it attains the status of a social-organization legal person from the date of its establishment.

Article 91: To establish a social-organization legal person, there shall be articles of association formulated in accordance with law. A social-organization legal person shall establish a governing body such as a members' assembly or a meeting of the members' representatives. A social-organization legal person shall establish an executive body such as a council. The chairman of the council, the president, or an individual with similar responsibilities shall, in accordance with the articles of association, act as the legal representative of the legal person.

Article 92: A foundation, social service institution, or any other institution established with donated property for the purpose of public welfare attains the status of a donation-funded legal person if it meets the requirements for being a legal person and is legally registered as such.

A site legally established to hold religious activities may be registered as a legal person and attains the status of a donation-funded legal person if it meets the requirements for being a legal person. Where there are laws or administrative regulations providing for the religious sites, such provisions shall be followed.

Article 93: To establish a donation-funded legal person, there shall be articles of association formulated in accordance with law.

A donation-funded legal person shall establish a decision-making body such as a council or any other form of democratic management body, and an executive body. The chairman of the council or an individual with similar responsibilities shall, in accordance with the articles of association, act as the legal representative of the legal person.

A donation-funded legal person shall establish a supervisory body such as a board of supervisors.

Article 94: A donor has the right to inquire into and provide comments and suggestions on the expenditure and management of the property he has donated to a donation-funded legal person, and the donation-funded legal person shall respond honestly and in a timely manner.

Where a decision is made by the decision-making body, executive body, or the legal representative of a donation-funded legal person, if the decision-making procedure is in violation of the laws, administrative regulations, or the legal person's articles of association, or, if the content of the decision violates the articles of association, a donor or any other interested person, or the competent authority may request the people's court to revoke the decision. Provided, however, that any civil juristic relationship already formed between the donation-funded legal person and a bona fide counterparty based on such a decision may not be affected.

Article 95: Upon termination, a non-profit legal person established for the purpose of public welfare may not distribute the residual assets among its capital contributors, incorporators, or members. The residual assets shall continue to be used for the purpose of public welfare, as is stipulated in the articles of association or the resolution made by the governing body; where it is not possible to dispose of such residual assets in accordance with the articles of association or the resolution made by the governing body, the competent authority shall take the charge transferring the assets to another legal person with the same or similar purposes and then make a public notice.

Section 4: Special Legal Persons

Article 96: For the purposes of this Section, State-organ legal persons, rural economic collective legal persons, urban and rural cooperative economic organization legal persons, and primary-level self-governing organization legal persons are special types of legal persons.

Article 97: A State organ with independent budgets or a legally chartered institution assuming administrative functions is qualified as a State-organ legal person from the date of its establishment and may engage in civil activities that are necessary for the performance of its responsibilities.

Article 98: A State-organ legal person is terminated when the State organ is closed, and its civil-law rights and obligations are enjoyed and assumed by the succeeding State-organ legal person; in the absence of a succeeding State organ, the said rights and obligations shall be enjoyed and assumed by the State-organ legal person that has made the decision to close it.

Article 99: A rural economic collective attains the status of a legal person in accordance with law. Where there are laws or administrative regulations providing for rural economic collectives, such provisions shall be followed.

Article 100: An urban or rural economic cooperative attains the status of a legal person in accordance with law. Where there are laws or administrative regulations providing for urban and rural economic cooperatives, such provisions shall be followed.

Article 101: An urban residents' committee or a villagers' committee, as a primary-level self-governing organization, attains the status of a legal person, and may engage in civil activities necessary for the performance of their responsibilities.

Where there is no village economic collective established, the villagers' committee may, in accordance with law, perform the responsibilities of a village economic collective.

Chapter IV: Unincorporated Organizations

An unincorporated organization is an organization which does not have the legal person status but may engage in civil activities in its own name in accordance with

Article 102: Unincorporated organizations include sole proprietorships, partnerships, professional service institutions that do not have the legal person status, and the like.

Article 103: Unincorporated organizations shall be registered in accordance with law. Where laws or administrative regulations provide that establishment of an unincorporated organization shall be subject to approval by the relevant authority, such provisions shall be followed.

Article 104: Where an unincorporated organization becomes insolvent, its capital contributors or founders shall assume unlimited liability for the debts of the organization, unless otherwise provided by law.

Article 105: An unincorporated organization may designate one or more members to represent the organization to engage in civil activities.

Article 106 : An unincorporated organization shall be dissolved under any of the following circumstances:

(1) the term stipulated in its articles of association expires or any other cause for dissolution as is stipulated in the articles of association occurs; (2) its capital contributors or founders decide to dissolve it; or (3) dissolution is required under any other circumstance as provided by law.

Article 107: Upon dissolution, an unincorporated organization shall be liquidated in accordance with law.

Article 108: In addition to the provisions in this Chapter, the provisions in Section 1 of Chapter III of this Book shall be applied to unincorporated organizations mutatis mutandis.

Chapter V: Civil-law Rights

Article 109: The personal liberty and dignity of a natural person is protected by law.

Article 110: A natural person enjoys the right to life, the right to corporeal integrity, the right to health, the right to name, the right to likeness, the right to reputation, the right to honor, the right to privacy, and the right to freedom of marriage.

A legal person or an unincorporated organization enjoys the right to entity name, the right to reputation, and the right to honor.

Article 111: A natural person's personal information is protected by law. Any organization or individual that needs to access other's personal information may only do so in accordance with law and guarantee the safety of such information, and may not illegally collect, use, process, or transmit other's personal information, or illegally trade, provide, or publicize such information.

Article 112: The personal rights of a natural person arising from a marital or familial relationship are protected by law.

Article 113: The proprietary rights of the persons of the civil law are equally protected by law.

Article 114: Persons of the civil law enjoy real rights in accordance with law. Real rights are the rights to directly and exclusively control a specific thing by the right holder in accordance with law, which consists of the ownership, right to usufruct, and security interests in the property.

Article 115: Property consists of immovable and movable property. Where the law provides that a right shall be treated as property over which a real right lies, such provisions shall be followed.

Article 116: The categories and contents of the real rights are provided by law.

Article 117: Where, for the purpose of public interests, immovable or movable property is expropriated or requisitioned according to the scope of authority and the procedure provided by law, fair and reasonable compensation shall be paid.

Article 118: Persons of the civil law have rights in personam in accordance with law. A right in personam is the right of an obligee to request a specific obligor to do or not to do a certain act, as arising from a contract, a tortious act, a negotiorum gestio, or unjust enrichment, or otherwise arising by operation of law.

Article 119: A contract formed in accordance with law is legally binding on the parties to the contract.

Article 120: Where a person's civil-law rights and interests are infringed upon due to a tortious act, the person is entitled to request the tortfeasor to bear tort liability.

Article 121: A person who, without a statutory or contractual obligation, engages in management activities to prevent another person from suffering loss of interests, is entitled to request the said other person who receives benefit therefrom to reimburse the necessary expenses thus incurred.

Article 122: Where a person obtains unjust interests at the expense of another person's loss without a legal cause, the person thus harmed is entitled to request the enriched person to make restitution.

Article 123: A person of the civil law enjoys intellectual property rights in accordance with law. Intellectual property rights are the exclusive rights enjoyed by the right holders in accordance with law over the following subject matters: (1) works; (2) inventions, new utility models, or appearance designs; (3) trademarks; (4) geographical indications; (5) trade secrets; (6) layout designs of integrated circuits; (7) new plant varieties; and (8) the other subject matters as provided by law.

Article 124: A natural person has the right to succession in accordance with law. Private property lawfully owned by a natural person may be transferred through inheritance in accordance with law.

Article 125: The persons of the civil law enjoy shareholder rights and other investor rights in accordance with law.

Article 126: The persons of the civil law enjoy other civil-law rights and interests as provided by law.

Article 127: Where there are laws particularly providing for the protection of data and online virtual assets, such provisions shall be followed.

Article 128: Where there are laws particularly providing for the protection of the civil-law rights of the minors, the elderly, the disabled, women, or the consumers, such provisions shall be followed.

Article 129: Civil-law rights may be acquired through the performance of a civil juristic act, the occurrence of an act de facto, the occurrence of an event as provided by law, or by other means provided by law.

Article 130: The persons of the civil law enjoy their civil-law rights according to their own will and in accordance with law free from any interference.

Article 131: While exercising civil-law rights, the persons of the civil law shall perform their obligations which are provided by law and agreed with the other parties.

Article 132: No person of the civil law shall abuse his civil-law rights and harm the interests of the State, the public interests, or the lawful rights and interests of others.

Chapter VI: Civil Juristic Acts

Section 1: General Rules

Article 133: A civil juristic act is an act through which a person of the civil law, by expression of intent, creates, alters, or terminates a civil juristic relationship.

Article 134: A civil juristic act may be accomplished through a consensus of expression of intent of two or more parties, or through one party's unilateral expression of intent. Where a legal person or an unincorporated organization makes a resolution in accordance with the procedure and voting method provided by law or stipulated in its articles of association, such a resolution is accomplished as a civil juristic act.

Article 135: A civil juristic act may be done in writing, orally, or in any other form; where a specific form is required by laws or administrative regulations, or agreed by the parties, it shall be done in such a form.

Article 136: Unless otherwise provided by law or agreed by the parties, a civil juristic act takes effect at the time it is accomplished.

A person that performs a civil juristic act may not change or revoke the act without authorization, unless doing so is in compliance with law or as consented to by the other party.

Section 2: Expression of Intent

Article 137: An expression of intent made through real-time communication becomes effective from the time the person to whom the intent is expressed is aware of its content.

An expression of intent made in a form other than real-time communication becomes effective from the time it reaches the person to whom the intent is expressed. Where such an expression of intent is made through an electronic data message and the person to whom the intent is expressed has designated a specific data-receiving system, it becomes effective from the time such a data message enters that system; where no data-receiving system is specifically designated, it becomes effective from the time the person to whom the intent is expressed knows or should have known that the data message has entered the system. Where the parties have agreed otherwise on the effective time of the expression of intent made in the form of an electronic data message, such an agreement shall prevail.

Article 138: Where an expression of intent is not made to any specific person, it becomes effective when the expression is completed, unless otherwise provided by law.

Article 139: An expression of intent made through public notice becomes effective upon the time the public notice is posted.

Article 140: A person performing a civil juristic act may make an expression of intent either expressly or implicitly. Silence is deemed as an expression of intent only when it is so provided by law, agreed by the parties, or accords with the course of dealing between the parties.

Article 141: A person performing a civil juristic act may withdraw an expression of intent. The notice of withdrawal of the expression of intent shall reach the counterparty prior to or at the same time with the counterparty's receipt of the expression of intent.

Article 142: Where an expression of intent is made to a specific person, the meaning of the expression shall be interpreted according to the words and sentences used, with reference to the relevant terms, the nature and purpose of the civil juristic act, the custom, and the principle of good faith.

Where an expression of intent is not made to any specific person, the true intent of the person performing a civil juristic act may not be interpreted solely on the words and sentences used, but along with the relevant terms, the nature and purpose of the civil juristic act, custom, and the principle of good faith.

Section 3: Effect of a Civil Juristic Act

Article 143: A civil juristic act is valid if the following conditions are satisfied: (1) the person performing the act has the required capacity for performing civil juristic acts; (2) the intent expressed by the person is true; and (3) the act does not violate any mandatory provisions of laws or administrative regulations, nor offend public order or good morals.

Article 144: A civil juristic act performed by a person who has no capacity for performing civil juristic acts is void.

Article 145: A civil juristic act, performed by a person with limited capacity for performing civil juristic acts, which is purely beneficial to the person or is appropriate to the age, intelligence, or mental status of the person is valid; any other civil juristic act performed by such a person is valid if a consent or ratification is obtained from his legal representative.

A third person involved in the act performed by a person with limited capacity for performing civil juristic acts may request the legal representative of the latter to ratify the act within 30 days from receipt of the notification. Inaction of the legal representative is deemed as refusal of ratification. Before such an act is ratified, a bona fide third person is entitled to revoke the act. The revocation shall be made by notice.

Article 146: A civil juristic act performed by a person and another person based on a false expression of intent is void. Where an expression of intent deliberately conceals a civil juristic act, the validity of the concealed act shall be determined in accordance with the relevant laws.

Article 147: Where a civil juristic act is performed based on serious misunderstanding, the person who performs the act has the right to request the people's court or an arbitration institution to revoke the act.

Article 148: Where a party by fraudulent means induces the other party to perform a civil juristic act against the latter's true intention, the defrauded party has the right to request the people's court or an arbitration institution to revoke the act.

Article 149: Where a party knows or should have known that a civil juristic act performed by the other party is based on a third person's fraudulent act and is against the other party's true intention, the defrauded party has the right to request the people's court or an arbitration institution to revoke the civil juristic act.

Article 150: Where a party performs a civil juristic act against its true intention owing to duress of the other party or a third person, the coerced party has the right to request the people's court or an arbitration institution to revoke the civil juristic act.

Article 151: In situations such as where one party takes advantage of the other party that is in a desperate situation or lacks the ability of making judgment, and as a result the civil juristic act thus performed is obviously unfair, the damaged party is entitled to request the people's court or an arbitration institution to revoke the act.

Article 152: A party's right to revoke a civil juristic act is extinguished under any of the following circumstances: (1) the party has failed to exercise the right to revocation within one year from the date when it knows or should have known of the cause for revocation, or within 90 days from the date when the party who has performed the act with serious misunderstanding knows or should have known of the cause for revocation; (2) the party acting under duress has failed to exercise the right to revocation within one year from the date when the duress ceases; or (3) the party who becomes aware of the cause for revocation waives the right to revocation expressly or through its own conduct.

The right to revocation is extinguished if the party fails to exercise it within five years from the date when the civil juristic act has been performed.

Article 153: A civil juristic act in violation of the mandatory provisions of laws or administrative regulations is void, unless such mandatory provisions do not lead to invalidity of such a civil juristic act. A civil juristic act that offends the public order and good morals is void.

Article 154: A civil juristic act is void if it is conducted through malicious collusion between the actor and a counterparty and thus harms the lawful rights and interests of another person.

Article 155: A void or revoked civil juristic act does not have any legal force ab initio.

Article 156: If invalidation of a part of a civil juristic act does not affect the validity of the other part, the other part of the act remains valid.

Article 157: Where a civil juristic act is void, revoked, or is determined to have no legal effect, the property thus obtained by a person as a result of the act shall be returned, or compensation be made based on the appraised value of the property if it is impossible or meaningless to return the property. Unless otherwise provided by law, the loss thus incurred upon the other party shall be compensated by the party at fault, or, if both parties are at fault, by the parties proportionally.

Section 4: A Civil Juristic Act Subject to a Condition or a Term

Article 158: A condition may be attached to a civil juristic act unless the nature of the act denies such an attachment. A civil juristic act subject to a condition precedent becomes effective when the condition is fulfilled. A civil juristic act subject to a condition subsequent becomes invalid when the condition is fulfilled.

Article 159: Where a condition is attached to a civil juristic act, if a party, for the sake of its own interests, improperly obstructs the fulfillment of the condition, the condition is deemed as having been fulfilled; if a party improperly facilitates the fulfillment of the condition, the condition is deemed as not having been fulfilled.

Article 160: A term may be attached to a civil juristic act, unless the nature of such act denies such an attachment. A civil juristic act subject to a term of effectiveness becomes effective when the term begins. A civil juristic act subject to a term of termination becomes ineffective upon expiration of the term.

Chapter VII: Agency

Section 1: General Rules

Article 161: A person of the civil law may perform a civil juristic act through his agent. A civil juristic act may not be performed through an agent if the act must be performed by the principal himself in accordance with law, as agreed by the parties, or based on the nature of the act.

Article 162: A civil juristic act performed by an agent in the principal's name within the scope of authority is binding on the principal.

Article 163: Agency consists of agency by agreement and agency by operation of law. An agent under agreement shall act in accordance with the principal's authorization. An agent by operation of law shall act in accordance with law.

Article 164: An agent who fails to perform or fully perform his duty and thus causes harm to the principal shall bear civil liability.

Where an agent maliciously colludes with a third person, thus harming the lawful rights and interests of the principal, the agent and the third person shall bear joint and several liability.

Section 2: Agency by Agreement

Article 165: In an agency by agreement, if authority is conferred in writing, it shall clearly state in the letter of authorization the name of the agent, the authorized matters, as well as the scope and duration of the authority, and it shall be signed or sealed by the principal.

Article 166: Where two or more agents are authorized to deal with the same matter for the principal, the agents shall jointly exercise the authority unless otherwise agreed by the parties.

Article 167: Where an agent knows or should have known that handling the authorized matter is in violation of law but still acts as authorized, or, if a principal knows or should have known that an act of the agent is in violation of law but raises no objection, the principal and the agent shall bear joint and several liability.

Article 168: An agent may not, in the principal's name, perform a civil juristic act with himself, unless it is consented to or ratified by the principal. An agent who has been designated by two or more principals may not in the name of one principal perform a civil juristic act with another principal whom he concurrently represents, unless it is consented to or ratified by both principals.

Article 169: Where an agent needs to re-delegate his authority to a third person, he shall obtain consent or ratification from the principal. If the re-delegation of authority to a third person is consented to or ratified by the principal, the principal may directly instruct the third person to do the authorized task, and the agent shall be liable only for the selection of such a third person and the instructions given to the third person by the agent himself.

If re-delegation of authority to a third person is not consented to or ratified by the principal, the agent shall be liable for the acts performed by the third person, unless the agent re-delegates his authority to a third person in an emergency situation in order to protect the interests of the principal.

Article 170: A civil juristic act performed by a person for fulfilling his responsibilities assigned by a legal person or an unincorporated organization, within the scope of authority and in the name of the legal person or the unincorporated organization, is binding on the legal person or unincorporated organization.

Restrictions imposed by a legal person or an unincorporated organization on the scope of authority of a person who performs the responsibilities assigned by the legal person or unincorporated organization are not effective against a bona fide counterparty.

Article 171: An act performed by a person without authority, beyond the authority, or after the authority is terminated is not effective against the principal who has not ratified it. A counterparty may urge the principal to ratify such an act within 30 days after receipt of the notification. Inaction of the principal is deemed as a refusal of ratification. Before such an act is ratified, a bona fide counterparty has the right to revoke the act. The revocation shall be made by notice.

Where the aforementioned act is not ratified, a bona fide counterparty has the right to request the person who has performed the act to fulfill the obligations or compensate for the loss thus incurred. Provided, however, that the amount of compensation may not exceed the amount of benefit the counterparty would have received had the principal ratified the act.

Where a counterparty knows or should have known that the person performing the act has no authority, the counterparty and the said person shall bear the liability in proportion to their fault.

Article 172: An act performed by a person without authority, beyond the authority, or after the authority is terminated is effective if the counterparty has reasons to believe that the said person has authority.

Section 3: Termination of Agency

Article 173: An agency by agreement is terminated under any of the following circumstances: (1) the term of agency expires or the authorized tasks have been completed; (2) the principal revokes the agency or the agent resigns; (3) the agent loses his capacity for performing civil juristic acts; (4) the agent or the principal deceases; or (5) the legal person or unincorporated organization who is the agent or the principal is terminated.

Article 174: An act performed by an agent under agreement after the principal deceases remains valid under any of the following circumstances: (1) the agent does not know or should not have known of the death of the principal; (2) the act is ratified by the heirs of the principal; (3) it is clearly stated in the letter of authorization that the agency is terminated only upon completion of the authorized tasks; or (4) the agent has started the act before the principal deceases and continues to act in the interests of the heirs of the principal. The preceding paragraph shall be applied mutatis mutandis where the principal who is a legal person or an unincorporated organization is terminated.

Article 175: An agency by operation of law is terminated under any of the following circumstances: (1) the principal obtains or regains full capacity for performing civil juristic acts; (2) the agent loses the capacity for performing civil juristic acts; (3) the agent or the principal deceases; or (4) there exists any other circumstance as provided by law.

CHAPTER VIII: CIVIL LIABILITY

Article 176: A person of the civil law shall perform civil-law obligations and bear civil liability in accordance with law or the agreement of the parties.

Article 177: Where two or more persons assume shared liability in accordance with law, each person shall bear the liability in proportion to their respective share of fault if such share can be determined, or in equal share if such share cannot be determined.

Article 178: Where two or more persons assume joint and several liability in accordance with law, the right holder has the right to request some or all of them to bear the liability. The persons subjected to joint and several liability shall each bear the liability in proportion to their respective share of fault, or in equal share if such share cannot be determined. A person who has assumed the liability more than his share of fault has the right to contribution against the other person(s) subjected to the joint and several liability. Joint and several liability shall be either provided by law or agreed upon by the parties.

Article 179: The main forms of civil liability include: (1) cessation of the infringement; (2) removal of the nuisance; (3) elimination of the danger; (4) restitution; (5) restoration; (6) repair, redoing, or replacement; (7) continuance of performance; (8) compensation for losses; (9) payment of liquidated damages; (10) elimination of adverse effects and rehabilitation of reputation; and (11) extension of apologies.

Where punitive damages are available as provided by law, such provisions shall be followed. The forms of civil liability provided in this Article may be applied separately or concurrently.

Article 180: A person who is unable to perform his civil-law obligations due to force majeure bears no civil liability, unless otherwise provided by law. "Force majeure" means objective conditions which are unforeseeable, unavoidable, and insurmountable.

Article 181: A person who causes harm to the tortfeasor out of a justifiable defense bears no civil liability. A person who, when acting out of justifiable defense, exceeds the necessary limit and thus causes undue harm to the tortfeasor shall bear appropriate civil liability.

Article 182: Where a person when seeking to avoid a peril in response to an emergency causes harm to others, the person who creates the peril shall bear civil liability. Where the peril is caused by natural forces, the person who causes harm to others when seeking to avoid the peril bears no civil liability, but may make appropriate compensation.

Where the measures adopted by a person seeking to avoid a peril in response to an emergency are improper or exceed the necessary limit and thus cause undue harm to others, the person shall bear appropriate civil liability.

Article 183: Where a party is injured for protecting the civil-law rights and interests of another person, the tortfeasor shall bear civil liability, and the beneficiary may make appropriate compensation to the injured person. In the absence of a tortfeasor, or if the tortfeasor flees or is incapable of assuming civil liability, upon request of the injured person, the beneficiary shall make appropriate compensation.

Article 184: A person who voluntarily engages in rescuing another person in an emergency situation and thus causes harm to the latter person bears no civil liability.

Article 185: A person who infringes upon the name, likeness, reputation, or honor of a hero or a martyr and thus harms the social public interests shall bear civil liability.

Article 186: Where a party's breach of contract causes harm to the other party's personal or proprietary rights and interests, the latter party may elect to request the former to bear liability either for breach of contract or for commission of tort.

Article 187: Where a person of the civil law has to concurrently bear civil, administrative, and criminal liabilities as a result of the same act performed by him, the assumption of administrative or criminal liabilities by the person may not affect the civil liability he should bear. If the assets of the person are insufficient to pay for all the liabilities, the civil liability shall be paid first.

Chapter IX: Limitation of Action

Article 188: The limitation period for a person to request the people's court to protect his civil-law rights is three years, unless otherwise provided by law.

Unless otherwise provided by law, the limitation period begins from the date when the right holder knows or should have known that his right has been harmed and that who is the obligor. However, no protection to a right is to be granted by the people's court if 20 years have lapsed since the date when the injury occurs, except that the people's court may, upon request of the right holder, extend the limitation period under special circumstances.

Article 189: Where the parties agree on payment of a debt by installment, the limitation period begins from the date when the last installment is due.

Article 190: The limitation period for a person with no or limited capacity for performing civil juristic acts to bring a claim against his legal representative begins from the date when the agency by operation of law is terminated.

Article 191: The limitation period for a minor to bring a sexual molestation claim against the offender begins from the date when the minor reaches the age of eighteen.

Article 192: Expiration of the limitation period may be used by an obligor as a defense against a claim of non-performance.

An obligor who agrees to perform a prior obligation after the limitation periodexpires may not later on use the expiration of the limitation period as a defense, and35an obligor who has voluntarily performed such a prior obligation may not later on demand for restitution.

Article 193: The people's court may not apply the provisions on limitation periods on its own initiative.

Article 194: The limitation period is suspended if, within the last six months of the limitation period, a right holder is unable to exercise the right to claim owing to the existence of one of the following obstacles: (1) where there is force majeure; (2) where the right holder with no or limited capacity for performing civil juristic acts has no legal representative, or his legal representative deceases or loses the capacity for performing civil juristic acts or the right to representation; (3) where no heir or administrator of an estate has been determined after the opening of succession; (4) where the right holder is controlled by the obligor or another person; or (5) where there are other obstacles that cause the right holder unable to exercise the right to claim. The limitation period shall expire six months after the date when the cause for suspension is removed.

Article 195: A limitation period is interrupted under any of the following circumstances, and the limitation period shall run anew from the time of interruption or the time when the relevant proceeding is completed: (1) the right holder requests the obligor to perform the obligation; (2) the obligor agrees to perform the obligation; (3) the right holder initiates a lawsuit or arbitration proceeding against the obligor; or (4) there exists any other circumstance that has the same effect as initiating a lawsuit or arbitration proceeding by the right holder.

Article 196: The limitation period does not apply to the following rights to claim: (1) a claim for cessation of the infringement, removal of the nuisance, or elimination of the danger; (2) a claim for return of property of a person who has a real right in immovable or registered movable property; (3) a claim for payment of child support or support for other family members; or (4) any other claim to which the limitation period is not applicable in accordance with law.

Article 197: The time period, counting methods, and the grounds for suspension and interruption of the limitation period are provided by law, and any arrangement otherwise agreed by the parties is void. An anticipatory waiver of one's interests in the limitation period made by the parties is void.

Article 198: Any provisions of law regulating the limitation period for arbitration shall be followed; in the absence of such provisions, the provisions on limitation period for litigation provided herein shall be applied mutatis mutandis.

Article 199: The time period within which a right holder may exercise certain rights, such as the right to revocation and the right to rescission, which are provided by law or agreed by the parties shall begin, unless otherwise provided by law, from the date when the right holder knows or should have known that he has such a right, and the provisions on the suspension, interruption, or extension of the limitation period are not be applicable. Upon expiration of the time period, the right to revocation, the right to rescission, and the like rights are extinguished.

Chapter X: Counting of Periods of Time

Article 200: Time periods referred to in the civil law are counted by year, month, day, and hour according to the Gregorian calendar.

Article 201: Where a time period is counted by year, month, and day, the day on which the time period begins is not counted in and the period runs from the following day. Where a time period is counted by hour, the period begins to run from the hour as provided by law or agreed by the parties.

Article 202: Where a time period is counted by year and month, the corresponding date of the due month is the last day of the time period; in the absence of such a corresponding date, the last day of that month is the last day of the time period.

Article 203: Where the last day of a time period falls on a legal holiday, the day after the holiday is deemed as the last day of the period. The last day shall end at 24:00 hours; where a business hour is applied, the last day shall end at the time the business is closed.

Article 204: The counting of a time period shall be governed by the provisions of this Code, unless otherwise provided by law or agreed by the parties.

Appendix D

The Law on Foreign Relations of the People's Republic of China

http://en.npc.gov.cn.cdurl.cn/laws.html
   Adopted at the Third Meeting of the Standing Committee of the 14th National People's Congress on June 28, 2023

TABLE OF CONTENTS

Chapter I   General Principles
Chapter II   Functions and Powers for the Conduct of Foreign Relations
Chapter III   Goals and Mission of Conducting Foreign Relations
Chapter IV   The System of Foreign Relations
Chapter V   Support for the Conduct of Foreign Relations
Chapter VI   Supplementary Provision

CHAPTER I: GENERAL PRINCIPLES

Article 1: This Law is enacted pursuant to the Constitution of the People's Republic of China to conduct foreign relations to:

- safeguard China's sovereignty, national security and development interests;
- protect and promote the interests of the Chinese people;
- build China into a great modernized socialist country;
- realize the great rejuvenation of the Chinese nation;

- promote world peace and development; and
- build a community with a shared future for mankind.

Article 2: This Law shall apply to the conduct by the People's Republic of China of diplomatic relations with other countries, its exchanges and cooperation with them in the economic, cultural and other areas, and its relations with the United Nations and other international organizations.

Article 3: The People's Republic of China conducts foreign relations and promotes friendly exchanges under the guidance of Marxism-Leninism, Mao Zedong Thought, Deng Xiaoping Theory, the Important Thinking of Three Represents, the Scientific Outlook on Development and Xi Jinping Thought on Socialism with Chinese Characteristics for a New Era.

Article 4: The People's Republic of China pursues an independent foreign policy of peace, and observes the five principles of mutual respect for sovereignty and territorial integrity, mutual non-aggression, mutual non-interference in internal affairs, equality and mutual benefit, and peaceful coexistence. The People's Republic of China keeps to a path of peaceful development and adheres to the fundamental policy of opening to the outside world and a strategy of opening-up for mutual benefit. The People's Republic of China observes the purposes and principles of the Charter of the United Nations, and endeavors to safeguard world peace and security, promote global common development, and build a new type of international relations. It is committed to settling international disputes by peaceful means and opposes the use of force or threat of force in international relations, hegemonism and power politics. It remains true to the principle that all countries are equal regardless of size, strength or level of development and respects the development paths and social systems decided upon independently by the people of all countries.

Article 5: The conduct of foreign relations by the People's Republic of China is under the centralized and overall leadership of the Communist Party of China.

Article 6: The State institutions, armed forces, political parties, people's organizations, enterprises, public institutions, other social organizations, and citizens have the responsibility and obligation to safeguard China's sovereignty, national security, dignity, honor and interests in the course of international exchanges and cooperation.

Article 7: The State encourages friendly people-to-people exchanges and cooperation with foreign countries. Those who make outstanding contribution to international exchanges and cooperation shall be honored and awarded pursuant to applicable regulations of the State.

Article 8: Any organization or individual who commits acts that are detrimental to China's national interests in violation of this Law and other applicable laws in the course of engaging in international exchanges shall be held accountable by law.

Chapter II: Functions and Powers for the Conduct of Foreign Relations

Article 9: The central leading body for foreign affairs is responsible for policy making, deliberation and coordination relating to the conduct of foreign relations. It considers and formulates the State's foreign relations strategy and related major principles and policies, and provides guidance for their implementation. It is responsible for top-level design, coordination and holistic advancement of work concerning foreign relations, and supervises its implementation.

Article 10: The National People's Congress and its Standing Committee ratify or denounce treaties and important agreements concluded with other countries, and exercise functions and powers relating to foreign relations pursuant to the Constitution and other laws. The National People's Congress and its Standing Committee actively conduct international exchanges, and strengthen exchanges and cooperation with parliaments of foreign countries as well as international and regional parliamentary organizations.

Article 11: The President of the People's Republic of China represents the People's Republic of China, conducts affairs of state, and exercises functions and powers relating to foreign relations pursuant to the Constitution and other laws.

Article 12: The State Council manages foreign affairs, concludes treaties and agreements with foreign countries, and exercises functions and powers relating to foreign relations pursuant to the Constitution and other laws.

Article 13: The Central Military Commission organizes and conducts international military exchanges and cooperation and exercises functions and powers relating to foreign relations pursuant to the Constitution and other laws.

Article 14: The Ministry of Foreign Affairs of the People's Republic of China conducts foreign affairs in accordance with the law and undertakes matters relating to diplomatic exchanges of Party and State leaders with foreign leaders. The Ministry of Foreign Affairs enhances guidance, coordination, management and service for international exchanges and cooperation conducted by other government departments and localities. Other central and government departments conduct international exchanges and cooperation according to their respective scope of responsibilities.

Article 15: Diplomatic missions of the People's Republic of China abroad, including embassies and consulates in foreign countries as well as permanent missions to the United Nations and other international intergovernmental organizations, represent the People's Republic of China abroad. The Ministry of Foreign Affairs exercises overall leadership over the work of Chinese diplomatic missions abroad.

Article 16: Provinces, autonomous regions and cities directly under central government jurisdiction shall carry out international exchanges and cooperation within the specific scope of mandate authorized by the central authorities. People's governments of provinces, autonomous regions and cities directly under central government jurisdiction shall manage matters relating to international exchanges and cooperation in areas under their administration in accordance with their functions and powers.

Chapter III: Goals and Mission of Conducting Foreign Relations

Article 17: The People's Republic of China conducts foreign relations to uphold its system of socialism with Chinese characteristics, safeguard its sovereignty, unification and territorial integrity, and promote its economic and social development.

Article 18: The People's Republic of China calls for putting into action the Global Development Initiative, the Global Security Initiative and the Global Civilization Initiative, and endeavors to advance a foreign affairs agenda on multiple fronts, at different levels, in various areas and of multiple dimensions. The People's Republic of China works to promote coordination and sound interaction with other major countries and grow relations with its neighboring countries in accordance with the principle of amity, sincerity, mutual benefit and inclusiveness and the policy of enhancing friendship and partnership with its neighbors. Guided by the principle of sincerity, delivering outcomes, affinity and good faith and the vision of promoting common good and shared interests, it works to strengthen solidarity and cooperation with other developing countries. The People's Republic of China upholds and practices multilateralism and participates in the reform and development of the global governance system.

Article 19: The People's Republic of China upholds the international system with the United Nations at its core, the international order underpinned by international law, and the fundamental norms governing international relations based on the purposes and principles of the Charter of the United Nations. The People's Republic of China stays true to the vision of global governance featuring extensive consultation and joint contribution for shared benefits. It participates in the development of international rules, promotes democracy in international relations, and works for economic globalization that is more open, inclusive, balanced and beneficial to all.

Article 20: The People's Republic of China stays true to the vision of common, comprehensive, cooperative, and sustainable global security, and endeavors to strengthen international security cooperation and its participation in mechanisms of global security governance. The People's Republic of China fulfills its responsibilities as a permanent member of the United Nations Security Council; it is committed to safeguarding international peace and security and upholding the authority and stature of the United Nations Security Council. The People's Republic of China supports and participates in peacekeeping operations mandated by the United Nations Security Council, observes the basic principles of the peacekeeping operations, respects the territorial integrity and political independence of sovereign countries concerned, and maintains a position of fairness. The People's Republic of China is committed to upholding international regimes of arms control, disarmament and non-proliferation. It is against arms race; it opposes and prohibits proliferation of weapons of mass destruction in any form, fulfills relevant international obligations, and is engaged in international cooperation on non-proliferation.

Article 21: The People's Republic of China stays true to the vision of global development which is equitable, inclusive, open, cooperative, comprehensive, well-coordinated, innovation-driven and interconnected. It endeavors to promote coordinated and sustainable development of the economy, the society and the environment and well-rounded human development.

Article 22: The People's Republic of China respects and protects human rights; it is committed to the principle of universality of human rights and its observance in light of the realities of countries. The People's Republic of China promotes comprehensive and coordinated development of all human rights, carries out international exchanges and cooperation in the field of human rights on the basis of equality and mutual respect, and works for the sound development of the global cause of human rights.

Article 23: The People's Republic of China calls on all countries to rise above national, ethnic and cultural differences and uphold peace, development, equity, justice, democracy and freedom, which are common values of humanity.

Article 24: The People's Republic of China stays true to the vision of equality, mutual learning, dialogue and inclusiveness among civilizations, respects diversity of civilizations, and promotes exchanges and dialogue among civilizations.

Article 25: The People's Republic of China plays an active part in global environmental and climate governance and endeavors to strengthen international cooperation on green and low-carbon development; it is committed to jointly enhancing global ecological conservation and building a global system of environmental and climate governance that is fair, equitable, cooperative and beneficial to all.

Article 26: The People's Republic of China is committed to advancing high-standard opening-up. It develops foreign trade, actively promotes and protects, in accordance with the law, inbound foreign investment, encourages external economic cooperation including outbound investment, and promotes high-quality development of the Belt and Road Initiative. It is committed to upholding the multilateral trading system, opposes unilateralism and protectionism, and works to build an open global economy.

Article 27: The People's Republic of China provides foreign aid in the form of economic, technical, material, human resources, management, and other assistance to boost economic development and social advances of other developing countries, build up their capacity for sustainable development, and promote international development cooperation. The People's Republic of China carries out international humanitarian cooperation and assistance, strengthens international cooperation on disaster prevention, mitigation and relief and helps recipient countries respond to humanitarian emergencies. In providing foreign aid, the People's Republic of China respects the sovereignty of recipient countries and does not interfere in their internal affairs or attach any political conditions to its aid.

Article 28: The People's Republic of China carries out, as needed in the conduct of foreign relations, exchanges and cooperation in educational, science and technology, cultural, public health, sports, social, ecological, military, security, the rule of law and other fields.

Chapter IV: The System of Foreign Relations

Article 29: The State advances the rule of law in both domestic and foreign affairs and strengthens foreign-related legislative work and the system of rule of law in foreign affairs.

Article 30: The State concludes or accedes to treaties and agreements in accordance with the Constitution and other laws and fulfills in good faith obligations stipulated in such treaties and agreements. Treaties and agreements that the State concludes or accedes to shall not contravene the Constitution.

Article 31: The State takes due measures to implement and apply treaties and agreements to which it is a Party. The implementation and application of treaties and agreements shall not undermine the sovereignty of the State, national security and public interests.

Article 32: The State shall strengthen the implementation and application of its laws and regulations in foreign-related fields in conformity with the fundamental principles of international law and fundamental norms governing international relations. The State shall take law enforcement, judicial or other measures in accordance with the law to safeguard its sovereignty, national security and development interests and protect the lawful rights and interests of Chinese citizens and organizations.

Article 33: The People's Republic of China has the right to take, as called for, measures to counter or take restrictive measures against acts that endanger its sovereignty, national security and development interests in violation of international law or fundamental norms governing international relations. The State Council and its departments adopt administrative regulations and departmental rules as necessary, establish related working institutions and mechanisms, and strengthen inter-departmental coordination and cooperation to adopt and enforce measures mentioned in the preceding paragraph. Decisions made pursuant to the first and second paragraphs of this Article are final.

Article 34: The People's Republic of China, on the basis of the one-China principle, establishes and develops diplomatic relations with other countries in accordance with the Five Principles of Peaceful Coexistence. The People's Republic of China, in accordance with treaties and agreements it concludes or accedes to as well as the fundamental principles of international law and fundamental norms governing international relations, may take diplomatic actions as necessary including changing or terminating diplomatic or consular relations with a foreign country.

Article 35: The State takes steps to implement sanction resolutions and relevant measures with binding force adopted by the United Nations Security Council in accordance with Chapter VII of the Charter of the United Nations. The Ministry of Foreign Affairs issues notices to release the sanction resolutions and measures mentioned in the preceding paragraph. The government departments concerned and the people's governments of provinces, autonomous regions, and cities directly under central government jurisdiction shall take actions to implement such sanction resolutions and measures within the scope of their respective functions and powers. Organizations and individuals in the Chinese territory shall comply with the notices issued by the Ministry of Foreign Affairs and related actions taken by government departments and localities, and shall not engage in any activity in violation of the above-mentioned sanction resolutions and measures.

Article 36: The People's Republic of China confers privileges and immunities to diplomatic institutions and officials of other countries, and to international organizations and their officials in accordance with relevant laws as well as treaties and agreements it concludes or accedes to. The People's Republic of China confers immunities to foreign states and their properties in accordance with relevant laws as well as treaties and agreements it concludes or accedes to.

Article 37: The State shall take measures as necessary in accordance with the law to protect the safety, security, and legitimate rights and interests of Chinese citizens and organizations overseas and safeguard China's overseas interests against any threat or infringement. The State shall strengthen the systems and working mechanisms and build the capacity to protect its overseas interests.

Article 38: The People's Republic of China protects the lawful rights and interests of foreign nationals and foreign organizations in its territory in accordance with the law. The State has the power to permit or deny a foreign national entry, stay or residence in its territory, and regulates, in accordance with the law, activities carried out in its territory by foreign organizations. Foreign nationals and foreign organizations in the territory of China shall abide by its laws, and shall not endanger China's national security, undermine social and public interests or disrupt social and public order.

Article 39: The People's Republic of China strengthens multilateral and bilateral dialogue on the rule of law and promotes international exchanges and cooperation on the rule of law. The People's Republic of China shall engage in international cooperation in law enforcement and judicial fields with other countries and international organizations in accordance with treaties and agreements it concludes or accedes to or in line with the principles of equality and reciprocity. The State strengthens and expands its working mechanisms for international cooperation in law enforcement, improves its systems and mechanisms for judicial assistance, and promotes international cooperation in law enforcement and judicial fields. The State strengthens international cooperation in areas such as combating transnational crimes and corruption.

Chapter V: Support for the Conduct of Foreign Relations

Article 40: The State shall improve its system of integrated support for conducting foreign relations and strengthen its capacity to conduct foreign relations and safeguard national interests.

Article 41: The State shall provide funding required for conducting foreign relations and establish a funding mechanism that meets the need of conducting foreign relations and is commensurate with China's economic development.

Article 42: The State shall strengthen capacity building of personnel working in foreign relations and take effective steps in related work such as training, employment, management, service and support.

Article 43: The State shall promote public understanding of and support for its conduct of foreign relations through various forms.

Article 44: The State shall strengthen capacity building for international communication, enable the world to learn more about and better understand China, and promote exchanges and mutual learning between different civilizations.

Chapter VI: Supplementary Provision

Article 45: This Law shall come into force on July 1, 2023.

Appendix E

Supervision Law of the PRC (2018)

By China Law Translate on 2018/03/21
 Source of text: http://www.npc.gov.cn/npc/xinwen/2018-03/21/content_2052362.htm; https://www.chinalawtranslate.com/en/supervision-law-of-the-prc-2018/

Supervision Law of the People's Republic of China

The National People's Congress Supervision Law of the People's Republic of China (passed on March 20, 2018 by the first meeting of the 13th Session of the National People's Congress)

CONTENTS

Supervision Law of the People's Republic of China
Chapter I: General Provisions
Chapter II: Supervision Organs and Their Duties
Chapter III: Scope of Supervision and Jurisdiction
Chapter IV: Scope of Supervision Authority
Chapter V: Supervision Procedures
Chapter VI: International Cooperation Against Corruption
Chapter VII: Oversight of Supervision Organs and Supervision Personnel
Chapter VIII: Legal Responsibility
Chapter IX: Supplementary Provisions

Chapter I: General Provisions

Article 1: This Law is formulated on the basis of the Constitution so as to deepen the reform of the state supervision system, to strengthen oversight of all public employees who exercise public power, to bring about full coverage of state supervision, to thoroughly carry out Anti-Corruption efforts, and to advance the modernization of the national governance system and governance capacity.

Article 2: Persist in the leadership of the Communist Party of China over state supervision work, and be guided by Marxism-Leninism, Mao Zedong Thought, Deng Xiaoping Theory, the Theory of "Three Represents," the Scientific Outlook on Development, and Xi Jinping Thought on Socialism with Chinese Characteristics for a New Era, to build a state supervision system with Chinese characteristics that is centralized and unified, authoritative and highly efficient.

Article 3: The Supervision Commissions of all levels are the specialized organs for the exercise of state supervision functions, and are to follow this Law to conduct supervision of all public employees exercising public power (hereinafter public employees), investigate violations and crimes abusing public office, carry out efforts to establish a clean government and fight corruption, and preserve the dignity of the Constitution and laws.

Article 4: The Supervision Commissions exercise supervision power independently, in accordance with the provisions of law, and not subject to interference by any administrative organ, social group, or individual.

Supervision Organs handling cases of violations or crimes abusing public office, shall mutually cooperate with and mutually restrict the adjudicatory organs, procuratorial organs, and law enforcement departments.

Where the Supervision Organs need assistance in their work, the relevant organs and units shall give assistance in accordance with law, as requested by the Supervision Organs.

Article 5: State supervision work is to strictly conform to the Constitution and laws, have the facts as its basis with the laws as their measure, and apply the laws equally to all; ensure parties' lawful rights and interests, have authority corresponding to responsibility, and strict oversight; and punishment is to be combined with education, leniency combined with severity.

Article 6: State supervision work is to persist in treating both symptoms and root causes, and in comprehensive administration; it is to strengthen oversight and accountability, and strictly punish corruption; it is to deepen reforms and complete the rule by law [法治], it is to effectively restrain and oversee power; and it is to strengthen education on law and ethics, promote the outstanding traditional Chinese culture, and establish long-term and effective mechanisms making it so that no one dares to be corrupt, no one is able to be corrupt, and no one wants to be corrupt.

Chapter II: Supervision Organs and Their Duties

Article 7: The State Supervision Commission of the People's Republic of China is the highest Supervision Organ.

Provinces, autonomous regions, directly governed municipalities, autonomous prefectures, counties, autonomous counties, cities, and municipal districts, are to establish Supervision Commissions.

Article 8: The State Supervision Commission is created by the National People's Congress, and is responsible for supervision work nationwide.

The State Supervision Commission is composed of a director, several deputy directors and several members; with the director elected by the National People's Congress and the deputy directors and members appointed or removed by proposal of the director of the State Supervision Commission to the Standing Committee of the National People's Congress.

The term of office of the State Supervision Commission Director is the same as that for the National People's Congress, and they must not serve for more than two consecutive terms.

The State Supervision Commission is responsible to the National People's Congress and its Standing Committee, and is to accept their oversight.

Article 9: Local Supervision Commissions are created by the people's congress at the corresponding level, and are responsible for supervision work in their respective administrative regions.

All levels of local Supervision Commission are to be composed of a director, several deputy directors and several members; with the director elected by the people's congress at the corresponding level and the deputy directors and members appointed or removed by proposal of the director of the Supervision Commission to the standing committee of the people's congress at the corresponding level.

The term of office for directors of all levels of local Supervision Commissions is the same as that for the people's congress at the corresponding level.

All levels of local Supervision Commissions are responsible to the people's congresses and their standing committees at the same level, and to the Supervision Commission at the level above, and are to accept their oversight.

Article 10: The State Supervision Commission leads the work of local Supervision Commissions at all levels, and higher Supervision Commissions lead the work of lower Supervision Commissions.

Article 11: Supervision Commissions carry out the duties of oversight, investigation, and disposition in accordance with this Law and relevant laws:

(1) Carry out education for public employees in clean governance, and oversee and inspect their performance of duties in accordance with law, just use of authority, clean governance, and ethical conduct;

(2) Conduct investigations into violations and crimes abusing public office, such as suspected corruption, bribery, abuse of power, dereliction of duty, rent-seeking, siphoning benefits, twisting the law for personal gain, and wasting State assets;

(3) Make decisions on governmental sanctions for public employees who break the law; hold accountable those leadership personnel who perform their duties ineffectively or who shirk their duties and responsibilities; transfer the investigative conclusions on suspected crimes abusing public office to the people's procuratorates to initiate public prosecutions in accordance with law; and issue supervision recommendations to the units of the targets of supervision.

Article 12: All levels of Supervision Commission may station or dispatch supervision bodies or Supervision Commissioners in organs of the Communist Party of China, state organs, or organizations and units authorized by laws or regulations or retained to administer public affairs at the corresponding levels, as well as to the administrative regions or state-owned enterprises under their jurisdiction.

The supervision bodies or commissioners are responsible to the Supervision Commissions that stationed or dispatched them.

Article 13: As authorized, stationed or dispatched supervision bodies or Supervision Commissioners are to conduct oversight of public employees and issue supervision recommendations in accordance with the scope of their management authority; and are to lawfully investigate and handle public employees.

Article 14: The State is to implement a supervision official system, lawfully determining systems such as for the hierarchical setup, appointment and removal, evaluation, and promotion of supervision officials.

CHAPTER III: SCOPE OF SUPERVISION AND JURISDICTION

Article 15: Supervision Organs are to conduct supervision of the following public employees and relevant personnel:

(1) Officials of Chinese Communist Party organs, organs of people's congresses and their standing committees, people's governments, Supervision Commissions, people's courts, people's procuratorates, organs of CPPCC committees at all levels, democratic party organs, and organs of the federations of industry and commerce, and persons managed with reference to the "People's Republic of China Law on Public Officials";

(2) Personnel engaged in public affairs at organizations authorized by laws or regulations, or lawfully retained by state organs, to manage public affairs;

(3) Management of state-owned enterprises;

(4) Personnel engaged in management in public education, scientific research, culture, health care, sports and other such units;

(5) Personnel engaged in collective affairs management at basic-level autonomous mass organizations;

(6) Other personnel who perform public duties in accordance with law.

Article 16: In accordance with the scope of their management authority, all levels of Supervision Organ are to have jurisdiction over supervision matters in their jurisdictional region that involve the personnel provided for in article 15 of this Law.

A higher-level Supervision Organ may handle the supervision matters in the jurisdiction of the Supervision Organ at the level below, and when necessary, may also handle supervision matters in the jurisdiction of the Supervision Organs at any level within its jurisdiction.

Where there are disputes between the Supervision Organs over the jurisdiction of supervision matters, they shall be determined by their common higher-level Supervision Organ.

Article 17: Higher level Supervision Organs may designate a lower level Supervision Organ as having jurisdiction over supervision with its jurisdiction, or may appoint a different Supervision Organ to have jurisdiction over a supervision matter in the jurisdiction of a lower level Supervision Organ.

Where Supervision Organs find that supervision matters over which they have jurisdiction are major or complicated, and need to have a higher level Supervision Organ take jurisdiction, they may request that a higher Supervision Organ take jurisdiction.

CHAPTER IV: SCOPE OF SUPERVISION AUTHORITY

Article 18: Supervision Organs exercising their oversight and investigation authority have the right to learn of circumstances and gather or collect evidence from relevant units or individuals in accordance with law. Relevant units and individuals shall truthfully provide it.

Supervision Organs and their staffs shall preserve the confidentiality of the state secrets, commercial secrets or personal privacy that they learn of in the course of oversight and investigations.

Evidence must not be fabricated, concealed, or destroyed by any unit or individual.

Article 19: In accordance with their management authority, the Supervision Organs may, either directly or by retaining relevant organs or personnel, talk with or request explanations of situations from targets of supervision that might have illegally abused public office.

Article 20: During the course of investigation, Supervision Organs may request that persons under investigation for suspected illegal abuse of public office give statements regarding the suspected illegal conduct, and when necessary, issue a written notice to the person under investigation.

The Supervision Organs may conduct an interrogation and request a truthful statement about the suspected crime from those under investigation for suspected embezzlement and bribery, dereliction of duty, and other such crimes abusing public office.

Article 21: During the course of an investigation, the Supervision Organs may question witnesses and other such persons.

Article 22: Where the persons under investigation are suspected of serious violations or crimes abusing public office such as corruption, bribery, or dereliction of duty, and the Supervision Organs already have a handle on some of the facts and evidence on the violations or crimes, but still have important issues that need further investigation, then after review and approval by the Supervision Organ in accordance with law, they may be retained in custody at a designated location in any of the following circumstances:

(1) the case is major or complicated;

(2) they might flee or commit suicide;

(3) They might collude testimony or fabricate, conceal, or destroy evidence;

(4) They might have other conduct obstructing investigation.

Persons implicated in cases of suspected bribery or joint crimes abusing public office, may be retained in custody by the Supervision Organs on the basis of the preceding paragraph.

The setup, management, and oversight of sites for retention in custody are to be implemented in accordance with relevant state provisions.

Article 23: When investigating corruption, bribery, dereliction of duty, or other serious violations or crimes abusing public office, the Supervision Organs may, as necessary for work, make inquiries into and freeze assets of units and persons implicated in the case, such as savings, remittances, bonds, stocks and fund shares, in accordance with the provisions. Relevant units and individuals shall cooperate. Relevant units and individuals shall cooperate.

Where frozen assets are shown to be unrelated to the case through investigation, they shall be unfrozen and returned within three days.

Article 24: Supervision Organs may conduct searches of the persons, items, domiciles, and other places related to the persons being investigated for crimes abusing public office as well as of persons who might be hiding the persons under investigation or criminal evidence. When conducting searches, search documents shall be presented and an authenticating witness, such as the persons being searched or their family members, shall be present.

Searches of women's persons shall be carried out by female personnel.

When conducting searches, the Supervision Organs may request that the public security organs cooperate as necessary for work. The public security organs shall provide assistance in accordance with law.

Article 25: During the course of investigations, the Supervision Organs may collect, seal, or seize information such as property, documents, and electronic data that are to be used to prove the violations or crimes of which the person under investigation is suspected. In taking measures to collect, seal, or seize, the original item shall be taken, and each item is to be photographed, registered, and numbered, collaboratively with the person in possession, custodian, or authenticating witness, and a catalog is to be made and signed by those at scene, and a copy of the catalog is to be given the person in possession or custodian.

The Supervision Organs shall establish special accounts and locations, and designate specialized personnel, for appropriately storing property and documents they collect, seal or seize, strictly perform formalities for their transfer and collection, and it must not be damaged or used for other purposes. Items for which the value is unclear shall be promptly appraised, and they shall be specially sealed in storage.

Where the sealed or seized property or documents are shown to be unrelated to the case through investigation, they shall be unsealed or unseized and returned within three days.

Article 26: During the course of investigations, the Supervision Organs may, directly or by appointment, employ personnel with specialized knowledge or qualifications to carry out inspections or examinations presided over by the investigators. A written record shall be made of the results of the inspection or examination, to be signed or have a seal affixed by the inspecting or examining personnel and the authenticating witnesses.

Article 27: During the course of investigations, the Supervision Organs may appoint or employ persons with specialized knowledge to conduct evaluations of specialized issues in the cases. After conducting appraisals, the appraisers shall write and sign appraisal opinions.

Article 28: When conducting investigations of suspected crimes abusing public office such as major corruption or bribery, the Supervision Organs may, as necessary and upon completing strict approval procedures, employ technical investigation measures and follow provisions to have the relevant organs carry them out.

The approval decision shall clearly state the type of technical investigative measures and their target, and be effective for three months of its issue; where the period is completed in a complicated or challenging case and it is still necessary to continue employing technical investigative measures, the period may be extended upon approval, but each time must not exceed three months. Where it is not necessary to continue employing technical investigation measures, they shall be promptly lifted.

Article 29: If the persons under investigation who shall be lawfully retained in custody are at large, the Supervision Organs may decide to list them as wanted within their respective administrative regions, and the public security organs are to issue a wanted notice and seek to bring them in. Where the scope of the wanted bulletin exceeds that administrative region, it shall be reported to a higher Supervision Organ with authority to make the decision.

Article 30: In order to prevent the persons under investigation and related personnel from escaping outside the mainland territory, Supervision Organs may, with the approval of the Supervision Organ at or above the provincial level, take measures to limit the persons under investigation and related personnel from leaving the mainland territory, and the public security organs are to enforce them in accordance with law. Where it is not necessary to continue employing measures restricting exit from the mainland territory, they shall be promptly lifted.

Article 31: Where persons under investigation for suspected crimes abusing public office voluntarily admit guilt and accept punishment, and have any of the following circumstances, then after collective research by the leadership personnel, and reporting to the Supervision Organ at the level above for approval, the Supervision Organs may issue a recommendation for lenient punishment when they are transferred to the people's procuratorate:

(1) voluntarily surrenders and truly acknowledges and repents the crime;

(2) actively cooperates with the investigation and truthfully confesses illegal or criminal acts of which the Supervision Organ has not yet been aware;

(3) proactively returns the spoils and reduces damages;

(4) made a major meritorious contribution or where the case involved major State interests.

Article 32: Where persons implicated in cases of violations or crimes abusing public office reveal violations or crimes abusing public office that prove true; or provide important leads that assist in the investigation of other cases; then after collective research by the leadership, and reporting to the Supervision Organ at the next higher level for approval, the Supervision Organs may issue a recommendation for lenient punishment when the case is transferred to the procuratorate.

Article 33: Evidence collected by Supervision Organs in accordance with this law, including physical evidence, documentary evidence, witness testimony, confessions or explanations by the investigation subject, audiovisual materials and electronic data, may be used as evidence in criminal cases.

When collecting, fixing, examining and using evidence, the Supervision Organs shall be consistent with the evidentiary requirements and standards for criminal adjudication.

Evidence collected by illegal means shall be excluded in accordance with law, and must not be used as the basis for the case disposition.

Article 34: Where people's courts, people's procuratorates, public security organs, auditing organs and other state organs discover in their work any leads about suspected corruption, bribery, dereliction of duty, or other violations or crimes abusing public office by public employees, they shall transfer them to the Supervision Organs, and the Supervision Organs are to investigate and handle them in accordance with law.

Where persons under investigation are suspected of both serious violations or crimes abusing public office, and other illegal or criminal acts, the Supervision Organ shall generally take the lead in the investigation, and other organs are to assist.

CHAPTER V: SUPERVISION PROCEDURES

Article 35: Supervision Organs shall accept and handle reports or informant reports, in accordance with the relevant regulations. Those that do not come within their respective jurisdictions shall be transferred to the competent organs for disposition.

Article 36: The Supervision Organs shall carry out their work in strict accordance with procedures, and shall establish working mechanisms for mutual assistance and mutual restraint in the various departments that handle, investigate, and hear issues and leads.

The Supervision Organs shall strengthen the oversight and management over the entire process of investigation and disposition, set up corresponding work departments for management of leads, oversight and inspections, urging handling, statistical analysis, and other management coordination functions.

Article 37: The Supervision Organs shall follow relevant provisions to submit opinions on disposition of leads regarding problems with the targets of supervision, perform review and approval formalities, and conduct categorical handling. The disposition of leads shall be summarized and circulated at regular intervals, and have inspections and spot checks at relevant intervals.

Article 38: Where it is necessary to adopt preliminary verification methods to handle issues and leads, the Supervision Organs shall perform review and approval procedures in accordance with law, and form a verification team. After the preliminary verification is completed, the verification team shall write a report on the preliminary verification situation, and put forward suggestions on how to handle it. The undertaking departments shall put forward categorized opinions on handling. The preliminary verification reports and categorized handling opinion reports are to be reported to the principal responsible person of the Supervision Organs for review and approval.

Article 39: Where upon preliminary verification, there are suspected violations or crimes abusing public office that need to be pursued for legal responsibility, the Supervision Organs are to handle the formalities for filing the case in accordance with the scope of their authority and procedures.

After approving the filing of cases in accordance with law, the principal responsible persons of Supervision Organs shall preside over special meetings, study and determine the investigation plan, and decide on what investigative measures need to be taken.

The decision to file and investigate a case shall be announced to the person under investigation and reported to relevant organizations. Where serious violations or crimes abusing public office are suspected, the family of the persons under investigation shall be informed, and they shall be announced to the public.

Article 40: In cases of violations or crimes abusing public office, the Supervision Organs shall investigate and gather evidence of whether the persons under investigation have broken the law or committed a crime and of the seriousness of the circumstances, and ascertain the facts of the violations or crimes, to form a mutually corroborative, complete and stable chain of evidence.

The gathering of evidence by threats, enticements, fraud, and other illegal means is strictly prohibited; and berating, striking, abusing, and direct or covert corporal punishment of the persons under investigation, and persons implicated in the case, is strictly prohibited.

Article 41: When investigators employ investigation measures such as interrogation, questioning, retention in custody, searches, collection, sealing, seizure, inspection, or examination, they shall always follow regulations to present documents, issue a written notice, have two or more people carrying it out, and compose written materials such as notes or reports, and have the relevant personnel sign them and affix a seal.

When investigators conduct interrogations and important evidence gathering efforts such as searches, sealing, or seizures, they shall make an audiovisual recording of the entire process, and retain it for future reference.

Article 42: Investigators shall strictly implement the investigation plan, and must not freely expand the scope of the investigation or change its targets and matters.

Important matters in the course of the investigation shall be collectively studied and then reported for instruction in accordance with procedures.

Article 43: Supervisory Organs' employment of retention in custody measures shall be upon collective study and decision of the Supervisory Organ's leadership. Employment of retention in custody measures by Supervisory Organs at or below the districted city level, shall be reported to the Supervisory Organ at the level above for approval. Provincial level Supervisory Organ employment of retention in custody shall be reported to the State Supervision Commission for recording.

The period of retention in custody must not exceed three months. Under special circumstances, it may be extended once, and the extension period must not exceed three months. Where a Supervision Organ at the provincial level or below employs retention in custody measures, the extension of the period of retention in custody shall be reported to the Supervision Organ at the next higher level for approval. Where the Supervision Organs find that the employment of retention in custody measures is inappropriate, they shall promptly lift them.

Supervision Organs employing retention in custody measures may request that the public security organs cooperate, as necessary for work. The public security organs shall provide assistance in accordance with law.

Article 44: After a person under investigation is retained in custody, the unit or family of the person retained in custody shall be informed within 24 hours, except where there might be circumstances that would impede the investigation such as destruction or fabrication of evidence, disrupting witnesses from testifying, or colluding testimony. After the circumstances obstructing the investigation have been eliminated, the person being retained in custody's unit and family shall be immediately informed.

The Supervision Organs shall ensure the diet, rest, and safety of persons retained in custody, and provide medical services. Interrogation of persons retained in custody shall have reasonably arranged interrogation times and lengths, and the interrogation records are to be signed by the persons being interrogated after they read them.

Where persons retained in custody who are suspected of crimes are transferred to the judicial organs and then lawfully sentenced to controlled release, short-term detention, or fixed-term imprisonment; every day they were retained in custody is to reduce controlled release by two days, or reduce short-term detention or imprisonment by one day.

Article 45: Based on the results of oversight and investigation, the Supervision Organs are to make the following dispositions in accordance with law:

(1) For public employees who have broken the law by abusing public office but the circumstance were more minor, follow the scope of authority to, either directly or by retaining a relevant organ or personnel, talk with them and remind them, criticize and educate them, order inspections, or admonish them;

(2) Give public employees who have broken the law a warning, demerit, major demerit, demotion, removal, expulsion, or other governmental sanction decision in accordance with procedures.

(3) For leadership personnel who have responsibility for the nonperformance or incorrect performance of duties, follow the scope of management authority to either directly make a decision to hold them responsible, or make an accountability recommendation to an organ with authority to make decisions on accountability;

(4) For those suspected of crimes abusing public office, where upon investigation the Supervision Organs find that the facts of the crime are clear and the evidence is credible and sufficient, they are to draft written opinions in support of prosecution and transfer them, along with the case file materials and evidence, to the people's procuratorates to have public prosecutions initiated in accordance with law;

(5) Issue a Supervision Recommendation on problems that exist in the clean governance establishment and performance of duties by the units of the subjects of the investigations.

After investigation, the Supervision Organs shall withdraw cases where there is no evidence proving that the persons under investigations have engaged in illegal or criminal acts, and report this the person under investigation's unit.

Article 46: After investigation, the Supervision Organs are to confiscate and recover any illegally obtained property, or order its return.

Article 47: In cases transferred by the Supervision Organs, the people's procuratorate is to employ compulsory measures against the person under investigation in accordance with the "Criminal Procedure Law of the People's Republic of China."

Where through investigation the people's procuratorate finds that the facts of the crime are already clear and the evidence is credible and sufficient, and that criminal responsibility shall be pursued in accordance with law, they shall make a decision to prosecute.

Where after examination, the people's procuratorate finds it is necessary to supplement or verify, it shall return it to the supervision organ for supplementary investigation, and, when necessary, may supplement the investigation on its own. In cases where investigation is supplemented, the supplementation shall be completed within one month. Supplementation of investigation is limited to two times.

Where there are circumstance for non-prosecution as provided for in the "Criminal Procedure Law of the People's Republic of China," upon reporting to the people's procuratorate at the level above, the people's procuratorate is to make a non-prosecution decision in accordance with law. Where the Supervision Organ finds that the decision not to prosecute is in error, it may request a reconsideration from the people's procuratorate at the level above.

Article 48: Where the person under investigation by the Supervision Organs for corruption, bribery, dereliction of duty or other crimes abusing public office has escaped or died during the course of investigation, and there is a need to continue investigating, upon approval of the Supervision Organ at the provincial level or above the investigation shall be continued and a conclusion made. Where the person under investigation has escaped and cannot be brought in after being listed as wanted for one year, or has died, the Supervision Organs shall request that the people's procuratorates follow legally prescribed procedures to apply to the people's courts for confiscating any unlawful gains.

Article 49: Where the targets of supervision are dissatisfied with decisions made by the Supervision Organs' involving them, they may apply for a re-examination to the Supervision Organ that made the decision within one month of receiving the decision, and the re-examination organ shall issue a re-examination decision within one month; where the target of supervision is still dissatisfied with the re-examination decision, they may apply to the Supervision Organ at the level above for a review within one month of receiving the review decision; and the review organ shall make a review decision within two months. Enforcement of the handling decision is not suspended during the period for re-examination or review. Where the organ accepting the review finds that there is an error in the handling decision, the original handling organ shall promptly correct it.

CHAPTER VI: INTERNATIONAL COOPERATION AGAINST CORRUPTION

Article 50: The State Supervision Commission is to carry out overall planning and coordination for international Anti-Corruption communication and cooperation with other nations, regions, and international organizations, and to organize efforts on the implementation of international Anti-Corruption treaties.

Article 51: The State Supervision Commission is to organize coordination with the relevant parties to strengthen cooperation with relevant countries, regions and international organizations in areas such as Anti-Corruption law enforcement, extradition, judicial assistance, custody transfer of sentenced persons, asset recovery, and information exchanges.

Article 52: The State Supervision Commission is to strengthen the organization and coordination of Anti-Corruption efforts such as international pursuit of stolen assets and fleeing persons and preventing escapes, and to spur the relevant units to do a good job of relevant work:

(1) In cases of crimes abusing public office, such as major corruption, bribery and dereliction of duty, where the persons under investigation have escaped outside the country (mainland territory) and the Supervision Organ has already obtained more conclusive evidence, bring them in through means such as carrying out overseas pursuit;

(2) Making requests to the country where stolen assets or goods are located to make inquiries, freeze, seize, confiscate, recover, or return the assets involved with the case;

(3) Make inquiries of or monitor public employees suspected of crimes abusing public office and related persons in their entry and exit from the

country (mainland territory) and the flow of cross-territorial funds, and set up procedures for preventing escape in the course of investigating cases.

Chapter VII: Oversight of Supervision Organs and Supervision Personnel

Article 53: All levels of Supervision Commission shall accept oversight by the people's congress of that level and its standing committee

Standing committees of people's congresses at all levels are to hear and deliberate special work reports of the Supervision Commissions at the corresponding level, and organize law enforcement inspections.

When people's congresses and their standing committees at any level at the county level or above hold a meeting, the people's congress delegates or members of the standing committee may, in accordance with the procedures prescribed by law, raise inquiries or questioning about issues in supervision work.

Article 54: The Supervision Organs shall make information on Supervision work public in accordance with law, and accept democratic oversight, social oversight and public opinion oversight.

Article 55: Through measures such as establishing internal special oversight bodies, the Supervision Organs shall strengthen oversight of the supervision personnel's performance of their duties and compliance with the law, and establish a supervision corps that that is loyal, clean, and responsible.

Article 56: Supervision personnel must be models of compliance with the Constitution and the laws; be devoted to their duties, and enforce the law impartially; be honest and upright, and keep secrets; they must have good political character, be familiar with supervision operations, and possess the abilities such as using the laws, regulations, policies, and investigating to collect evidence; and conscientiously accept oversight.

Article 57: Where supervision personnel inquire into case circumstances or pry into a case, intercede or intervene, the supervision personnel handling the supervision matter shall promptly report it. Relevant circumstances shall be registered and filed for the record.

Where it is discovered that Supervision Personnel handling a supervision matter have, without permission, had contact with the persons under investigation, persons implicated in the case, and their designated associates, those who are aware shall promptly make a report. Relevant circumstances shall be registered and filed for the record.

Article 58: Where Supervision Personnel handling a supervision matter have any of the following circumstances, they shall voluntarily recuse themselves, and the targets of supervision, informants, or other relevant persons, also have the right to request recusal:

(1) Is a close relative of the target of the supervision or the informant;

(2) has served as a witness in that case;

(3) They, or their close relatives, have an interest in the supervision matters being handled;

(4) Has other circumstances that may impact the fair handling of the matters for supervision.

Article 59: After leaving the post, Supervision Organs' personnel who are involved with secrets shall abide by the management provisions for the departure period and strictly perform their obligations to keep secrets, and must not divulge relevant secrets.

Within three years after the resignation or retirement of the Supervision personnel, they must not engage in professions in which conflicts of interest might occur in connection with the supervision and judicial work.

Article 60: Where Supervision Organs or their staffs exhibit any of the following conduct, the persons being investigated and their close relatives have the right to appeal to that organ:

(1) The period for retention in custody is complete, but it is not lifted;

(2) Seals, Seizes or freezes assets not related to the case;

(3) The sealing, seizure or freezing of assets should be lifted, but they do not do so;

(4) Embezzles, misappropriates, privately distributes, exchanges, or uses sealed, seized, or frozen assets in violation of regulations;

(5) Other conduct that violates laws and regulations or infringes upon the lawful rights and interests of the persons under investigation.

The Supervision Organ that accepts the appeal shall make a decision on its disposition within one month of receiving it. Where the complainant is dissatisfied with the disposition decision, they may apply for a review to the Supervision Organ at the level above within one month of receiving the disposition decision, and the Supervision Organ at level above shall handle make a decision on handling within two months of receiving the application for review, and where the circumstances are true, promptly make corrections.

Article 61: Where after the completion of the investigation, it is discovered that the bases for filing the case was insufficient or inaccurate, there were major mistakes in the handling of the case, or the Supervision personnel seriously violated the law, the responsible leaders and the directly responsible personnel shall be pursued for responsibility.

Chapter VIII: Legal Responsibility

Article 62: Where relevant units refuse to enforce a handling decision made by the Supervision Organs, or refuse to accept a supervision recommendation without legitimate reasons, the department in charge of them or the organ at the level above shall order it to make corrections and circulate a criticism of the unit; and sanctions are to be given to the responsible leaders and directly responsible personnel in accordance with law.

Article 63: Where relevant personnel violate the provisions of this Law with any of the following conduct, their unit, the competent department, the organ at the level above, or the Supervision Organ is to order corrections, and lawfully give sanctions;

(1) refusing to cooperate with the Supervision Organ such as by not providing materials as requested, or by refusing or obstructing the implementation of investigative measures;

(2) Providing false circumstances to conceal the truth;

(3) Colluding testimony, or fabricating, concealing, or destroying evidence;

(4) Preventing others from exposing and reporting or providing evidence;

(5) Having other conduct in violation of the provisions of this Law, where the circumstances are serious.

Article 64: Where targets of supervision retaliate against or frame an accuser, informant, witness, or supervision personnel; or where accusers, informants, or witnesses fabricate facts to falsely accuse or frame the targets of supervision, they are to be dealt with in accordance with law.

Article 65: Where the Supervision Organs or their staffs exhibit any of the following conduct, the responsible leaders and the directly responsible personnel are to be dealt with in accordance with law:

(1) Disposing of leads without permission or authorization, concealing and not reporting major case circumstances after discovering them, or keeping or handling the materials involved in the case without authorization;

(2) Exploiting their authority or the influence of their positions to interfere with investigative work or to seek a personal benefit from the case;

(3) Illegally stealing or disclosing investigation information or leaking information about reported matters, the acceptance of reports, and informants' information;

(4) Extorting or inducing confessions from the persons under investigation or persons implicated in the case, or insulting, beating, berating, abusing, physically punishing, or covertly physically punishing them;

(5) Disposing of sealed, seized, or frozen property in violation of regulations;

(6) Causing case-handling security incidents in violation of regulations, or concealing and not reporting security incidents after they occur, making untruthful reports, or mishandling them;

(7) Employing retention in custody measures in violation of regulations;

(8) Restricting others from exiting the Mainland territory in violation of regulations, or not following regulations to lift restrictions on exiting the Mainland territory;

(9) Other conduct abusing authority, dereliction of duties, or improper conduct for personal gain.

Article 66: Where a violation of the provisions of this Law constitutes a crime, criminal responsibility is to be pursued in accordance with law.

Article 67: Where Supervision Organs and their staffs, in performing their duties, infringe on the lawful rights and interests of citizens, legal persons, and other organizations and cause harm, they shall pay state compensation in accordance with law.

CHAPTER IX: SUPPLEMENTARY PROVISIONS

Article 68: Based on the provisions of this law, the Central Military Commission is to formulate specific provisions on the carrying out of supervision work by the Chinese People's Liberation Army and the Chinese people's armed police forces.

Article 69: This Law takes effect on the date of promulgation. "The Administrative Supervision Law of the PRC" is simultaneously abolished.

Glossary

an quan shi ying daoli 安全是硬道理
bainian weiyou zhi dabianju 百年未有之大变局
bu wang chu xin 不忘初心
chi ren 吃人
chou guan, chou fu 仇官, 仇富
cong yan zhi dang 从严治党
da yi tong 大一统
dang da hai shi fa da 党大还是法大
dang zheng fen jia 党政分家
dao bi gai ge 倒逼改革
datong 大同
dongchang, xichang 东厂西厂
du jiang yan 都江堰
fazhan shi yingdaoli 发展是硬道理
fen shu keng ru 焚书坑儒
gaobie geming 告别革命
guanxi 关系
gong tong fu yu 共同富裕
guojin mintui 国进民退
guo xue yuan 国学院
He Shang 河殇
Huawei 华为
jian cha 监察
jin yi wei 锦衣卫
jiu wang yadao qimeng 救亡压倒启蒙
Kuomintang 国民党
lilun zixin 理论自信

liuzhi 留置
mei you guo, na you jia 没有国，哪有家
min ke you zhi, bu ke zhi zhi 民可由之，不可知之
qi zhe, qi ye 妻者齐也
ren lei mingyun gongtongti 人类命运共同体
Renminbi 人民币
Renmin de mingyi 人民的名义
ru fa zhi zheng 儒法之争
shang shan ruo shui 上善若水
shehui cunzai 社会存在
shehui yishi 社会意识
Shuanggui 双规
Shun 舜
siqing 四清
tao guang yang hui 韬光养晦
tian ming 天命
tianxia 天下
tiaoli 条例
tu cheng 屠城
tuo gu gai zhi 托古改制
wei jun zi 伪君子
wending yadao yiqie 稳定压倒一切
wenhua zixin 文化自信
Wu Quan Xian Fa 五权宪法
wu-tuo-bang 乌托邦
xin minzhu zhuyi geming 新民主主义革命
Xiongnu 匈奴
xiaokang 小康
xinyang que shi 信仰缺失
Yao 尧
yi chushi zhixin zuo rushi zhishi 以出世之心，做入世之事
yi de bao yuan 以德报怨
yi de zhi guo 以德治国
yushi dafu 御史大夫
zhan lang wai jiao 战狼外交
Zhong Nan Hai 中南海
zhongyuan 中原
zi jin ren 紫禁城
zui ji zhao 罪己诏

Notes

Chapter 1

1. I use the term "Chinese Dream," which implies a cultural phenomenon, rather than "China Dream," which connotes the country itself.

2. Zhonggong zhongyang wenxian yanjiushi, ed., *Xi Jinping guanyu shixian Zhonghua minzu weida fuxing de Zhongguo meng: Lunshu gaobian* [Xi Jinping on Realizing the China Dream of the Great Rejuvenation of the Chinese Nation: Discussion Edition] (Beijing: Zhongyang wenxian chubanshe, December 2013), 3, 5.

3. Liu Qibao, "Guanyu zhongguo tese shehui zhuyi lilun tixi de jidian renshi [Some points of understanding concerning the theoretical structure of socialism with Chinese characteristics], *Renmin Ribao* July 8, 2013. http://opinion.people.com.cn/n/2013/0708/c1003-22109528.html.

4. Hua Shiping, "Yifazhiguo de wenhua rentong," [Cultural acceptance of rule according to law], *Renmin luntan* November 17, 2014. http://theory.rmlt.com.cn/2014/1028/335879.shtml.

5. Xinhua News Agency, "Guanyu zhonguomeng, Xi Jinping zongshuji shi zheyang miaohuide [On the Chinese Dream, General Party Secretary Xi Jinping Has This to Say] November 30, 2016. http://news.cctv.com/2016/11/30/ARTIANwy45Nvn1PRGbNqhASG161130.shtml.

6. He Qinhua, "Bainian fazhilu, huihuang zhongguomeng" [A century long road to rule according to the law, the glorious Chinese Dream] *zhongguo sifa*, no. 7, 2022, https://mp.weixin.qq.com/s?__biz=MzI5MzkxMDQ4NQ==&mid=2247511013&idx=2&sn=46d97ec800404addcc61a3437c632fa8&chksm=ec68095fdb1f80491d2fe7261787d31e4b6ce6b3a0963a6a1d7658bfeb43d3ea7b41742981a7&scene=27.

7. Datong literally refers to a Chinese Utopian vision of the world in which everyone and everything is at peace. More details will follow in chapter 2.

8. Xiaokang, a moderately prosperous society, will be discussed in detail in chapter 2.

9. Xinhua News Agency, "Guanyu zhonguomeng, Xi Jinping zongshuji shi zheyang miaohuide (General Party Secretary Xi Jinping Has This To Say on the Chinese Dream).

10. Guo Liangping, "Minzu fuxing ying ju pushi yiyi" (National Rejuvenation Should Embody Universal Values) *Lianhe caobao*, December 23, 2022, https://www.zaobao.com.sg/forum/views/story20221223-1346279.

11. William Callahan, "History, Tradition and the China Dream: Socialist Modernization in the World of Great Harmony," *Journal of Contemporary China* 24, no. 96 (2017): 983–1001, http://dx.doi.org/10.1080/10670564.2015.1030915.

12. Cited in Samuel P. Huntington, *The Clash of Civilizations and the Remaking of World Order* (New York: Simon & Schuster Press, 2011), 109.

13. Chinese Ministry of Foreign Affairs, "Xi Jinping Attends the CPC in Dialogue with World Political Parties High-level Meeting and Delivers a Keynote Speech," March 16, 2023, 23:00, https://www.mfa.gov.cn/eng/zxxx_662805/202303/t20230317_11043656.html.

14. N. Stephen Broadberry, Hanhui Guan, and David D. Li, "China, Europe and the Great Divergence: A Study in Historical National Accounting," *CEPR Discussion Paper* no. DP11972 (April 2017): 980–1850. Available at SSRN: https://ssrn.com/abstract=2957511. Also, https://worldeconomics.com/Share-of-Global-GDP/China.aspx.

15. Zhen Sun, "Utopia, nostalgia, and femininity: visually promoting the Chinese Dream," *Visual Communication* 18, no. 1 (2017): 107–133, https://doi.org/10.1177/1470357217740394.

16. John K. Fairbank, *The United States and China* (Cambridge, MA: Harvard University Press, 1983).

17. Sun Tzu, *The Art of War*, Samuel B. Griffith, trans., B. H. Liddell Hart (foreword) (New York: Oxford University Press, 1971).

18. Peter Zarrow, "Liberalism and Utopianism in the New Culture Movement: Case Studies of Chen Duxiu and Hu Shi," in *Utopia and Utopianism in the Contemporary Chinese Context*, ed. David Der-wei Wang, Angelia Ki Che Leung, and Zhang Yinde (Hong Kong: Hong Kong University Press, 2020), 36–52.

19. Hang Tu, "Anticipatory Utopia and Redemptive Utopia in Post-revolutionary China," in *Utopia and Utopianism in the Contemporary Chinese Context*, ed. David Der-wei Wang, Angela Ki Che Leung and Yinde Zhang.

20. Xin Yuxi, "Songchao zhe san ge huangdi jing jujue dengji, bu kendang huangdi" [The three emperors of Song don't want to be the emperors], blog, March 24, 2023 14:45:01, http://zs.aipingxiang.com/ls/13252.html.

21. Shiping Hua, *Scientism and Humanism: Two Cultures in Post-Mao China* (Albany: State University of New York Press, 1996).

22. This study is also a continuation of my monograph, *Chinese Utopianism: A Comparative Study of Reformist Thought of Japan and Russia* (Stanford, 2009) in which I found that after waves of Chinese utopianism during the twentieth century, it finally subsided during the Dengist period.

23. Guanghua Yu, *The Roles of Law and Politics in China's Development* (New York: Springer, 2014).

24. Albert H. Y. Chen, "China's Long March towards Rule of Law or China's Turn against Law" *The Chinese Journal of Comparative Law* 4 (2016): 1–35, http://doi.org/ 10.1093/cjcl/cxw003.

25. Larry Catá Backer, "The Rule of Law, The Chinese Communist Party, and Ideological Campaigns: Sange Daibiao (The "Three Represents," Socialist Rule of Law, and Modern Chinese Constitutionalism) *Journal of Transnational L & Contemporary Problems* 16, no. 1 (2006).

26. Jacques deLisle, "Law in the China Model 2.0: Legality, Developmentalism and Leninism under Xi Jinping,"

27. Shiping Hua, "A Reversal of the Reform? China's Fifth Constitutional Amendment," *Asian Survey* 60, no. 6 (November/December 2020): 1172–93.

28. Robert G. Sutter, *US-China Relations: Perilous Past, Uncertain Present* (Lanham, MD: Rowman & Littlefield, 2022).

29. Elizabeth C. Economy, "The Third Revolution: Xi Jinping and the New Chinese State," https://www.csis.org/podcasts/chinapower/xi-jinpings-vision-china-conversation-dr-elizabeth-economy. Retrieved June 20, 2023.

30. Mary E. Gallagher, *Authoritarian Legality in China: Law, Workers, and the State* (Cambridge: Cambridge University Press, 2017).

31. Carl Minzner, *The End of an Era: How China's Authoritarian Revival is Undermining its Rise* (New York: Oxford University Press, 2020).

32. Jacques deLisle, "Law in the China Model 2.0: Legality, Developmentalism and Leninism under Xi Jinping."

33. Jeffrey E. Thomas, Chapter 2: "Rule of Law with Chinese Characteristics," in Shiping Hua ed. *Chinese Legality: Ideology, Law and Institutions* (London: Routledge 2022).

34. Rogier J. E. H. Creemers, Susan Trevaskes, *Law and the Party in China: Ideology and Organization* (Cambridge: Cambridge University Press, 2021).

35. Roderick MacFarquar, "China: The Superpower of Mr. Xi," *New York Review of Books* (2013), http://www.nybooks.com/articles/2015/08/13/china-superpower-mr-xi/.

36. Michael A. Peters (2017) "The Chinese Dream: Xi Jinping thought on Socialism with Chinese characteristics for a new era," *Educational Philosophy and Theory* 49, no. 14 (2017): 1299–1304, http://doi.org/10.1080/00131857.2017.1407578.

37. He Qinhua, "Bainian fazhilu, huihuang zhongguomeng" [A century long road to rule according to law, glorious Chinese Dream].

38. Suk-Wai Cheong, "Singapore's sovereignty 'never a given': Bilahari Kausikan," *The Straits Times*, January 30, 2016, http://www.straitstimes.com/singapore/singapores-sovereignty-never-a-givenbilahari-kausikan.

39. Michael X. Y. Feng "The 'Chinese Dream' Deconstructed: Values and Institutions," *Journal of Chinese Political Science* no. 20 (2015): 163–83, http://doi.org/10.1007/s11366-015-9344-4.

40. Christopher A. Ford, "The Party and the Sage: Communist China's Use of Quasi-Confucian Rationalizations for One-party Dictatorship and Imperial ambition," *Journal of Contemporary China* 24, no. 96 (2015): 1032–47, http://dx.doi.org/10.1080/10670564.2015.1030954.

41. William A. Callahan, "History, Tradition and the China Dream: Socialist Modernization in the World of Great Harmony," *Journal of Contemporary China* 24, no. 96 (2015): 983–1001; William A. Callahan, *China Dreams: 20 Visions of the Future* (Oxford: Oxford University Press, 2013).

42. "A Foreign Investment Law is planned to integrate and harmonize long-developing and still-fragmented laws that govern diverse legal vehicles," Jacques deLisle, "Law in the China Model 2.0: Legality, Developmentalism and Leninism under Xi Jinping."

43. Lao Tzu, Stephen Mitchell, trans., *Tao Te Ching*: A New English Version (New York: Harper Perennial Modern Classics, 2006).

44. Kerry Brown, *China's Dream: The Culture of Chinese Communism and the Secret Sources of its Power* (London: Polity, 2018).

Chapter 2

1. James Truslow Adams was the first historian to coin the term "American Dream" in *The Epic of America* (New York: Simon & Schuster, 2001).

2. David B. Gosset, "Xi Jinping—Person of the Year 2013," *The Huffington Post*, December 4, 2013. https://www.huffpost.com/entry/xi-jinping-person-of-the_b_4381233 Retrieved January 20, 2023.

3. Ye Zicheng and Long Quanlin, *Hua Xi Zhuyi* (China-ism) (Beijing: Renmin Chubanshe, 2017), 224–25.

4. He Huifeng, "Parents Angry at Removal of Lu Xun's Works from China's School Textbooks," *South China Morning Post,* September 8, 2013, https://www.scmp.com/news/china/article/1305905/parents-angry-removal-lu-xuns-works-chinas-school-textbooks.

5. Andrea Ghiselli, "Revising China's Strategic Culture: Contemporary Cherry-Picking of Ancient Strategic Thought," *The China Quarterly* 233 (2018): 166–85.

6. Suisheng Zhao, "Rethinking the Chinese World Order: The Imperial Cycle and the Rise of China," *Journal of Contemporary China* 24, no. 96 (2015): 961–82, http://dx.doi.org/10.1080/10670564.2015.1030913.

7. Peng Ming, ed., *Cong kongxiang dao kexue: Zhongguo shehui zhuyi sixiang fazhan de lishi kaocha* (From utopia to science: historical overview of the development of China's socialist thought) (Beijing: Zhongguo Renmin Daxue Chubanshe, 1986), 43.

8. For the translation, see W. T. de Bary, ed., *Sources of Chinese Tradition*, Volume 1 (New York: Columbia University Press, 1960), 176.

9. Charles Snyder identifies three key elements of hope: goals, pathways, and motivation, specifically, you need to have focused thoughts, you must develop strategies in advance in order to achieve these goals, and you have to be motivated to make the effort required to actually reach these goals. C. R. R. Snyder, *Psychology of Hope: You Can Get Here from There* (New York: Free Press, 2003).

10. Shiping Hua, *Chinese Utopianism: A Comparative Study of Reformist Thought of Japan and Russia* (Stanford, CA: Stanford University Press, 2009).

11. Angela Duckworth, *Grit: The Power of Passion and Perseverance* (New York: Scribner, 2018).

12. Karl Mannheim and Louis Wirth, *Ideology and Utopia: An Introduction to the Sociology of Knowledge*, 196.

13. Thomas M. Magstadt and Peter M. Schotten, *Understanding Politics: Ideas, Institutions, and Issues* (New York: St. Martin's Press, 1984).

14. Susan L. Shirk, *China: Fragile Superpower* (London: Oxford University Press, 2008).

15. Chen Zhengyan and Lin Qiyan, *Zhongguo gudai datong sixiang yanjiu* (A study of utopian thought in ancient China) (Shanghai: Renmin Chubanshe, 1986): 84.

16. This is how the *Shi Jing* describes xiaokang: "Now the Great Way has become hidden and the world is the possession of private families. Each regards as parents only his own parents, as sons only his own sons; goods and labor are employed for selfish ends. Hereditary offices and titles are granted by ritual law while walls and moats must provide security. Ritual and rightness are used to regulate the relationship between ruler and subject, to ensure affection between father and son, peace between brothers and harmony between husband and wife, to set up social institutions, organize the farms and villages, honor the brave and wise, and bring merit to the individual. Therefore intrigue and plotting come about and men take up arms. Emperor Yu, Kings Tang, Wen, Wu, Cheng, and the Duke of Zhou achieved eminence for this reason: that all six rulers were constantly attentive to ritual, made manifest their rightness, and acted in complete faith. They exposed error, made humanity their law and humility their practice, showing the people wherein they should constantly abide. If there were any who did not abide by these principles, they were dismissed from their positions and regarded by the multitude as dangerous. This is the period of Lesser Prosperity." For the translation, see William Theodore de Bary and Irene Bloom, *Sources of Chinese Tradition*, Vol. 1, 2nd ed. (New York: Columbia University Press, 1999), 343.

17. Qian Mu, *Zhongguo wenhuashi daolun* (Introduction to Chinese cultural history) (Beijing: Shangwu Chubanshe, 2023).

18. Weber said legitimacy lies in history, charismatic leader, and legal procedure Max Weber, *The Religion of China: Confucianism and Taoism Max Weber, Religion in China* (Springfield, OH: Collier-Macmillan, 1964).

19. Sun Yat-sen, *Sun Zhongshan Quanji*, Vol. 2 (Beijing: Zhonghua Shuju, 1981) 337–39.

20. *Minli Bao,* September 10, 1921.

21. Sun Yat-sen, *Sun Zhongshan Quanji*, 2:524.

22. Huang Jilu, *Yanjiu zhongshan xiansheng de shiliao yu shixue* (Study of Sun Yat-sen Historical Research Center) (Taipei: zhonghua minguo shiliao yanjiu zhongxin, 1981): 557–65.

23. Mao Zedong, *On the People's Democratic Dictatorship: Ideals and Ideologies* (London: Routledge, 2019).

24. Guo Moruo, "Makesi jin wen miao" (Marx enters the Confucian temple), *Hong Shui,* no. 7, 1926.

25. Shiping Hua, "The Deng Reforms and the Gorbachev Reforms Revisited: A Political Discourse Analysis," *Problems of Post Communism* 53, no. 3 (May/June 2006), 3–16.

26. Roderick MacFarquhar, *The Origins of the Cultural Revolution, Vol. 1: Contradictions among the People 1956–1957* (New York: Columbia University Press, 1974). Jiaqi Yan and Gao Gao, *Turbulent Decade: A History of the Cultural Revolution* (Honolulu: University of Hawaii Press, 1996).

27. Liu Zehua, ed., *Zhongguo gudai zhengzhi sixiang shi* (A history of Chinese political thought in pre-modern times) (Tianjin: Nankai Daxue Chubanshe, 1994), 381–95.

28. The concept of "primary stage socialism" that was developed in the late 1970s and early 1980s is the belief that Maoism violated Marxist rules of historical materialism by skipping a stage of the development of capitalism. In order to develop real socialism and communism, China needs to make up the lesson of capitalism.

29. Chen Fong-ching and Jin Guantao. *From Youthful Manuscripts to River Elegy: The Chinese Popular Cultural Movement and Political Transformation 1979–1989* (Hong Kong: Chinese University of Hong Kong Press, 1997), 215–37.

30. Li Zehou and Liu Zaifu, *Gaobie Geming: Huiwang ershi shiji Zhongguo* (Farewell, revolution: Twentieth century China in retrospect) (Hong Kong: Tiandi Tushu youxian gongsi, 1995).

31. Peter Zarrow, *Abolishing Boundaries: Global Utopias in the Formation of Modern Chinese Political Thought (1880–1940)* (Albany: State University of New York Press, 2021); Maurice J. Meisner, *Marxism, Maoism, and Utopianism: Eight Essays* (Madison: University of Wisconsin Press, 1982); Kung-Chuan Hsiao, *Modern China and a New World: Kang Youwei, Reformer and Utopian, 1858–1927* (Seattle: University of Washington Press, 1975); Stuart R. Schram, "To Utopia and Back: A Cycle in the History of the Chinese Communist Party," *The China Quarterly,* no. 87 (September 1981): 407–39; Shiping Hua, *Chinese Utopianism: A Comparative Study of the Reformist Thought of Japan and Russia* (Stanford, CA: Stanford University Press, 2009).

32. Meisner and Hsiao believe that when Western scholars describe Western utopias, they tend to refer to "no place;" when they describe Chinese utopias, they tend to refer to a "better place. Maurice J. Meisner, *Marxism, Maoism, and Utopianism: Eight Essays*, 3, 13; Kung-Chuan Hsiao, *A Modern China and a New World: K'ang Yu-wei, Reformer and Utopian, 1858–1927*, 412.

33. Henry Kissinger, *On China* (New York: Penguin Books, 2012).

34. Thomas A. Metzger, *Escape from Predicament: Neo-Confucianism and China's Evolving Political Culture* (New York: Columbia University Press, 1986).

35. Wolfgang Bauer, *China and the Search for Happiness: Recurring Themes in Four Thousand Years of Chinese Cultural History* (New York: Seabury Press, 1976).

36. There are complex reasons as to why few gigantic social engineering movements have occurred in the West. The most important factor seems to be the lack of a strong state in the West during most historical periods.

37. National Intelligence Council, "Tracking the Dragon: National Intelligence Estimate on China during the Era of Mao, 1948–1976," May 13, 1967 and "Economic Outlook for Communist China," May 25, 1965 (Washington DC: National Intelligence Council, 2004), 494.

38. Similarly, Stuart Schram observes that, for the Chinese, "the subjective creates the objective." Stuart R. Schram, "To Utopia and Back: A Cycle in the History of the Chinese Communist Party," 422.

39. For Plato, wisdom and morality are the same, and the bottom line of his wisdom is logic, rationality, and consistency. Plato believed that humans are not naturally kind and that good people often do not have a good ending. Plato, *The Republic* trans. Richard W. Sterling and William C. Scott (New York: W. W. Norton, 1985): 48–49, 56–61.

40. In the words of Roger Ames, Greek thought is rational, while traditional Chinese thought is "biographical." Roger Ames, "New Confucianism: A Native Response to Western Philosophy," in Shiping Hua ed., *Chinese Political Culture* (Armonk, NY: M. E. Sharpe, 2001), 70–102.

41. Li Zehou and Liu Zaifu, *Gaobie Geming: Huiwang ershi shiji Zhongguo* (Farewell, revolution: Twentieth Century China in retrospect), 82.

42. Metzger, *Escape from Predicament*, 154–158, see also 220.

43. Karl Mannheim and Louis Wirth, et al. *Ideology and Utopia: An Introduction to the Sociology of Knowledge* (Eastford, CT: Martino Fine Books, 2015), 196.

44. Karl Marx, "The German Ideology" [1846], in Robert C. Tucker, ed., *The Marx-Engels Reader* (New York: W. W. Norton, 1978): 163.

45. Karl Marx, "Preface to a Contribution to the Critique of Political Economy" [1859], in Robert C. Tucker, ed., *The Marx-Engels Reader*.

46. Karl Marx and Friedrich Engels, "Manifesto of the Communist Party" [1848], in Robert C. Tucker, ed., *The Marx-Engels Reader*, 475.

47. Shiping Hua, "The Deng Reforms and the Gorbachev Reforms Revisited: A Political Discourse Analysis."

48. Jiaqi Yan, Gao Gao, *Turbulent Decade: A History of the Cultural Revolution* (Shaps Library of Translations) (Honolulu: University of Hawaii Press, 1996).

49. "Legalism" is a school of Chinese philosophy that became influential during the Warring States era (475–221 BCE) developed by the philosophers Shang Yang, Li Si, and Han Fei, that was instrumental in the establishment of China's first imperial dynasty, the Qin (221–207 BCE). Legalism insists that for good governance laws should be strictly applied instead of using arbitrary personal control. This is discussed further in Chapter 2.

50. Mao favored Legalism, because of the widely held belief that Legalism helped the Qin Empire to unify China. Another ambiguity is that Mao promoted Confucian datong but rejected Confucianism as a way of life.

51. World Bank data, https://data.worldbank.org/indicator/NE.TRD.GNFS.ZS?locations=CN. Retrieved August 31, 2023.

52. "Rule by law" is a concept that views the governing authority as above the law, with the power to make and enforce law wherever it is useful, regardless of the impact on human freedom. Examples include Qin's control of people through laws rather than arbitrary personal oppression; Nazi Germany's imprisonment of Jews in concentration camps in accordance with a law that permitted such abuse; and South Africa's apartheid regime's use of racially discriminatory laws against the Blacks.

53. Ai Siqi. *Bianzheng weiwu zhuyi he lishi weiwu zhuyi* (Dialectical materialism and historical materialism) (Beijing: Renmin Chubanshe, 1961).

54. Shiping Hua, "Yifazhiguo de wenhua rentong" (Cultural integration of rule of law), *Renmin Luntan*, 459, November 1, 2014.

55. Lynn White, "Chinese Constitutional Currents." *Modern China* 36, 1 (2010): 100–114.

56. Xinhua News Agency, "Guanyu zhongguomeng, Xi Jinping zongshuji shi zheyang miaohuide (On the Chinese dream, General Party Secretary Xi Jinping has this to say).

57. Scott Kennedy," The Myth of the Beijing Consensus," *Journal of Contemporary China* 19, no. 65 (2010): 461–477; 470.

58. Barry Naughton, Kellee S. Tsai, eds. *State Capitalism, Institutional Adaptation, and the Chinese Miracle* (Comparative Perspectives in Business History) (New York: Cambridge University Press, 2015). Also, Margaret M. Pearson, Meg Rithmire, Kellee Tsai, *The State and Capitalism in China* (Elements in Politics and Society in East Asia) (New York: Cambridge University Press, 2023).

59. For the connection between market and law in general and that during the Xi era in particular, please refer to Max Weber, *The Religion of China: Confucianism and Taoism Max Weber, Religion in China* (Springfield, OH: Collier-Macmillan, 1964); Jacques deLisle, "Law in the China Model 2.0: Legality, Developmentalism

and Leninism under Xi Jinping" *Journal of Contemporary China*, 26, no. 103 (2017): 68–84. http://dx.doi.org/10.1080/10670564.2016.1206299.

60. Xinhua News Agency, "Guanyu zhonguomeng, Xi Jinping zongshuji shi zheyang miaohuide [On Chinese Dream, General Party Secretary Xi Jinping Has This to Say].

61. Barry Naughton and Kellee S. Tsai eds. *State Capitalism, Institutional Adaptation, and the Chinese Miracle* (London: Cambridge University Press, 2015); Margaret M. Pearson and Meg Rithmire and Kellee Tsai, *The State and Capitalism in China* (London: Cambridge University Press, 2023).

62. Xinhua News Agency, "Xi Jinping: Rang shichang ze ziyuan peizhizhong qi jueding zuoyong, bu neng huidao jihuajingji de laolushang qu (Xi Jinping: Let the market play a decisive role: We can't go back to planned economy), May 23, 2020, https://www.gov.cn/xinwen/2020-05/23/content_5514220.htm. Retrieved February 20, 2023.

63. Xinhua News Agency, "Guanyu zhonguomeng, Xi Jinping zongshuji shi zheyang miaohuide (On the Chinese dream, General Party Secretary Xi Jinping has this to say).

64. Rainer Zitelmann, "State capitalism? No, the private sector was and is the main driver of China's economic growth," *Forbes*, September 30, 2019, https://www.forbes.com/sites/rainerzitelmann/2019/09/30/state-capitalism-no-the-private-sector-was-and-is-the-main-driver-of-chinas-economic-growth/?sh=64504db527cb. Retrieved March 20, 2023.

65. Max Weber, *The Religion of China*, 149.

66. This is based on a talk by Renmin University Professor Wen Tiejun, https://quanmin.baidu.com/sv?source=shareh5&pd=qm_share_search&vid=4934058254553649271. Retrieved August 1, 2023.

67. Tianlei Huang and Nicolas Véron, "The Private Sector's Share of China's Largest Listed Companies Continued to Decline to 43 Percent in the Second Half of 2022," Peterson Institute for International Economics, February 2, 2023, https://www.piie.com/blogs/realtime-economics/private-sectors-share-chinas-largest-listed-companies-continued-decline-43. Retrieved April 10, 2023.

68. Weber, *The Religion of China*, 241.

69. Katrin Blasek, *Rule of Law in China: A Comparative Approach* (New York: Springer, 2015).

70. Karen G. Turner, "Rule of Law Ideals in Early China?" *Columbia Journal of Asian Law* 6, no. 1 (1992): 1–44. See also Karen G. Turner, *The Limits of the Rule of Law in China* (Seattle: University of Washington Press, 2000).

71. Jacques deLisle, "Law in the China Model 2.0: Legality, Developmentalism and Leninism under Xi Jinping."

72. Jacques deLisle, "Law in the China Model 2.0: Legality, Developmentalism and Leninism under Xi Jinping."

73. Chris Buckley, "China Internal Security Jumps Past Army Budget," *Reuters*, March 5, 2011.

74. Congyan Cai, "Enforcing a New National Security—China's National Security Law and International Law," *Journal of East Asia & International Law* 10, no. 65 (2017): 65–81, 70.

75. Dong Xiaobo and Zhang Yafang. "Translation and Research of Traditional Chinese Legal Classics." *China Legal Science* 9, no. 3 (May 2021): 23–58.

76. Dong Xiaobo and Zhang Yafang. "Translation and Research of Traditional Chinese Legal Classics."

77. Isaac Kardon, "Rule by Law: China's Increasingly Global Legal Reach." Carnegie Endowment for International Peace, May 4, 2023, https://carnegieendowment.org/sada/89688. Retrieved July 20, 2023; Jeffrey E. Thomas, "Rule of Law with Chinese Characteristics," Chapter 2; Haig Patapan, "Legalism and the Xi Jinping Thought: Han Fei's Influence on Contemporary Chinese Politics and Law," Chapter 4, in Shiping Hua, ed., *Chinese Legality: Ideology, Law and Institutions* (London: Routledge, 2022).

78. Chen Zhiwu, *wenming de luoji* (The logic of civilizations) (Beijing: Zhongxin Chubanshe, 2022).

79. Congyan Cai, "Enforcing a New National Security—China's National Security Law and International Law," *Journal of East Asia & International Law*, Vol. 10, no. 65 (2017), 70.

80. Ye Zicheng, and Long Quanlin, *Hua Xia Zhuyi (China-ism)* (Beijing: Renmin Chubanshe, 2017), 224.

81. *Han Fei Tzu: Basic Writings*, Translated by Burton Watson (New York: Columbia University Press, 2003).

82. The Xi regime is also described as "neo-totalitarian." David Shambaugh, "The Evolution of American Contemporary China Studies: Coming Full Circle?," *Journal of Contemporary China*, 2023, http://doi.org/10.1080/10670564.2023.2237918.

83. Fu Zhengyuan, *China's Legalists: The Earliest Totalitarians and their Art of Ruling* (Armonk and London: M. E. Sharpe, 1996).

84. Chungying Cheng, "Legalism versus Confucianism: A Philosophical Appraisal," *Journal of Chinese Philosophy* 8 (1981): 271–302.

85. Shang Yang, *The Book of Lord Shang. a Classic of the Chinese School of Law* (New York: Lawbook Exchange Ltd., 2011): 20, 121.

86. Shang Yang, *The Book of Lord Shang: A Classic of the Chinese School of Law*, 17: 101.

87. Burton Watson, *Han Fei Tzu: Basic Writings*.

88. Ibid.

Chapter 3

1. Shiping Hua, *Chinese Legal Culture and Constitutional Order*, chapter 9 (London: Routledge, 2019).

2. Robert Sutter believed that "the Obama government remained positive about US–Chinese relations to the end of its tenure"; Robert Sutter, "The United States and Asia in 2017: The Impact of the Trump Administration," *Asian Survey* 58, no. 1 (February 2018): 10–20.

3. Neil J. Diamant, Stanley Lubman, and Kevin O'Brien, *Engaging the Law in China: State, Society and Possibilities for Justice* (Stanford, CA: Stanford University Press, 2005), 4; Ma Jihong, "The Constitutional Law of the People's Republic of China and its Development." *Columbia Journal of Asian Law* 23, no. 1 (2009) 175; Randall Peerenboom, "Law and Development of Constitutional Democracy: Is China a Problem Case?" *The Annals of the American Academy of Political and Social Science* 603 (2006): 192, 8; Lynn White, "Chinese Constitutional Currents," *Modern China* 36, no. 1 (2010): 100–14; Randall Peereboom, *China's Long March toward Rule of Law* (London: Cambridge University Press, 2002), 44.

4. Jianfu Chen, "The Revision of the Constitution in the PRC: A Great Leap Forward or a Symbolic Gesture?" *China Perspectives* 53 (2004): 1–20.

5. Kerry Brown, "Ideology in the Era of Xi Jinping."

6. Jiang Zemin, *Lun sange daibiao (On Three Represents)* (Beijing: Zhongyang wenxian chubanshe. 2001), 168–70.

7. Klimeš and Marinelli, "Introduction: Ideology, Propaganda, and Political Discourse in the Xi Jinping Era."

8. Full text of Xi Jinping's report at 19th CPC National Congress. http://www.xinhuanet.com/english/special/2017-11/03/c_136725942.htm.

9. Suisheng Zhao, "The Ideological Campaign in Xi's China Rebuilding Regime Legitimacy."

10. CCP Central Committee Party History Research Office, "Treating the Two Periods Before and After the Reform Correctively," *People's Daily*, November 8, 2013, 6.

11. http://news.dwnews.com/global/news/2018-09-10/60083752.html.

12. Wang Weiguang, "There is s Nothing Wrong with Adhering to the People's Democratic Dictatorship," *Qiushi*, September 23, 2014, http://www.qstheory.cn/dukan/hqwg/2014-09/23/c_1112586776.htm.

13. Deng Xiaoping, *Help the People Understand the Importance of the Rule of Law,* http://web.peopledaily.com.cn/english/dengxp/vol3/text/c1540.html.

14. The following was cut: "The party leadership largely refers to the leadership in the areas of politics, ideology and organization." The following was added: "The CCP is the key feature of socialism with Chinese characteristics."

15. https://mp.weixin.qq.com/s/7hvuKhCoCAA_lXZeg9rzBQ?.

16. http://www.wenxuecity.com/news/2018/08/28/7577533.html.

17. Zhao, "The Ideological Campaign in Xi's China Rebuilding Regime Legitimacy."

18. Xu Chongde, "Peng Zhen yu 1982 nian xianfa de xiugai gongzuo," (Peng Zhen and the revision of the 1982 Constitution), July 16, 2015, CCP History website: http://www.zgdsw.org.cn/n/2015/0716/c244516-27316121.html.

19. General Outline: the following was added: "Mao Zedong thought, theory of Deng Xiaoping, Three Represents' thought, scientific development outlook and the Xi Jiping thought about socialism with Chinese characteristics in the new era. Also, in Article 23, the following was added: "in the Central Military Commission, the Chairman is in charge."

20. http://www.wenxuecity.com/news/2018/03/08/7043819.html.

21. Francis Fukuyama, "China's Bad Emperors," *Washington Post*, https://www.washingtonpost.com/news/theworldpost/wp/2018/03/06/xi/?nid&utm_term=.cfee54a2f020; Elizabeth C. Economy, "China's Imperial President," *Foreign Affairs* (November–December 2014).

22. General Outline: the phrase with a line through it was cut: "At the present, the main contradiction of the Chinese society is between the people's increasing desire for a higher living standard and the backward social productivity and the unbalanced, underdevelopment,"https://mp.weixin.qq.com/s/s5emniSZ1EDYvixOA-NBGg.

23. Actually, Western scholars found some similarity between Zhu Yuanzhang and Mao Zedong. Anita M. Andrew and John A. Rapp, *Autocracy and China's Rebel Founding Emperors: Comparing Chairman Mao and Ming Taizu* (Lanham, MD: Rowman & Littlefield, 2000).

24. Jonathan Spence, God's Chinese Son: The Taiping Heavenly Kingdom of Hong Xiuquan (New York: W. W. Norton & Company, 1996).

25. http://www.chinadaily.com.cn/a/201803/11/WS5aa5471da3106e7dcc140e7c.html.

26. Franz Schurmann, *Ideology and Organization of Communist China* (Berkeley: University of California Press, 1966).

27. Ai Siqi, *Bianzheng weiwu zhuyi, lishi weiwu zhuyi (Dialectical Materialism and Historical Materialism)* (Beijing: Renmin chubanshe, 1983).

28. Roderick MacFarquhar, *The Origins of the Cultural Revolution* 3 (New York: Columbia University Press, 1999).

29. Maurice Meissner, "Marxism, Maoism, and Social Change: A Reexamination of the 'Voluntarism' in Mao's Strategy and Thought. A Response, F Wakeman," *Modern China* 3, no. 2 (1977): 161–68.

30. Jiang, *Lun Sange Daibiao (On Three Represents)*, 19, 49.

31. Shiping Hua, "All Roads Lead to Democracy," *Bulletin of Concerned Asian Scholars* (now *Critical Asian Studies*) 24, no. 1 (January–March 1992): 43–56.

32. Zhang Wei, "shehuizhuyi chujijieduan lilun de lishi fazhan yuqishi" (The theory of primary stage of socialism's development and insights) *Guangxi shehui kexue* 164, no. 2 (2009): 6–9.

33. David Shambaugh, "Contemplating China's Future," *Journal of Chinese Political Science* (2018): 23, 1–7.

34. Yang Guangbin, "Xi Jinping Zhongzhi sixiang tixi chutan" (A Primary Study on Xi Jinping's Political Thought System), *Xue Hai*, no. 4, 2017, *Renmin University*, https://mp.weixin.qq.com/s/wC1ed9f1y9zqCmEW58JdEA.

35. http://www.china.com.cn/guoqing/2015-08/31/content_36459844.htm.

36. Yang, "Xi Jinping Zhongzhi sixiang tixi chutan" (A Primary Study on Xi Jinping's Political Thought System).

37. Kerry Brown, "Ideology in the Era of Xi Jinping."

38. Yang, "Xi Jinping Zhongzhi sixiang tixi chutan" (A Primary Study on Xi Jinping's Political Thought System).

39. Xi Jinping, *How to Deepen Reform Comprehensively* (Beijing: Foreign Languages Press, 2014), 9.

40. Yang, "Xi Jinping Zhongzhi sixiang tixi chutan" (A Primary Study on Xi Jinping's Political Thought System).

41. Ibid.

42. Xinhua News Agency, "Guanyu zhongguomeng, Xi Jinping zongshuji shi zheyang miaohuide [On Chinese Dream, General Party Secretary Xi Jinping has this to say] November 30, 2016, http://news.cctv.com/2016/11/30/ARTIANwy45 Nvn1PRGbNqhASG161130.shtml.

43. Xi Jinping, "Xi Jinping zai zhongfa jianjiao 50 zhoujian jinian dahui shangde jianghua," (Speech on the 50th Anniversary of the Establishment of Sino-French Diplomatic Relations), https://news.12371.cn/2014/03/28/ARTI1395961336034916.shtml.

44. Xi Jinping, "Xieshou xiaochu pinkun, cujin gongtong fazhan," (Eliminating poverty hand in hand, promote joint development) *Renmin Ribao*, October 17, 2015, http://cpc.people.com.cn/n/2015/1017/c64094-27709112.html.

45. Lu Xun, *The Real Story of Ah-Q and Other Tales of China: The Complete Fiction of Lu Xun* (London: Penguin, 2010).

46. Wang Min, *Lilun yu shijian yanjiu: Jiang Zemin shehuizhuyi wenhua jianshe* (Studies of theories and practice: Jiang Zemin's socialist cultural construction) (Jinan: Shangdong Renmin Chubanshe, 2005), 635.

47. Jiang Zemin. *Lun sange daibiao* (On Three Represents) (Beijing: Zhongyang Wenxian Chubanshe. 2001): 37.

48. "Jiaoyubu fawen: Yiwu jiaoyu bude shiyong jingwai jiaocai (Free Education Can't Use Foreign Text Materials). *Xinjing Bao*, January 7, 2020, https://view.inews.qq.com/wxn/20200107A07VKV00?tbkt=B5&pushid=2020010702&strategy=&openid=o04IBAHH7C8vWnfXMxtBJ4VAIvxs&uid=&sharer=o04IBAHH7C8vWnfXMxtBJ4VAIvxs&shareto=&key=&version=1800272c&devicetype=iOS16.5.1&wuid=oDdoCt8Zf30JhT5j7TJ6jJAwkntU&openwith=wxmessage&hiter=false&originPath=w2.

49. Xi Jinping: Jiejian lishi youxiu lianzheng wenhua, buduan tigao jufu fangbian nengli (Make use of the Clean Governance Experience in Chinese Culture, Raise the Capacity of Anti-Corruption), 2013. *Renmin Net*, http://politics.people.com.cn/n/2013/0420/c1001-21214843.html.

50. The following was added: "glorifying the traditional Chinese virtues and morality" (Art. 3 [8]).

51. Qiu Feng, "Rujia zuowei xiandai Zhongguo zhi jiangouzhe" (Confucianism as the constructor of modern China) *Wenhua zongheng* (Beijing), February 2014, 68–73.

52. https://www.worldbank.org/en/news/press-release/2022/04/01/lifting-800-million-people-out-of-poverty-new-report-looks-at-lessons-from-china-s-experience.

53. https://data.worldbank.org/country/china. https://data.worldbank.org/indicator/SI.POV.GINI?locations=CN.

54. Jesse Turiel, Edward Cunningham, and Anthony Saich, "To Serve the People: Income, Region and Citizen Attitudes towards Governance in China (2003–2016)" *The China Quarterly*, no. 906 (2019): 906–935.

55. Mao Zedong, "Where Do Correct Ideas Come From?," in *The Chinese Cultural Revolution: Selected Documents,* ed. K. H. Fan (New York: Monthly Review Press, 1968), 31–32.

56. https://www.bbc.com/news/magazine-30483762.

57. Full text of Xi Jinping's report at the 19th CPC National Congress. http://www.xinhuanet.com/english/special/2017-11/03/c_136725942.htm.

58. https://www.business-standard.com/article/international/china-lifting-800-million-people-out-of-poverty-is-historic-world-bank-117101300027_1.html.

59. Bob Davis, "What's a Global Recession?," *Wall Street Journal*, April 22, 2009.

60. Hu Angang stated that China will surpass the United States in economic power by 1.15 times, science and technology by 1.31 times and overall country power by 1.36 times by 2016; Hu Angang, "dui zhongmei zonghe guoli de pinggu" (1990–2013) (Evaluation of the Country Power of the United States and China), *Journal of Tsinghua University (Philosophy and Social Sciences)* no. 1 (2015), https://mp.weixin.qq.com/s/aZhkA_y-3_pxFJa75nCNYQ.

61. Adam Tooze, *Crashed: How a Decade of Financial Crises Changed the World* (New York: Viking, 2018).

62. Francis Fukuyama, "America: The Failed State." *Prospect,* January 2017.

63. https://www.worldbank.org/en/news/speech/2018/11/01/world-bank-group-president-jim-yong-kim-remarks-at-the-international-forum-on-chinas-reform-and-opening-up-and-poverty-reduction.

64. Samuel Huntington, *The Third Wave: Democratization in the Late 20th Century* (Oklahoma: University of Oklahoma Press, 1993).

65. Arch Puddington and Tyler Roylance, "Anxious Dictators, Wavering Democrats," *Journal of Democracy* 27, no. 2 (2016): 86–100; Lowell Dittmer, "Asia in 2017 Return of the Strongman," *Asian Survey* 58, no. 1 (January/February 2018): 1–9.

66. Francis Fukuyama, *The End of History and the Last Man* (New York: Free Press, 2006).

67. Francis Fukuyama, *Political Order and Political Decay: From the Industrial Revolution to the Present Day* (New York: Farrar, Straus and Giroux, 2014).

68. Eric Hobsbawm, *The Age of Extremes: The Short Twentieth Century, 1914–1991* (New York: Vintage, 1994).

69. Joseph A. Schumpeter, *Capitalism, Socialism and Democracy* (New York: Harper Perennial Modern Classics, 2008).

70. "Xi Jinping's Anticorruption Campaign: How Big is its Scope? What is its Goal (*Xi Jinping* defanfu yundong: fanwei youduoguang Mubiao shishenme)" BBC, October 23, 2017. http://www.bbc.com/zhongwen/simp/chinese-news-41719314.

71. https://asia.nikkei.com/Spotlight/China-People-s-Congress-2018/China-spending-puts-domestic-security-ahead-of-defense.

72. Zhongyang Dangxiao zhongguo tese shehuizhuyi lilun tixi yanjiuzhongxin, "Xi Jinping xinshidai zhongguo teseshehuizhuyi sixiang shi yige xitongwanzheng, luojiyanmi de kexue lilun tixi," (Xi Jinping New Era Socialist Thought with Chinese Characteristics Is a Comprehensive and Logically Tight Scientific Theory), *Guangming Ribao*, November 28, 2017.

73. The term refers to those children of the first-generation revolutionaries.

74. Haig Patapan and Yi Wang, "The Hidden Ruler: Wang Huning and the Making of Contemporary China," *Journal of Contemporary China* 27, no. 109 (2018): 47–60, https://doi.org/10.1080/10670564.2017.1363018.

Chapter 4

1. Weixing Hu, "Xi Jinping's 'Big Power Diplomacy' and China's Central National Security Commission (CNSC)," *Journal of Contemporary China* 25, no. 98 (2016): 163–77, http://dx.doi.org/10.1080/10670564.2015.1075716; Ji You, "China's National Security Commission: Theory, Evolution and Operations," *Journal of Contemporary China*, 25, no. 98 (2016): 178–96, http://dx.doi.org/10.1080/10670564.2015.1075717.

2. Joel Wuthnow, "China's Much-Heralded NSC Has Disappeared: Is It a Sign of Beijing's Secrecy or Xi Jinping's Weakness?" *Foreign Policy*, June 30, 2016, https://foreignpolicy.com/2016/06/30/chinas-much-heralded-national-security-council-has-disappeared-nsc-xi-jinping/ (accessed September 26, 2023).

3. David Lampton, "Xi Jinping and the National Security Commission: Policy Coordination and Political Power," *Journal of Contemporary China* 24, no. 95 (2015): 759–77.

4. A. Wolfers, "National Security as an Ambiguous Symbol," *Political Science Quarterly* 67 (1952).

5. Hitoshi Nasu, "The Expanded Conception of Security and International Law," *Amsterdam Law Forum* 3, no. 20 (2011).

6. Anton Grizold, "The Concept of National Security in the Contemporary World," *International Journal on World Peace*, 11, no. 3 (September 1994): 37–53.

7. Congyan Cai, "Enforcing a New National Security—China's National Security Law and International Law," *Journal of East Asia and International Law* 10, no. 65 (2017): 65–89.

8. Edward Wong, "Security Law Suggests a Broadening of China's 'Core Interests,'" *New York Times*, July 2, 2015, https://archive.nytimes.com/www.nytimes.com/2015/07/03/world/asia/security-law-suggests-a-broadening-of-chinas-core-interests.html.

9. Hu, "Xi Jinping's 'Big Power Diplomacy' and China's Central National Security Commission (CNSC)."

10. Jeremy Brown, *June Fourth: The Tiananmen Protests and Beijing Massacre of 1989* (Cambridge: Cambridge University Press, 2021).

11. Wang Yi, "Speech on China's Diplomacy," December 31, 2014, http://www.fmprc.gov.cn/mfa_chn/wjb_602314/wjbz_602318/zyjhs/t1224950.shtml.

12. https://blogs.worldbank.org/trade/trade-and-development-chart-rise-china (accessed January 14, 2024).

13. You, "China's National Security Commission: Theory, Evolution and Operations," *Journal of Contemporary China*.

14. Kenneth Lieberthal, "Introduction: the 'Fragmented Authoritarianism' Model and its Limitations, in Kenneth Lieberthal and David M. Lampton, eds, *Bureaucracy, Politics, and Decision Making in Post-Mao China* (Berkeley, CA: University of California Press, 1992): 6–8.

15. You, "China's National Security Commission: Theory, Evolution and Operations," *Journal of Contemporary China*.

16. Joel Wuthnow, "China's New Black Box: Problems and Prospects for the Central National Security Commission," *The China Quarterly* 232, no. 886 (2017).

17. Ankit Panda, "The Truth About China's New National Security Law," *The Diplomat*, https://thediplomat.com/2015/07/the-truth-about-chinas-new-national-security-law/ (accessed September 29, 2023).

18. Aadil Brar, "Xi Says 'National Security' 50 Times at Party Congress & China Sees Rare Protest against Him," *The Print*, https://theprint.in/opinion/chinascope/xi-says-national-security-50-times-at-party-congress-china-sees-rare-protest-against-him/1170804/ (accessed September 29, 2023).

19. Ralf Emmers, "Securitization," in *Contemporary Security Studies*, ed. Alan Collins (Oxford: Oxford University Press, 2010), 142.

20. Tang Aijun, "Ideological Security as National Security," CSIS, edited by Jude Blanchette, December 2020, https://www.csis.org/analysis/ideological-security-national-security.

21. Mao Zedong, *The Chinese Revolution and the Chinese Communist Party* (Beijing: Foreign Languages Press, 1968).

22. Core socialist values are the national values of "prosperity," "democracy," "civility," and "harmony;" the social values of "freedom," "equality," "justice" and the "rule of law;" and the individual values of "patriotism," "dedication," "integrity" and "friendship." Frank N. Pieke, *Knowing China* (Cambridge: Cambridge University Press, 2016), 24.

23. Jeffrey S. Lantis, "Strategic Culture and National Security Policy," *International Studies Review* 4, no. 3 (Autumn 2002): 87–113.

24. Tang, "Ideological Security as National Security."

25. Xinhua News Agency, "Focus on Five Points in the New National Security Law," (jujiao xin guojia anquanfa wu da liangdian), July 1, 2015, http://www.xinhuanet.com//politics/2015-07/01/c_1115787097_2.htm.

26. Tang, "Ideological Security as National Security."

27. Anthony J. Spires, "Lessons from Abroad: Foreign Influences on China's Emerging Civil Society," *China Journal* 68 (July 2012): 125–46.

28. From 2007 through 2012, Xi Jinping was the President of the Central Party School.

29. National Defense University of China, "Jiaoliang wusheng (Silent Competition)," April 27, 2019, https://www.youtube.com/watch?v=-TjJsRi3VMg (accessed September 29, 2023).

30. Karrie J. Koesel, "The Rise of a Chinese House Church: The Organizational Weapon," *The China Quarterly* 572, no. 215 (2013): 572–89.

31. Shiping Hua and Ming Xia, eds., "The Battle between the Chinese Government and the Falun Gong," *Chinese Law and Government*, 32, no. 5 (September–October 1999).

32. Koesel, "The Rise of a Chinese House Church: The Organizational Weapon."

33. Ibid.

34. Ronald Inglehart and Christian Welzel, *Modernization, Cultural Change, and Democracy* (New York: Cambridge University Press, 2005).

35. Surya P. Subedi, "China's Approach to Human Rights and the UN Human Rights Agenda," *Chinese Journal of International Law* 14, no. 3 (2015): 437–64.

36. Peter Lorentzen and Suzanne Scoggins, "Understanding China's Rising Rights Consciousness," *China Quarterly* 223 (2015): 638–57.

37. Tang, "Ideological Security as National Security."

38. https://www.c-span.org/video/?c4813522/user-clip-jiang-zemin-gettysburg-address.

39. Xiaohui Wu, "From Assimilation to Autonomy: Realizing Ethnic Minority Rights in China's National Autonomous Regions," *Chinese Journal of International Law* 13, no. 1 (2014): 55–90.

40. Ben Hillman and Graw Tuttle eds., *Ethnic Conflict and Protest in Tibet and Xinjiang: Unrest in China's West* (New York: Columbia University Press, 2016).

41. John Powers, *Introduction to Tibetan Buddhism* (Ithaca, NY: Snow Lion Publications, 2007).

42. Wu, "From Assimilation to Autonomy: Realizing Ethnic Minority Rights in China's National Autonomous Regions."

43. United Nations, "China: UN Experts Alarmed by Separation of 1 Million Tibetan Children from Families and Forced Assimilation at Residential

Schools," February 6, 2023, https://www.ohchr.org/en/press-releases/2023/02/china-un-experts-alarmed-separation-1-million-tibetan-children-families-and.

44. Lindsay Maizland, "China's Repression of Uyghurs in Xinjiang," September 22, 2022, Council on Foreign Relations, https://www.cfr.org/backgrounder/china-xinjiang-uyghurs-muslims-repression-genocide-human-rights.

45. BBC, "Hong Kong National Security Law: What Is It and Is It Worrying?" June 28, 2022, https://www.bbc.com/news/world-asia-china-52765838.

46. Stephan Ortmann "Legality and the Hong Kong Protests," in *Chinese Legality: Ideology, Law and Institutions*, ed. Shiping Hua (London: Routledge, 2019).

47. Shiping Hua, ed., *Reflections on the Triangular Relations of Beijing-Taipei-Washington since 1995: Status Quo at the Taiwan Strait?* (New York: Palgrave Macmillan, 2006).

48. Yan Siqi, "Taiwan chaoye yizhi fandui dalu guojia anquanfa (Taiwan's Ruling and Oppositions Parties Are against National Security Law)," BBC, July 2, 2015, https://www.bbc.com/zhongwen/trad/china/2015/07/150702_taiwan_china_security-law_reax.

49. Chinese Ministry of Foreign Affairs, "Set Aside Dispute and Pursue Joint Development," https://www.fmprc.gov.cn/eng/ziliao_665539/3602_665543/3604_665547/200011/t20001117_697808.html (accessed September 29, 2023).

50. Andrew S. Ericksona and Adam P. Liffb, "Installing a Safety on the 'Loaded Gun'? China's Institutional Reforms, National Security Commission and Sino–Japanese Crisis (In)stability," *Journal of Contemporary China*, 25, no. 98 (2016): 197–215, http://dx.doi.org/10.1080/10670564.2015.1075713.

51. Jennifer Jett, "China's New Map Outrages its Neighbors," September 1, 2023, NBC, https://www.nbcnews.com/news/world/china-new-map-anger-india-south-china-sea-border-disputes-rcna102921.

52. M. Taylor Fravel, *Strong Borders, Secure Nation: Cooperation and Conflict in China's Territorial Disputes* (Princeton: Princeton University Press, 2008).

53. Kevin Breuninger and Eamon Javers "Communist Party Cells Influencing U.S. Companies' China Operations, FBI Director Wray says," CNBC, July 12, 2023. https://www.cnbc.com/2023/07/12/communist-cells-influence-companies-in-china-fbi-director.html.

54. Reuters, "China Wants to Mobilise Entire Nation in Counter-espionage," August 1, 2023, https://www.reuters.com/world/china/china-wants-mobilise-entire-nation-counter-espionage-2023-08-01/?utm_source=Sailthru&utm_medium=-Newsletter&utm_campaign=Daily-Briefing&utm_term=080123.

55. https://www.nytimes.com/2023/07/12/magazine/semiconductor-chips-us-china.html (accessed on January 14, 2024).

56. Prabir Purkayastha, "US Chip Ban De Facto Declaration of War on China?" *Asia Times*, October 29, 2022, https://asiatimes.com/2022/10/us-chip-ban-de-facto-declaration-of-war-on-china/.

57. *Qiu Shi Net*, 2023-09-27, https://mp.weixin.qq.com/s/jyjrBhWWJYt8C_z Bvstaew.

58. The United States government accused Beijing of having "reinforced a zero-sum dynamic in the world economy where China's growth and prosperity come at the expense of workers and economic opportunity here in the U.S. and other market-based democratic economies," https://ustr.gov/about-us/policy-offices/press-office/speeches-and-remarks/2021/october/remarks-prepared-delivery-ambassador-katherine-tai-outlining-biden-harris-administrations-new.

59. For how the United States tried to shape the policy choices of China during the reform era, see Christensen (2015).

60. Mackenzie Eaglen, "10 Ways the United States Is Falling Behind China in National Security," American Enterprise Institute, https://www.jstor.org/stable/resrep52691, accessed September 17, 2023.

61. Song Zhihong, "National Security vs. Privacy Protection: Research on Practices in the United States after the September 11 Attacks," *China Legal Science*, 2, no. 4 (2014): 88–114.

62. Cai, "Enforcing a New National Security—China's National Security Law and International Law."

63. Stephanie D. Hinnershitz, *Japanese American Incarceration* (Philadelphia: University of Pennsylvania Press, 2022).

64. Rein Mullerson, "Human Rights Are Neither Universal Nor Natural," *Chinese Journal of International Law* 17, no. 4 (2018): 925–42.

65. Shiping Hua, *Chinese Utopianism: A Comparative Study of Reformist Thought with Japan and Russia (1898–1997)* (Stanford, CA: Stanford University Press, 2009).

66. Chris Hogg, "China Ends Death Penalty for 13 Economic Crimes." BBC, February 25, 2011.

67. Chenjie Ma, "China's Death Penalty Practice Undermines the Integrity of the Death Penalty as a Sentencing Option," *Australian Journal of Asian Law*, 15, no. 2 (2014): 151–67.

68. Wu, "From Assimilation to Autonomy: Realizing Ethnic Minority Rights in China's National Autonomous Regions."

69. Cai, "Enforcing a New National Security—China's National Security Law and International Law."

70. *The Guardian*, "US, Japan, EU Team Up to Warn China of Concerns over New Security Laws," March 1, 2016, https://www.theguardian.com/world/2016/mar/01/us-japan-eu-team-up-to-warn-china-of-concerns-over-new-security-laws (accessed September 29, 2023).

71. United Nations Human Rights, "UN Human Rights Chief Says China's New Security Law is Too Broad and Vague," https://www.ohchr.org/en/press-releases/2015/07/un-human-rights-chief-says-chinas-new-security-law-too-broad-too-vague#:~:text=China%20%2F%20new%20law%20on%20national%20security&

text=%E2%80%9CThis%20law%20raises%20many%20concerns,%2C%E2%80%9D%20High%20Commissioner%20Zeid%20said (accessed September 29, 2023).

72. Chun Han Wong, "China Adopts Sweeping National-Security Law," *Wall Street Journal*, https://www.wsj.com/articles/china-adopts-sweeping-national-security-law-1435757589 (accessed September 29, 2023).

73. Ankit Panda, "The Truth about China's New National Security Law," *The Diplomat*, https://thediplomat.com/2015/07/the-truth-about-chinas-new-national-security-law/ (accessed September 29, 2023).

74. Elizabeth Economy, "China's Imperial President: Xi Jinping Tightens his Grip," *Foreign Affairs* (November/December 2014): 80–91; Kathleen McLaughlin, "Chinese Power Play: Xi Jinping Creates a National Security Council," *Christian Science Monitor*, November 13, 2013, http://www.csmonitor.com/World/Asia-Pacific/2013/1113/Chinese-powerplay-Xi-Jinping-creates-a-national-security-council (accessed September 29, 2023).

75. You, "China's National Security Commission: Theory, Evolution and Operations."

76. https://baike.baidu.com/item/人民的名义/17545218?fr=ge_ala.

77. https://www.britannica.com/biography/Jack-Ma (accessed November 8, 2023).

Chapter 5

1. It was passed by the NPC in 1997 and revised in 2010.

2. Kilkon Ko and Cuifen Weng, "Critical Review of Conceptual Definitions of Chinese Corruption: A Formal-Legal Perspective," *Journal of Contemporary China* 20, no. 70 (2011): 359–78.

3. Tobias Smith, "Power Surge: China's New National Supervisory Commission," in *China Story Yearbook 2018: Power*, eds. Jane Golley, Linda Jaivin, Paul J. Farrelly, and Sharon Strange (Canberra: Australian National University Press, 2018), 32–35; J. T. Deng, "The National Supervision Commission: A New Anti-Corruption Model in China," *International Journal of Law Crime and Justice* 52 (2018): 58–73; Li Li and Peng Wang, "From Institutional Interaction to Institutional Integration: The National Supervisory Commission and China's New Anti-Corruption Model," *The China Quarterly* 240 (2019): 967–89.

4. Tian Linan, "On the Procedural Supervision over Interrogation in Investigation," *China Legal Science* 9, no. 5 (2021): 111–36.

5. Liu Mingyu, "Nature of New Power of Supervision and Judicial Supervision," *China Legal Science* 7 (2019): 123–25; Zheng Yinglong and Yang Ping, "Three Significant Dimensions in the Connection of Supervision System Reform and Judicial System Reform in China," *China Legal Science* 85, no. 5 (2021): 85.

6. Li Li and Peng Wang, "From Institutional Interaction to Institutional Integration: The National Supervisory Commission and China's New Anti-Corruption Model."

7. Louise Shelley, "The Soviet Police and the Rule of Law," *Police Innovation and Control of the Police Problems of Law, Order, and Community*, ed. Lorraine Green, David Weisburd, and Craig Uchida (New York: Springer, 1993), 127–44.

8. Zhou Zhen, "Jianguo chuqi Xin San Fan Yundong Shuping," [A new interpretation of the Three Antis in the early 1950s], *Journal of UESTC* 13, no. 2 (2011): 77–82.

9. Roderick MacFarquhar, *The Hundred Flowers Campaign and the Chinese Intellectuals* (New York: Praeger, 1960).

10. Lowell Dittmer, *Liu Shaoqi and the Chinese Cultural Revolution* (Armonk, NY: M. E. Sharpe, 1997).

11. Zheng Chang "Understanding the Corruption Networks Revealed in the Current Chinese Anti-Corruption Campaign: A Social Network Approach," *Journal of Contemporary China* 27, no. 113 (2018): 113, 735–47.

12. Ting Gong, "Dangerous Collusion: Corruption as a Collective Venture in Contemporary China," *Communist and Post-Communist Studies* 35 no. 1 (2002): 85–103.

13. Max Weber, *The Religion of China: Confucianism and Taoism* (New York: Free Press, 1968).

14. Angang Hu, "Corruption and Social Inequality," *Jiangsu Social Sciences* no. 3 (2001): 51–53.

15. Melanie Manion, *Corruption by Design-Building Clear Government in Mainland China and Hong Kong* (Cambridge, MA: Harvard University Press, 2004).

16. Cheng Chen, "Ideology-Building under Hu Jintao: Reacting to Jiang and Paving the Way for Xi," in *Chinese Ideology* ed. Shiping Hua (London: Routledge, 2021).

17. Chris Buckley, "China Internal Security Jumps Past Army Budget," *Reuters*, March 5, 2011.

18. Jin Guantao and Liu Qingfeng, *Xingsheng yu Weiji: Zhongguo shehui chao wending jiegou* [Ultra-stable structure of China's feudal system] (Beijing: falu chubanshe, 2011).

19. The first peasant rebellion occurred around the eighth century. In the following eight hundred years, there were only about seven or eight peasant rebellions in the several dozen countries in Western Europe. Above all, none of the dynasties was overthrown by peasant rebellions. Zhang Hongjie, *Daming wangchao de qige miankong (Seven faces of the Ming Empire)* (Guangzhou: Guangdong renmin chubanshe, 2016).

20. Mencius, *Mencius*, D. C. Lau, trans. (London: Penguin, 2005).

21. Han Fei Tzu, *Basic Writings,* Burton Watson, trans. (New York: Columbia University Press, 1964).

22. Dong Xiaobo and Zhang Yafang, "Translation and Research of Traditional Chinese Legal Classics," *China Legal Science* 9, no. 3 (May 2021): 23–58.

23. Roger T. Ames and Henry Rosemont, *The Analects of Confucius: A Philosophical Translation* (New York: Ballantine, 1999), 35.

24. Norman P. Ho, "The Legal Thought of Emperor Taizong of the Tang Dynasty (618–907)," *Frontiers of Law in China* 12, no. 4 (2017): 584–625.

25. Chen Si, "Mao Zedong yu 24 shi," (Mao Zedong and the 24 histories), *Xue Xi Shi bao,* August 7, 2019, http://dangshi.people.com.cn/n1/2019/0807/c85037-31280331.html?ivk_sa=1024320u.

26. Yang Shang, *The Book of Lord Shang. a Classic of the Chinese School of Law* (Clark, NJ: Lawbook Exchange, 2011).

27. Patricia Buckley Ebrey, ed., *Chinese Civilization: A Sourcebook* (New York: Free Press, 1993), 205–6.

28. Zhu Gongliang, "Zhu Yuanzhan zhili jintan xi" (An analysis of Zhu Yuanzhang's Anti-Corruption efforts) *She Hui Kexue* (Social Science) 11 (1991); Anita M. Andrew and John A. Rapp, *Autocracy and China's Rebel Founding Emperors* (Lanham, MD: Rowman & Littlefield, 2000).

29. Confucius, *The Analects.* 2/3. Cited in Roger T. Ames and Henry Rosemont, Jr., *The Analects of Confucius* (New York: Ballantine, 1998).

30. Ho, "The Legal Thought of Emperor Taizong of the Tang Dynasty (618–907)."

31. Wang Zhonghan, "Tian Weijing Zhuan," [Biography of Tian Wenjing] in *Qing Shi Lie Zhuan* ed., Wang Zhonghan (Biographies of Qing), Vol. 13 (Beijing: Zhong Hua Shuju, 2016), 961.

32. Wenshan Jia, *The Remaking of the Chinese Character and Identity in the 21st Century: The Chinese Face Practices* (Westport, CT: Praeger, 2001).

33. "Nearly 1 Million People Sit China's Civil Servant Exam," *China Daily,* December 2, 2018, https://www.chinadaily.com.cn/a/201812/02/WS5c03fee3a310eff30328e850_5.html.

34. Joseph Fewsmith, "Balances, Norms and Institutions: Why Elite Politics in the CCP Have Not Institutionalized," *The China Quarterly* 248 (2021): 265–82.

35. Minxin Pei, "China in 2017: Back to Strongman Rule," *Asian Survey* 58, no. 1 (2018): 21–32; Murray Scot Tanner, "China in 2015: China's Dream, Xi's Party, *Asian Survey* 56, no. 1 (2016): 19–33.

36. Larry Catá Backer, "The Rule of Law, the CCP and Ideological Campaigns," *Journal of Transnational Law and Contemporary Problems* 16 no. 1 (2006): 6.

37. Patricia M. Thornton, "The Advance of the Party: Transformation or Takeover of Urban Grassroots Society," *The China Quarterly* 213 (2013): 1–18.

38. Li Li and Peng Wang, "From Institutional Interaction to Institutional Integration: The National Supervisory Commission and China's New Anti-Corruption Model."

39. Joseph Fewsmith, "Balances, Norms and Institutions: Why Elite Politics in the CCP Have Not Institutionalized," *The China Quarterly*, no. 248 (2021): 265–82.

40. Hualing Fu, "China's Striking Anti-Corruption Adventure: A Political Journey towards the Rule of Law?" in *The Beijing Consensus? How China Has Changed the Western Ideas of Law and Economic Development*, ed. Weitseng Chen (Cambridge: Cambridge University Press, 2016), 249–74.

41. Li Li and Peng Wang, "From Institutional Interaction to Institutional Integration: The National Supervisory Commission and China's New Anti-Corruption Model."

42. CGTN "China's Draft Supervision Law: What Is It, Why Does It Matter?." March 13, 2018, https://news.cgtn.com/news/346b6a4d796b7a6333566d54/index.html.

43. Li Li and Peng Wang, "From Institutional Interaction to Institutional Integration: The National Supervisory Commission and China's New Anti-Corruption Model."

44. Li Li and Peng Wang, "From Institutional Interaction to Institutional Integration: The National Supervisory Commission and China's New Anti-Corruption Model."

45. Carolin Kautz, "Power Struggle or Strengthening the Party: Perspectives on Xi Jinping's Anticorruption Campaign, *Journal of Chinese Political Science* no. 25 (2020): 501–11.

46. Xuezhi Guo, "Controlling Corruption in the Party: China's Central Discipline Inspection Commission," *The China Quarterly* 597 (2014): 597–624.

47. Ting Gong, "Managing Government Integrity under Hierarchy: Anti-Corruption Efforts in Local China," *Journal of Contemporary China* 24, no. 94 (2015): 684–700, http://dx.doi.org/10.1080/10670564.2014.978151.

48. Hui Li, Ting Gong, Hanyu Xiao, "The Perception of Anti-Corruption Efficacy in China: An Empirical Analysis," *Social Indicators Research* 3 (2016): 885–903.

49. G. Z. Chen, "Several Views on the Reform of China's Supervisory System," *Global Law Review* 2 (2017): 115–17.

50. Ling Li, "The 'Organisational Weapon' of the Chinese Communist Party China's Disciplinary Regime from Mao to Xi Jinping," in *Law and the Party in China: Ideology and Organization*, ed. R. Creemers and S. Trevaskes (Cambridge: Cambridge University Press, 2020).

51. Jinting Deng, "The National Supervision Commission: A New Anti-Corruption Model in China," *International Journal of Law, Crime and Justice* 52 (2018): 58–73.

52. *Renmin Ribao*, March 14, 2018.

53. Jin Guantao and Liu Qingfeng, *Xingsheng yu Weiji: Zhongguo shehui chao wending jiegou* (Ultra-stable structure of China's feudal system) (Beijing: falu chubanshe, 2011).

54. Carl Minzner, *The End of an Era: How China's Authoritarian Revival is Undermining Its Rise* (New York: Oxford University Press, 2020).

55. Shiping Hua, "Yifazhiguo de wenhua rentong" [Cultural Integration of Rule of Law], *Renmin Luntan*, 459, November 1, 2014.

56. Shuanggui is also based on 2010 Administrative Supervision Law (xin zheng jian cha fa) and the 1994 "CCP Discipline Inspection Institutions Cases Investigation Statutes" (zhonguo gongchandang jilu jiancha jiguan anjian jiancha tiaoyue).

57. Article 20 of the 2010 Supervision Law states that "supervision officials cannot detain or quasi-detain those under investigation."

58. Li Li and Peng Wang, "From Institutional Interaction to Institutional Integration: The National Supervisory Commission and China's New Anti-Corruption Model."

59. Amnesty International, "China: New Supervision Law a Systemic Threat to Human Rights," 2018, https://www.amnesty.org/en/latest/news/2018/03/china-new-supervision-law-threat-to-human-rights/.

60. Jianchi sige zixin, buwang chuxin jixuqianjin [Stick to four self-confidences, remember the original belief and march forward], July 10, 2016, *hualong net*, https://finance.ifeng.com/a/20160710/14581205_0.shtml.

61. John Foley, "Zhu Rongji Merits China's Admiration Not Imitation," *Reuters*, August 14, 2014.

62. Abby Liu, "Hiding $2.34 Trillion in China," *Global Voices*, March 7, 2013, http://global voicesonline.org/2013/03/07/chinese-households-have-2-34-trillion-in-hidden-income/.

63. Hou Liqiang, "Chinese Transfer $458.3 Billion Overseas in 2011," *China Daily*, January 22, 2014, http://europe.chinadaily.com.cn/business/2014-01/22/content_17253790.htm.

64. John Kennedy, "China Has at Least 1.8 Million Ready-to-Flee 'Naked Officials,' Anti-Corruption Rant Reveals," *South China Morning Post*, February 27, 2013.

65. Dexter Roberts, "Almost Half of China's Rich Want to Emigrate," *Bloomberg Business Week*, September 15, 2014, http://www.businessweek.com/articles/2014-09-15/almost-half-of-chinas-richwant-to-emigrate, Retrieved August 6, 2023.

66. Samuel Rubenfeld, "Report: Corrupt Chinese Officials Take $123 Billion Overseas," *Wall Street Journal*, June 16, 2011, https://www.wsj.com/articles/BL-CCB-4598.

67. Rahul Karan Reddy, "China's Anti-Corruption Campaign: Tigers, Flies, and Everything in Between." *The Diplomat*, May 12, 2022, https://thediplomat.com/2022/05/chinas-Anti-Corruption-campaign-tigers-flies-and-everything-in-between/.

68. *CCTV Net*: http://news.cctv.com/2019/01/29/ARTI6iircEygj7E2tCFNQxsN190129.shtml (accessed August 7, 2023).

69. Rahul Karan Reddy, "China's Anti-Corruption Campaign: Tigers, Flies, and Everything in Between."

70. Sebastian Rotella and Kirsten Berg, "Operation Fox Hunt: How China Exports Repression Using a Network of Spies Hidden in Plain Sight." July 22, 2021.

Propublica, https://www.propublica.org/article/operation-fox-hunt-how-china-exports-repression-using-a-network-of-spies-hidden-in-plain-sight.

71. https://freedomhouse.org/report/transnational-repression/china (accessed August 31, 2023).

72. Bertram Lang, "China's Anti-graft Campaign and International Anti-Corruption Norms: Towards a New International Anti-Corruption Order?," *Crime Law and Social Change* 70 (2018): 331–47.

73. Bradley Jardine and Natalie Hall, "The International Community Must Resist China's Abuse of Interpol." *Newsweek*, November 19, 2021, https://www.newsweek.com/international-community-must-resist-chinas-abuse-interpol-opinion-1650890.

74. Jiangnan Zhu, "Out of China's Reach: Globalized Corruption Fugitives," *The China Journal* 86, no. 4 (2021): 90–113.

75. About 43 percent of countries require their public servants to disclose their income to the public: https://www.worldbank.org/en/news/press-release/2012/11/08/only-fourty-three-percent-countries-disclose-public-officials-financial-assets-says-world-bank.

76. Li Li and Peng Wang, "From Institutional Interaction to Institutional Integration: The National Supervisory Commission and China's New Anti-Corruption Model."

77. Xinhua News Agency, "Supervision Law Gives Legal Teeth to China's Graft-Busting Agency," March 20, 2018, http://www.chinadaily.com.cn/a/201803/20/WS5ab1172da3106e7dcc143eef.html.

78. *Beijing ribao*, "Guojia jianwei chengli yizhounian, ganle zhexie dashi" [NSC has done the following big things since its establishment a year ago] March 23, 2019, https://baijiahao.baidu.com/s?id=1628761705695287129&wfr=spider&for=pc.

79. Andrew Wedeman, "Policing the Police, Party, and State: Corruption and Anti-Corruption in China," Chapter 11 in *Chinese Legality: Ideology, Law and Institutions*, ed. Shiping Hua (London: Routledge, 2022).

80. https://www.transparency.org/en/cpi/2021/index/chn (accessed August 2, 2023).

81. *Zhongguo jianchabao*, "Shinianlai fafubai douzheng chengxiao youmu gongdu, chenggong zouchu yikao zhidu youshi,fazhi youshi fafubai zhilu," [Everybody can see that the Anti-Corruption campaign has achieved a lot. The achievement is because of the superiority of the system, and rule according to law], October 16, 2022. http://fanfu.people.com.cn/n1/2022/1016/c64371-32546268.html. Retrieved July 20, 2023.

Chapter 6

1. Xianchu Zhang, "The New Round of Civil Law Codification in China," *University of Bologna Law Review* 1, no. 1 (2016): 106–37.

2. Michael Gow, "The Core Socialist Values of the Chinese Dream: Towards a Chinese Integral State," *Critical Asian Studies* 49, no. 1 (2017): 92–116.

3. Wei Wen, "China's New General Provisions of Civil Law: Changes and Advancements for the Better," *LAWASIA Journal* (January 2018). https://papers.ssrn.com/sol3/papers.cfm?abstract_id=3171363.

4. Larry A DiMatteo and Lei Chen, eds., *Chinese Contract Law: Civil and Common Law Perspectives* (Cambridge: Cambridge University Press, 2017).

5. Mark D. Kielsgard and Lei Chen, "The Emergence of Private Property Law in China and Its Impact on Human Rights," *Asian-Pacific Law & Policy Journal* 15, no. 1 (2014): 94–134.

6. Tiantian Zhai and Yen-Chiang Chang. "The Contribution of China's Civil Law to Sustainable Development: Progress and Prospects," *Sustainability* 11, no. 1 (2019): 294.

7. Bing Ling, "The New Contract Law in the Chinese Civil Code," *Chinese Journal of Comparative Law* 8, no. 3 (2020): 558–634.

8. Suisheng Zhao, "Deng Xiaoping's Southern Tour: Elite Politics in Post-Tiananmen China," *Asian Survey* 33, no. 8 (1991): 739–56.

9. "Primary stage socialism" is based on the historical materialism's belief that human society progresses through different stages, from lower level to higher level of development: from slavery society, to feudal society, to capitalist society and then finally to communist society. Socialism is the primary stage communism. Chinese theoreticians at the beginning of the reform believed that Mao made the mistake of trying to skip the stage of capitalism and jump into communism prematurely. Ai Siqi, *Bianzheng weiwu zhuyi, lishi weiwu zhuyi (Dialectical Materialism and Historical Materialism)* (Beijing: Renmin chubanshe, 1983).

10. Lei Chen, "The Historical Development of the Civil Law Tradition in China: A Private Law Perspective," *Legal History Review* 78, no. 1 (September 2009): 159–81.

11. Robert Service, *A History of Twentieth-Century Russia* (Cambridge, MA: Harvard University Press, 1997): 124–25.

12. Hua-yu Li, "The Political Stalinization of China: The Establishment of One-Party Constitutionalism, 1948–1954," *Journal of Cold War Studies* 3 (2001): 28–47.

13. Shiping Hua, *Chinese Legal Culture and Constitutional Order* (London: Routledge, 2019).

14. Yen-lin Chung, "The Witch-Hunting Vanguard: The Central Secretariat's Roles and Activities in the Anti-Rightist Campaign," *China Quarterly* 206 (2011): 391–411.

15. Roderick MacFarquhar, *The Origins of the Cultural Revolution*, Volume 3 ed. (New York: Columbia University Press, 1999).

16. Stuart R. Schram, "Economics in Command? Ideology and Policy Since the Third Plenum, 1978–84," *China Quarterly* 99 (September 1984): 417–61.

17. Jude Howell, "NGOs and Civil Society: The Politics of Crafting a Civic Welfare Infrastructure in the Hu-Wen Period," *China Quarterly* 237 (2019): 58–81.

18. Cheng Chen, "Ideology-Building Under Hu Jintao: Reacting to Jiang and Paving the Way for Xi," in *Chinese Ideology*, ed. Shiping Hua (London: Routledge, 2021).

19. Chris Buckley, "China Internal Security Spending Jumps Past Army Budget," *Reuters*, March 4, 2011.

20. Keith Zhai, Gabriel Crossley, and Yew Lun Tian, "China Set to Implement Its First Civil Code, as Private Investment Slows," *Reuters*, May 21, 2020, http://www.reuters.com/article/us-china-parliament-civil-code/china-set-to-implement-its-first-civil-code-as-private-investment-slows-idUSKBN22X0TC.

21. Ibid.

22. Chris Chung, "Drawing the U-Shaped Line: China's Claim in the South China Sea, 1946–1974," *Modern China* 42, no. 1 (2016): 38–72.

23. Huo Zhengxin, "China Enters an Era with a Civil Code," *C. J. Observer*, May 29, 2020, www.chinajusticeobserver.com/a/china-enters-an-era-with-a-civil-code.

24. Hua, *Chinese Legal Culture and Constitutional Order*.

25. Zhai, et al., "China Set to Implement Its First Civil Code, as Private Investment Slows."

26. Charlie Chen, "Waiting for China's Precarious Housing Bubble to Burst," *The Politic* (accessed April 25, 2021), https://thepolitic.org/waiting-for-chinas-precarious-housing-bubble-to-burst/.

27. Youqin Huang, Shenjing He, and Li Gan, "Introduction to Special Issue: Unpacking the Chinese Dream of Homeownership." *Journal of Housing and the Built Environment* 36 (2021): 1–7.

28. Rödl and Partner, "China's Civil Code" (accessed April 27, 2021), http://www.roedl.com/insights/china-civil-code/china-adopts-civil-code.

29. Ibid.

30. Huo, "China Enters an Era with a Civil Code."

31. Wu Guo, "Why the Chinese People Are Invisible in US Media" (accessed April 26, 2021), http://www.thinkchina.sg/why-chinese-people-are-invisible-us-media.

32. Daxue Consulting, "Behind the Industry of Counterfeit Products in China and Lawsuit Success Cases" (accessed April 27, 2021), https://daxueconsulting.com/counterfeit-products-in-china/.

33. Reedsmith, "The Adoption of the Chinese Civil Code and Its Implications on Contracts Relating to China."

34. CSIS, "How Well-off Is China's Middle Class?" (accessed April 27, 2021), https://chinapower.csis.org/china-middle-class/.

35. Shiping Hua, "The Politics of Gender in the Chinese New Cinema," *Hong Kong Journal of Social Sciences* 12 (Autumn 1998): 53–65.

36. Yuxiao Shan and Han Wei, "In Depth: Decoding China's First Civil Code," *Politics & Law*, June 1, 2020, http://www.caixinglobal.com/2020-06-01/in-depth-decoding-chinas-first-civil-code-101561290.html.

37. G. A. Cohen, "The Labor Theory of Value and the Concept of Exploitation," *Philosophy and Public Affairs* 8, no. 4 (1979): 338–60.

38. Yang Yang, "Over 84% Companies in China Are Private," *China Daily*, November 28, 2019.

39. Rebecca Hamlin, "Civil Rights," *Britannica* (accessed May 11, 2021), http://www.britannica.com/topic/civil-rights.

40. *Stanford Encyclopedia of Philosophy* (accessed May 11, 2021), https://plato.stanford.edu/entries/civil-rights/.

41. H. Jiao, "Wuquanfa (Cao'an) de Hexianxing Fenxi" [Constitutional Analysis on the Property Law]. *Legal Science* 3 (2006): 39–41.

42. Scott Ikeda, "China's New Civil Code Would Be a Historic Expansion of Privacy Rights—Assuming It's Consistently Enforced." *CPO Magazine*, June 11, 2020, http://www.cpomagazine.com/data-protection/chinas-new-civil-code-would-be-a-historic-expansion-of-privacy-rights-assuming-its-consistently-enforced/.

43. Keith Zhai, Gabriel Crossley, and Yew Lun Tian, "China Set to Implement Its First Civil Code, as Private Investment Slows." *Reuters*, May 21, 2020, http://www.reuters.com/article/us-china-parliament-civil-code/china-set-to-implement-its-first-civil-code-as-private-investment-slows-idUSKBN22X0TC.

44. Ikeda, "China's New Civil Code Would Be a Historic Expansion of Privacy Rights—Assuming It's Consistently Enforced."

45. Chris Gill, "Insights Into China's New Civil Code." *Asia Times Financial*, May 31, 2020, http://www.asiatimesfinancial.com/insights-into-china-s-new-civil-code.

46. Zhai et al., "China Set to Implement Its First Civil Code, as Private Investment Slows."

47. Ikeda, "China's New Civil Code Would Be a Historic Expansion of Privacy Rights—Assuming It's Consistently Enforced."

48. Zhai, etc., "China Set to Implement Its First Civil Code, as Private Investment Slows."

49. Ikeda, "China's New Civil Code Would Be a Historic Expansion of Privacy Rights—Assuming It's Consistently Enforced."

50. Di Wang, "Jia, as in Guojia: Building the Chinese Family into a Filial Nationalist Project." *China Law and Society Review* 5 no. 1 (2020): 1–32.

51. Chris Gill, "Insights Into China's New Civil Code." *Asia Times Financial*, May 31, 2020, http://www.asiatimesfinancial.com/insights-into-china-s-new-civil-code.

52. BBC. 2021. "The Rising Cost of a Chinese Bride Price." *BBC*, http://www.bbc.com/news/blogs-trending-35727057.

53. Tian Lu, "First-ever Chinese Civil Code Adopted at National Legislature: No 'IP Section,' Yet Still Relevant." *IPKIT*, May 31, 2020, http://ipkitten.blogspot.com/2020/05/first-ever-chinese-civil-code-adopted.html.

54. Shan et al., "In Depth: Decoding China's First Civil Code."

55. Peter Moody, "Some Reflections on Xi Jinping's Political Thought." In *Chinese Ideology*, ed. Shiping Hua (London: Routledge, 2021); Chris Buckley, "China Enshrines 'Xi Jinping Thought,' Elevating Leader to Mao-Like Status," *New York Times*, October 24, 2017.

56. David J. Lorenzo, "Sun Yat-sen and The San Min Chu I Lectures as Ideology," in *Chinese Ideology*, ed. Shiping Hua (London: Routledge, 2021).

57. Anthony H. F. Li, "Centralisation of Power in the Pursuit of Law-based Governance Legal Reform in China Under the Xi Administration," *China Perspectives* 2 (2016): 63–68.

58. Michael W. Dowdle, "Heretical Laments: China and the Fallacies of 'Rule of Law,'" *Cultural Dynamics* 11 no. 2 (1999): 287.

59. Democracy (Jiang and Wallace, Sept. 3, 2000).

60. Yiu-chung Wong, "Assessing the Era of Jiang Zemin," in *Chinese Ideology*, ed., Shiping Hua.

61. Guangcheng Chen, "The Supreme Court Rules That If the Law Did Not Stipulates, Then the Judge Can Rule Based on Ideological Considerations," *Radio Free Asia*, March 17, 2021.

62. Radio France International 2021.

63. Yizhu Yu, "Cong xibai wenge dao huifu lishixing dingxing, zhongguo jiaokeshu xiugai beihou fasheng le shenmo (From *White Wash the Cultural Revolution to Restore the Renouncing it, What Is Going on Behind the Chinese Textbook Revisions*)." *Duowei News*, September 7, 2020, http://www.dwnews.com/中国/60210791/

64. See *South China Morning Post*: "Xi Jinping: China to stick to Communist rule and its own path to cope with 'unimaginable' perils," https://www.scmp.com/news/china/politics/article/2178471/xi-china-stick-communist-rule-and-its-own-path-cope-unimaginable.

65. Randall Peerenboom, *China Modernizes: Threat to the West or Model for the Rest?* (New York: Oxford University Press, 2008); Alvin Y. So, *Social Change and Development: Modernization, Dependency and World-System Theories* (Newbury Park, CA: SAGE, 1990).

66. Samuel Huntington, *The Third Wave: Democratization in the Late 20th Century* (Oklahoma City: University of Oklahoma Press, 1993).

67. Guobin Zhu, Jian Qu, and Han Zhai, "Paradigm Shift in Chinese Legal Studies," in *Paradigm Shifts in Chinese Studies*, ed. Shiping Hua (London: Palgrave Macmillan, 2021).

68. Kielsgard et al., "The Emergence of Private Property Law in China and Its Impact on Human Rights."

69. Donald F. Lach, "Leibniz and China." *Journal of the History of Ideas* 6, no. 4 (1945): 436–55.

70. Xianchu Zhang, "The New Round of Civil Law Codification in China." *University of Bologna Law Review* 1, no. 1 (2016): 106–37.

Chapter 7

1. VOA, "zhongguo duiwai guanxifa: quefa xinyi de fanzhi xuanyan" (China's Foreign Relations Law: A Declaration on Sanctions that is Lack of Novelty) July 7, 2023. https://www.voachinese.com/a/china-launches-foreign-relations-law-in-response-to-suppression-of-its-development-20230707/7171283.html.

2. "Xi Jinping zongshuji guanyu zhongguo meng de jiqing huayu" (General Secretary Xi Jinping's Excellent Statements on the Chinese Dream),' *Renmin Ribao*, November 30, 2012, 1.

3. Björn Alexander Düben, "Xi Jinping and the End of Chinese Exceptionalism," *Problems of Post-Communism*, 67, no. 2 (2020): 111–28, http://doi.org/10.1080/10758216.2018.1535274. Also see Rein Müllerson, "The Nation-State: Not Yet Ready for the Dustbin of History?," *Chinese Journal of International Law* 20 (2021): 699–725.

4. Public Trust in Government: 1958–2023, *Pew Research*, https://www.pewresearch.org/politics/2023/09/19/public-trust-in-government-1958-2023/.

5. Chinese intellectuals who either directly or indirectly advise the Chinese government. Shiping Hua, "One Servant, Two Masters: The Dilemma of Chinese Establishment Intellectuals," *Modern China* 20, no. 1 (1994) 92–121.

6. Peter J. Katzenstein, *The End of the American Order* (Ithaca, NY: Cornell University Press, 2022).

7. Gordon Barrass and Nigel Inkster, "Xi Jinping: The Strategist Behind the Dream," *Survival*, 60, no. 1 (2018): 41–68.

8. Tsinghua University, CISS, fabu [zhongguo ren de guoji Anquan guan "minyi diaocha baogao (2023) (Chinese People's View on International Security: Public Opinion Survey Report) https://m.thepaper.cn/baijiahao_23190848 accessed in September 29, 2024.

9. Andrea Ghiselli, "Revising China's Strategic Culture: Contemporary Cherry-Picking of Ancient Strategic Thought," *The China Quarterly* 233 (2018) 166–185.

10. "Zhongguo ren de guoji Anquan guan minyi diaocha baogao" (Chinese People's International Security View: A Survey) https://mp.weixin.qq.com/s/Il6CdcCEMFpL4Gfz3ENM5g (accessed September 29, 2023).

11. Weixing Hu, "Xi Jinping's 'Major Country Diplomacy': The Role of Leadership in Foreign Policy Transformation," *Journal of Contemporary China*, 28, no. 115 (2019): 1–14.

12. James Char and Richard A. Bitzinger, "A New Direction in the People's Liberation Army's Emergent Strategic Thinking, Roles and Missions," *China Quarterly* 232 (2017): 841–65.

13. Björn Alexander Düben, "Xi Jinping and the End of Chinese Exceptionalism," *Problems of Post-Communism*, 67, no. 2 (2020): 111–28.

14. Steve Tsang, "Party-state Realism: A Framework for Understanding China's Approach to Foreign Policy," *Journal of Contemporary China*, 29, no. 122 (2020): 304–18.

15. *South China Morning Post*, June 29, 2023.

16. Ignacio de la Rasilla and Yayezi Hao, "The Community of Shared Future for Mankind and China's Legalist Turn in International Relations," *Chinese Journal of International Law* 20, no. 2 (2021): 341–79.

17. VOA, "Zhongguo duiwai guanxifa: quefa xinyi de fanzhi xuanyan" (China's Foreign Relations Law: A Declaration on Sanctions that is Lack of Novelty) July 7, 2023, https://www.voachinese.com/a/china-launches-foreign-relations-law-in-response-to-suppression-of-its-development-20230707/7171283.html.

18. Bingna Guo, James Hsiao, Bob Li, and Royston C. Tan, "The Law on Foreign Relations of the People's Republic of China Became Effective on 1 July 2023," *Whitecase* July 20, 2023. https://www.whitecase.com/insight-alert/law-foreign-relations-peoples-republic-china-became-effective-1-july-2023.

19. *Voice of Germany* "Fazhi xifang zhicai, zhongguo tui duiwai guanxifa" (Counter Sanctions of the West, China Promulgated Foreign Relations Law), June 29, 2023.

20. Ministry of Foreign Affairs, "Xi Jinping Attends the CPC in Dialogue with World Political Parties High-level Meeting and Delivers a Keynote Speech," March 16, 2023, https://www.mfa.gov.cn/eng/zxxx_662805/202303/t20230317_11043656.html.

21. Zhao Tingyang, *Tianxia tixi: Shijie zhidu zhexue daolun (The Under-Heaven System: The Philosophy for the World Institution)* (Beijing: Zhongguo Renmin Chubanshe, 2011): 1.

22. Editorial, "Never Relax Ideological Works: Implementing the National Propaganda and Thought Work Conference Spirit," *Qiushi*, no. 17, September 1, 2013, http://www.qstheory.cn/zxdk/2013/201317/201308/t20130827_264732.htm.

23. Jacques deLisle, "Law in the China Model 2.0: Legality, Developmentalism and Leninism under Xi Jinping," *Journal of Contemporary China*, 26, no. 103 (2017): 68–84.

24. Francis Fukuyama, *The End of History and the Last Man* (New York: Free Press, 2006).

25. Liu Xiang, *Zhan Guo Ce* 5 (Shanghai: Shanghai Guji Chubanshe, 1978), 190.

26. Confucius, *The Analects*, Li ji, Liyun.

27. Sheng Hong, "Rujia de waijiao yuanze jiqi dangdai yiyi," (Confucian Foreign Policy Principles and Contemporary Significance) *Wenhua zongheng*, no. 8 (2012): 17, 45.

28. Ge Zhaoguang, "Dui tianxia de xiangxiang—yige wutuobang xiangxian beihou de zhengzhi, sixiang, yu xueshu" (An Imagination of Tianxia—The Politics, Ideas and Scholarship behind a Utopia) *gu ge er yishu*, October 19, 2022. https://mp.weixin.qq.com/s/r7AknZhownURh6Rvf-fFag.

29. Lin Gang, "Zhengfu yu suijing—wenming kuozhan de guancha yu bijiao" (Conquest and Appeasement: Expansion of Civilizations' Observation and Comparison) *Beijing Daxue Xuebao,* no. 5 (2012): 68–78.

30. Xu Jilin, "Duoyuan wenming shidai de Zhongguo shiming" (Multi-Civilizations and China's Destiny) *Wenhua Zongheng,* 87 (June 2013).

31. Ye Zicheng, *Inside China's Grand Strategy: The Perspective from the People's Republic.* trans. Guoli Liu and Steven I. Levine. Lexington: University Press of Kentucky, 2011. Guo Shuyong, *Zhongguo ruanshili zhanlue* (China's Soft Power Strategy) (Beijing: Shishi Chubanshe, 2012).

32. Zhao Tingyang, "Political Realism and the Western Mind Exploring an Alternative Based upon 'Relational Rationality' and 'Confucian Improvement' " (pp. 23–36) in *The Edinburgh Companion to Political Realism,* ed. Robert Schuett and Miles Hollingworth (Edinburgh: Edinburgh University Press, 2018), http://www.jstor.org/stable/10.3366/j.ctv2f4vqhm.

33. Xiang Shuchen, "Tianxia and Its Decolonial Counterparts: 'China' as Civilization, Not Ethnicity," *China Review,* 23, no. 2 (2023): 165–87.

34. When Chinese Premier Zhou Enlai met members of the Indian Government Delegation on December 31, 1953, he put forward for the first time the Five Principles of Peaceful Co-existence, namely, mutual respect for each other's territorial integrity and sovereignty, mutual nonaggression, noninterference in each other's internal affairs, equality and mutual benefit, and peaceful co-existence.

35. June T. Dreyer, "The 'Tianxia Trope': Will China Change the International System," *Journal of Contemporary China* 24, no. 96 (2015): 1015–31.

36. Barry Buzan, "Goujian yige duoyuan wenming geju, zhongguo keyi zuoshenmo" (What Can China Do in Order to Construct a Pluralistic International society) IPP International Meeting on 8 October 202e; Feng Zhang and Barry Buzan, "The Relevance of Deep Pluralism for China's Foreign Policy," *Chinese Journal of International Politics,* 15, no. 3 (2022): 246–71.

37. Samuel P. Huntington, *The Clash of Civilizations and the Remaking of World Order* (New York: Simon & Schuster, 1996); Feng Zhang and Barry Buzan, "The Relevance of Deep Pluralism for China's Foreign Policy," *Chinese Journal of International Politics* 15, no. 3 (2022): 246–71.

38. John K. Fairbank, *The United States and China* (Cambridge, MA: Harvard University Press, 1983).

39. Sun Tzu, *The Art of War,* Samuel B. Griffith (trans.), B. H. Liddell Hart (foreword) (Oxford: Oxford University Press, 1971).

40. See https://www.hnn.us/article/representative-ike-skeltons-book-list.

41. Confucius, *The Analects.*

42. Xiongnu are nomadic people who at the end of the 3rd century BCE formed a tribal league that was able to dominate much of Central Asia for more than five hundred years.

43. Wang Dongyue *renlei de moluo (Decline of Mankind)* (Xian: Shaanxi chuban jituan, 2010).

44. Samuel P. Huntington, *The Clash of Civilizations and the Remaking of World Order* (New York: Simon & Schuster Press, 2011).

45. Paul Varley, *Japanese Culture*. 4th ed. (Honolulu: University of Hawaii Press, 2000).

46. Joseph S Nye Jr, *Soft Power: The Means to Success in World Politics* (New York: Public Affairs, 2005).

47. Rudy J. Rummel *Death by Government: Genocide and Mass Murder Since 1900*, 5th ed. (London: Routledge, 1997).

48. Max Weber, *The Religion of China: Confucianism and Taoism Max Weber, Religion in China* (Springfield, OH: Collier-Macmillan, 1964): 227–48.

49. Arnold Toynbee and Daisaku Ikeda, *Choose Life: A Dialogue (Echoes and Reflections)* (London: I. B. Tauris, 2007).

50. Samuel P. Huntington, *The Clash of Civilizations and the Remaking of World Order* (New York: Simon & Schuster Press, 2011), 201, 205, 51.

51. Wu Zhicheng, "Xieshou tuidong 'sanda quanqio changyi,' luodizoushi yinling renlei fanzhan maixiang guangming weilai" (Promote Three Global Initiatives, Lead Mankind on a March to a Bright Future), *Guangmin Daily*, September 12, 2023. http://theory.people.com.cn/n1/2023/0912/c40531-40075578.html. Also, http://vienna.china-mission.gov.cn/eng/zgbd/202302/t20230221_11028594.htm.

52. Chinese Ministry of Foreign Affairs, "Xi Jinping Delivers a Keynote Speech at the Opening Ceremony of the Boao Forum for Asia Annual Conference 2022," March 21, 2022, https://www.fmprc.gov.cn/eng/zxxx_662805/202204/t20220421_10671083.html.

53. Jiangyu Wang and Hua Cheng, "China's Approach to International Law: From Traditional Westphalianism to Aggressive Instrumentalism in the Xi Jinping Era," *The Chinese Journal of Comparative Law* 10, no. 1 (2022): 140–53. https://doi.org/10.1093/cjcl/cxac020.

54. Wei Liu, *China in the United Nations* (Singapore: World Scientific Press, 2014).

55. In the name of the UN, sixteen countries participated in the war against the North Korean invasion of the South: United States, United Kingdom, Australia, Netherlands, Canada, France, New Zealand, Philippines, Turkey, Thailand, South Africa, Greece, Belgium, Luxembourg, Ethiopia and Colombia. The United States contributed the bulk of the forces.

56. Ministry of Foreign Affairs, "Xi Jinping Delivers a Keynote Speech at the Opening Ceremony of the Boao Forum for Asia Annual Conference 2022," March 21, 2022. 10:59 https://www.fmprc.gov.cn/eng/zxxx_662805/202204/t20220421_10671083.html.

57. Suisheng Zhao, "The Ideological Campaign in Xi's China Rebuilding Regime Legitimacy"; Tang Aijun, "Ideological Security as National Security," CSIS, edited by Jude Blanchette, December 2020, https://www.csis.org/analysis/ideological-security-national-security.

58. Ministry of Foreign Affairs, "Xi Jinping Attends the CPC in Dialogue with World Political Parties High-level Meeting and Delivers a Keynote Speech," March 16, 2023, https://www.mfa.gov.cn/eng/zxxx_662805/202303/t20230317_11043656.html.

59. Ben Hillman and Gray Tuttle, eds., *Ethnic Conflict and Protest in Tibet and Xinjiang: Unrest in China's West* (New York: Columbia University Press, 2016).

60. *Global Times*, July 1, 2017.

61. Xinhua News Agency, January 31, 2021.

62. An Baijie, "Hard work is path to happiness, Xi says," *China Daily*, May 2, 2018.

63. Xinhua News Agency, "Xi Focus Quotable Quotes: Xi Jinping on Freedom," March 4, 2021, http://www.xinhuanet.com/english/2021-03/04/c_139783183.htm.

64. Zhongyan Wang, "Democracy with Chinese Adjectives: Whole-process Democracy and China's Political Development," in *CPC Futures: The New Era of Socialism with Chinese Characteristics*," ed. Frank N. Pieke and Bert Hofman (Singapore: National University of Singapore Press, 2022).

65. Tang Aijun, "Ideological Security as National Security," CSIS, edited by Jude Blanchette, December 2020, https://www.csis.org/analysis/ideological-security-national-security.

66. Sun Tzu *The Art of War* (New York: Peter Pauper Press, 2022).

67. "Bandung Spirit." In 1958, leaders from twenty-nine Asian and African countries attended the Bandung Conference in Bandung, Indonesia, giving birth to the Bandung spirit of solidarity, friendship and cooperation, among countries in Asia, Africa and Latin America. See https://www.fmprc.gov.cn/eng/zxxx_662805/202204/t20220421_10671083.html.

68. The 2023 International Forum for Trilateral Cooperation (in Qingdao), https://www.globaltimes.cn/page/202307/1293640.shtml (accessed October 16, 2023).

69. David C. Kang, "International Order in Historical East Asia: Tribute and Hierarchy Beyond Sinocentrism and Eurocentrism," *International Organization* (2019): 1–29. https://doi.org/10.1017/S0020818319000274; Zhang Yongjin and Barry Buzan, "The Tributary System as International Society in Theory and Practice," *Chinese Journal of International Politics* 5 (2012): 3–36.

70. Ezra F. Vogel, *China and Japan: Facing History* (Cambridge: MA: Harvard University Press, 2019).

71. Editorial Board, *Jixiu siku quanshu* (Vol. 735) (Shanghai: Shanghai Guji Chubanshe): 509.

72. Wu Han, ed., *Lichao shilu zhong de Zhongguo shiliao*, Vol. 1 (History Materials in the Archives of the Past Dynasties) (Beijing: Zhonghua Shuju, 1980), 115.

73. Ge Zhaoguang, "Dui tianxia de xiangxiang—yige wutuobang xiangxian beihou de zhengzhei, sixiang, yu xueshu" (An Imagination of Tianxia—the Politics, Ideas and Scholarship behind a Utopia) *gu ge er yishu*, October 19, 2022.

74. Hans Morgenthau, *Scientific Man versus Power Politics* (Chicago: University of Chicago Press, 1946).

75. Chin-Hao Huang, *Power and Restraint in China's Rise* (New York: Columbia University Press, 2022).

76. David C. Kang, *China Rising: Peace, Power, and Order in East Asia* (New York: Columbia University Press, 2010): 198; David C. Kang, *East Asia before the West Five Centuries of Trade and Tribute* (New York: Columbia University Press, 2010): 167–69.

77. Alastair Iain Johnston, *Cultural Realism: Strategic Culture and Grand Strategy in Chinese History* (Princeton, NJ: Princeton University Press, 1995), xi.

78. Joseph Z. Reday, "Reparations from Japan," *Far Eastern Survey* 18, no. 13 (June 29, 1949): 145–51.

79. Guangqiu Xu, "Eight Foreign Armies Invasion of China," *In China at War: An Encyclopedia*, ed., Xiaobing Li (New York: Bloomsbury Academic, 2012).

80. Edwin O. Reischauer and Marius B. Jansen, *The Japanese Today: Change and Continuity* (Cambridge, MA: Harvard University Press, 1995).

81. Louis Hayes, *Introduction to Japanese Politics* (London: Routledge, 2018).

82. Andrea Ghiselli, "Revising China's Strategic Culture: Contemporary Cherry-Picking of Ancient Strategic Thought," *China Quarterly* 233 (2018): 166–85.

83. Suisheng Zhao, "Rethinking the Chinese World Order: The Imperial Cycle and the Rise of China," *Journal of Contemporary China*, 24, no. 96 (2015): 961–82.

84. William Callahan, "History, Tradition and the China Dream: Socialist Modernization in the World of Great Harmony," *Journal of Contemporary China* 24, no. 96 (2017): 983–1001.

85. Angus Maddison, *Chinese Economic Performance in the Long Run*, 2nd ed. (Paris, OECD, 2007): 213.

86. Treaty of Shimonoseki (*Maguan Tiaoyue*), April 17, 1895, https://www.britannica.com/event/Treaty-of-Shimonoseki.

87. Ho Ping-ti, *Studies on the Population of China, 1368–1953* (Cambridge, MA: Harvard University Press, 1959): 252.

88. Martin Jacques, *When China Rules the World: The Rise of the Middle Kingdom and the End of the Western World* (London: Penguin, 2012): 98.

89. Graham Allison, "The Thucydides Trap: Are the U.S. and China Headed for War?" *The Atlantic*. September 24, 2015, https://www.theatlantic.com/international/archive/2015/09/united-states-china-war-thucydides-trap/406756/.

90. Huntington, *The Clash of Civilizations and the Remaking of World Order*, chaps. 3–4.

91. Christopher Layne, "The Global Power Shift from West to East," *National Interest*, April 25, 2012: https://nationalinterest.org/article/the-global-power-shift-west-east-6796.

92. Bingna Guo, James Hsiao, Bob Li, and Royston C. Tan, "The Law on Foreign Relations of the People's Republic of China Became Effective on 1 July 2023," *Whitecase*, https://www.whitecase.com/insight-alert/law-foreign-relations-peoples-republic-china-became-effective-1-july-2023 (accessed October 17, 2023).

93. China Ministry of Foreign Affairs, "Xi Jinping Attends the General Debate of the 76th Session of the United Nations General Assembly and Delivers an Important Speech," September 22, 2021, https://www.fmprc.gov.cn/mfa_eng/wjb_663304/zzjg_663340/gjs_665170/gjsxw_665172/202109/t20210923_9580159.html.

94. Cao Desheng, "Law on Foreign Relations to Act as Safeguard," *China Daily*, June 30, 2023.

95. Ka Zeng, "Complementary Trade Structure and U.S.–China Negotiations over Intellectual Property Rights," *East Asia* 20 (2002): 54–80, https://doi.org/10.1007/s12140-002-0003-y.

96. Chalmers Johnson, *MITI and the Japanese Miracle: The Growth of Industrial Policy, 1925–1975* (Stanford, CA: Stanford University Press, 1982); Gregory Shank, "Japan–U.S. Trade War?" *Social Justice* 21, no. 2 (Summer 1994): 20–23.

97. See https://wid.world/ (accessed November 7, 2023).

98. Bingna Guo, James Hsiao, Bob Li, and Royston C. Tan, "The Law on Foreign Relations of the People's Republic of China Became Effective on 1 July 2023."

99. Cao Desheng, "Law on Foreign Relations to Act as Safeguard," *China Daily*, June 30, 2023.

100. Katie Tarasov, "Inside TSMC, the Taiwanese Chipmaking Giant that's Building a New Plant in Phoenix," *CNBC*, October 16, 2021, https://www.cnbc.com/2021/10/16/tsmc-taiwanese-chipmaker-ramping-production-to-end-chip-shortage.html.

101. Dan Blumenthal, Gregory Graff, and Christian Curriden, *How China Views It: Sino-American Technology Competition* (Washington, DC: American Enterprise Institute for Public Policy, 2022).

102. Gregory C. Allen, *Choking off China's Access to the Future of AI* (Washington, DC: Center for Strategic and International Studies, 2022).

103. Juncheng Cao, "A Case Study of Extradition: United States v. Meng Wanzhou." *International Journal of Law, Ethics, and Technology* 20 (2021): 21–46.

104. Camila Domonoske, "China Imposes Export Controls on 2 Metals Used in Semiconductors and Solar Panels," *NPR*, July 4, 2023, https://www.npr.org/2023/07/04/1185940293/china-imposes-export-controls-on-two-metals-used-in-semiconductors-and-solar-pan.

105. Suisheng Zhao, "China's Belt-Road Initiative as the Signature of President Xi Jinping Diplomacy: Easier Said than Done," *Journal of Contemporary China* 29, no. 123 (2020): 319–35. https://doi.org/10.1080/10670564.2019.1645483.

106. Eyck Freymann, *One Belt One Road: Chinese Power Meets the World* (Cambridge, MA: Harvard University Press, 2020).

Chapter 8

1. Jude Howell and Jane Duckett, "Reassessing the Hu-Wen Era: A Golden Age or Lost Decade for Social Policy in China," *The China Quarterly*, no. 2 (2019): 1–14.

2. Freedom House, "Marking 50 Years in the Struggle for Democracy," https://freedomhouse.org/report/freedom-world/2023/marking-50-years (accessed on December 11, 2023).

3. Pew, "Public Trust in Government: 1958–2023." https://www.pewresearch.org/politics/2023/09/19/public-trust-in-government-1958-2023/ accessed on December 11, 2023.

4. World Bank data, https://data.worldbank.org/indicator/NE.TRD.GNFS.ZS?locations=CN (accessed August 31, 2023).

5. Shiping Hua, ed., *Chinese Political Culture* (1989–2000) (Armonk, NY: M. E. Sharpe, 2001).

6. James B. Lewis, *The East Asian War, 1592–1598: International Relations, Violence and Memory* (London: Routledge, 2014).

7. Lu Hsun, "A Madman's Diary," *Selected Stories of Lu Hsun* (Beijing: Foreign Languages Press, 1972).

8. Cheng Chong-ying, "Legalism Versus Confucianism: A Philosophical Appraisal." *Journal of Chinese Philosophy*, 8 no. 3 (1981): 271–302. https://doi.org/10.1163/15406253-00803001.

9. Confucius, *The Analects*, Chapter 17, Yang Huo. 《论语•第十七章•阳货篇》.

10. Ban Gu, *Bai Hu Tong*. Jia Qu 班固《白虎通. 嫁娶》: "妻者, 齐也。与夫齐体。

11. For instance, the Catholics often cite "the chance for a rich man to go to heaven is like a camel running through the eye of the needle," thus showing an antibusiness attitude. But the Calvinists like to cite the Bible story of three persons who inherit properties to use them for different purpose, to consume, to bury, or to invest. The Lord favors the one who invests, thus showing the attitude in favor of entrepreneurship. See Max Weber, *The Protestant Ethic and the "Spirit" of Capitalism and Other Writings* (London: Penguin, 2002).

12. Shiping Hua, *Chinese Utopianism: A Comparative Study of the Reformist Thought with Japan and Russia* (Stanford: Stanford University Press, 2009).

13. Chih-yu Shih, *Post-Chineseness: Cultural Politics and International Relations* (Albany: State University of New York Press, 2022).

14. Sima Qian, *Shi Ji*, Fa Ju and Cai Ze Biographies 史记•范睢蔡泽列传.

15. Timothy Brook, ed. *Documents on the Rape of Nanjing* (Ann Arbor: University of Michigan Press, 1999).

16. Lois Mai Chan, "The Burning of the Books in China, 213 B.C.," *Journal of Library History*, 7 no. 2 (1972): 101–8.

17. Lao Tzu, *Dao De Jing (The Book of the Way)* (Berkeley: University of California Press, 1997).

18. Michael Loewe, "Dong Zhongshu," *A Biographical Dictionary of the Qin, Former Han and Xin Periods (221 BC–AD 24)* (Leiden: Brill, 2000), 70–73.

19. Yasheng Huang, *The Rise and Fall of the EAST: How Exams, Autocracy, Stability, and Technology Brought China Success, and Why They Might Lead to Its Decline* (New Haven, CT: Yale University Press, 2023).

20. Thomas H. Reilly, *The Taiping Heavenly Kingdom: Rebellion and the Blasphemy of Empire* (Seattle: University of Washington Press, 2004).

21. Edwin O. Reischauer and Marius B. Jansen, *The Japanese Today: Change and Continuity* (Cambridge, MA: Harvard University Press, 1995).

22. Jin Guantao *Xing sheng yu wei ji: Lun Zhongguo she hui chao wen ding jie gou* (Prosperity and Crisis: China's Ultra-stable Social System) (Hong Kong: Chinese University of Hong Kong Press, 1992).

23. Mencius. *Mencius*, D. C. Lau, trans. (London: Penguin, 2005).

24. Karl A. Wittfogel, *Oriental Despotism: A Comparative Study of Total Power* (New Haven, CT: Yale University Press, 1957).

25. Thomas M. Magstadt, *Understanding Politics: Ideas, Institutions, and Issues* (Boston, MA: Cengage Learning, 2016).

26. Chenshan Tian, *Chinese Dialectics: From Yijing to Marxism* (Lanham, MD: Lexington, 2005).

27. Alan K. L. Chan, *Mencius: Contexts and Interpretations* (Honolulu: University of Hawaii Press, 2002).

28. Louis-Frédéric Nussbaum and Käthe Roth, *Japan Encyclopedia* (Cambridge, MA: Harvard University Press, 2005).

29. Fa Shuzhi, *Chongzhen Zhuan (Biography of Chongzhen)* (Beijing: Zhonghua shuju, 2021).

30. Confucius, *The Analects* (London: Penguin, 1998).

31. Ezra F. Vogel, *China and Japan: Facing History* (Cambridge, MA: Harvard University Press, 2019).

32. Steven Hess, "The Flight of the Affluent in Contemporary China," *Asian Survey* 56, no. 4 (2016): 629–50.

33. See https://www.worldbank.org/en/news/press-release/2022/04/01/lifting-800-million-people-out-of-poverty-new-report-looks-at-lessons-from-china-s-experience.

34. Ronald Inglehart *Modernization and Postmodernization: Cultural, Economic, and Political Change in 43 Societies* (Princeton, NJ: Princeton University Press, 2020).

35. Milton Friedman, *Capitalism and Freedom* (Chicago: University of Chicago Press, 2002); Richard Ebeling, *Political Economy, Public Policy and Monetary Economics: Ludwig von Mises and the Austrian Tradition* (New York: Routledge, 2010).

36. Karl Marx, *Economic and Philosophic Manuscripts of 1844* (Garden City, NY: Dover Books, 2007).

37. Gabriel Abraham Almond, *A Discipline Divided: Schools and Sects in Political Science* (Thousand Oaks, CA: SAGE, 1989).

38. David H. Pinkney, "Nationalization of Key Industries and Credit in France after the Liberation," *Political Science Quarterly* 62, no. 3 (1947): 368–80; William A. Robson, *Nationalised Industries in Britain and France* (London: Cambridge University Press, 2013).

39. Phenix TV: "An On-Line Survey about the Cultural Revolution. The Result Is Not Good." See https://nam11.safelinks.protection.outlook.com/?url=

https%3A%2F%2Fmp.weixin.qq.com%2Fs%2FKjffHVzfZsCRqMcYy0n5
Ag&data=05%7C01%7Cshiping.hua%40louisville.edu%7Cb7de6254465047
dd064308db1f7a08fb%7Cdd246e4a54344e158ae391ad9797b209%7C0%7C0%
7C638138381213321547%7CUnknown%7CTWFpbGZsb3d8eyJWIjoiMC4wLjAw
MDAiLCJQIjoiV2luMzIiLCJBTiI6Ik1haWwiLCJXVCI6Mn0%3D%7C3000%7
C%7C%7C&sdata=byBPcEdadXjkBPCELSDrz3hekt1q2ZTV4cb5GlmobkE%3D&
reserved=0.

40. Albert Walter, *The Future of China's Past: Reflections on the Meaning of China's Rise* (Albany: State University of New York Press, 2023).

41. Jude Blanchette *China's New Red Guards: The Return of Radicalism and the Rebirth of Mao Zedong* (London: Oxford University Press, 2019).

42. Tony Saich, Jesse Turiel, and Edward Cunningham, "Understanding CCP Resilience: Surveying Chinese Public Opinion Through Time." Harvard University Kennedy School, Ash Center, 2020, https://ash.harvard.edu/files/ash/files/final_policy_brief_7.6.2020.pdf.

43. Huang, *The Rise and Fall of the East*.

44. Cheng Li, *Middle Class Shanghai: Reshaping U.S.-China Engagement* (Washington, DC: Brookings Institution Press, 2021).

45. *Phenix Finance*: Long Yongtu: "Gap of Economic Power Still Exists between China and US. We Need to Have a Sense of Urgency." https://finance.ifeng.com/a/20180222/15991952_0.shtml (accessed December 15, 2023).

46. *New York Times*, October 3, 2018. https://www.nytimes.com/2018/10/03/business/china-economy-private-enterprise.html?smid=nytcore-ios-share.

47. Chen Xiao, "Gaoxiao bianzhi gaige dui jiaoyu zhiyuan zhuanye hua fazhan yingxiang," (The impact on professionalism of the staff of the higher education by the restructuring of personnel policy), *Beijing jiaoyu*, no. 1, 2018, http://www.jyb.cn/zcg/xwy/wzxw/201801/t20180122_940959.html.

48. General Outline: the phrase with a line cutting through was cut: "At the present, the main contradiction of the Chinese society is between the people's increasing desire for a higher living standard and the backward social productivity and the unbalanced, underdevelopment," https://mp.weixin.qq.com/s/s5emniSZ1EDYvixOA-NBGg.

49. BBC, September 17, 2018, http://www.wenxuecity.com/news/2018/09/17/7638014.html.

50. I. de Soysa, and K. C. Vadlamannati, "Free Market Capitalism and Societal Inequities: Assessing the Effects of Economic Freedom on Income Inequality and the Equity of Access to Opportunity, 1990–2017," *International Political Science Review*, 44 no. 4 (2023): 471–91. https://doi.org/10.1177/01925121211039985.

51. Richard Holton, "Industrial Politics in France: Nationalisation under Mitterrand, *West European Politics*, 9 no. 1 (1986): 67–80, http:/doi.org/10.1080/01402388608424563.

52. M. Steven Fish, "The Hazards of Half-Measures: Perestroika and the Failure of Post-Soviet Democratization," *Demokratizatsiya*, 13, no. 2 (2005): 241+.

link.gale.com/apps/doc/A135818429/AONE?u=anon~a7266bbd&sid=googleScholar&xid=9c815913.

53. Ma Linghe, ed., Zhongguo jindai shi 1840–1949 (Modern China History) (Beijing: Renmin Jieoyu chubanshe, 2015): 135–37.

54. Roderick MacFarquhar, *The Origins of the Cultural Revolution: Volume III, the Coming of the Cataclysm 1961–1966* (New York: Columbia University Press, 1999).

55. Richard Baum, "Revolution and Reaction in the Chinese Countryside: The Socialist Education Movement in Cultural Revolutionary Perspective," *China Quarterly* 38, no. 38 (1969): 92–119.

56. Yan Jiaqi and Gao Gao, *Turbulent Decade: A History of the Cultural Revolution* (Honolulu: University of Hawaii Press, 1996).

57. Bruce Gilley *Tiger on the Brink: Jiang Zemin and China's New Elite* (Berkeley: University of California Press, 1998).

58. Tse-Tung Chow, *The May Fourth Movement* (Cambridge, MA: Harvard University Press, 2013).

59. Hua, *Chinese Legal Culture and Constitutional Order*.

60. The impact of culture is also found in the fact that among the former Soviet bloc countries, those that are located geographically near the West, such as the Baltic states, Poland, Czech, and East Germany are more successful in transforming themselves into liberal democracies. Ukraine is torn between the East and West: sometimes it leans towards Russia, like Petro Poroshenko who is Volodymyr Zelenskyy's predecessor; sometimes it is more liberal, like the current regime. Belarus is pro-Russia largely because it is located in the East. Asian countries are profoundly influenced by China, with more emphasis on the collective, especially the state, and has less concern for individuals; these traits give rise to authoritarianism. All communist countries except one are located in Asia: China, Vietnam, Laos, and North Korea. Japan, Taiwan, and South Korea; these countries also have authoritarian cultural traditions but have become successful democracies, partly because of the economic support and security protection of the United States.

61. Having said this, I would like to add that the future is hard to predict. In fact, some Western scholars are quite optimistic about the possibility that Chinese-style civilization may replace the Western one. Samuel Huntington quoted Carroll Quigley as saying: "Western civilization did not exist about A.D. 500; it did exist in full flower about A.D. 1500, and it will surely pass out of existence at some time in the future, perhaps before A.D. 2500. New civilizations in China and India, replacing those destroyed by the West will then move into their stages of expansion and threaten both Western and Orthodox civilizations." See Carroll Quigley, *The Evolution of Civilizations: An Introduction to Historical Analysis* (Indianapolis: Liberty Press, 1979), 127, 164–66. Cited in Huntington, *The Clash of Civilizations and the Remaking of World Order* (New York: Simon & Schuster, 2011), 303. Also see Arnold J. Toynbee, Daisaku Ikeda *Choose Life* (London: I.B. Tauris, 2007).

Bibliography

Adams, James Truslow. *The Epic of America*. New York: Simon & Schuster, 2001.
Ai, Siqi, *Bianzheng weiwu zhuyi, lishi weiwu zhuyi (Dialectical Materialism and Historical Materialism)*. Beijing: Renmin chubanshe, 1983.
Allen, Gregory C. *Choking off China's Access to the Future of AI*. Washington, DC: Center for Strategic and International Studies, 2022.
Allison, Graham. "The Thucydides Trap: Are the U.S. and China Headed for War?" *The Atlantic*. September 24, 2015, https://www.theatlantic.com/international/archive/2015/09/united-states-china-war-thucydides-trap/406756/.
Almond, Gabriel Abraham. *A Discipline Divided: Schools and Sects in Political Science*. Thousand Oaks, CA: Sage Publications, 1989.
Ames, Roger. "New Confucianism: A Native Response to Western Philosophy," in Shiping Hua ed., *Chinese Political Culture*. Armonk, NY: M. E. Sharpe, 2001, 70–102.
Ames, Roger. *The Analects of Confucius: A Philosophical Translation*. New York: Ballantine Books, 1999, 35.
Amnesty International. "China: New Supervision Law a Systemic Threat to Human Rights" (2018), https://www.amnesty.org/en/latest/news/2018/03/china-new-supervision-law-threat-to-human-rights/. Retrieved January 2, 2023.
Andrew, Anita M. and John A. Rapp. *Autocracy and China's Rebel Founding Emperors: Comparing Chairman Mao and Ming Taizu*. Lanham, MD: Roman & Littlefields, 2000.
Backer, Larry Catá. "The Rule of Law, The Chinese Communist Party, and Ideological Campaigns: Sange Daibiao," *Journal of Transnational L & Contemporary Problems* 16, no. 1 (2006).
Ban, Gu. *Bai Hu Tong*. Jia Qu 班固《白虎通. 嫁娶》:"妻者, 齐也。与夫齐体。
Barrass, Gordon, Nigel Inkster Gordon Barrass, and Nigel Inkster. "Xi Jinping: The Strategist Behind the Dream," *Survival* 60, no. 1 (2018): 41–68. doi: 10.1080/00396338.2018.1427363.
Bauer, Wolfgang. *China and the Search for Happiness: Recurring Themes in Four Thousand Years of Chinese Cultural History*. New York: Seabury Press, 1976.

Baum, Richard. "Revolution and Reaction in the Chinese Countryside: The Socialist Education Movement in Cultural Revolutionary Perspective." *The China Quarterly* 38, no. 38 (1969): 92–119.

BBC. "Weilai qianjing buming, zhongguo saying qiye yi pian huangkong (The future is uncler, China's private enterprises are scared) September 17, 2018. http://www.wenxuecity.com/news/2018/09/17/7638014.html accessed December 15, 2023.

BBC. "Hong Kong national Security Law: What Is it and Is It Worrying?" June 28, 2022. https://www.bbc.com/news/world-asia-china-52765838.

BBC. "The Rising Cost of a Chinese Bride Price." *BBC*. Accessed May 1, 2021. www.bbc.com/news/blogs-trending-35727057.

BBC. "Xi Jinping's Anticorruption Campaign: How Big is its Scope? What is its Goal (*Xi Jinping defanfu yundong: fanwei youduoguang Mubiao shishenme*)" in the *BBC*, October 23, 2017. http://www.bbc.com/zhongwen/simp/chinese-news-41719314.

Beijing ribao, "Guojia jianwei chengli yizhounian, ganle zhexie dashi" [NSC has done the following big things since its establishment a year ago] March 23, 2019, https://baijiahao.baidu.com/s?id=1628761705695287129&wfr=spider&for=pc. Retrieved August 10, 2023.

Blanchette, Jude. *China's New Red Guards: The Return of Radicalism and the Rebirth of Mao Zedong*. London: Oxford University Press, 2019.

Blasek, Katrin. *Rule of Law in China: A Comparative Approach*. New York: Springer, 2015.

Blumenthal, Dan, Gregory Graff, and Christian Curriden. *How China Views It: Sino-American Technology Competition*. Washington, DC: American Enterprise Institute for Public Policy, 2022.

Brar, Aadil. "Xi Says 'National Security' 50 Times at Party Congress & China Sees Rare Protest against Him," *The Print* https://theprint.in/opinion/chinascope/xi-says-national-security-50-times-at-party-congress-china-sees-rare-protest-against-him/1170804/ accessed September 29, 2023.

Brown, Kerry. *China's Dream: The Culture of Chinese Communism and the Secret Sources of its Power*. London: Polity, 2018.

Breuninger, Kevin, and Eamon Javers. "Communist Party cells influencing U.S. companies' China operations, FBI Director Wray says," CNBC, July 12, 2023 https://www.cnbc.com/2023/07/12/communist-cells-influence-companies-in-china-fbi-director.html accessed September 29, 2023.

Broadberry, Stephen N., Hanhui Guan, and David D. Li. "China, Europe and the Great Divergence: A Study in Historical National Accounting," *CEPR Discussion Paper* no. DP11972 (April 2017): 980–1850. https://ssrn.com/abstract=2957511.

Brook, Timothy, ed. *Documents on the Rape of Nanjing*. Ann Arbor: University of Michigan Press, 1999.

Brown, Jeremy. *June Fourth: The Tiananmen Protests and Beijing Massacre of 1989.* London: Cambridge University Press, 2021.
Brown, Kerry, and Una Aleksandra Bērziņa-Čerenkova. "Ideology in the Era of Xi Jinping" *Journal of Chinese Political Science* 23, no. 3 (September 2018): 323–39.
Buckley, Chris. "China Enshrines 'Xi Jinping Thought,' Elevating Leader to Mao-Like Status." *New York Times,* October 24, 2017.
Buckley, Chris. "China Internal Security Jumps Past Army Budget," *Reuters,* March 5, 2011.
Buzan, Barry. "goujian yige duoyuan wenming geju, zhongguo keyi zuoshenmo" (What can China do in order to construct a pluralistic international society) *IPP International Meeting* 2023-10-08 09. https://m.thepaper.cn/baijiahao_19727873 accessed January 27, 2024.
Buzan, Barry. "The Relevance of Deep Pluralism for China's Foreign Policy," *Chinese Journal of International Politics* 15, no. 3 (2022): 246–271.
Buzan, Barry. "The Tributary System as International Society in Theory and Practice," *The Chinese Journal of International Politics,* 5 (2012): 3–36.
Cabestan, Jean-Pierre. "China's Institutional Changes in the Foreign and Security Policy Realm Under Xi Jinping: Power Concentration vs. Fragmentation Without Institutionalization," *East Asia: An International Quarterly* 34 (2017): 113–31.
Cai, Congyan. "Enforcing a New National Security—China's National Security Law and International Law," *Journal of East Asia & International Law* 10, no. 65 (2017): 65–89, 70.
Callahan, William. "History, Tradition and the China Dream: Socialist Modernization in the World of Great Harmony," *Journal of Contemporary China* 24, no. 96 (2017): 983–1001. http://dx.doi.org/10.1080/10670564.2015.1030915.
Callahan, William. *China Dreams: 20 Visions of the Future.* Oxford: Oxford University Press, 2013.
Callahan, William. "History, Tradition and the China Dream: Socialist Modernization in the World of Great Harmony." *Journal of Contemporary China* 24, no. 96 (2017): 983–1001. http://dx.doi.org/10.1080/10670564.2015.1030915.
Cao, Desheng. "Law on Foreign Relations to act as safeguard," *China Daily,* June 30, 2023.
Cao, Juncheng. "A Case Study of Extradition: United States v. Meng Wanzhou." *International Journal of Law, Ethics, and Technology* (IJLET), 20 (2021): 21–46.
CCP Central Committee Party History Research Office. "Treating the Two Periods Before and After the Reform Correctively," *People's Daily,* November 8, 2013, p. 6. http://news.dwnews.com/global/news/2018-09-10/60083752.html.
CCP Central Committee Party History Research Office. "CCP Discipline Inspection Institutions Cases Investigation Statutes" (zhongguo gongchandang jilu jiancha jiguan anjian jiancha gongzuo tiaoli) https://baike.baidu.com/item/%E4%B8%AD%E5%9B%BD%E5%85%B1%E4%BA%A7%E5%85%9A%E7%BA%AA%E5%BE%8B%E6%A3%80%E6%9F%

A5%E6%9C%BA%E5%85%B3%E6%A1%88%E4%BB%B6%E 6%A3%80%E6%9F%A5%E5%B7%A5%E4%BD%9C%E6%9D %A1%E4%BE%8B/6790689?fr=ge_ala accessed January 29, 2024.

CCTV Net. "2018 nian zhuihui waitao renyuan 1335, zhuihui 3.541 bilian yuan—jiancha tizhi gaige zhuli guoji zhuitao zhui zang shoseixian xintupo" (In 2018, we brought back 1335 who escaped abroad, retrieved 3.541 yuan—the reform of supervision system help international chase those who escaped abroad with embezzled funds). http://news.cctv.com/2019/01/29/ARTI6iircEygj7E2t CFNQxsN190129.shtml, Retrieved August 7, 2023.

CGTN. "China's Draft Supervision Law: What Is It, Why Does It Matter?." March 13, 2018, https://news.cgtn.com/news/346b6a4d796b7a6333566d54/index.html.

Chan, Alan K.L. *Mencius: Contexts and Interpretations.* Honolulu: University of Hawaii Press, 2002.

Chan, Lois Mai. "The Burning of the Books in China, 213 B.C." *The Journal of Library History* 7, no. 2 (1972): 101–8.

Chang, Zheng. "Understanding the Corruption Networks Revealed in the Current Chinese Anti-Corruption Campaign: A Social Network Approach," *Journal of Contemporary China* 27, no. 113 (2018): 735–47.

Char, James, and Richard A. Bitzinger. "A New Direction in the People's Liberation Army's Emergent Strategic Thinking, Roles and Missions," *The China Quarterly* 232 (2017): 841–65.

Chen, Albert H.Y. "China's Long March towards Rule of Law or China's Turn against Law." *The Chinese Journal of Comparative Law* (2016): 4, 1–35.

Chen, Charlie. "Waiting for China's Precarious Housing Bubble to Burst." *The Politic.* April 25, 2021. https://thepolitic.org/waiting-for-chinas-precarious-housing-bubble-to-burst/ accessed January 27, 2024.

Chen, Cheng. *The Return of Ideology: The Search for Regime Identities in Postcommunist Russia and China.* Ann Arbor: University of Michigan Press, 2016.

Chen, Cheng. "Ideology-Building under Hu Jintao: Reacting to Jiang and Paving the Way for Xi," Chapter 13, in *Chinese Ideology* edited by Shiping Hua. London: Routledge, 2021.

Chen, G. Z. "Several Views on the Reform of China's Supervisory System," *Global Law Review* 2 (2017): 115–17.

Chen, Guangcheng. "The Supreme Court Rules That If the Law Did Not Stipulate, Then the Judge Can Rule Based on Ideological Considerations." *Radio Free Asia,* March 17, 2021.

Chen, Fong-ching, Chen and Jin Guantao. *From Youthful Manuscripts to River Elegy: the Chinese Popular Cultural Movement and Political Transformation 1979–1989.* Hong Kong: Chinese University of Hong Kong Press, 1997, 215–37.

Chen, Jianfu. "The Revision of the Constitution in the PRC: A Great Leap Forward or a Symbolic Gesture?" *China Perspectives,* 53 (2004): 1–20.

Chen, Lei. "The Historical Development of the Civil Law Tradition in China: A Private Law Perspective." *The Legal History Review* 78, no. 1 (September 2009). http://doi.org/10.2139/ssrn.1479442.

Chen, Si. "Mao Zedong yu 24 shi," (Mao Zedong and the 24 histories), *Xue Xi Shi bao*, August 7, 2019, http://dangshi.people.com.cn/n1/2019/0807/c85037-31280331.html?ivk_sa=1024320u.

Chen, Xiao. "gaoxiao bianzhi gaige dui jiaoyu zhiyuan zhuanye hua fazhan yingxiang," (The impact on professionalism of the staff of the higher education by the restructuring of personnel policy), *Beijing jiaoyu*, no. 1, 2018. http://www.jyb.cn/zcg/xwy/wzxw/201801/t20180122_940959.html.

Chen, Zhengyan, and Lin Qiyan. *Zhongguo gudai datong sixiang yanjiu* (A study of utopian thought in ancient China) Shanghai: Renmin Chubanshe, 1986, 84.

Chen, Zhiwu. *wenming de luoji* (The logic of civilizations) Beijing: Zhongxin Chubanshe, 2022.

Cheng, Chun-gying. "Legalism versus Confucianism: A Philosophical Appraisal." *Journal of Chinese Philosophy* 8 (1981): 271–302.

Cheong, Suk-Wai. "Singapore's sovereignty 'never a given': Bilahari Kausikan." *The Straits Times*, January 30, 2016, http://www.straitstimes.com/singapore/singapores-sovereignty-never-a-givenbilahari-kausikan.

China Daily. "Nearly 1 Million People Sit China's Civil Servant Exam." December 2, 2018, https://www.chinadaily.com.cn/a/201812/02/WS5c03fee3a310eff303 28e850.html.

China Ministry of Foreign Affairs. "Xi Jinping Attends the General Debate of the 76th Session of the United Nations General Assembly and Delivers an Important Speech," September 22, 2021. https://www.fmprc.gov.cn/mfa_eng/wjb_663304/zzjg_663340/gjs_665170/gjsxw_665172/202109/t20210923_9580159.html

China Ministry of Foreign Affairs. "Set Aside Dispute and Pursue Joint Development." https://www.fmprc.gov.cn/eng/ziliao_665539/3602_665543/3604_6655 47/200011/t20001117_697808.html accessed September 29, 2023.

China Ministry of Foreign Affairs. "Xi Jinping Attends the CPC in Dialogue with World Political Parties High-level Meeting and Delivers a Keynote Speech," March 16, 2023, 23:00, https://www.mfa.gov.cn/eng/zxxx_662805/202303/t20230317_11043656.html. Retrieved August 31, 2023.

China Ministry of Foreign Affairs. "Xi Jinping Delivers a Keynote Speech at the Opening Ceremony of the Boao Forum for Asia Annual Conference 2022," 2022-04-21 10:59. https://www.fmprc.gov.cn/eng/zxxx_662805/202204/t20 220421_10671083.html.

Cohen, G. A. "The Labor Theory of Value and the Concept of Exploitation." *Philosophy and Public Affairs* 8 (1979): 338–60.

Confucius. *The Analects.* 2/3. Cited in Roger T. Ames and Henry Rosemont Jr. *The Analects of Confucius.* New York: Ballantine Books, 1998.

Confucius. *The Analects*, Chapter 17, Yang Huo.《论语·第十七章·阳货篇》.
Confucius. *The Analects*, Li ji, Liyun.
Chow, Tse-Tung. *The May Fourth Movement* (Harvard East Asian) Cambridge, MA: Harvard University Press, 2013.
Chung, Chris. "Drawing the U-Shaped Line: China's Claim in the South China Sea, 1946–1974." *Modern China* 42 (2016): 38–72.
Chung, Yen-lin. "The Witch-Hunting Vanguard: The Central Secretariat's Roles and Activities in the Anti-Rightist Campaign." *The China Quarterly* 206 (2011): 391–411.
Creemers, Rogier J. E. H., Susan Trevaskes, *Law and the Party in China: Ideology and Organization*. Cambridge: Cambridge University Press, 2021.
CSIS. 2021. "How Well-off Is China's Middle Class?" April 27, 2021. https://chinapower.csis.org/china-middle-class/. Accessed January 27, 2024.
CSIS and Tsinghua University, "Zhongguo ren de guoji Anquan guan minyi diaocha baogao (Chinese People's International Security View: A Survey) May 24, 2023. https://mp.weixin.qq.com/s/Il6CdcCEMFpL4Gfz3ENM5g Accessed on September 29, 2023.
Davis, Bob. "What's a Global Recession?" *The Wall Street Journal*, April 22, 2009.
Daxue Consulting. "Behind the Industry of Counterfeit Products in China and Lawsuit Success Cases." April 27, 2021. https://daxueconsulting.com/counterfeit-products-in-china/.
de Bary, William Theodore and Irene Bloom. *Sources of Chinese Tradition*, Vol. 1, 2nd ed. New York: Columbia University Press, 1999, 343, 176.
De Jong, Alice. "The Demise of the Dragaon: Background to the Chinese Film "River Elegy" *China Information* 4, no. 3 (December 1989): 28–43. http://doi.org/10.1177/0920203X8900400304. S2CID 220801020.
de la Rasilla, Ignacio and Yayezi Hao, "The Community of Shared Future for Mankind and China's Legalist Turn in International Relations." *Chinese Journal of International Law* 20, no. 2 (June 2021): 341–79. https://doi.org/10.1093/chinesejil/jmab021.
deLisle, Jacques. "Law in the China Model 2.0: Legality, Developmentalism and Legalism under Xi Jinping." *Journal of Contemporary China* 26, no. 68 (2016): 1–17.
Deng, Jinting. "The National Supervision Commission: A New Anti-Corruption Model in China." *International Journal of Law, Crime and Justice* 52 (2018): 58–73.
de Soysa, Indre and K. C. Vadlamannati. "Free Market Capitalism and Societal Inequities: Assessing the Effects of Economic Freedom on Income Inequality and the Equity of Access to Opportunity, 1990–2017," *International Political Science Review* 44, no. 4 (2023): 471–91. https://doi.org/10.1177/01925121211039985.

Deng, Xiaoping. "*Help The People Understand The Importance Of The Rule Of Law,*" http://web.peopledaily.com.cn/english/dengxp/v

Dittmer, Lowell. *Liu Shaoqi and the Chinese Cultural Revolution.* Armonk, NY: M. E. Sharpe, 1997.

Dittmer, Lowell. "Asia in 2017 Return of the Strongman," *Asian Survey* 58, no. 1 (January/February 2018): 1–9.

Diamant, Neil J., Stanley Lubman, and Kevin O'Brien. *Engaging the Law in China: State, Society and Possibilities for Justice.* Stanford, CA: Stanford University Press, 2005, 4.

DiMatteo Larry A., and Lei Chen, eds. *Chinese Contract Law: Civil and Common Law Perspectives.* Cambridge: Cambridge University Press, 2017.

Domonoske, Camila. "China imposes export controls on 2 metals used in semiconductors and solar panels," *NPR,* July 4, 2023. https://www.npr.org/2023/07/04/1185940293/china-imposes-export-controls-on-two-metals-used-in-semiconductors-and-solar-pan.

Dong, Xiaobo, and Zhang Yafang. "Translation and Research of Traditional Chinese Legal Classics." *China Legal Science* 9, no. 3 (May 2021): 23–58.

Dowdle, Michael W. "Heretical Laments: China and the Fallacies of 'Rule of Law.'" *Cultural Dynamics* 11 (1999): 287–314.

Dreyer, June T. "The 'Tianxia Trope': Will China Change the International System," *Journal of Contemporary China* 24, no. 96 (2015): 1015–1031, http://dx.doi.org/10.1080/10670564.2015.1030951.

Düben, Björn Alexander. "Xi Jinping and the End of Chinese Exceptionalism," *Problems of Post-Communism* 67, no. 2 (2020): 111–128. doi: 10.1080/10758 216.2018.1535274.

Duckworth, Angela. *Grit: The Power of Passion and Perseverance.* New York: Scribner, 2018.

Eaglen, Mackenzie. American Enterprise Institute, "10 Ways the United States Is Falling Behind China in National Security," https://www.jstor.org/stable/resrep52691. Accessed January 27, 2024.

Ebeling, Richard. *Political Economy, Public Policy and Monetary Economics: Ludwig von Mises and the Austrian Tradition.* New York: Routledge, 2010.

Ebrey, Patricia Buckley, ed. *Chinese Civilization: A Sourcebook.* New York: The Free Press, 1993, 205–206.

Economy, Elizabeth C. "China's Imperial President: Xi Jinping Tightens His Grip." *Foreign Affairs* (November/December 2014): 80–91.

Economy, Elizabeth C. *The Third Revolution: Xi Jinping and the New Chinese State.* London: Oxford University Press, 2018. Preface.

Economy, Elizabeth C. "The Third Revolution: Xi Jinping and the New Chinese State," https://www.csis.org/podcasts/chinapower/xi-jinpings-vision-china-conversation-dr-elizabeth-economy. Accessed June 20, 2023.

Emmers, Ralf. "Securitization," in Alan Collins, ed., *Contemporary Security Studies*. Oxford: Oxford University Press, 2010, 142.

Ericksona, Andrew S., and Adam P. Liffb. "Installing a Safety on the 'Loaded Gun'? China's institutional reforms, National Security Commission and Sino–Japanese crisis (in)stability," *Journal of Contemporary China* 25, no. 98 (2016): 197–215.

Fa, Shuzhi. *Chongzhen Zhuan (Biography of Chongzhen Emperor)* Beijing: Zhonghua shuju, 2021.

Fairbank, John K. *The United States and China*. Cambridge, MA: Harvard University Press, 1983.

Fairbank, John K. *The Chinese World Order*. Cambridge, MA: Harvard University Press, 1968.

Feng, Michael X. Y. "The 'Chinese Dream' Deconstructed: Values and Institutions," *Journal of Chinese Political Science*, no. 20 (2015): 163–83, http://doi.org/10.1007/s11366-015-9344-4.

Feng, Qiu. "Rujia zuowei xiandai Zhongguo zhi jiangouzhe" (Confucianism as the constructor of modern China) *Wenhua zongheng* (Beijing) (February 2014): 68–73.

Fewsmith, Joseph. "Balances, Norms and Institutions: Why Elite Politics in the CCP Have Not Institutionalized." *The China Quarterly*, no. 248 (2021): 265–82.

Fish, M. Steven. "The Hazards of Half-Measures: Perestroika and the Failure of Post-Soviet Democratization." *Demokratizatsiya* 13, no. 2 (Spring 2005): 241. http://www.gale.com/apps/doc/A135818429/AONE?u=anon~a7266bbd&sid=googleScholar&xid=9c815913.

Foley, John. "Zhu Rongji Merits China's Admiration Not Imitation." *Reuters*. August 14, 2014.

Ford, Christopher A. "The Party and the Sage: Communist China's Use of Quasi-Confucian Rationalizations for One-party Dictatorship and Imperial ambition." *Journal of Contemporary China* 24 no. 96 (2015): 1032–47. http://dx.doi.org/10.1080/10670564.2015.1030954.

Fukuyama, Francis. "America: The Failed State." *Prospect*, January 2017.

Fukuyama, Francis. "China's Bad Emperors," *Washington Post*, March 6, 2018. https://www.washingtonpost.com/news/theworldpost/wp/2018/03/06/xi/?nid&utm_term=.cfee54a2f020.

Fukuyama, Francis. *Political Order and Political Decay: From the Industrial Revolution to the Present Day*. New York: Farrar, Straus and Giroux, 2014.

Fukuyama, Francis. *The End of History and the Last Man*. New York: Free Press, 2006.

Fravel, M. Taylor. *Strong Borders, Secure Nation: Cooperation and Conflict in China's Territorial Disputes*. Princeton: Princeton University Press, 2008.

Freedom House. "Marking 50 Years in the Struggle for Democracy." https://freedomhouse.org/report/freedom-world/2023/marking-50-years. Accessed December 15, 2023.

Freymann, Eyck. *One Belt One Road: Chinese Power Meets the World*. Cambridge, MA: Harvard University Press, 2020.
Friedman, Milton. *Capitalism and Freedom*. Chicago: University of Chicago Press, 2002.
Fu, Hualing. "China's Striking Anti-Corruption Adventure: A Political Journey towards the Rule of Law?" In *The Beijing Consensus? How China Has Changed the Western Ideas of Law and Economic Development*, edited by Weitseng Chen. Cambridge: Cambridge University Press, 2016, 249–74.
Fu, Zhengyuan. *China's Legalists: The Earliest Totalitarians and their Art of Ruling*. Armonk and London: M. E. Sharpe, 1996.
Gallagher, Mary E. *Authoritarian Legality in China: Law, Workers, and the State*. Cambridge: Cambridge University Press, 2017.
Gang, Lin. "Zhengfu yu suijing—wenming kuozhan de guancha yu bijiao" (Conquest and appeasement: expansion of civilizations' observation and comparison) *Beijing Daxue Xuebao*, no. 5 (2012): 68–78.
Ge, Zhaoguang. "dui tianxia de xiangxiang—yige wutuobang xiangxian beihou de zhengzhei, sixiang, yu xueshu" (An imagination of tianxia—the politics, ideas and scholarship behind a utopia) *gu ge er yishu*, October 19, 2022. https://mp.weixin.qq.com/s/r7AknZhownURh6Rvf-fFag.
Ghiselli, Andrea. "Revising China's Strategic Culture: Contemporary Cherry-Picking of Ancient Strategic Thought," *The China Quarterly* 233 (2018): 166–85.
Gill, Chris. "Insights Into China's New Civil Code." *Asia Times Financial*, May 31, 2020. www.asiatimesfinancial.com/insights-into-china-s-new-civil-code.
Gilley, Bruce. *Tiger on the Brink: Jiang Zemin and China's New Elite*. Berkeley: University of California Press, 1998.
Jin, Guantao, and Liu Qingfeng, *Xing sheng yu wei ji: Lun Zhongguo she hui chao wen ding jie gou* (Prosperity and Crisis: China's Ultra-stable Social System) Hong Kong: Chinese University of Hong Kong Press, 1992.
Gong, Ting. "Dangerous Collusion: Corruption as a Collective Venture in Contemporary China," *Communist and Post-Communist Studies* 35, no. 1 (2002): 85–103.
Gong, Ting. "Managing Government Integrity under Hierarchy: Anti-Corruption Efforts in Local China," *Journal of Contemporary China* 24, no. 94 (2015): 684–700. http://dx.doi.org/10.1080/10670564.2014.978151.
Gosset, David B. "Xi Jinping—Person of the Year 2013," *The Huffington Post*, December 4, 2013. https://www.huffpost.com/entry/xi-jinping-person-of-the_b_4381233 Retrieved January 20, 2023.
Gow, Michael. "The Core Socialist Values of the Chinese Dream: Towards a Chinese Integral State." *Critical Asian Studies* 49 (2017): 92–116.
Grizold, Anton. "The Concept of National Security in the Contemporary World." *International Journal on World Peace* 11, no. 3 (September 1994): 37–53.
Guo, Bingna, James Hsiao, Bob Li, Royston C. Tan. "The Law on Foreign Relations of the People's Republic of China became effective on 1 July

2023." *Whitecase* July 20, 2023. https://www.whitecase.com/insight-alert/law-foreign-relations-peoples-republic-china-became-effective-1-july-2023.

Guo, Liangping. "Minzu fuxing ying ju pushi yiyi," *Lianhe caobao*, December 23, 2022. https://www.zaobao.com.sg/forum/views/story20221223-1346279.

Guo, Moruo. "Makesi jin wen miao" (Marx enters the Confucian temple), *Hong Shui*, no. 7 (1926).

Guo, Shuyong. *Zhongguo ruanshili zhanlue* (China's Soft Power Strategy) Beijing: Shishi Chubanshe, 2012.

Guo, Xuezhi. "Controlling Corruption in the Party: China's Central Discipline Inspection Commission." *The China Quarterly* 597 (2014): 597–624.

Han, Fei. *Basic Writings*, Burton Watson, trans. New York: Columbia University Press, 1964.

Hamlin, Rebecca. "Civil Rights." *Britannica*. www.britannica.com/topic/civil-rights. Accessed January 27, 2024.

Hayes, Louis. *Introduction to Japanese Politics*. London: Routledge, 2018.

He, Huifeng. "Parents Angry at Removal of Lu Xun's Works from China's School Textbooks," *South China Morning Post*, September 8, 2013, https://www.scmp.com/news/china/article/1305905/parents-angry-removal-lu-xuns-works-chinas-school-textbooks. Retrieved August 1, 2023.

He, Qinghua. "Bainian fazhilu, huihuang zhongguomeng," (Hundred year on rule accordingly to law and the Chinese Dream) *zhongguo sifa*, no. 7, 2022. https://mp.weixin.qq.com/s?__biz=MzI5MzkxMDQ4NQ==&mid=2247511013&idx=2&sn=46d97ec800404addcc61a3437c632fa8&chksm=ec68095fdb1f80491d2fe7261787d31e4b6ce6b3a0963a6a1d7658bfeb43d3ea7b41742981a7&scene=27 Retrieved August 31, 2023.

Hess, Steven. "The Flight of the Affluent in Contemporary China," *Asian Survey* 56, no. 4 (2016): 629–50.

Hillman, Ben and Graw Tuttle eds. *Ethnic Conflict and Protest in Tibet and Xinjiang: Unrest in China's West*. New York: Columbia University Press, 2016.

Hinnershitz, Stephanie D. *Japanese American Incarceration*. Philadelphia: University of Pennsylvania Press, 2022.

Ho, Norman P. "The Legal Thought of Emperor Taizong of the Tang Dynasty (618–907)" *Frontiers of Law in China* 12, no. 4 (2017): 584–625.

Ho, Ping-ti. *Studies on the Population of China, 1368–1953*. Cambridge, MA: Harvard University Press, 1959, 252.

Hobsbawm, Eric. *The Age of Extremes: The Short Twentieth Century, 1914–1991*. New York: Vintage, 1994.

Hogg, Chris. "China Ends Death Penalty for 13 Economic Crimes." BBC, February 25, 2011.

Holton, Richard. "Industrial politics in France: Nationalisation under Mitterrand," *West European Politics* 9, no. 1 (1986): 67–80. http://doi.org/10.1080/01402388608424563.

Hou, Liqiang. "Chinese Transfer $458.3 Billion Overseas in 2011," *China Daily*, January 22, 2014, http://europe.chinadaily.com.cn/business/2014-01/22/content_17253790.htm.
Howell, Jude. "NGOs and Civil Society: The Politics of Crafting a Civic Welfare Infrastructure in the Hu-Wen Period." *China Quarterly* 237 (2019): 58–81.
Howell, Jude. "Reassessing the Hu-Wen Era: A Golden Age Or Lost Decade for Social Policy in China." *The China Quarterly*, no. 2 (2019): 1–14.
Hsiao, Kung-Chuan. *Modern China and a New World: Kang Youwei, Reformer and Utopian, 1858–1927*. Seattle: University of Washington Press, 1975.
Hu, Angang. "Tian fu yu pinfu bujun" (Corruption and Social Inequality). *Jiangsu Social Sciences*, no. 3 (2001): 51–53.
Hu, Angang. "Dui zhongmei zonghe guoli de pinggu (1990–2013) (Evaluation of the Country Power of the United States and China), *Journal of Tsinghua University Philosophy and Social Sciences* no. 1, 2015. https://mp.weixin.qq.com/s/aZhkA_y-3_pxFJa75nCNYQ.
Hu, Weixing. "Xi Jinping's 'Big Power Diplomacy' and China's Central National Security Commission (CNSC)." *Journal of Contemporary China* 25, no. 98 (2016): 163–77. http://dx.doi.org/10.1080/10670564.2015.1075716.
Hu, Weixing. "Xi Jinping's 'Major Country Diplomacy': The Role of Leadership in Foreign Policy Transformation," *Journal of Contemporary China* 28, no. 115 (2019): 1–14 https://doi.org/10.1080/10670564.2018.1497904.
Hualong Net. "Jianchi sige zixin, buwang chuxin jixuqianjin" [Stick to four self-confidences, remember the original belief and march forward], July 10, 2016, https://finance.ifeng.com/a/20160710/14581205_0.shtml.
Hua, Shiping, ed. *Chinese Political Culture (1989–2000)*. Armonk, NY: M. E. Sharpe, 2001.
Hua, Shiping. "All Roads Lead to Democracy," *Bulletin of Concerned Asian Scholars (Now Critical Asian Studies)* 24, no. 1 (January–March, 1992): 43–56.
Hua, Shiping. "A Reversal of the Reform? China's Fifth Constitutional Amendment," *Asian Survey* 60, no. 6 (November/December 2020): 1172–93.
Hua, Shiping. *Chinese Legal Culture and Constitutional Order*, London: Routledge, 2019.
Hua, Shiping. *Chinese Utopianism: A Comparative Study of Reformist Thought with Japan and Russia (1898–1997)*. Redwood, CA: Stanford University Press, 2009.
Hua, Shiping. "One Servant, Two Masters: The Dilemma of Chinese Establishment Intellectuals." *Modern China* 20, no. 1 (January 1994): 92–121.
Hua, Shiping. *Reflections on the Triangular Relations of Beijing-Taipei-Washington since 1995: Status Quo at the Taiwan Strait?*. New York: Palgrave-Macmillan, 2006.
Hua, Shiping. *Scientism and Humanism: Two Cultures in Post-Mao China*. Albany: State University of New York Press, 1996.
Hua, Shiping. "The Battle between the Chinese Government and the Falun Gong," *Chinese Law and Government* 32, no. 5 (September/October 1999).

Hua, Shiping. "The Deng Reforms and the Gorbachev Reforms Revisited: A Political Discourse Analysis." *Problems of Post Communism* 53, no. 3 (May/June 2006): 3–16.
Hua, Shiping. "The Politics of Gender in the Chinese New Cinema." *Hong Kong Journal of Social Sciences* 12 (Autumn 1998): 53–65.
Hua, Shipping. "Yifazhiguo de wenhua rentong" (Cultural integration of rule of law), *Renmin Luntan,* 459, November 1, 2014.
Hua, Shipping. "Yifazhiguo de wenhua rentong," (Cultural acceptance of rule according to law) *Renmin luntan* November 17, 2014.
Huang, Chin-Hao. *Power and Restraint in China's Rise*. New York: Columbia University Press, 2022.
Huang, Jilu. *Yanjiu zhongshan xiansheng de shiliao yu shixue* (Study of Sun Yat-sen Historical Research Center) Taipei: zhonghua minguo shiliao yanjiu zhongxin, 1981, 557–565.
Huang, Tianlei and Nicolas Véron. "The Private Sector's Share of China's Largest Listed Companies Continued to Decline to 43 Percent in the Second Half of 2022," Peterson Institute for International Economics, February 2, 2023, https://www.piie.com/blogs/realtime-economics/private-sectors-share-chinas-largest-listed-companies-continued-decline-43.
Huang, Yasheng. *The Rise and Fall of the EAST: How Exams, Autocracy, Stability, and Technology Brought China Success, and Why They Might Lead to Its Decline*. New Haven, CT: Yale University Press, 2023.
Huang, Youqin, Shenjing He, and Li Gan. "Introduction to Special Issue: Unpacking the Chinese Dream of Homeownership." *Journal of Housing and the Built Environment* (2021): 1–7.
Huntington, Samuel. *The Clash of Civilizations and the Remaking of World Order*. New York: Simon & Schuster, 2011): 201, 205, 51, chapters 3–4.
Huntington, Samuel. *The Third Wave: Democratization in the Late 20th Century*. Oklahoma City: University of Oklahoma Press, 1993.
Huo Zhengxin. "China Enters an Era With a Civil Code." *C. J. Observer,* May 29, 2020. www.chinajusticeobserver.com/a/china-enters-an-era-with-a-civil-code. Accessed April 4, 2021.
Ikeda, Scott. "China's New Civil Code Would Be a Historic Expansion of Privacy Rights—Assuming It's Consistently Enforced." *CPO Magazine*, June 11, 2020. www.cpomagazine.com/data-protection/chinas-new-civil-code-would-be-a-historic-expansion-of-privacy-rights-assuming-its-consistently-enforced/. Accessed May 11, 2021.
Inglehart, Ronald. *Modernization and Postmodernization: Cultural, Economic, and Political Change in 43 Societies*. Princeton, NJ: Princeton University Press, 2020.
Inglehart, Ronald. *Modernization, Cultural Change, and Democracy*. New York: Cambridge University Press, 2005.
Inglehart, Surya P. "China's Approach to Human Rights and the UN Human Rights Agenda." *Chinese Journal of International Law* 14, no. 3 (2015): 437–64.

Jacques, Martin. *When China Rules the World: The Rise of the Middle Kingdom and the End of the Western World.* London: Penguin, 2012, 98.

Jardine, Bradley, and Natalie Hall. "The International Community Must Resist China's Abuse of Interpol." *Newsweek,* November 19, 2021. https://www.newsweek.com/international-community-must-resist-chinas-abuse-of-interpol-opinion-1650890.

Jett, Jennifer. "China's new map outrages its neighbors," September 1, 2023, NBC https://www.nbcnews.com/news/world/china-new-map-anger-india-south-china-sea-border-disputes-rcna102921.

Jia, Wenshan. *The Remaking of the Chinese Character and Identity in the 21st Century: The Chinese Face Practices.* Westport, CT: Praeger Publishers, 2001.

Jiang, Zemin, *Lun sange daibiao (On Three Represents).* Beijing: Zhongyang wenxian chubanshe. 2001, 19, 37, 49, 168–170.

Jiang interviewed by Mike Wallace, September 3, 2000. Accessed May 1, 2021. http://www.youtube.com/watch?v=1tNMH2M_jJ0.

Jiao, H. "Wuquanfa de xianxing Fenxi" (Analysis on of the Five Powers Constitution in the light of the current situation]. *Legal Science* (2006): 39–41.

Jin, Guantao, Jin and Liu Qingfeng. *Xingsheng yu Weiji: Zhongguo shehui chao wending jiegou* [Ultra-stable structure of China's feudal system] Beijing: falu chubanshe, 2011.

Johnson, Chalmers. *MITI and the Japanese Miracle: The Growth of Industrial Policy, 1925–1975.* Stanford, CA: Stanford University Press, 1982.

Johnston, Alastair Iain. *Cultural Realism: Strategic Culture and Grand Strategy in Chinese History.* Princeton, NJ: Princeton University Press, 1995, xi.

Kang, David C. *China Rising: Peace, Power, and Order in East Asia.* New York: Columbia University Press, 2010, 198.

Kang, David C.*East Asia before the West Five Centuries of Trade and Tribute.* New York: Columbia University Press, 2010, 167–69.

Kang, David C. "International Order in Historical East Asia: Tribute and Hierarchy Beyond Sinocentrism and Eurocentrism." *International Organization* (2019): 1–29. https://doi.org/10.1017/S0020818319000274.

Kardon, Isaac. "Rule by Law: China's Increasingly Global Legal Reach." Carnegie Endowment for International Peace, May 4, 2023. https://carnegieendowment.org/sada/89688.

Katzenstein, Peter J. *The End of the American Order.* Ithaca, NY: Cornell University Press, 2022.

Kautz, Carolin. "Power Struggle or Strengthening the Party: Perspectives on Xi Jinping's Anticorruption Campaign," *Journal of Chinese Political Science,* no. 25 (2020): 501–11.

Kennedy, John. "China Has at Least 1.8 Million Ready-to-Flee 'Naked Officials,' Anti-Corruption Rant Reveals," *South China Morning Post,* February 27, 2013.

Kennedy, Scott. "The Myth of the Beijing Consensus," *Journal of Contemporary China* 19, no. 65 (2010): 461–477, 470.

Kielsgard, Mark D., and Lei Chen. "The Emergence of Private Property Law in China and Its Impact on Human Rights." *Asian-Pacific Law & Policy Journal* 15 (2014): 94–134.

Kissinger, Henry. *On China*. New York: Penguin Books, 2012.

Klimeš, Ondřej and Maurizio Marinelli. "Introduction: Ideology, Propaganda, and Political Discourse in the Xi Jinping Era," *Journal of Chinese Political Science*, 23 (2018): 313–22.

Ko, Kilkon, and Cuifen Weng. "Critical Review of Conceptual Definitions of Chinese Corruption: A Formal-Legal Perspective," *Journal of Contemporary China* 20, no. 70 (2011): 359–78.

Koesel, Karrie J. "The Rise of a Chinese House Church: The Organizational Weapon," 2013. *The China Quarterly* 572, no. 215 (2013): 572–89.

Lach, Donald F. "Leibniz and China." *Journal of the History of Ideas* 6 (1945): 436–55.

Lampton, David. "Xi Jinping and the National Security Commission: Policy Coordination and Political Power." *Journal of Contemporary China* 24, no. 95 (2015): 759–77.

Lang, Bertram. "China's Anti-graft Campaign and International Anti-Corruption Norms: Towards a New International Anti-Corruption Order?," *Crime Law and Social Change* 70 (2018): 331–47.

Lantis, Jeffrey S. "Strategic Culture and National Security Policy," *International Studies Review* 4, no. 3 (Autumn, 2002): 87–113.

Lao, Tzu, Stephen Mitchell, trans. *Tao Te Ching*: A New English Version. New York: Harper Perennial Modern Classics, 2006.

Layne, Christopher. "The Global Power Shift from West to East," *National Interest*, April 25, 2012.: https://nationalinterest.org/article/the-global-power-shift-west-east-6796.

Layne, Christopher. "Leninism under Xi Jinping" *Journal of Contemporary China* 26, no. 103 (2017): 68–84. http://dx.doi.org/10.1080/10670564.2016.1206299.

Lewis, James B. *The East Asian War, 1592–1598: International Relations, Violence and Memory*. London: Routledge, 2014.

Li, Anthony H. F. "Centralization of Power in the Pursuit of Law-based Governance Legal Reform in China Under the Xi Administration." *China Perspectives* 2 (2016): 63–68.

Li, Cheng. *Chinese politics in the Xi Jinping era: Reassessing collective leadership*. Washington, D.C.: The Brookings Institution, 2016.

Li, Cheng. *Middle Class Shanghai: Reshaping U.S.-China Engagement*. Washington, DC.: Brookings Institution Press, 2021.

Li, Hua-yu. "The Political Stalinization of China: The Establishment of One-Party Constitutionalism, 1948–1954." *Journal of Cold War Studies* 3 (2001): 28–47.

Li, Hui, Ting Gong, and Hanyu Xiao, "The Perception of Anti-Corruption Efficacy in China: An Empirical Analysis," *Social Indicators Research* 3 (2016): 885–903.

Li, Li, and Peng Wang. "From Institutional Interaction to Institutional Integration: The National Supervisory Commission and China's New Anti-Corruption Model." *The China Quarterly* 240 (2019): 967–89.

Li, Ling. "The 'Organisational Weapon' of the Chinese Communist Party China's Disciplinary Regime from Mao to Xi Jinping." In *Law and the Party in China: Ideology and Organisation*. Edited by R. Creemers and S. Trevaskes. Cambridge: Cambridge University Press, 2020.

Li, Zehou, and Liu Zaifu. *Gaobie Geming: Huiwang ershi shiji Zhongguo* (Farewell, revolution: twentieth century China in retrospect) Hong Kong: Tiandi Tushu youxian gongsi, 1995, 82.

Lieberthal, Kenneth. "Introduction: The Fragmented Authoritarianism Model and Its Limitations." In *Bureaucracy, Politics, and Decision Making in Post-Mao China*, edited by Kenneth Lieberthaland David M. Lampton. Berkeley: University of California Press, 1992, 6–8.

Ling, Bing. "The New Contract Law in the Chinese Civil Code." *The Chinese Journal of Comparative Law* 8 (2020): 558–634.

Liu, Abby. "Hiding $2.34 Trillion in China," *Global Voices*, March 7, 2013, http://global voicesonline.org/2013/03/07/chinese-households-have-2-34-trillion-in-hidden-income/.

Liu, Mingyu. "Nature of New Power of Supervision and Judicial Supervision." *China Legal Science* 7 (2019): 123–25.

Liu, Qibao. "Guanyu zhongguo tese shehui zhuyi lilun tixi de jidian renshi," *Renmin Ribao* July 8, 2013. http://opinion.people.com.cn/n/2013/0708/c1003-22109528.html.

Liu, Wei. *China in the United Nations*. Singapore: World Scientific Press, 2014.

Liu, Xiang. *Zhan Guo Ce*, Vol. 5, Shanghai: Shanghai Guji Chubanshe, 1978, 190.

Liu, Zehua, ed. *Zhongguo gudai zhengzhi sixiang shi* (A history of Chinese political thought in pre-modern times). Tianjin: Nankai Daxue Chubanshe, 1994, 381–95.

Loewe, Michael. "Dong Zhongshu." In *A Biographical Dictionary of the Qin, Former Han and Xin Periods (221 BC–AD 24)* Leiden: Brill, 2000, 70–73.

Long, Yongtu: "Gap of Economic Power Still Exists between China and US. We need to have a Sense of Urgency." *Phenix Finance*: https://finance.ifeng.com/a/20180222/15991952_0.shtml. Accessed December 15, 2023.

Lorentzen, Peter, and Suzanne Scoggins. "Understanding China's Rising Rights Consciousness," *The China Quarterly* 223 (2015): 638–57.

Lorenzo, David J. "Sun Yat-sen and The San Min Chu I Lectures as Ideology." In *Chinese Ideology*, edited by Shiping Hua. London: Routledge, 2021.

Lu, Hsun. (Lu Xun) "A Madman's Diary," *Selected Stories of Lu Hsun*. Beijing: Foreign Languages Press, 1972.

Lu, Hsun. (Lu Xun). *The Real Story of Ah-Q and Other Tales of China: The Complete Fiction of Lu Xun.* London: Penguin, 2010.

Lu, Tian. "First-ever Chinese Civil Code Adopted at National Legislature: No 'IP Section,' Yet Still Relevant." *IPKIT*, May 31, 2020. http://ipkitten.blogspot.com/2020/05/first-ever-chinese-civil-code-adopted.html.

Ma, Chenjie. "China's Death Penalty Practice Undermines the Integrity of the Death Penalty as a Sentencing Option," *Australian Journal of Asian Law* 15, no. 2 (2014): 151–67.

Ma, Jihong. "The Constitutional Law of the People's Republic of China and its Development." *Columbia Journal of Asian Law* 23, no. 1 (2009): 175.

Ma, Linghe, ed., *Zhongguo jindai shi 1840–1949* (Modern China History). Beijing: Renmin Jieoyu chubanshe, 2015, 135–37.

MacFarquar, Roderick. "China: The Superpower of Mr. Xi." *New York Review of Books*, August 8, 2013. http://www.nybooks.com/articles/2015/08/13/china-superpower-mr-xi/.

MacFarquar, Roderick. *The Hundred Flowers Campaign and the Chinese Intellectuals.* New York: Praeger, 1960. *The Origins of the Cultural Revolution, Vol. 1: Contradictions among the People 1956–1957.* New York: Columbia University Press, 1974.

MacFarquar, Roderick. *The Origins of the Cultural Revolution: Volume III, the Coming of the Cataclysm 1961–1966.* New York: Columbia University Press, 1999.

McLaughlin, Kathleen. "Chinese Power Play: Xi Jinping Creates a National Security Council." *Christian Science Monitor,* November 13, 2013.

Maddison, Angus. *Chinese Economic Performance in the Long Run*, 2nd ed. Paris, OECD (2007): 213.

Magstadt, Thomas M. *Understanding Politics: Ideas, Institutions, and Issues.* Boston, MA: Cengage Learning, 2016.

Maizland, Lindsay. Council on Foreign Relations, "China's Repression of Uyghurs in Xinjiang," September 22, 2022. https://www.cfr.org/backgrounder/china-xinjiang-uyghurs-muslims-repression-genocide-human-rights.

Manion, Melanie. *Corruption by Design-Building Clear Government in Mainland China and Hong Kong.* Cambridge, MA: Harvard University Press, 2004.

Mannheim, Karl, and Louis Wirth, et al. *Ideology and Utopia: An Introduction to the Sociology of Knowledge.* Eastford, CT: Martino Fine Books, 2015, 196.

Mao, Zedong. *On the People's Democratic Dictatorship: Ideals and Ideologies.* London: Routledge, 2019.

Mao, Zedong. *The Chinese Revolution and the Chinese Communist Party* (Beijing: Foreign Languages Press, 1968).

Mao, Zedong. "Where Do Correct Ideas Come From?" In *The Chinese Cultural Revolution: Selected Documents,* edited by K.H. Fan. New York: Monthly Review Press, 1968, 31–32.

Marx, Karl. "Economic and Philosophic Manuscripts of 1844." Garden City, NY: Dover Books, 2007.

Marx, Karl. "Manifesto of the Communist Party." In Robert C. Tucker, ed., *The Marx-Engels Reader*, 475.

Marx, Karl. "Preface to a Contribution to the Critique of Political Economy." In Robert C. Tucker, ed., *The Marx-Engels Reader*.

Marx, Karl. "The German Ideology." In Robert C. Tucker, ed., *The Marx-Engels Reader*. New York: W. W. Norton, 1978, 163.

Mei, Hong. "Ruhe zhengque pingjia gaige kaifang qianhou de liangge 30nian," *Renmin Wang*, February 19, 2013, https://dangshi.people.com.cn/n/2013/0219/c85037-20530313.html.

Meisner, Maurice J. *Marxism, Maoism, and Utopianism: Eight Essays* Madison: University of Wisconsin Press, 1982.

Meissner, Maurice. "Marxism, Maoism, and Social Change: A Reexamination of the 'Voluntarism' in Mao's Strategy and Thought. A Response, F Wakeman." *Modern China* 3, no. 2 (1977): 161–68.

Mencius. *Mencius*, D. C. Lau, trans. London: Penguin, 2005.

Metzger, Thomas. *Escape from Predicament*, Columbia University Press. Reprint ed. October 15, 1986, 154–158, 220.

Minzer, Carl. "Legal Reform in the Xi Jinping Era," *Asia Policy*, Number 20 (July 2015): 4–9.

Minzner, Carl. *The End of an Era: How China's Authoritarian Revival is Undermining Its Rise*. New York: Oxford University Press, 2020.

Monitor (13 November 2013), http://www.csmonitor.com/World/Asia-Pacific/2013/1113/Chinese-powerplay-Xi-Jinping-creates-a-national-security-council.

Moody, Peter. "Some Reflections on Xi Jinping's Political Thought." In *Chinese Ideology*, edited by Shiping Hua. London: Routledge, 2021.

Mu, Qian. *Zhongguo wenhuashi daolun* (Introduction to Chinese cultural history) Beijing: Shangwu Chubanshe, 2023.

Mu¨llerson, Rein. "The Nation-State: Not Yet Ready For the Dustbin of "Human Rights Are Neither Universal Nor Natural *Chinese Journal of International Law* 17, no. 4 (2018): 925–42.

Nasu, Hitoshi. "The Expanded Conception of Security and International Law." *Amsterdam Law Forum* 3, no. 20 (2011).

National Defense University of China. "Jiaoliang wusheng (Silent Competition)" https://www.youtube.com/watch?v=-TjJsRi3VMg accessed September 29, 2023.

National Intelligence Council. "Tracking the Dragon: National Intelligence Estimate on China during the Era of Mao, 1948–1976," May 13, 1967, and "Economic Outlook for Communist China," May 25, 1965. Washington DC: National Intelligence Council, 2004, 494.

Naughton, Barry, and Kellee S. Tsai, eds. *State Capitalism, Institutional Adaptation, and the Chinese Miracle* (Comparative Perspectives in Business History) London: Cambridge University Press, 2015.

Nussbaum, Louis-Frédéric, and Käthe Roth. *Japan Encyclopedia*. Cambridge, MA: Harvard University Press, 2005.

Nye, Joseph S. Jr. *Soft Power: The Means To Success In World Politics*. New York: Public Affairs, 2005.

Ortmann, Stephan. "Legality and the Hong Kong protests," in *Chinese Legality: Ideology, Law and Institutions*, edited by Shiping Hua. London: Routledge, 2019.

Panda, Ankit. "The Truth About China's New National Security Law." *The Diplomat*, https://thediplomat.com/2015/07/the-truth-about-chinas-new-national-security-law/. Accessed September 29, 2023.

Patapan, Haig, and Yi Wang. "The Hidden Ruler: Wang Huning and the Making of Contemporary China." *Journal of Contemporary China* 27, no. 109 (2018): 47–60. https://doi.org/10.1080/10670564.2017.1363018.

Patapan, Haig, and Yi Wang. "Legalism and the Xi Jinping Thought: Han Fei's Influence on Contemporary Chinese Politics and Law," Chapter 4, in *Chinese Legality: Ideology, Law and Institutions*, edited by Shiping Hua. London: Routledge, 2022.

Pearson, Margaret M., Meg Rithmire, and Kellee Tsai. *The State and Capitalism in China* (Elements in Politics and Society in East Asia) New York: Cambridge University Press, 2023.

Peerenboom, Randall. *China's Long March toward Rule of Law*. London, Cambridge University Press, 2002. 44.

Peerenboom, Randall. *China Modernizes: Threat to the West or Model for the Rest?* New York: Oxford University Press, 2008.

Peerenboom, Randall. "Law and Development of Constitutional Democracy: Is China a Problem Case?" *The Annals of the American Academy of Political and Social Science* 603 (2006): 192, 198.

Pei, Minxin. "China in 2017: Back to Strongman Rule." *Asian Survey* 58, no. 1 (2018): 21–32.

Peng, Ming, ed. *Cong kongxiang dao kexue: Zhongguo shehui zhuyi sixiang fazhan de lishi kaocha* (From utopia to science: historical overview of the development of China's socialist thought) Beijing: Zhongguo Renmin Daxue Chubanshe (1986), 43.

Peters, Michael A. "The Chinese Dream: Xi Jinping Thought on Socialism with Chinese Characteristics for a New Era," *Educational Philosophy and Theory* 49, no. 14 (2017): 1299–1304. http://doi.org/10.1080/00131857.2017.1407578.

Pew, "Public Trust in Government: 1958–2023." https://www.pewresearch.org/politics/2023/09/19/public-trust-in-government-1958-2023/ Accessed on December 11, 2023.

Phenix TV, "An On-Line Survey about the Cultural Revolution. The Result Is Not Good." https://nam11.safelinks.protection.outlook.com/?url=https%3A

%2F%2Fmp.weixin.qq.com%2Fs%2FKjffHVzfZsCRqMcYy0n5Ag&data= 05%7C01%7Cshiping.hua%40louisville.edu%7Cb7de6254465047dd064 308db1f7a08fb%7Cdd246e4a54344e158ae391ad9797 b209%7C0%7C0%7C 638138381213321547%7CUnknown%7CTWFpbGZiI6Ik1sb3d8eyJWI joiMC4wLjAwMDAiLCJQIjoiV2luMzIiLCJBThaWwiLCJXVCI6Mn 0%3D%7C3000%7C%7C%7C&sdata=byBPcEdadXjkBPCELSDrz3hekt 1q2ZTV4cb5GlmobkE%3D&reserved=0.

Pieke, Frank N. *Knowing China.* Cambridge: Cambridge University Press, 2016, 24.

Pinkney, David H. "Nationalization of Key Industries and Credit in France After the Liberation," *Political Science Quarterly* 62, no. 3 (1947): 368–380.

Plato, *The Republic* trans. Richard W. Sterling and William C. Scott. New York: W. W. Norton, 1985, 48–49, 56–61.

Powers, John. *Introduction to Tibetan Buddhism.* Ithaca, New York: Snow Lion Publications, 2007.

Puddington, Arch and Tyler Roylance. "Anxious Dictators, Wavering Democrats," *Journal of Democracy* 27, no. 2 (2016): 86–100.

Purkayastha, Prabir. "US Chip Ban De Facto Declaration of War on China?" *Asia Times*, October 29, 2022. https://asiatimes.com/2022/10/us-chip-ban-de-facto-declaration-of-war-on-china/.

Quigley, Carroll. *The Evolution of Civilizations: An Introduction to Historical Analysis.* Indianapolis: Liberty Press, 1979.

Qiu Shi. "Yongyuan fuyao fangqi yishixingtai gongzuo," (Never Relax Ideological Works) no. 17, September 1, 2013.

Radio France International. www.wenxuecity.com/news/2021/04/15/10486255.html. Accessed April 5, 2021.

Reday, Joseph Z. "Reparations from Japan," *Far Eastern Survey* 18, no. 13 (1949): 145–51.

Reddy, Rahul Karan. "China's Anti-Corruption Campaign: Tigers, Flies, and Everything in Between." *The Diplomat*, May 12, 2022, https://thediplomat.com/2022/05/chinas-Anti-Corruption-campaign-tigers-flies-and-everything-in-between/.

Reedsmith. "The Adoption of the Chinese Civil Code and Its Implications on Contracts Relating to China." www.reedsmith.com/en/perspectives/2020/06/the-adoption-of-the-chinese-civil-code-and-its-implications-on-contracts. Accessed April 28, 2021.

Reilly, Thomas H. *The Taiping Heavenly Kingdom: Rebellion and the Blasphemy of Empire.* Seattle: University of Washington Press, 2004.

Reischauer, Edwin O. and Marius B. Jansen. *The Japanese Today: Change and Continuity.* Cambridge, MA: Harvard University Press, 1995.

Reuters. "China Wants to Mobilise Entire Nation in Counter-espionage." August 1, 2023. https://www.reuters.com/world/china/china-wants-mobilise-entire-nation-counter-espionage-2023-08-01/?utm_source=Sailthru&utm_medium=-Newsletter&utm_campaign=Daily-Briefing&utm_term=080123.

Renmin ribao. "Xi Jinping zongshuji guanyu zhongguo meng de jiqing huayu" (General Secretary Xi Jinping's excellent statements on the Chinese dream), November 30, 2012, 1.
Roberts, Dexter. "Almost Half of China's Rich Want to Emigrate," *Bloomberg Business Week*, September 15, 2014, http://www.businessweek.com/articles/2014-09-15/almost-half-of-chinas-richwant-to-emigrate.
Robson, William A. *Nationalised Industries in Britain and France*. London: Cambridge University Press, 2013.
Rödl & Partner. "China's Civil Code." www.roedl.com/insights/china-civil-code/china-adopts-civil-code. Accessed April 27, 2021.
Rotella, Sebastian, and Kirsten Berg. "Operation Fox Hunt: How China Exports Repression Using a Network of Spies Hidden in Plain Sight." July 22, 2021. *Propublica*, https://www.propublica.org/article/operation-fox-hunt-how-china-exports-repression-using-a-network-of-spies-hidden-in-plain-sight.
Rubenfeld, Samuel. "Report: Corrupt Chinese Officials Take $123 Billion Overseas." *Wall Street Journal*, June 16, 2011. https://www.wsj.com/articles/BL-CCB-4598.
Rummel, Rudy J. *Death by Government: Genocide and Mass Murder Since 1900*, 5th ed. London: Routledge, 1997.
Schram, Stuart R. "Economics in Command? Ideology and Policy Since the Third Plenum, 1978–84." *The China Quarterly* 99 (September 1984): 417–61.
Schram, Stuart R. "To Utopia and Back: A Cycle in the History of the Chinese Communist Party." *The China Quarterly*, no. 87 (September 1981): 407–39, 422.
Schumpeter, Joseph A. *Capitalism, Socialism and Democracy*. New York: Harper Perennial Modern Classics, 2008.
Schurmann, Franz. *Ideology and Organization of Communist China*. Berkeley: University of California Press, 1966.
Service, Robert. *A History of Twentieth-Century Russia*, 124–25. Cambridge, MA: Harvard University Press, 1997.
Shambaugh, David. "Contemplating China's Future." *Journal of Chinese Political Science* (2018): 1–7, 23.
Shambaugh, David. "The Evolution of American Contemporary China Studies: Coming Full Circle?," *Journal of Contemporary China*, 2023. http://doi.org/10.1080/10670564.2023.2237918.
Shan, Yuxiao, and Han Wei. "In Depth: Decoding China's First Civil Code." *Politics & Law*, June 1, 2020. www.caixinglobal.com/2020-06-01/in-depth-decoding-chinas-first-civil-code-101561290.html.
Shang, Yang. *The Book of Lord Shang. a Classic of the Chinese School of Law*. Clark, NJ: Lawbook Exchange, 2011.
Shank, Gregory. "Japan—U.S. Trade War?" *Social Justice* 21, no. 2 (Summer 1994): 20–23. https://wid.world/.
Shelley, Louise. "The Soviet Police and the Rule of Law," *Police Innovation and Control of the Police Problems of Law, Order, and Community*, eds. Lorraine Green, David Weisburd, and Craig Uchida. New York: Springer, 1993, 127–144.

Sheng, Hong. "Rujia de waijiao yuanze jiqi dangdai yiyi," (Confucian Foreign Policy Principles and Contemporary Significance) *Wenhua zongheng*, no. 8, 2012, 17, 45.

Shih, Chih-yu. *Post-Chineseness: Cultural Politics and International Relations*. Albany: State University of New York Press, 2022.

Shirk, Susan L. *China: Fragile Superpower*. London: Oxford University Press, 2008.

Sima, Qian, *Shi Ji*, Fa Ju and Cai Ze Biographies《史记•范雎蔡泽列传》

Shi Ji, Chapter 73: Bai Qi and Wang Jia Biographies 《三家注史记•卷七十三•白起王翦列传第十三》

Smith, Tobias. "Power Surge: China's New National Supervisory Commission." In *China Story Yearbook 2018: Power*, edited by Jane Golley, Linda Jaivin, Paul J. Farrelly and Sharon Strange. Canberra: Australian National University Press, 2018, 32–35.

Snyderm, C.R.R. *Psychology of Hope: You Can Get Here from There*. New York: Free Press, 2003.

So, Alvin Y. *Social Change and Development: Modernization, Dependency and World-System Theories*. Newbury Park, CA: SAGE, 1990.

Spence, Jonathan. *God's Chinese Son: The Taiping Heavenly Kingdom of Hong Xiuquan*. New York: W. W. Norton & Company, 1996.

Spires, Anthony J. "Lessons from Abroad: Foreign Influences on China's Emerging Civil Society," *The China Journal*, 68 (July 2012): 125–46.

Song, Zhihong. "National Security vs. Privacy Protection: Research on Practices in the United States after the September 11 Attacks," *China Legal Science* 2, no. 4 (2014): 88–114.

Sun, Tzu. *The Art of War*, edited and translated by Samuel B. Griffith, B. H. Liddell Hart. New York: Oxford University Press, 1971.

Sun, Yat-sen. *Sun Zhongshan Quanji* (Works of Sun Yat-sen), Vol. 2. Beijing: Zhonghua Shuju, 1981, 337–339, 524.

Sun, Zhen. "Utopia, nostalgia, and femininity: visually promoting the Chinese Dream," *Visual Communication* 18, no. 1 (2017): 107–133. https://doi.org/10.1177/1470357217740394.

Sutter, Robert. "The United States and Asia in 2017: The Impact of the Trump Administration." *Asian Survey* 58, no. 1 (February 2018): 10–20.

Sutter, Robert. *US-China Relations: Perilous Past, Uncertain Present*. Lanham, MD: Rowman & Littlefield, 2022.

Tang, Aijun. "Ideological Security as National Security," CSIS, edited by Jude Blanchette (December 2020). https://www.csis.org/analysis/ideological-security-national-security.

Tanner, Murray Scot. "China in 2015: China's Dream, Xi's Party," *Asian Survey* 56, no. 1 (2016): 19–33.

Tarasov, Katie. "Inside TSMC, the Taiwanese Chipmaking Giant That's Building a New Plant in Phoenix," *CNBC*, October 16, 2021. https://www.cnbc.com/2021/10/16/tsmc-taiwanese-chipmaker-ramping-production-to-end-chip-shortage.html.

The Guardian. "US, Japan, EU Team Up to Warn China of Concerns Over New Security Laws." March 1, 2016, https://www.theguardian.com/world/2016/mar/01/us-japan-eu-team-up-to-warn-china-of-concerns-over-new-security-laws.

Thomas, Jeffrey E. Chapter 2: "Rule of Law with Chinese Characteristics," in *Chinese Legality: Ideology, Law and Institutions*, edited by Shiping Hua. London: Routledge 2022.

Thornton, Patricia M. "The Advance of the Party: Transformation or Takeover of Urban Grassroots Society," *The China Quarterly* 213 (2013): 1–18.

Tian, Chenshan. *Chinese Dialectics: From Yijing to Marxism*. Lanham, MD: Lexington, 2005.

Tian, Linan. "On the Procedural Supervision over Interrogation in Investigation." *China Legal Science* 9, no. 5 (2021): 111–136.

Tooze, Adam. *Crashed: How a Decade of Financial Crises Changed the World*. New York: Viking, 2018.

Toynbee, Arnold and Daisaku Ikeda. *Choose Life: A Dialogue (Echoes and Reflections)*. London: I.B. Tauris, 2007.

Treaty of Shimonoseki (*Maguan Tiaoyue*), April 17, 1895, https://www.britannica.com/event/Treaty-of-Shimonoseki.

Tsang, Steve. "Party-state Realism: A Framework for Understanding China's Approach to Foreign Policy." *Journal of Contemporary China* 29, no. 122 (2020): 304–18. https://doi.org/10.1080/10670564.2019.1637562.

Tsinghua University, CISS, fabu [zhongguo ren de guoji Anquan guan "minyi diaocha baogao (2023) (Chinese People's View on International Security: Public Opinion Survey Report). https://m.thepaper.cn/baijiahao_23190848.

Tu, Hang. "Anticipatory Utopia and Redemptive Utopia in Post-revolutionary China." In *Utopia and Utopianism in the Contemporary Chinese Context*, edited by David Der-wei Wang, Angela Ki Che Leung and Yinde Zhang. Hong Kong: Hong Kong University Press, 2020, 99–114.

Turiel, Jesse, Edward Cunningham, and Anthony Saich. "To Serve the People: Income, Region and Citizen Attitudes towards Governance in China (2003–2016)." *The China Quarterly*, no. 906 (2019): 906–35.

Turner, Karen G. "Rule of Law Ideals in Early China?" *Columbia Journal of Asian Law* 6, no. 1 (1992): 1–44. *The Limits of the Rule of Law in China*. Seattle: University of Washington Press, 2000.

United Nations. "China: UN experts alarmed by separation of 1 million Tibetan children from families and forced assimilation at residential schools," February 6, 2023 https://www.ohchr.org/en/press-releases/2023/02/china-un-experts-alarmed-separation-1-million-tibetan-children-families-and.

United Nations Human Rights. "UN human rights chief says China's new security law is too broad and vague," https://www.ohchr.org/en/press-releases/2015/07/un-human-rights-chief-says-chinas-new-security-law-too-broad-too-vague#:~:text=China%20%2F%20new%20law%20on%20national%20security&text=%E2%80%9CThis%20law%20raises%20many%20concerns,%2C%E2%80%

80%9D%20High%20Commissioner%20Zeid%20said. Accessed September 29, 2023.
Varley, Paul. *Japanese Culture*. 4th Edition. Honolulu: University of Hawaii Press, 2000.
VOA. "zhongguo duiwai guanxifa: quefa xinyi de fanzhi xuanyan" (China's Foreign Relations Law: A declaration on sanctions that is Lack of Novelty) July 7, 2023. https://www.voachinese.com/a/china-launches-foreign-relations-law-in-response-to-suppression-of-its-development-20230707/7171283.html.
Vogel, Ezra F. *China and Japan: Facing History*. Cambridge, MA: Harvard University Press, 2019.
Voice of Germany "fazhi xifang zhicai, zhongguo tui "duiwai guanxifa (Counter sanctions of the West, China Promulgated Foreign Relations Law), 29 June 2023.
Walter, Albert. *The Future of China's Past: Reflections on the Meaning of China's Rise*. Albany: State University of New York Press, 2023.
Wang, Di. "Jia, as in Guojia: Building the Chinese Family into a Filial Nationalist Project." *China Law and Society Review* 5 (2020): 1–32.
Wang, Dongyue. *renlei de moluo (Decline of Mankind)*. Xian: Shaanxi chuban jituan, 2010.
Wang, Jiangyu, and Hua Cheng. "China's Approach to International Law: From Traditional
Wang, Jiangyu, and Hua Cheng. "Westphalianism to Aggressive Instrumentalism in the Xi Jinping Era." *The Chinese Journal of Comparative Law* 10, no. 1 (2022): 140–53. https://doi.org/10.1093/cjcl/cxac020.
Wang, Min. *Lilun yu shijian yanjiu: Jiang Zemin shehuizhuyi wenhua jianshe* (Studies of theories and practice: Jiang Zemin's socialist cultural construction) Jinan: Shangdong Renmin Chubanshe, 2005, 635.
Wang, Weiguang. "There is s Nothing Wrong with Adhering to the People's Democratic Dictatorship," *Qiushi*, September 23, 2014. http://www.qstheory.cn/dukan/hqwg/2014-09/23/c_1112586776.htm.
Wang, Yi. 'Speech on China's Diplomacy," December 31, 2014. http://www.fmprc.gov.cn/mfa_chn/wjb_602314/wjbz_602318/zyjhs/t1224950.shtml.
Wang, Zhonghan. "Tian Weijing Zhuan" [Biography of Tian Wenjing]. In *Qing Shi Lie Zhuan* edited by Wang Zhonghan (Biographies of Qing), Vol. 13. Beijing: Zhong Hua Shuju, 2016, 961.
Wang, Zhongyan. "Democracy with Chinese Adjectives: Whole-process Democracy and China's Political Development," in *CPC Futures: The New Era of Socialism with Chinese Characteristics*," edited by Frank N. Pieke and Bert Hofman. Singapore: National University of Singapore Press, 2022.
Watson, Burton. *Han Feizi—Basic Writings*, 2. New York: Columbia University Press, 2003.
Weber, Max. *The Protestant Ethic and the "Spirit" of Capitalism and Other Writings*. London: Penguin, 2002.
Weber, Max. *The Religion of China: Confucianism and Taoism*. Springfield, OH: Collier-Macmillan, 1964, 227–248, 241.

Wedeman, Andrew. "Policing the Police, Party, and State: Corruption and Anti-Corruption in China," Chapter 11 in *Chinese Legality: Ideology, Law and Institutions*, edited by Shiping Hua. London: Routledge, 2022.

Wen, Wei. "China's New General Provisions of Civil Law: Changes and Advancements for the Better." *LAWASIA Journal* (January 2018). https://papers.ssrn.com/sol3/papers.cfm?abstract_id=3171363.

White, Lynn. "Chinese Constitutional Currents." *Modern China* 36, no. 1 (2010): 100–14.

Wittfogel, Karl A. *Oriental Despotism: A Comparative Study of Total Power*. New Haven, CT: Yale University Press, 1957.

Wolfers, Arnold. "National Security as an Ambiguous Symbol," *Political Science Quarterly* 67 (1952): 481–502.

Wong, Chun Han. "China Adopts Sweeping National-Security Law." *Wall Street Journal*, https://www.wsj.com/articles/china-adopts-sweeping-national-security-law-1435757589. Accessed September 29, 2023.

Wong, Edward. "Security Law Suggests a Broadening of China's 'Core Interests,'" *New York Times*, July 2, 2015. https://archive.nytimes.com/www.nytimes.com/2015/07/03/world/asia/security-law-suggests-a-broadening-of-chinas-core-interests.html.

Wong, Yiu-chung. "Assessing the Era of Jiang Zemin." In *Chinese Ideology*, edited by Shiping Hua. London: Routledge. World Bank data. 2021. https://data.worldbank.org/indicator/NY.GDP.MKTP.KD.ZG?locations=CN.

World Bank Data. https://data.worldbank.org/indicator/NE.TRD.GNFS.ZS?locations=CN. Retrieved August 31, 2023.

Wu, Han, ed., *Lichao shilu zhong de Zhongguo shiliao*, Vol. 1 (History materials in the archives of the past dynasties) Beijing: Zhonghua Shuju, 1980, 115.

Wu, Guo. "Why the Chinese People Are Invisible in US Media." Accessed April 26, 2021. www.thinkchina.sg/why-chinese-people-are-invisible-us-media.

Wu, Xiaohui. "From Assimilation to Autonomy: Realizing Ethnic Minority Rights in China's National Autonomous Regions." *Chinese Journal of International Law* 13, no. 1 (2014): 55–90.

Wu, Zhicheng. "xieshou tuidong "sanda quanqio changyi," luodizoushi yinling renlei fanzhan maixiang guangming weilai," (Promote three global initiatives, lead the mankind to march to the bright future), *Guangmin Daily*, September 12, 2023. http://theory.people.com.cn/n1/2023/0912/c40531-40075578.html.

Wuthnow, Joel. "China's Much-Heralded NSC Has Disappeared: Is it a sign of Beijing's secrecy or Xi Jinping's weakness?" *Foreign Policy*, June 30, 2016. https://foreignpolicy.com/2016/06/30/chinas-much-heralded-national-security-council-has-disappeared-nsc-xi-jinping/.

Wuthnow, Joel. "China's New Black Box: Problems and Prospects for the Central National Security Commission." *The China Quarterly* 232, no. 886 (2017).

Xi, Jinping. *How to Deepen Reform Comprehensively*. Beijing: Foreign Languages Press, 2014, 9.

Xi, Jinping. "Xieshou xiaochu pinkun, cujin gongtong fazhan," (Eliminating poverty hand in hand, promote joint development) *Renmin Ribao,* October 17, 2015, http://cpc.people.com.cn/n/2015/1017/c64094-27709112.html.

Xi Jinping's report at 19th CPC National Congress. http://www.xinhuanet.com/english/special/2017-11/03/c_136725942.htm. Accessed January 27, 2024.

Xiang, Shuchen. "Tianxia and Its Decolonial Counterparts: "China" as Civilization, Not Ethnicity." *The China Review* 23, no. 2 (May 2023): 165–87.

Xin, Yuxi. "Songchao zhe san ge huangdi jing jujue dengji, bu kendang huangdi," blog, March 24, 2023, 14:45:01. http://zs.aipingxiang.com/ls/13252.html.

Xinhua News Agency. "Jujiao xin guojia anquanfa wudaliangdian" (Focus on Five Points in the New National Security Law) July 1, 2015, http://www.xinhuanet.com//politics/2015-07/01/c_1115787097_2.htm.

Xinhua News Agency. "Guanyu zhongguomeng, Xi Jinping zongshuji shi zheyang miaohuide [On Chinese Dream, General Party Secretary Xi Jinping has this to say] November 30, 2016, http://news.cctv.com/2016/11/30/ARTIANwy45Nvn1PRGbNqhASG161130.shtml.

Xinhua News Agency. "Supervision Law Gives Legal Teeth to China's Graft-Busting Agency." March 20, 2018, http://www.chinadaily.com.cn/a/201803/20/WS5ab1172da3106e7dcc143eef.html.

Xinhua News Agency. "Xi Focus-Quotable Quotes: Xi Jinping on freedom," March 4, 2021. http://www.xinhuanet.com/english/2021-03/04/c_139783183.htm.

Xinhua News Agency. "Xi Jinping: Jiejian lishi youxiu lianzheng wenhua, buduan tigao jufu fangbian nengli" (Make use of the Clean Governance Experience in Chinese Culture, Raise the Capacity of Anti-Corruption), 2013. *Renmin Wang,* http://politics.people.com.cn/n/2013/0420/c1001-21214843.html.

Xinhua News Agency. "Xi Jinping: Rang shichang ze ziyuan peizhizhong qi jueding zuoyong, bu neng huidao jihuajingji de laolushang qu (Xi Jinping: Let the market play a decisive role: We can't go back to planned economy), May 23, 2020, https://www.gov.cn/xinwen/2020-05/23/content_5514220.htm.

Xinhua News Agency. "Xi Jinping zai zhongfa jianjiao 50 zhoujian jinian dahui shangde jianghua," (Speech on the 50th Anniversary of the Establishment of Sino-French Diplomatic Relations), https://news.12371.cn/2014/03/28/ARTI1395961336034916.shtml.

Xin Jing Bao. "Jiaoyubu fawen: Yiwu jiaoyu bude shiyong jingwai jiaocai (Free Education Can't Use Foreign Text Materials). January 7, 2020, https://view.inews.qq.com/wxn/20200107A07VKV00?tbkt=B5&pushid=2020010702&strategy=&openid=o04IBAHH7C8vWnfXMxtBJ4VAIvxs&uid=&sharer=o04IBAHH7C8vWnfXMxtBJ4VAIvxs&shareto=&key=&version=1800272c&devicetype=iOS16.5.1&wuid=oDdoCt8Zf30JhT5j7TJ6jJAwkntU&openwith=wxmessage&hiter=false&originPath=w2.

Xu, Chongde. "Peng Zhen yu 1982 nian xianfa de xiugai gongzuo," (Peng Zhen and the 1982 constitution revision) July 16, 2015, CCP History http://www.zgdsw.org.cn/n/2015/0716/c244516-27316121.html.

Xu, Keyue. "Wang Yi calls on Japan, S.Korea to practice open regionalism, resist coercion Trilateral cooperation mechanism expected to restart under joint efforts," "The 2023 International Forum for Trilateral Cooperation." (In Qingdao) https://www.globaltimes.cn/page/202307/1293640.shtml. Accessed October 16, 2023.

Xu, Guangqiu. "Eight Foreign Armies Invasion of China." In *China at War: An Encyclopedia*, edited by Xiaobing Li. New York: Bloomsbury Academic, 2012.

Xu, Jilin. "Duoyuan wenming shidai de Zhongguo shiming" (Multi-civilizations and China's Destiny," *Wenhua Zongheng* 87 (June 2013).

Xue, Yujie. "Jack Ma's School for Business Elites Drops 'University' from Its Name." *South China Morning Post*, May 17, 2021. https://www.scmp.com/tech/big-tech/article/3133783/jack-mas-school-business-elites-drops-university-its-name.

Yan, Jiaqi, and Gao Gao. *Turbulent Decade: A History of the Cultural Revolution* (Shaps Library of Translations) Honolulu: University of Hawaii Press, 1996.

Yan, Siqi. "Taiwan chaoye yizhi fandui dalu guojia anquanfa (Taiwan's Ruling and Oppositions Parties Are Against National Security Law), BBC, July 2, 2015. https://www.bbc.com/zhongwen/trad/china/2015/07/150702_taiwan_china_security-law_reax.

Yang, Feng. "The Future of China's Personal Data Protection Law: Challenges and Prospects." *Asia Pacific Law Review* (September 2019): 62–82. Published online: August 5.

Yang, Guangbin. "Xi Jinping Zhongzhi sixiang tixi chutan" (A Primary Study on Xi Jinping's Political Thought System), *Xue Hai*, no. 4, 2017, Renmin University, https://mp.weixin.qq.com/s/wC1ed9f1y9zqCmEW58JdEA.

Yang, Yang. "Over 84% Companies in China Are Private." *China Daily*, November 28, 2019.

Ye, Zicheng, and Long Quanlin. "*Hua Xia Zhuyi (China-ism)*" Beijing: Renmin Chubanshe 2017, 224–25.

Ye, Zicheng, and Long Quanlin. *Inside China's Grand Strategy: The Perspective from the People's Republic*. trans. by Guoli Liu and Steven I. Levine. Lexington, KY: University Press of Kentucky, 2011.

You, Ji. "China's National Security Commission: Theory, Evolution and Operations," *Journal of Contemporary China* 25, no. 98 (2016): 178–96. https://www.britannica.com/biography/Jack-Ma.

"China's National Security Commission: Theory, Evolution and Operations." https://baike.baidu.com/item/人民的名义/17545218?fr=ge_ala.

Yu, Guanghua. *The Roles of Law and Politics in China's Development*. New York: Springer, 2014.

Yu, Yizhu. "Cong xibai wenge dao huifu lishixing dingxing, zhongguo jiaokeshu xiugai beihou fasheng le shenmo (From White Wash the Cultural Revolution to Restore the Renouncing it, What Is Going on Behind the Chinese Textbook Revisions)." *Duowei News*, September 7. Accessed May 11, 2021.

www.dwnews.com/中国/60210791/从洗白文革到恢复历史定性中国教科书修改背后发生了什么.

Yuan, Li. "*Private Businesses Built Modern China. Now the Government Is Pushing Back. New York Times*, October 3, 2018. https://www.nytimes.com/2018/10/03/business/china-economy-private-enterprise.html?smid=nytcore-ios-share.

Zarrow, Peter. *Abolishing Boundaries: Global Utopias in the Formation of Modern Chinese Political Thought (1880–1940)* Albany: State University of New York Press, 2021.

Zarrow, Peter. "Liberalism and Utopianism in the New Culture Movement: Case Studies of Chen Duxiu and Hu Shi," pp. 36–52 in David Der-wei Wang, Angelia Ki Che Leung, and Zhang Yinde, eds., *Utopia and Utopianism in the Contemporary Chinese Context*. Hong Kong: Hong Kong University Press, 2020.

Zeng, Ka. "Complementary Trade Structure and U.S.-China Negotiations over Intellectual Property Rights." *East Asia* 20 (2002): 54–80. https://doi.org/10.1007/s12140-002-0003-y.

Zhai, Keith, Gabriel Crossley, and Yew Lun Tian. "China Set to Implement Its First Civil Code, as Private Investment Slows." *Reuters*, May 21, 2020. www.reuters.com/article/us-china-parliament-civil-code/china-set-to-implement-its-first-civil-code-as-private-investment-slows-idUSKBN22X0TC.

Zhai, Tiantian, and Yen-Chiang Chang. "The Contribution of China's Civil Law to Sustainable Development: Progress and Prospects." *Sustainability* 11 (2019).

Zhang, Hongjie. *Daming wangchao de qige miankong (Seven faces of the Ming Empire)* Guangzhou, Guangdong renmin chubanshe, 2016.

Zhang, Laney. "Chinese Law on Private Ownership of Real Property." *Library of Congress*, March 10, 2015. Accessed April 25, 2021. https://blogs.loc.gov/law/2015/03/chinese-law-on-private-ownership-of-real-property/.

Zhang, Wei. "shehuizhuyi chujijieduan lilun de lishi fazhan yuqishi" (The theory of primary stage of socialism's development and insights) *Guangxi shehui kexue*, 164, 2 (2009): 6–9.

Zhang, Xianchu. "The New Round of Civil Law Codification in China." *University of Bologna Law Review* 1 (2016).

Zhao, Suisheng. "China's Belt-Road Initiative as the Signature of President Xi Jinping Diplomacy: Easier Said than Done," *Journal of Contemporary China* 29, no. 123 (2020): 319–35. https://doi.org/10.1080/10670564.2019.1645483.

Zhao, Suisheng. "Deng Xiaoping's Southern Tour: Elite Politics in Post-Tiananmen China." *Asian Survey* 33 (1993): 739–56.

Zhao, Suisheng. "Rethinking the Chinese World Order: The Imperial Cycle and the Rise of China," *Journal of Contemporary China* 24, no. 96 (2015): 961–82. http://dx.doi.org/10.1080/10670564.2015.1030913.

Zhao, Suisheng. "Xi Jinping's Maoist Revival," *Journal of Democracy* 27, no. 3 (July 2016): 83–97.

Zhao, Tingyang. *Tianxia tixi: Shijie zhidu zhexue daolun (The Under-Heaven System: The Philosophy for the World Institution)* Beijing: Zhongguo Renmin Chubanshe, 2011, 1.

Zhao, Tingyang. "Political Realism and the Western Mind Exploring an alternative based upon 'relational rationality' and 'Confucian improvement." In *The Edinburgh Companion to Political Realism,* edited by Robert Schuett and Miles Hollingworth. Edinburgh: Edinburgh University Press, 2018, 23–36. http://www.jstor.org/stable/10.3366/j.ctv2f4vqhm.

Zheng, Yinglong, and Yang Ping. "Three Significant Dimensions in the Connection of Supervision System Reform and Judicial System Reform in China." *China Legal Science* 85, no. 5 (2021): 85.

Zhou, Zhen. "Jianguo chuqi Xin San Fan Yundong Shuping," [A new interpretation of the Three Antis in the early 1950s]. *Journal of UESTC* 13, no. 2 (2011): 77–82.

Zhonggong zhongyang wenxian yanjiushi, ed., *Xi Jinping guanyu shixian Zhonghua minzu weida fuxing de Zhongguo meng: Lunshu gaobian* (Xi Jinping on the rejuvenation of the Chinese nation): Beijing: Zhongyang wenxian chubanshe (December 2013): 3, 5.

Zhongguo jianchabao, "Shinianlai fafubai douzheng chengxiao youmu gongdu, chenggong zouchu yikao zhidu youshi,fazhi youshi fafubai zhilu," (Everybody can see that the Anti-Corruption campaign has achieved a lot. The achievement is because of the superiority of the system, and rule according to law), October 16, 2022, http://fanfu.people.com.cn/n1/2022/1016/c64371-32546268.html.

Zhongyang Dangxiao zhongguo tese shehuizhuyi lilun tixi yanjiuzhongxin. "Xi Jinping xinshidai zhongguo teseshehuizhuyi sixiang shi yige xitongwanzheng,luojiyanmi de kexue lilun tixi," (Xi Jinping New Era Socialist Thought with Chinese Characteristics Is a Comprehensive and Logically Tight Scientific Theory), *Guangming Ribao,* November 28, 2017.

Zhu, Gongliang. "Zhu Yuanzhan zhili jintan xi" (An analysis of Zhu Yuanzhang's Anti-Corruption efforts) *She Hui Kexue* (Social Science), 11 (1991).

Zhu, Guobin, Jian Qu, and Han Zhai. "Paradigm Shift in Chinese Legal Studies." In *Paradigm Shifts in Chinese Studies*, edited by Shiping Hua. London: Palgrave Macmillan, 2021.

Zhu, Jiangnan. "Out of China's Reach: Globalized Corruption Fugitives." *The China Journal* 86, no. 4 (2021): 90–113.

Zitelmann, Rainer. "State capitalism? No, the private sector was and is the main driver of China's economic growth," *Forbes,* September 30, 2019, https://www.forbes.com/sites/rainerzitelmann/2019/09/30/state-capitalism-no-the-private-sector-was-and-is-the-main-driver-of-chinas-economic-growth/?sh=64504db527cb.

Index

Administrative Supervision Law of the People's Republic of China (2010), 59, 71
Administrative Supervision Statutes of the People's Republic of China (1990), 59
Adoption Law, 81
All-China Federation of Industry and Commerce, 22
Almond, Gabriel, 123
Ames, Roger, 64, 217n40
an quan shi ying daoli (security is the hard truth), 55
The Analects (Confucius), 12
anti-corruption strategies, 26. *See also* Administrative Supervision Law of the People's Republic of China; Administrative Supervision Statutes of the People's Republic of China; National Supervision Law; supervision laws
  centralization of, 70
  criticism of, 75
  domestic, 70–75
  efficient governance traditions and, 121
  guanxi and, 61, 75
  during Ming dynasty, 60
  Operation Fox Hunt and, 73–74
  overseas, 70–75
  in People's Republic of China, 61–62
  as selective, 75
  in Soviet Union, 60–61
  under Xi Jinping, 76, 121–122
Anti-Espionage Law, China, 51
APEC. *See* Asia-Pacific Economic Cooperation
The Art of War (Sun Tzu), 95, 100, 107–108, 112–113
Asia-Pacific Economic Cooperation (APEC), 74–75
authoritarianism
  in China, 34, 125–126
  fragmented authoritarianism model, 45

bainian weiyou zhi dabianju (a great change that has not happened in a hundred years), 82
Bandung Spirit, 244n67
Belt and Road Initiative (BRI), 109
Bequelin, Nicholas, 72
Biden, Joseph, 96, 98–99, 103
Blanchette, Jude, 123
Book of Lord Shang, 26
BRI. *See* Belt and Road Initiative
bu wang chu xin (never forget about the original goals of CCP), 91

280 | Index

Buddhism, 48
Buzan, Barry, 45, 100

capitalism. *See also* private property; state capitalism
  in China, 35
  failures of, 40
  political, 23
  Sun Yat-sen and, 22
CASS. *See* Chinese Academy of Social Sciences
CCDI. *See* Central Commission of Disciplinary Inspection
CCP. *See* Chinese Communist Party
CDIs. *See* Commission of Disciplinary Inspections
Central Commission of Disciplinary Inspection (CCDI), 60, 66–68
Chen, Albert, 4
Chen Boda, 32
Chen Zhiwu, 24–25
Cheng (King), 215n16
chi ren (cannibalism), 117
China (People's Republic of China) (PRC). *See also* Chinese Communist Party; Civil Code; constitutional law; Fifth Constitutional Amendment; Republic of China; *specific leaders*; *specific topics*
  Administrative Supervision Law of the People's Republic of China, 59, 71
  Administrative Supervision Statutes of the People's Republic of China, 59
  Adoption Law, 81
  Anti-Corruption campaigns in, 26
  anti-corruption strategies in, 61–62
  Anti-Espionage Law, 51
  authoritarianism in, 34, 125–126
  Biden administration and, 96
  broadcasting media in, 31
  capitalism in, 35
  civil rights in, 83–86
  Constitution of, 20
  constitutional amendments and reforms in, 30–31
  constitutionalism in, 21
  Contracts Law, 81
  Criminal Procedure Law, 71–72
  emergence of middle class in, 85
  Five Principles of Peaceful Coexistence, 100, 102, 105, 242n34
  foreign investment in, 20
  Foreign Investment Law, 22, 214n42
  freedom in, 104
  global GDP for, 2–3, 108
  hegemonic power in East Asia, 102
  human rights conventions in, 53
  Hundred Flowers Movement in, 61
  Hundred-Years of Humiliation in, 112–113
  Inheritance Law, 81
  International Convention on the Elimination of All Forms of Racial Discrimination in, 53
  in Interpol, 75
  Japanese invasion of, 106, 108
  Law on National Regional Autonomy of 1984, 48–49
  Manchus society in, 100–101
  Marriage Law of 1980, 81
  Marxism in, 19–21
  Mongol society in, 100–101
  new global order for, 95–97
  nongovernmental organizations in, 46
  opposition to unilateralist political approaches, 96
  peasant rebellion in, 17
  People's Police Law, 71
  pluralism and, 96

political reform failures in, 20
Property Law, 87
Rights in Rem Law, 81
San Fan Movement in, 61
Soviet influences in, 19–21
Taiping Rebellion, 31, 119
Tort Liability Law, 81
trade war with U.S., 52, 78
Transparency International assessment of, 76
Trump administration and, 95–96
Westphalian principles in, 103
in World Trade Organization, 72, 123–124
Xinhua News Agency and, 2
Chinese Academy of Social Sciences (CASS), 30
democracy concept in, 105
Chinese civilization. *See also* Civilization Initiative
characteristics of, 99–102
tianxia and, 99–101
Chinese Communist Party (CCP)
Chinese Dream and, 1
civil liberties and, 115–116
Constitutions influenced by, 30–31
Four Constitutional Amendments and, 38–39
legitimacy of, 66–67
political security and, 45–46
under Xi Jinping, 97
Chinese Dream. *See also* datong
Chinese Communist Party and, 1
conceptual approach to, 1–3
cultural traditions in, 37
definition of, 2
democracy and, 2, 7
Foreign Relations Law and, 95
freedom and, 2, 6–7
hope and, 11
through law, 6–8, 19–23
meaning of, 211n1

socialism and, 2
state capitalism and, 7, 19
utopianism and, 3, 7, 11–19
variability of, 6
Xi Jinping and, 1
Xi regime and, 1
xiaokang in, 13
Chinese utopias, 217n32
Chin-Hao Huang, 106
Chongzhen (Emperor), 120
chou fu (people hated the rich), 55
chou guan (people hated the government), 55
Christianity, hope of afterlife in, 13
Civil Code of 1898, in Japan, 82
Civil Code of the People's Republic of China, 1, 22, 65
civil juristic acts under, 170–174
civil laws under, 77, 168–169
civil liability under, 176–178
civil rights under, 83–86, 152–154
conceptual approach to, 77–79
constitutional amendments as influence on, 82–83
contract laws and, 77, 89–90
cultural traditions and, 89–90
death declarations, 157–159
Deng Xiaoping and, 78
divorce regulations under, 89
Draft Civil Code and, 79
early Chinese constitutions as influence on, 80
early history of, 77, 79–83
economic impact of, 78, 92
Fifth Constitutional Amendment and, 82–83, 90–91
foreign experiences with, 89–90
general provisions of, 151–152
guardianship mechanisms in, 154–157
historical context for, 90–93
household management under, 159

Civil Code of the People's Republic of China *(continued)*
  Hu Jintao and, 81
  human rights protections under, 54
  illegal detentions under, 88–89
  Japanese influences on, 79
  legal persons under, 160–167
  limitations of actions under, 178–180
  marriage rights, 89
  missing person declarations, 157–159
  modernization and, 89–90, 92
  natural persons under, 152–159
  Pandekten system as influence on, 90
  personal agency in, 174–176
  pragmatic characteristics of, 79
  primary stage socialism and, 90
  privacy protections in, 85–86, 88
  private property laws and, 77
  Qin dynasty and, 79
  sexual harassment definitions in, 85
  social goals of, 78–79
  socialism under, 86
  Soviet Civil Code as influence on, 80
  state's rights under, 87–89
  structural elements of, 77
  theoretical context for, 90–93
  time periods in, 180
  unincorporated organizations under, 167
  U.S.-China trade war and, 78
  World Trade Organization and, 81
  Xi regime and, 81–82
civil juristic acts
  under Civil Code of the People's Republic of China, 170–174
  conditions of, 173–174
  effects of, 171–173
  expression of intent, 170–171
civil laws, under Civil Code of the People's Republic of China, 77, 168–169
civil liberties, 115–116
civil rights. *See also* Civil Code
  under Civil Code of the People's Republic of China, 83–86
  during COVID-19 crisis, 84
  definitions of, 86
  political rights and, 87
  rights of a legal person, 83–84
  rights of a natural person, 84–86
  states' rights and, 87
Civilization Initiative
  in Foreign Relations Law, 98–102
  goals of, 98–99
  Xi Jinping and, 98–102
von Clausewitz, Carl, 100
Cohen, Jerome, 54
Commission of Disciplinary Inspections (CDIs), 68–70
communism, 16. *See also* Union of Soviet Socialist Republic; *specific topics*
  Fifth Constitutional Amendment and, 42
  Maoist concept of, 15
  as national tradition, 41
Communist International, Kuomintang membership in, 15
community of shared future. *See* ren lei mingyun gongtongti
confidence in Chinese culture. *See* wenhua zixin
confidence in theories. *See* lilun zixin
Confucianism
  corruption and, 62, 64
  datong and, 2, 13, 117–118
  as dominant ideology, 38
  Legalism and, 64
  modern implications of, 11–12
  tian ming, 120
  Xi Jinping and, 12

Confucius, 12
  ethics and, 18
  Kang Youwei on, 14–15
cong yan zhi dang, 67
Congyan Cai, 44
considerations of stability override everything else. See wending yadao yiqie
constitutional amendments, constitutional reforms and. See also Fifth Constitutional Amendment
  analysis of, 41–42
  in China, 29–31
  Chinese Communist Party and, 38–39
  Civil Code of the People's Republic of China influenced by, 82–83
  under Deng Xiaoping, 27
  Four Constitutional Amendments, 38–39
  Fourth Constitutional Amendment, 28
constitutional law. See also Fifth Constitutional Amendment
  reform of, 4
constitutionalism. See also Fifth Constitutional Amendment
  in China, 21
  thin, 21
Constitutions, in China, 20. See also Fifth Constitutional Amendment
  Chinese Communist Party and, 30–31
  Civil Code of the People's Republic of China influenced by, 80
  cult of personality as influence on, 31–32
  Five Powers Constitution, 28
  human rights in, 27
  under Jiang Zemin, 28
  1975 Constitution, 30

1978 Constitution, 30
1982 Constitution, 27–32
  Xi Jinping, 31–32
contracts, contract law and
  in China, 20
  under Civil Code of the People's Republic of China, 77, 89–90
Contracts Law, 81
corruption, in China
  Confucianism and, 62, 64
  Corruption Perception Index, 76
  economic losses from, 62
  guanxi and, 61, 75
  history of, 62–65
  under Supervision Law of the People's Republic of China, 204–205
Corruption Perception Index, 76
cosmopolitanism, 100
COVID-19 pandemic, civil rights in China during, 84
Criminal Procedure Law, 71–72
The Critique of Political Economy (Marx), 33
cult of personality. See also Deng Xiaoping; Hu Jintao; Wen Jiabao; Xi Jinping; Xi regime
  Constitutions influenced by, 31–32
cultural pluralism, 36
Cultural Revolution
  historical legacy of, 92
  Legalism and, 20
  Mao Zedong and, 3, 17
  New Economic Policy compared to, 126
  recurrence of, 123
  revisionist approach to, 30
cultural traditions, Chinese. See also datong; specific topics
  in Chinese Dream, 37
  Civil Code of the People's Republic of China influenced by, 89–90

cultural traditions, Chinese *(continued)*
  cosmopolitanism in, 100
  criticisms of, 37
  efficient governance traditions, 120–122
  modern reinterpretation of, 12
  under new economic reforms, 36–38
  by political regime, 37
culture, in post-Soviet bloc countries, 250n60

Da Tong Shu (The Book of Datong) (Kang), 14
da yi tong, 70
dang da hai shi fa da, 60
dang zheng fen jia, 60
dao bi gai ge, 123
datong (Great Harmony)
  in communities, 12–13
  Confucianism and, 2, 13, 117–118
  hope and, 11–13, 117–118
  Kang Youwei and, 117
  Mao Zedong and, 16, 117
  meaning of, 211n7
  Sun Yat-sen and, 15, 117
  utopianism and, 17–19, 211n7
  Xi Jinping and, 3, 117
  Xi regime and, 36
  xiaokang and, 117
deLisle, Jacques, 23
Demers, John, 74
democracy. *See also* liberal democracy
  China definition of, 105
  in Chinese Dream, 2, 7
  efficient governance traditions instead of, 120–122
  New Democracy, 16, 20, 33
  Third Wave of Democratization, 39–40
Deng Xiaoping
  Civil Code and, 78
  constitutional reforms under, 27
  cultural traditions under, 37
  foreign policy objectives under, 97
  Four Cardinal Principles, 42
  leadership personality of, 65–66
  1982 Constitution under, 28
  responsibility system for, 80
  Southern Tour and, 34, 78
  United Nations and, 103
  U.S.-China trade war under, 52
Deng Xiaoping Theory, 128, 192, 222n19
Development Initiative
  Belt and Road Initiative, 109
  economic structural change in, 109–111
  export/import limitations in, 111–112
  in Foreign Relations Law, 109–112
  Huawei and, 109–111
  income growth in, 110–111
  protectionist policies in, 109, 113
domestic security issues, 48–49
Dong Zhongshu, 118–119
dongchang (Eastern Yard), 63
Dreyer, June, 100
du jiang yan (irrigation system), 120
Duke of Zhou, 215n16

economic development is the hard truth. *See* fazhan shi yingdaoli
economic reform, political reform and, 35
economic security
  Anti-Espionage Law and, 51
  of China, 51–52
  under National Security Law of 2015, 51
  in U.S., 51–52
enforced detention. *See* liuzhi
ethics, for Confucius, 18
ethnic separatism, 49
European Union (EU), General Data Protection Regulation in, 86
everything under heaven. *See* tianxia

Fairbank, John King, 102
fake gentleman. *See* wei jun zi
Falun Gong cult, 47
Fan Ju, 118
fazhan shi yingdaoli (economic development is the hard truth), 55
fen shu keng ru, 118
Fifth Constitutional Amendment, 1, 19, 127–133
　anti-corruption elements in, 70
　Civil Code of the People's Republic of China and, 82–83, 90–91
　Commissions of Supervision in, 134–135
　communism and, 42
　as exception, 8
　methodological approach to, 27–29
　National Supervision Law compatibility with, 75
　Xi Jinping and, 27–28
Five Powers Constitution (Wu Quan Xian Fa), 28
Five Principles of Peaceful Coexistence, 100, 102, 105, 242n34
Foreign Investment Law, 22, 214n42
Foreign Relations Law (FRL), 12
　Chinese Dream and, 95
　Civilization Initiative in, 98–102
　Development Initiative in, 109–112
　foreign policy goals and missions under, 184–186
　foreign relations conduct and power in, 183–184, 189
　foreign relations systems in, 186–189
　general principles of, 181–183
　international human rights under, 104
　Security Initiative in, 102–109, 112–113
　supplementary provisions in, 189
　UN Charter and, 103–104
　U.S. relations and, 95–96
　Western responses to, 95
　Xi Jinping and, 95–97
for-profit legal persons, 162–164
Four Cardinal Principles, 42
Four Self-Confidences, 72
Fourth Constitutional Amendment, National People's Congress and, 28
fragmented authoritarianism model, 45
freedom
　China definition of, 104
　in Chinese Dream, 2, 6–7
　statism and, 118–120
　Xi Jinping on, 113
French Civil Code of 1804, 82
Friedman, Milton, 122–123
FRL. *See* Foreign Relations Law
Fukuyama, Francis, 40, 98

gaobie geming, 17
GDP. *See* gross domestic product
General Data Protection Regulation, in EU, 86
General Principles of Civil Law, 81
Germany
　Civil Code of 1896, 82
　Pandekten system in, 90
Global South, 99
gong tong fu yu, 38
Gorbachev, Mikhail, 91
great change that has not happened in a hundred years. *See* bainian weiyou zhi dabianju
Great Depression, 39–40
Great Financial Crisis of 2008, 39
Great Harmony. *See* datong
Great Leap Forward
　failures of, 125
　Mao Zedong and, 3, 17
Grizold, Anton, 43–44
gross domestic product (GDP), China's global share of, 2–3, 108

guanxi (personal connection), 61, 75
Guo Moruo, 11, 16
guo xue yuan (School of Chinese Studies), 37
guojin mintui, 22

Hall, Natalie, 75
Han dynasty, 119
Han Fei, 26, 62, 218n49
Hart, Little, 100
Hayes, Louis, 107
He Shang, 17
Hideyoshi, Toyotomi, 117
hiding one's capabilities to bide one's time. *See* tao guang yang hui
Hinduism, hope of afterlife in, 13
historical materialism, 216n28
    Marxism and, 20
    primary stage socialism and, 35
    voluntarism and, 32
Hobsbawm, Eric, 40
Hong Kong
    National Security Law for Hong Kong, 49
    under Sino-British Joint Declaration, 49–50, 104
    territorial security and, 49–51
Hong Xiuquan, 31
hope
    Chinese conception of, 18
    in Christianity, 13
    datong and, 11–13, 117–118
    elements of, 215n9
    in Hinduism, 13
    in Shintoism, 13
    Snyder on, 215n9
    xiaokang and, 13–17
Hu, Richard, 43
Hu Angang, 124
Hu Jintao
    Civil Code of the People's Republic of China and, 81

    cultural traditions under, 37
    harmony for, 62
    ideology of, 91
    ideology tsar for, 42
    leadership of, 65
    philosophical influences on, 12
    political legacy of, 41
    as technocrat, 41
Huang Xing, 125
Huawei, 109–111
human rights
    China as signatory for, 53
    in Chinese constitutions, 27
    under Civil Code, 54
    under Foreign Relations Law, 104
    International Convention on the Elimination of All Forms of Racial Discrimination, 53
    modernization theory and, 47–48
    national security and, 53–54
    under National Security Law of 1993, 46–48, 54, 56t
    under National Security Law of 2015, 46–48, 54, 56t
    under National Supervision Law, 54
    political security and, 46–48
    during World War II, 53
Hundred Flowers Movement, 61
Hundred-Years of Humiliation, 112–113
Huntington, Samuel, 98, 102, 250n61
husbands and wives are equals. *See* qi zhe, qi ye
Hu-Wen, 97

idealism, 99
ideology, in political systems
    Confucianism, 38
    of Hu Jintao, 91
    of Jiang Zemin, 91
    of National Supervision Law, 65–70
    political security and, 45–46

socialist core values, 29
  of Xi Jinping, 91, 115
IMF. *See* International Monetary Fund
Inheritance Law, 81
intellectual property rights, in China, 84–85
International Monetary Fund (IMF), 39
international relations theory, 99, 101–102

Japan
  China invaded by, 106, 108
  Civil Code of 1898, 82
  Civil Code of the People's Republic of China influenced by, 79
  cultural traditions in, 101, 116–117
  economic development in, 110
  Meiji Restoration in, 15, 120
  militarist traditions in, 116–117
  modernization of, 14
  Nanjing Massacre, 118
  Perry expedition to, 126
  in Security Initiative, 105–107
  Taisho Democracy in, 117
  Tokugawa period, 116
Jardine, Bradley, 75
Ji You, 43
jian cha (supervision system), 67
Jianfu Chen, 28
Jiang Zemin
  constitutional amendments under, 28
  cultural traditions under, 37
  embrace of Western culture, 37
  ideological line for, 91
  leadership personality of, 65
  Marx as influence on, 33
  philosophical influences on, 12
  primary stage of socialism and, 33–35
  as technocrat, 41
  Theory of Three Represents, 42, 124, 128, 192, 222n19
Jin Guantao, 119

Jin period, 62
jin yi wei, 63
Jing (Emperor), 119
Jing Gangshan, 91
jiu wang yadao qimeng (the salvation of the Chinese nation precludes enlightenment), 37
Johnston, Alastair Iain, 107

Kang, David, 106–107
Kang Youwei, 3, 14–17, 37
  datong and, 117
Kennedy, Scott, 21
Kilcrease, Emily, 52
King Jie, 13–14
King Tang (Emperor), 13
King Zou (Emperor), 14
KMT. *See* Kuomintang
Korean War, 103
Kuomintang (KMT), 15
  Soviet constitutional model as influence on, 38
  Taiwan and, 50

Lai Ching-te, 50
Lamaism, 48
Lampton, David, 43
Lang, Bertram, 74–75
law. *See* legal models
Law on Foreign Relations, 1, 19
Law on National Regional Autonomy of 1984, 48–49
legal development, legal reform and, in China
  Chinese Dream and, 6–8, 19–23
  constitutional law reform, 4
  inequality of citizens and, 76
  instrumentalism as characteristic of, 76
  Kang Youwei as influence on, 37
  methodological approach to, 4–6, 8–9

legal development, legal reform and, in China *(continued)*
  National Supervision Law and, 62
  pragmatism as characteristic of, 75–76
  statism as characteristic of, 76
  traditional systems of, 24
  Western influences on, 21, 79
  under Xi Jinping, 70
legal models, Anglo-American, 21
legal persons
  under Civil Code of the People's Republic of China, 160–167
  civil rights for, 83–84
  for-profit, 162–164
  non-profit, 164–166
  private property rights for, 83–84
  special, 166–167
Legalism, Legalist approaches and, 19
  Confucianism and, 64
  Cultural Revolution and, 20
  historical development of, 25
  Mao Zedong and, 20, 218n50
  modern implications of, 11–12
  National Supervision Law and, 59–60, 62
  principles of, 25–26
  during Qin dynasty, 24–26
  Shang Yang and, 25
  during Warring States period, 24–25, 218n49
  Xi Jinping and, 7, 24–26
Leibniz, Gottfried Wilhelm, 93
Lenin, Vladimir, 33, 65, 80, 126. *See also* Marxism-Leninism
lesser prosperity. *See* xiaokang
Li Jianguo, 70
Li Shimin, 63
Li Si, 218n49
Li Zehou, 17
liberal democracy, 250n60
  modernization theory and, 122–125

liberalism, 41
Lieberthal, Kenneth, 45, 109
lilun zixin (confidence in theories), 90
Lin Gang, 99
Liu Shaoqi, 20, 80, 125
Liu Zaifu, 17
liuzhi (enforced detention), 6
Long Quanlin, 25
Long Yongtu, 123–124
Lorentzen, Peter, 48
Lu Hsun (Lu Xun), 12, 37, 117

Ma Zhengang, 1–2
Manchus society, in China, 100–101
Mandate of Heaven. *See* tian ming
Mao Zedong, 65
  communism and, 15
  Cultural Revolution and, 3
  cultural traditions under, 37
  datong and, 16, 117
  Great Leap Forward and, 3, 17
  Legalism and, 20
  New Democracy and, 16, 20, 33
  People's Commune and, 17
  philosophical voluntarism and, 32–38
  on social practices, 38–41
  Stalin as influence on, 19–20
  utopianism and, 3, 17
  Where Do Correct Ideas Come From?, 27
Mao Zedong Thought, 128, 192, 222n19
Maoism
  philosophical voluntarism and, 32–38
  primary stage socialism and, 216n28
  return to, 28–30
  voluntarism and, 32–35
Marriage Law of 1980, 81
marriage rights, under Civil Code of the People's Republic of China, 89

Marx, Karl, 33, 40, 65, 122–123
Marxism
 in China, 19–21
 historical materialism and, 20
 state capitalism and, 19
Marxism-Leninism, 6, 128, 192
materialism. *See* historical materialism
Matsuoka, Yoshimasa, 79
mei you guo, na you jia (without the state, how can family survive), 22
Meiji Restoration, in Japan, 15, 120
Meissner, Maurice, 32–33
Mencius, 16, 36
Meng Hongwei, 75
Meng Wanzhou, 111–112
min ke you zhi, bu ke zhi zhi (people should be allowed to know what things are; not why things are), 121
Ming dynasty, 23, 119, 120
 anti-corruption strategies during, 60
Minzner, Carl, 70
modernization theory
 human rights and, 47–48
 liberal democracy and, 122–125
 Marx and, 122–123
Mongol society, in China, 100–101
morality
 Plato on, 217n39
 wisdom and, 217n39
Muslims, 48

Nanjing Massacre, 118
National People's Congress (NPC)
 Fifth Constitutional Amendment and, 27–28
 Fourth Constitutional Amendment and, 28
 National Supervision Law and, 59
 political security and, 45
 Thirteenth, 27–28
National School of Administration, 66

national security. *See* security state
National Security Law for Hong Kong (NSLHK), 49
National Security Law of 1993 (SL93)
 conceptual approach to, 43–45
 Core Socialist Values in, 45–46
 foreign threats under, 46–48
 human rights protections under, 46–48, 54, 56t
 political security and, 45–48
 religious threats and, 46–48
 territorial security under, 48–51
National Security Law of 2015 (SL15), 1, 19, 87
 citizen's duties and rights under, 148–150
 conceptual approach to, 43–45
 Core Socialist Values in, 45–46
 crisis control structures, 147
 early warning systems, 146
 economic security under, 51
 examination structures in, 146
 foreign threats under, 46–48
 general principles of, 137–139
 goals of, 44
 human rights protections under, 46–48, 54, 56t
 institutional deficiency as reason for, 45
 intelligence and information collection under, 145–146
 national security guarantees, 148
 ordinary provisions in, 144–145
 organization's duties and rights under, 148–150
 political security and, 45–48
 religious threats under, 46–48
 risk prevention in, 146
 safeguarding duties in, 143–144
 supervision structures in, 146
 supplementary principles, 150
 tasks and security goals, 139–143

National Security Law of 2015 (SL15) (*continued*)
   territorial security under, 48–51
   under Xi Jinping, 25, 54
national security laws. *See also specific laws*
   as high politics, 24
   National Security Law for Hong Kong, 49
National Supervision Commission (NSC), 60, 67–68, 70, 74
National Supervision Law (NSL) (2018), 1, 12
   analysis of, 75–76
   anti-corruption operations under, 70–75
   Fifth Constitutional Amendment compatibility with, 75
   gray area income under, 73
   ideological orientation of, 65–70
   legal reform and, 62
   Legalism tradition and, 59–60, 62
   National People's Congress and, 59
   necessity of, 60–62
   scope of, 70–71
   structural issues for, 65–70
National Supervision Law (Supervision Law of the People's Republic of China) (NSL) (2018), 1, 12
nationalism, failures of, 40
natural persons
   under Civil Code of the People's Republic of China, 152–159
   civil rights for, 84–86
   private property rights for, 84–85
Nee, William, 54
never forget about the original goals of CCP. *See* bu wang chu xin
New Culture Movement, 125
New Democracy (xin minzhu zhuyi geming), 16, 20, 33

New Economic Policy, in USSR, 16, 80, 126
New Era Socialism with Chinese Characteristics, 90, 192, 222n19
NGOs. *See* nongovernmental organizations
nongovernmental organizations (NGOs), 46, 98
non-profit legal persons, 164–166
NPC. *See* National People's Congress
NSC. *See* National Supervision Commission
NSL. *See* National Supervision Law
NSLHK. *See* National Security Law for Hong Kong

Operation Fox Hunt, 73–74
Opium War, 2, 126

peasant rebellions, 17, 231n19
people hated the government. *See* chou guan
people hated the rich. *See* chou fu
people should be allowed to know what things are; not why things are. *See* min ke you zhi, bu ke zhi zhi
People's Commune, 17
People's Police Law, 71
People's Republic of China. *See* China
Perry, Matthew, 126
personal connection. *See* guanxi
philosophical voluntarism
   Mao Zedong and, 32–38
   as official ideology, 32–38
Plato
   on morality, 217n39
   reason for, 18
   The Republic, 217n39
   on wisdom, 217n39
Plekhanov, Georgi, 33

political capitalism, state capitalism as, 23
political reform, in China
  economic reform and, 35
  failures of, 20
  in post-Mao era, 55–56
  primary stage of socialism and, 20–21
political rights, civil rights and, 87
political security
  Chinese Communist Party and, 45–46
  foreign threats and, 46–48
  human rights awareness and, 46–48
  ideological threats and, 45–46
  Law on National Regional Autonomy of 1984, 48–49
  National People's Congress and, 45
  under National Security Law of 1993, 45–48
  under National Security Law of 2015, 45–48
  religious threats and, 46–48
Poroshenko, Petro, 250n60
PRC. *See* China
primary stage socialism, 216n28
  Civil Code of the People's Republic of China and, 90
  Deng Xiaoping and, 33
  historical materialism and, 35, 236n9
  Jiang Zemin and, 33–35
  political reform and, 20–21
privacy protections and rights
  in Civil Code of the People's Republic of China, 85–86, 88
  under General Data Protection Regulation, 86
private property rights, 22
  in Civil Code of the People's Republic of China, 77
  for intellectual property, 84–85
  for legal persons, 83–84
  for natural persons, 84–85
Property Law, in China, 87
public self-criticism. *See* zui ji zhao

qi zhe, qi ye (husbands and wives are equals), 117
Qian Long, 37
Qian Qichen, 96
Qin dynasty, 118, 218n49
Qing dynasty, 119, 125
  Civil Code of the People's Republic of China and, 79
  Legalism during, 24–26
  reforms during, 14–15
  utopianism during, 3
quasi-constitutionalism, 21
Quigley, Carroll, 250n61

realism, 99
reason, Plato on, 18
rebellions and protests
  by peasants, 17, 231n19
  Taiping Rebellion, 31, 119
  Yellow Turban Rebellion, 17
reform. *See* economic reform; political reform
ren lei mingyun gongtongti (community of shared future), 36
Ren Zhengfei, 111–112
Renmin de mingyi (In the Name of the People), 55
Renminbi (RMB) (currency), 39, 73–74, 110
The Republic (Plato), 217n39
Republic era, utopianism during, 3
Republic of China, 15
Rights in Rem Law, 81
RMB. *See* Renminbi
Rosemont, Henry, 64

royal censor. *See* yushi daifu
ru fa zhi zheng, 20
rule by law, 218n52
  state capitalism and, 21–23
  under Xi Jinping, 26
rule of law
  core elements of, 23
  cultural meaning of, 5
  World Bank and, 6
Russia. *See also* Union of Soviet Socialist Republics
  October Revolution in, 33
Russian-Ukraine War, 98–99

the salvation of the Chinese nation precludes enlightenment. *See* jiu wang yadao qimeng
San Fan Movement, 61
School of Chinese Studies. *See* guo xue yuan
Scientific Outlook on Development, 128, 182, 192, 222n19
Scoggins, Suzanne, 48
Second Revolution, 125
Security Initiative
  East Asia international relations in, 105–107
  Five Principles of Peaceful Coexistence and, 102, 105
  in Foreign Relations Law, 102–109, 112–113
  Japanese role in, 105–107
  origins of, 107–109
  United Nations and, 102–105
  universal values as part of, 102–105
security is the hard truth. *See* an quan shi ying daoli
security state, national security and. *See also specific laws*
  Chinese conception of, 44
  conceptual approach to, 43–45
  definition of, 43–44
  economic security, 51–52
  global security and, 44
  under Hu Jintao, 45
  human rights and, 53–54
  political security and, 45–48
  territorial security, 48–51
  under Wen Jiabao, 45
Senkaku Islands, territorial claims to, 50–51
Shambaugh, David, 34
Shang dynasty, 13–14
shang shan ruo shui, 119
Shang Yang, 25, 62, 218n49
shehui cunzai, 36
shehui yishi, 36
Shi Jing (Book of Odes), 13
  xiaokang in, 215n16
Shida, Kotaro, 79
Shihuang (Emperor), 25, 118
Shintoism, hope of afterlife in, 13
shuanggui, 60, 71
Shuchen Xiang, 99
Shun period, 12
si qing (Four Cleanings Campaign), 125
Sino-British Joint Declaration, for Hong Kong, 49–50, 104
Skelton, Ike, 100
SL15. *See* National Security Law of 2015
SL93. *See* National Security Law of 1993
Snyder, Charles, 215n9
socialism, 16
  in Chinese Dream, 2
  under Civil Code of the People's Republic of China, 86
  Core Socialist Values, 45–46, 226n22
  failures of, 40
  ideology in political systems and, 29
  in National Security Law of 1993, 45–46

in National Security Law of 2015, 45–46
New Era Socialism with Chinese Characteristics, 90, 192
primary stage, 20–21, 33–35, 90, 216n28, 236n9
Song dynasty, 37, 119
South China Sea region, territorial security for, 49–51
sovereignty, definition of, 102–103
Soviet Union. *See* Union of Soviet Socialist Republics
special legal persons, 166–167
Stalin, Joseph, 19–20, 80
state capitalism
  Chinese Dream and, 7, 19
  Marxist systems and, 19
  as political capitalism, 23
  rule by law and, 21–23
  scope of, 22
  Weber on, 23
statism, freedom and, 118–120
Su Shaozhi, 33
Sui dynasty, 119–120
Sun Tzu, 95, 100, 107–108, 112–113
  military doctrine influenced by, 12
Sun Yat-sen, 3, 37
  as anti-capitalist, 22
  datong and, 15, 117
  Five Powers Constitution and, 28
  Kuomintang and, 15
  leadership mobilization under, 91
  Second Revolution and, 125
  Three Principles of the People, 15–16
Supervision Law of the People's Republic of China (2018)
  compliance models, 205
  establishment of, 191
  general provisions of, 192–193
  international cooperation against corruption, 204–205

jurisdiction of, 194–195
legal responsibilities in, 207–208
supervision authority under, 199–206
supervision procedures under, 199–204
supplementary provisions in, 208
supervision laws. *See also* Administrative Supervision Law of the People's Republic of China; Administrative Supervision Statutes of the People's Republic of China; National Supervision Law
  Central Commission of Disciplinary Inspection, 60, 66–68
  Commission of Disciplinary Inspections, 68–70
  corruption as target of, 59
  National Supervision Commission, 60, 67–68, 70, 74
Sutter, Robert, 221n2

Taiping Rebellion, 31, 119
Taisho Democracy, in Japan, 117
Taiwan
  Kuomintang and, 50
  territorial security and, 49–51
Tang (King), 215n16
Tang Aijun, 46
Tang dynasty, 63, 119
Tang Wenming, 37
tao guang yang hui (hiding one's capabilities to bide one's time), 41
Taoism, modern implications of, 12
Tenghui, Lee, 50
territorial security
  domestic security, 48–49
  ethnic separatism and, 49
  for greater China area, 49–51
  Hong Kong and, 49–51
  under National Security Law of 1993, 48–51

territorial security *(continued)*
  under National Security Law of 2015, 48–51
  Senkaku Islands and, 50–51
  separatist movements and, 48–49
  of South China Sea region, 49–51
  Taiwan and, 49–51
Theory of Three Represents, 42, 124, 128, 192, 222n19
thin constitutionalism, 21
Third Wave of Democratization, 39–40
Three Principles of the People, 15–16
tian ming (Mandate of Heaven), 120
Tian Wenjing, 64
tianxia (everything under heaven), 99–101
tiaoli (supervision), 59
Tibet, separatist movement in, 48–49
Tokugawa period, in Japan, 116
Tong Zhiwei, 72
Tort Liability Law, 81
Toynbee, Arnold, 102
Transparency International, 76
Trump, Donald, 82
  political engagement with China, 95–96
tu cheng, 118
Tu Wei-ming, 118
tuo gu gai zhi, 14
Turner, Karen, 23

UN. *See* United Nations
UN General Assembly. *See* United Nations
UNESCO. *See* United Nations
Union of Soviet Socialist Republics (Soviet Union) (USSR)
  Civil Code in, 80
  corruption in, 60–61
  New Economic Policy in, 16, 80, 126

United Nations (UN)
  Deng Xiaoping and, 103
  Educational, Scientific and Cultural Organization, 103
  General Assembly, 2
  human rights conventions, 53
  International Convention on the Elimination of All Forms of Racial Discrimination, 53
  during Korean War, 103
  Security Initiative and, 102–105
  UN Charter, 103–104
  Xi Jinping at, 2
United States (U.S.)
  economic security for, 51–52
  Foreign Relations Law and, 95–96
  trade war with China, 52, 78
  UNESCO and, 103
USSR. *See* Union of Soviet Socialist Republics
utopianism
  Chinese Dream and, 3, 7, 11–19
  conceptual approach to, 5
  datong and, 17–19, 211n7
  Kang Youwei and, 3
  Mao Zedong and, 3, 17
  in modern Chinese history, 3
  during Qin dynasty, 3
  during Republic era, 3
  in twentieth century, 18
  Western scholarship on, 19, 217n32
utopias. *See* Western utopias

Vietnam War, 243n55
voluntarism
  historical materialism and, 32
  Maoist, 32–35
  philosophical, 32–38

Wademan, Andrew, 76
Wakeman, Frederic, 32–33

Walter, Albert, 123
Wang Dongyue, 101
Wang Huning, 42
Wang Jisi, 109
Wang Weiguang, 30
Wang Yangming, 18
Wang Yi, 97, 105, 109
Warring States period, Legalism during, 24–25, 218n49
Weber, Max, 23, 102
wei jun zi (fake gentleman), 64–65
Wei period, 62
Wen (King), 13, 119, 215n16
Wen Jiabao, 91
  political legacy of, 41
Wen Tiejun, 23
wending yadao yiqie (considerations of stability override everything else), 55
wenhua zixin (confidence in Chinese culture), 90
the West, Western world and
  The Art of War as influence in, 100
  Chinese legal development influenced by, 21, 79
  Foreign Relations Law and, 95
  international relations theory in, 99
  Washington Consensus and, 21
Western utopias, 217n32
Western Yard. *See* xichang
Where Do Correct Ideas Come From? (Mao Zedong), 27
Williamson, John, 21–22
wisdom
  morality and, 217n39
  Plato on, 217n39
without the state, how can family survive. *See* mei you guo, na you jia
World Bank, 5–6, 105

World Trade Organization
  China in, 72, 123–124
  Civil Code of the People's Republic of China and, 81
Wu (King), 13, 119, 215n16
Wu Jinglian, 124
Wu Quan Xian Fa (Five Powers Constitution), 28
Wuthnow, Joel, 43
wu-tuo-bang, 18

Xi Jinping. *See also* Fifth Constitutional Amendment; Foreign Relations Law; Xi regime; *specific topics*
  anti-corruption operations under, 76, 121–122
  Chinese Communist Party under, 97
  Chinese Dream and, 1
  Civilization Initiative for, 98–102
  Confucianism as influence on, 12
  Constitutions under, 31–32
  cultural pluralism and, 36
  datong and, 3
  Development Initiative, 109–112
  Fifth Constitutional Amendment and, 27–28
  Foreign Relations Law and, 95–97
  foreign threats and, 46
  Four Self-Confidences, 72
  on freedom, 113
  ideology of, 91, 115
  ideology tsar for, 42
  Jiang Zemin era and, 96
  leadership personality of, 66
  legal reform under, 70
  Legalism and, 7, 24–26
  National Security Law of 2015 under, 25, 54

Xi Jinping *(continued)*
  New Era Socialism with Chinese Characteristics and, 90, 192, 222n19
  as new generation of leader, 41
  rule by law under, 26
  Security Initiative, 102–109, 112–113
  at UN General Assembly, 2
Xi regime. *See also specific topics*
  Chinese Dream during, 1
  Civil Code of the People's Republic of China and, 81–82
  datong and, 36
  modernization discourse under, 36–37
  rejuvenation of Chinese nation in, 2
Xi Zhongxun, 41
Xia dynasty, 14
xiaokang (lesser prosperity), 2, 211n8, 215n16
  in Chinese Dream, 13
  as cultural tradition, 4
  datong and, 117
  hope and, 13–17
xichang (Western Yard), 63
xin minzhu zhuyi geming, 33. *See also* New Democracy
Xinhua news agency, 2
Xinjiang, separatist movement in, 48–49
xinyang que shi, 121
Xiongnu, 101, 242n42
Xu Jilin, 99

Xuezhi Guo, 69

Yang (Emperor), 120
Yang Guangbin, 34
Yao, 12
Ye Zicheng, 11–12, 25
Yellow Turban Rebellion, 17
yi chushi zhixin zuo rushi zhishi, 7
yi de bao yuan, 107
yi de zhi guo, 65
Yong Zheng (Emperor), 64
Yu (Emperor), 13
Yuan Shikai, 16
yushi daifu (royal censor), 67

Zelensky, Volodymyr, 250n60
Zeng Guofan, 119
zhan lang wai jiao, 106
Zhang Guozhong, 16
Zhang Lu, 17
Zhang Zhunqiao, 16
Zhao Lijian, 106
Zhao Tingyang, 98–99
Zheng Bijian, 96
Zheng Shuna, 45
Zhong Nan Hai, 65
zhongyuan, 101
Zhou Dynasty, 13
Zhou Enlai, 242n34
Zhou Yongkang, 26
Zhu Xi, 18
Zhu Yuanzhang, 23, 31, 60, 63–64, 106
zui ji zhao (public self-criticism), 120

www.ingramcontent.com/pod-product-compliance
Lightning Source LLC
Chambersburg PA
CBHW021834220426
43663CB00005B/236